Struggle for Survival in the Bush

World of Wildlife: AFRICA

Struggle for Survival in the Bush

From the original text by Dr Félix Rodríguez de la Fuente
Scientific staff: P. de Andres, J. Castroviejo, M. Delibes, C. Morillo, C. G. Vallecillo
English language version by John Gilbert
Consultant editor: Dr Maurice Burton
Creative director: Brian Innes

Contents

Acknowledgments

Bagel/Rapho: 176
Des Bartlett/Bruce Coleman: 94, 105, 144, 167, 170, 192, 214, 219, 225, 230, 236
Des Bartlett/Photo Researchers: 123
F. Bel/G. Vienne/Jacana: 262
C. Bevilacqua/Salmer: 141
R. Bousquet/Jacana: 250
J. Burton/Bruce Coleman: 64, 86, 95, 138, 161, 207, 211, 249, 252, 254, 258, 265
Bob Campbell/Bruce Coleman: 24, 196, 198, 209, 222
R. I. Campbell/Bruce Coleman: 182
Jean Carpenter/Bruce Coleman: 283
M. A. Castaños: 4, 58, 82, 202, 271, 283
E. Cerra: 51, 62, 92, 121, 122, 148, 192, 196, 235, 255
N. Cirani: 22, 25, 28, 291
Bruce Coleman: 30, 31
S. Dalton/Zardoya: 286
A. J. Deane/Bruce Coleman: 159, 269
Edistudio: 10, 126, 177
J. M. Fiévet/Jacana: 190, 203, 212, 242
Comandante Gatti: 35, 89
C. A. W. Guggisberg/Bruce Coleman: 130, 131, 173
Alfonso Gutiérrez/Edistudio: 12, 20, 41, 60, 70, 71, 124, 128, 133, 138, 180, 188, 190, 191, 204, 216
E. Hanumantha/Photo Researchers: 47
Hoa-Qui Editions: 145
E. Hosking: 52
B. Hunter/Photo Researchers: 110
C. de Klemm/Jacana: 109, 238, 250
J. Lalanda: 66, 97, 103, 129, 154, 160, 166, 174, 184, 186, 200, 230, 243, 248, 256, 261, 264, 273, 279, 290, 292, 293, 297
Lheriter/Afrique Photo: 285
Marka: 38
McWaren/Jacana: 269

W. T. Miller/F. W. Lane: 259
W. T. Miller/Popperfoto: 3, 52, 59, 75, 163, 175, 229, 262
J. Moss/Photo Researchers: 42
Norman Myers: 27
Norman Myers/Black Star: 153
Norman Myers/Bruce Coleman: 7, 48, 116, 137, 165, 167, 187, 265
Norman Myers/Okapia: 165, 288
Norman Myers/Popperfoto: 11, 14, 187, 189
Norman Myers/Salmer: 24
Naud/Afrique Photo: 109, 170, 208
D. Paterson/Bruce Coleman: 275
Jaime Pato/Prensa Española: 52, 59, 73, 76, 115, 117, 127, 147, 153, 154, 237, 241, 245, 246, 249
André Picou/Afrique Photo: 273, 299
G. D. Plage/Bruce Coleman: 297
Masood Quarishy/Bruce Coleman: 37, 40, 90, 138, 143, 156, 157
J. Robert/Jacana: 107, 195, 238
Félix Rodríquez de la Fuente: 3, 45, 60, 71, 96, 177, 245, 300
Alan Root/Okapia: 18, 23, 55, 111, 230, 276, 295
F. Roux/Jacana: 257
Salmer: 12, 148, 163
A. Sarro: 249
M. Socias: 8, 44, 78, 80, 81, 118, 181, 210
F. Sostres: 120
J. M. Terrase/Jacana: 203, 262
Time-Life Inc: 17, 26, 29, 30, 34, 91, 99, 101, 102
D. Thomas/Photo Researchers: 43
Simon Trevor/Bruce Coleman: 33, 55, 116, 134, 227, 232, 281
W. Schramal/Jacana: 46
J. P. Varin/Jacana: 204, 222, 223
Albert Visage/Jacana: 23, 150, 158, 249, 267
Z.F.A.: 9

Foreword

Africa today can be likened to a giant research laboratory of animal life. It was here, in prehistoric times, that animal species developed that were later to spread across the whole land-mass of the northern hemisphere; and now, in many thousands of square miles of wildlife reserves, more varieties of animal life are preserved than anywhere else in the world. But even where animals are protected by law they are still at risk: even apart from the dangers represented by poachers and the sudden outbreak of warfare, there are problems associated with any interference with the natural balance of nature. Elephants, no longer hunted by the native inhabitants. have increased their numbers in wildlife reserves so markedly that there is insufficient food to support the population; predators, themselves protected, have found their prey so plentiful that their natural patterns of behaviour have been changed. Sometimes it seems that man's efforts to preserve the animal population of Africa have been the greatest menace to its continuing existence.

Nevertheless, many rare and interesting species have been saved from extinction, and in some cases their numbers are already on the increase. This volume of *World of Wildlife* surveys the delicate balance of animal life which ensures survival in the African bush, and the dependence of one species upon another, from the termites in their strangely-shaped mounds of earth to the huge but placid white rhinoceros of Uganda. The bizarre but beautiful birds of the bush, the baboons and their relatives the green and red monkeys, the grotesque aardvark and the ravaging locust – they are all here, in this breathtaking panorama of life in the wild regions of Africa.

The hundreds of photographs, taken on safari throughout the continent, and the accompanying drawings, reveal the most intimate details of the animals' behaviour: their sex-lives and social relationships, their ways of fighting and feeding, and their relationships with other species. This is the true story of the struggle for survival in the bush.

CHAPTER 12

A giant in peril:
the white rhinoceros

In the Murchison Falls National Park of Uganda, notably those parts bordering Lake Albert, the tall elephant grass grows in abundance, covering the gently-rolling hillsides with a carpet of greenery. The shrubs and bushes that dot the savannah, the candelabra-shaped euphorbias whose images are reflected in the blue water of the lake and the small pools fed by rushing streams all provide ideal conditions for one of Africa's rarest animals – the white rhinoceros (*Ceratotherium simum*). In prehistoric times the enormous creature roamed all over the continent but today, in grave danger of extinction, this is one of its last remaining refuges.

Nobody with a genuine feeling for animals can fail to be concerned at the tragic plight of this peaceable creature, largest of all surviving members of the rhinoceros family. Though often regarded as a dangerous, quick-tempered beast, all studies of its behaviour indicate that it has been much maligned and that it cannot in any sense be considered an aggressive animal.

To confirm this judgment it is only necessary to watch a group of these rhinos at pasture on the savannah. A typical family unit may consist of one male, two females and a couple of youngsters. Their movements, as they graze with lowered heads on the succulent short grass, are slow and deliberate. On their backs perch the little white cattle egrets, which feed on the insects disturbed by the great pachyderms as they ponderously advance. The rhinos have not yet noticed the presence of the car from which observers are watching them, but when the group is about 50 yards or so from the vehicle one of the females suddenly lifts her head, sniffs the air and flicks her small ears in the direction of the intruders. The tapering, pointed horns look heavy and menacing. Noisily she lets out her breath and, as if responding to a signal, her companions imitate her. After a few seconds of hesitation they turn round and make off across the plain. For animals that weigh more than three tons, their trotting gait is remarkably speedy, relaxed and buoyant. When they have retired to what they consider is a safe distance, they come to an abrupt halt and resume their tranquil grazing. Around midday they wander off together to seek the shade of trees or bushes for an afternoon rest.

It is difficult to understand why these powerfully armed animals, feeding exclusively on grass and not harbouring any aggressive feelings towards other creatures, should find themselves on the very brink of extermination. Surely they should be immune to attack and well-nigh invulnerable. All one can reply is that prehistory and indeed more recent times have thrown up many examples of species that were apparently equally well endowed, but which nevertheless have disappeared from the earth. Species, like nations and individuals, have their moments of glory and then decline. They are born and eventually they die.

Fossil remains and the present African distribution of the white rhinoceros into two groups, some 1,100 miles apart from each other, seem to confirm the hypothesis that even before man arrived to aggravate an already precarious situation, geographical and climatic changes had combined to set the species on a downward path. In those long-distant days of prehistory, the ecological conditions necessary for the animals' survival could be found in nearly all parts of the great continent, which was then generously covered with savannahs of green grass, with shrubs and undergrowth, with springs, ponds, rivers and lakes. Nowadays such ideal conditions can only be found in a few regions—Sudan, Uganda and South Africa.

Over tens of millions of years the environment underwent vast changes. In the first place increased rainfall encouraged the growth of forests at the expense of plain and savannah, so that the rhinoceroses were forced to make a gradual retreat from habitats that no longer suited them. This failure to adapt may have been the chief reason for their splitting into two groups. Later, the return of a markedly drier period saw the process reversed, with an expansion of the open grass regions, which encroached upon the bounds of the forests. The former areas were now too dry to support the rhino populations, and since such conditions discouraged migration, the two groups failed to link up.

Horn and hide

In most adventure stories—and in more serious works of nonfiction as well—the white rhinoceros is traditionally described as a bad-tempered animal, looking for no excuse to charge madly at a stranger. Such accounts are either written by hunters, who have been more interested in seeing the animals dead than alive and who need the support of such a myth to glorify their feat, or by authors who have slavishly accepted the statement without making any effort to verify it. To be fair, some of these writers may have confused the white rhinoceros with the black, for the latter may, in certain circumstances, show hostile behaviour. But all those who have made a detailed study of the ways of the white rhinoceros report that it is an absolutely inoffensive creature.

Facing page (above) : White rhinoceroses are strict herbivores, preferring to live in gently undulating savannah country where the humidity content is high enough to encourage the growth of the grass that they require for sustenance. (*Below*) often seen in the company of these pachyderms are the little cattle egrets, birds that feed on insects disturbed by the rhinos as they graze and raise the alarm by taking flight should an intruder approach.

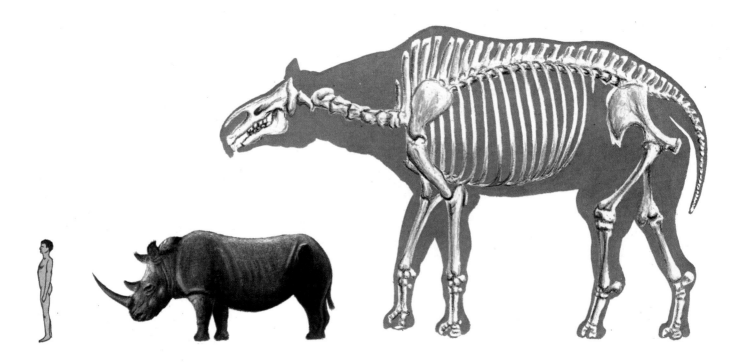

The white rhinoceros is the largest living species of the Rhinocerotidae and the second largest of living land mammals. Nevertheless, as can be seen from the comparative sizes in this diagram, it is small in relation to its colossal ancestor *Baluchitherium*, which lived about 30 million years ago.

Only on very rare occasions has it been known to attack a human, its immediate reaction in face of danger being to run away.

The white rhino, second largest of all land mammals (the African elephant takes first place), is curiously named. Far from being white, it is a greyish colour, admittedly somewhat lighter than its black relative. It was probably the Boers who first used the word *wyd* to describe the size of its mouth and the British, colonising the continent later, who misunderstood the term and referred to the creature as 'white'.

The arrival of the Europeans had immediate and tragic consequences for the white rhinoceros. Here was a rich prize indeed – a creature to be hunted for its edible flesh, its thick hide (out of which were fashioned a number of leather articles, including shields), and above all its horns, which were believed – quite wrongly – to contain magical and medicinal properties. By 1850 greed, ignorance and misplaced sporting zeal had brought about a drastic reduction in their numbers. The situation in the south was so grave that had not a few far-sighted individuals intervened, the animals would have been completely wiped out. Towards the end of the century it was in fact generally assumed that the species was extinct, for not many people knew of the existence of white rhinoceroses in Sudan and Uganda. Happily a handful had also managed to survive in the south, and in 1894 it was decided to create a game reserve in Zululand – in a region bounded to the north by the Black Umfolozi and to the south by the White Umfolozi – to save the last South African white rhinos.

In 1922 Vaughan Kirby reported that there were only 20 animals left in the Umfolozi reserve. There were in fact rather more, but a revelation of the true figure would doubtless have led the authorities to lift the ban on shooting the species. In 1929 there was another threat to their survival as the government debated the advisability of closing the reserve. Fortunately a member of the Natal Provincial Council, Douglas Mitchell, came to the rescue and succeeded in preventing the closure, thus enabling the rare animals to continue living under the protection of the

Parks Council of Natal. The results were staggering. Within a short time the white rhino population, previously so slim, grew to unmanageable proportions, far too dense to be supported by the limited pastures of the reserve. This posed a serious problem. Were the animals to be allowed to multiply unchecked and to destroy their habitat – in which case the species was surely doomed – or should selected individuals be killed so that the numbers could be controlled? It was an agonising dilemma, but happily a third solution was devised. Bearing in mind that the animals had once roamed freely over most of the continent, it was decided to capture a few and transfer them to another reserve in Africa. Thus the risk of overpopulation could be avoided and a new centre of population established where the rare creature would be able to breed and flourish. The first batch, consisting of ten rhinoceroses, were moved from Umfolozi to Mkuzi, farther north. Despite the efforts of poachers, the little group prospered.

For quite some time it was taken for granted that the white rhino's area of distribution was restricted to a region extending between the Orange and Zambezi rivers. But in 1900 a Major Gibbons of the British army killed a white rhinoceros on the west bank of the Nile, some 1,100 miles north of the Umfolozi reserve, thus proving the existence of two separate populations.

Some authors claim to find a sufficient number of anatomical differences to justify the two groups being considered as separate subspecies – that in the north-east being named *Ceratotherium simum cottoni* and the South African one *C. s. simum*. Other authorities, however, dispute this, pointing out that the distinction is purely fanciful and arguing that there are no significant variations between the two groups.

For a time it seemed that the northern population were in little serious danger. Not only had they survived, but their numbers were increasing satisfactorily. This happy state of affairs lasted until fairly recently. Then a sequence of violent political upheavals – civil war in Sudan and the fight for independence in the Congo – altered the situation. One consequence of the fighting in the Congo was the occupation by an armed contingent of the Garamba National Park, where the rhinos had formerly enjoyed protective security. When the conflict was over and the area evacuated, only 100 of the original 1,000 animals were left alive.

The situation in Uganda was equally grave. Here, poaching for rhinos' horns, with their allegedly aphrodisiac properties, was on the increase and to check the falling population a number of animals were transferred to the Murchison Falls National Park.

First catch your rhino

Transporting an enormous creature such as a rhinoceros from one area to another poses considerable problems, not the least of which is to capture it in the first place. It involves a proper team effort and since the enterprise is not without some danger, it also calls for much skill and courage. The rhinoceros is capable of moving over rough ground at about 25 miles per hour, so that the driver of the truck used for the operation must be pretty dexterous in threading his way across terrain dotted with trees and bushes,

WHITE RHINOCEROS
(*Ceratotherium simum*)

Class: Mammalia
Order: Perissodactyla
Family: Rhinocerotidae
Length of head and body: 175 inches (440 cm)
Height to shoulder: 72–78 inches (180–195 cm)
Weight: 6,600–8,800 lb (3,000–4,000 kg)
Food: grass
Gestation: 548–578 days
Number of young: one
Longevity: 40–50 years

Adults
The long head may measure up to 32 inches; the upper lip is truncated, whereas in other species it has a small prehensile appendage. The tiny eyes are laterally positioned; the ears are small and pointed. Two horns project from the nose region, the front one measuring from 40–60 inches in length, the other being shorter, seldom exceeding 8 inches. The greyish hide is thick, smooth and hairless, but the tail is tipped with a hairy tuft.

Young
Similar in appearance to the adult but with undeveloped horns. Sexual maturity is reached at about 5 years, though some females are already mature at 3 years.

Subspecies
The typical race, *Ceratotherium simum simum*, is nowadays confined to reserves in South Africa. What many experts consider a separate subspecies, *C. s. cottoni*, inhabits a limited area near the source of the Nile, comprising north-west Uganda, southern Sudan and part of the Congo.

/// Probable distribution around 1820

■ Modern distribution

Geographical distribution, past and present, of the white rhinoceros.

Facing page : The mud bath is an important daily ritual for the rhinoceros. It serves to regulate the animal's body temperature during the most intense heat of the day and also forms an enveloping crust which flakes off, together with irritating insects, when the rhino rubs itself against a tree.

and pitted with anthills and aardvark burrows. But the crucial stage comes when the rhino has been slowed down sufficiently for a direct attempt to be made to harness it. For this purpose one member of the team, stationed on top of the lorry, manipulates a lasso, attached to a long rod. This must be tossed over the animal's head while the other end, tied to the vehicle, prevents the rhino from escaping. The huge creature's reaction on feeling the noose tighten around its neck is to charge, battering its head against the sides of the lorry, but in due course it calms down so that its captors can safely approach, pass ropes around its legs, tumble it to the ground and render it helpless. Rollers are then used to hoist the massive animal into the lorry.

This method of capture can be both risky and protracted. The rhinoceros, once pinioned, is unlikely to be able to harm its captors, but by using its horns to charge repeatedly and vainly against the lorry, it may damage itself. To avoid such a possibility, the 'hunters' nowadays adopt a safer technique. The animal is located from the air by a helicopter, which directs the land-party to the spot. When the rhino is within range, a compressed-air rifle is used to shoot a syringe-dart, injecting the animal with an anaesthetic. This gradually paralyses the creature, which topples to the ground. Another drug is then injected by hand into a vein of the ear, which has the dual capacity of relaxing the effect of the anaesthetic and tranquillising the rhinoceros. The animal will then allow itself to be handled—as docile as a lamb.

The placid pachyderm

The favourite habitat of the white rhinoceros is well-watered, wooded savannah country, with gentle hills but no steep inclines. Given plenty of grass, a daily supply of drinking water and shade from the blazing sun (regulation of body temperature is of vital importance), the animal has all it needs for its placid life.

This colossal creature is certainly no beauty. It is enveloped in a thick hide, not unlike armour plating to look at, its neck is well muscled, and its huge head—higher at the rear than in the front—is generally furnished with two horns. The front one rises vertically from a quadrangular base and may, in some individuals, measure more than three feet long; the second one is much shorter and may even be absent. The length of the horns will vary according to the animal's age, those of the female being longer and thinner. The body is comparatively long, the legs short but strong, and a small projection of the backbone appears as a hump in the centre of the back. The tail terminates in a tuft of hair.

The rhino's eyes are very small and although the inadequacy of its vision has been exaggerated, it is certainly rather poor. One reason is that the prominent horns impede its view and force it to turn its head in order to see an object properly, and some experts suggest other physiological causes. To compensate for this, the sense of hearing is good and the sense of smell even more highly developed. The latter enables the rhinoceros both to find food and, by detecting the presence of natural scents, to avoid potential danger. Frequently, however, it is the cattle egrets, with their shrill alarm cries and sudden flight, which first notify the rhino

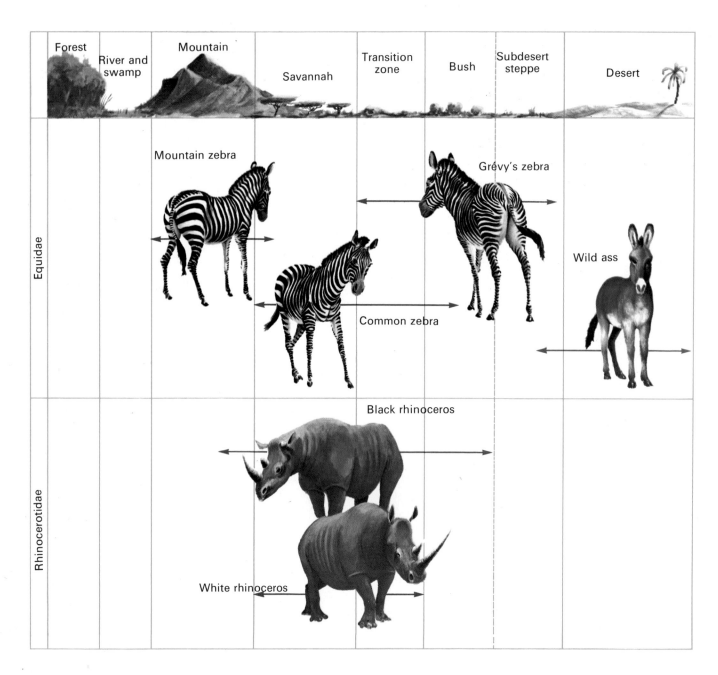

| Forest | River and swamp | Mountain | Savannah | Transition zone | Bush | Subdesert steppe | Desert |

Equidae

Mountain zebra

Grévy's zebra

Common zebra

Wild ass

Rhinocerotidae

Black rhinoceros

White rhinoceros

Among the perissodactyls of the Ethiopian region, the Equidae (zebras and wild asses) can be found in almost every habitat, with the exception of forests and swamps. The Rhinocerotidae, however, have a more restricted habitat. The white rhino, exclusively grass-eating, lives only in savannah terrain; the black rhino, although more adaptable and wide-ranging, is never found in forests, swamplands or deserts.

of an enemy's approach. The creature then lifts its heavy head, nervously flicks its ears and sniffs the wind. When it has pinpointed its adversary it takes a few hesitant steps and trots off in the opposite direction. If pursued, it will break into a run, but it is incapable of maintaining its speed for long. Should it be cornered by a human, it may turn and charge, but in normal circumstances loud shouts and frantic arm-flapping will be enough to precipitate the animal's headlong flight.

The white rhinoceros is a rather solitary creature. Adult males may sometimes be seen on their own or in company with a female; and a mother may often be found together with a youngster. Occasionally, however, male, females and young will form themselves into a family group of up to a dozen individuals. The daily routine will be unvarying. At daybreak the family will head slowly for a river or a waterhole to take a ritual mud bath. The main purpose of this is to get rid of parasites that may have lodged in the skin. When the creatures emerge from the water, caked in mud, they make for the nearest tree and begin rubbing themselves vigorously against the trunk, so that the insects drop off with the flaking muddy crust. As the sun becomes hotter, the rhinos seek the cooling shade of acacias or bushes. Here they remain throughout the heat of the day, lying on their sides or stretched out on their bellies, legs tucked beneath them and heads resting on the ground. Not until quite late in the afternoon will they get to their feet and prepare for the forthcoming night's activity. For although the white rhinoceros will sometimes graze during the day, its serious search for food is at night.

The species is very dependent on water—especially muddy pools—and this necessity conditions their movements all year round. In the Ugandan reserves near the Nile, during the dry season, all the paths trampled by the animals through the long grass seem to lead to the swampy banks of the great river, where they gather to drink and to bathe. When the rains arrive and the Nile overflows, they are content to spend much of their time in and around the cooling waters, but their tracks show that they return regularly to the open plains to graze.

These paths are clearly distinguished by reason of the huge piles of dung dropped by the animals on the way. Each rhino defecates on exactly the same spot, the heap of dung growing steadily until it may be several yards in diameter. It is a habit observed even more consistently and regularly by the black rhinoceros. The excrement of the white species is of some weight and black in colour—rather like horse dung, not surprisingly for an animal that has a similar grass-based diet—and quite different to that of the black rhino, which feeds on leaves. Examination of the undigested vegetable matter contained in the droppings provides a clear indication of the species responsible.

Since the territorial limits of the white rhinoceros are only vaguely defined, it does not appear that defecating plays any major role in the establishment of scent posts. In fact the places where the piles of dung are heaped are like crossroads, providing an infallible guide to the comings and goings of the huge creatures, and attracting many smaller animals which feed on the

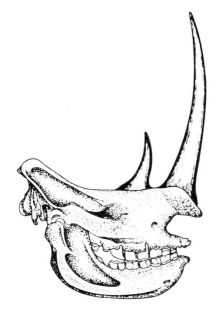

I: $\frac{(1)}{(1)}$ C: $\frac{0}{0}$ PM: $\frac{3}{3}$ M: $\frac{3}{3}$

Skull and dental formula of white rhinoceros.

Although the white rhino may sometimes be seen in family groups, including a male and a couple of females with their young, it is just as likely to be found alone on the savannah.

The front horn of the white rhinoceros may be several feet long, serving as a formidable natural weapon. Despite its fearsome appearance, however, the animal has a placid temperament and shows few aggressive tendencies, except occasionally towards rivals of its own species. The upper lip is flat, the muzzle square – suitable for cropping grass – whereas the upper lip of the black rhino, which browses on leaves, is more pointed and mobile.

Facing page: Young white rhinoceroses are carefully tended by their mothers until they are able to fend for themselves. Carnivores, including lions, are sometimes tempted to attack the babies but are liable to be foiled by the spirited defence put up by the adult female. The fully grown rhinoceros need fear no predator, apart from man.

waste matter. These include, first and foremost the dung beetles, then francolins and other birds, mongooses, reptiles such as the Nile monitor, and termites.

Although an atmosphere of calm hovers over the groups of pachyderms whether they are cropping the grass or wallowing in their mud bath, this pleasant tranquillity may sometimes be disturbed. During the mating season, for example, the adult males may engage in violent contests against each other. These dramatic battles may take place at any time of the year, though the normal breeding season for the southern population seems to be between July and September, and February or March for the northern group. The secreted odours given off by the females immediately attract the males, and two rivals will often clash in dangerous combat, their sharp horns inflicting deep wounds that may occasionally prove fatal. In the Umfolozi reserve, for example, between the years 1952 and 1957, game wardens came across the bodies of 30 dead rhinoceroses, most of which appeared to have been killed in fights with rivals for possession of a female.

The dominant male of a group may nevertheless display aggressive tendencies at other times as well, especially if he senses the threat of a potential rival – possibly one of his own offspring. When a young male attains the age of sexual maturity – at about five years – he is promptly expelled from the family unit. If he makes the slightest attempt to rejoin the group, he is summarily chased off by the dominant male, which shows hostility in snarls and menacing head-tossings. Occasionally the older animal will charge the younger, not with any evident intention to inflict a wound but rather to seal the latter's departure from the group.

Nobody really knows to what age the white rhinoceros will live in the wild. Examination of the state of wear and tear of teeth taken from skeletons, however, would seem to indicate a normal life expectancy of 40–50 years. Similar doubt surrounds the breeding habits of the species. Judging from studies of females accompanied by offspring, sexual maturity occurs at quite an early age – probably between three and five years old. The interval between successive births would therefore seem to be not more than three or four years.

The gestation period is believed to be about eighteen months – again the precise duration is not known – at the end of which the female gives birth to one baby. The newborn animal weighs approximately 100 lb and by the time it is a year and a half this will have risen to over half a ton. The mother evidently remains closely attached to her offspring until ready to conceive again.

The white rhinoceros has attained a gigantic size but is not unduly encumbered by its considerable weight. In fact it not only possesses great bodily strength but is amazingly light on its feet. With the aid of its primary natural weapons – the horns – the white rhino is well able to defend itself and its young against carnivores such as lions and hyenas. A female's relative lack of experience, however, may sometimes be sensed by a predator, and there have been cases of female rhinos having to abandon their young in such circumstances. But in general, as with most other wild animals of similar size and weight, the only real enemy to be feared is man himself.

FAMILY: Rhinocerotidae

Threatened with extinction, the rhinoceros family are nowadays confined to very limited parts of India, Malaysia and Indonesia, and to eastern and southern Africa. Yet not all that long ago, several different species of rhinoceros lived alongside the mammoth in many parts of Europe and Asia, and over most of the African continent.

One important reason for their present desperate plight is of course the pressure man himself has exerted on them through relentless hunting and poaching. But the gradual reduction of their numbers down the ages is also attributable to biological causes. The brain of the rhinoceros, for example, is very poorly developed in relation to the creature's immense size, and from this viewpoint alone it has evolved less than any other perissodactyl. A number of other primitive characteristics have also lingered on, which in most mammals have undergone evolutionary modification. To compensate for such shortcomings, however, the animal has a massive body, a thick hide and powerful horns that constitute a highly effective natural armoury to be employed in self-defence.

The rhinoceros's body varies in length, according to the species, from 8 to 14½ feet, its height from 6 to 7 feet and its weight from just under to over 3 tons. The legs are short but sturdy, with three toes on each foot, encased in incomplete hooves. The hard, tough hide, which on the back may be some 2 inches thick, is sometimes deeply folded, with horny plates, forming a kind of armour suiting. The skin surface is virtually hairless, apart from the edges of the ears and the tip of the tail. The sole exception is the Sumatran rhinoceros, which has a hairy coat.

The head is armed with either one or two horns—in the latter case one behind the other—and these are the animal's main weapons. These horns are not bony but fibrous in texture, growing out of the skin itself. Should they be accidentally broken, they will grow again.

The white rhinoceros, whose diet consists of grass, has a large, square muzzle well adapted for grazing. Other species that browse on leaves have a long, prehensile upper lip.

The incisor teeth are conically shaped and reduced in size. Those of the upper jaw are very small and absent altogether in aged animals. There are no canines and the large cheek teeth (premolars and molars) have transverse ridges on the crowns.

Rhinoceroses, with their tiny eyes, laterally placed, have poor vision, but their senses of hearing and, more especially, of smell are well developed. Open ground suits them best and in none of their habitats do they stray far from swamps and pools, where they regularly drink and bathe.

The Rhinocerotidae are classified, together with the Tapiridae, among the Ceratomorpha—a suborder of the Perissodactyla. They are further divided into two subfamilies—Rhinocerotinae and Dicerorhinae.

The former subfamily includes all those rhinoceroses with a single horn and a very thick, folded hide with prominent hard knobs interspersed between areas of thinner skin. They are Asiatic mammals, belonging to the genus *Rhinoceros*, represented by two species—the Indian rhinoceros (*Rhinoceros unicornis*) and the very rare Javan rhinoceros (*R. sondaicus*).

The Dicerorhinae consist of the two-horned species, all of which have thick hide, but with a smooth surface. There are three genera, each represented by a single species. The one Asiatic species is the Sumatran rhinoceros (*Dicerorhinus sumatrensis*), smallest of all the family. The two African species are the black rhinoceros (*Diceros bicornis*), fairly widespread in distribution, from Ethiopia southwards to Rhodesia, and the much rarer white rhinoceros (*Ceratotherium simum*), confined to Central and South Africa, the populations of the two zones being completely separated geographically.

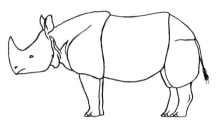
Indian rhinoceros
(*Rhinoceros unicornis*)

Javan rhinoceros
(*Rhinoceros sondaicus*)

Sumatran rhinoceros
(*Dicerorhinus sumatrensis*)

Black rhinoceros
(*Diceros bicornis*)

White rhinoceros
(*Ceratotherium simum*)

Above : The five surviving species of rhinoceros.
Facing page : The Rhinocerotidae are among the most primitive of the perissodactyls as well as the heaviest. They are divided into four genera and five species, of which three are Asian and two African. The one-horned species (*above*) are recognisably Asiatic, whereas the two-horned rhinos (*below*) are found in both continents.

CHAPTER 13

The African elephant: largest land animal

The elephant is the best known of all wild animals – familiar through books, cinema and television, a popular circus performer and affectionately admired by all visitors to the zoo. But although we can get a pretty good idea of the creature's size and strength from seeing it in captivity, its true nature and behaviour can only be assessed by patient study in its wild surroundings.

We are concerned here only with the African elephant (*Loxodonta africana*) which, together with the Indian elephant (*Elephas maximus*), belongs to the order Proboscidea. This is the largest land animal in the world, standing as high as 11 feet and weighing about 6 tons. There are two races of African elephant, which show certain anatomical differences. The bush elephant (*Loxodonta africana africana*) is larger in overall size but has a shorter head than the forest elephant (*L. a. cyclotis*).

Unlike other African mammals of considerable size – such as the rhinoceros and hippopotamus – the elephant has managed to adapt itself to widely different habitats. It may be found in savannah, bush, forest and even mountain country, as on the slopes of Mt Kilimanjaro or Mt Cameroon – at altitudes of up to 11,000 feet. Moreover, although many herds confine themselves to humid regions with an abundance of lakes and rivers, others appear to be quite content to live in desert-like conditions – as on the plain of El Aagher in Mauritania. This area is of some interest because the animals that live there are descended from those once inhabiting the fertile area now covered by the Sahara. Nowadays water is very scarce in these parts and vegetation thinly distributed. Bearing in mind the large quantity of vegetable matter consumed daily by an elephant as well as the plentiful supply of water needed for drinking and bathing, it seems extraordinary that it can survive in a region receiving so little rainfall.

Facing page : A magnificent male African elephant – though lacking one tusk – in typical savannah country at the foot of Mt Kilimanjaro. This is the largest of all land mammals, its range more restricted than formerly, but still widespread through Central, East and West Africa.

AFRICAN ELEPHANT
(*Loxodonta africana*)

Class: Mammalia
Order: Proboscidea
Family: Elephantidae
Length (including trunk): 240–300 inches (600–750 cm)
Height to shoulder: 96–132 inches (240–330 cm)
Weight: male, up to 6 tons; female, up to 4 tons
Food: vegetation (mainly branches, leaves, bark, fruit)
Gestation: 22 months
Number of young: one, occasionally twins
Longevity: 70–85 years

Adults
Large head with enormous ears almost covering shoulders. The upper incisors (tusks) diverge slightly at the base, the tips being curved inwards. The males are heavier than the females and have longer tusks. The trunk, an elongated nose, has nostrils at the tip, and two 'lips' (the Indian elephant only having one). The feet are rounded and the toes indistinguishable, only the nails being visible. The skin is almost naked; the tail terminates in two hairy tufts. Normal body temperature is about the same as man's (98 °F, 36·7 °C or slightly above), and the pulse rate, when at rest, 49 per minute, rising to 90 or 100 after exercise. The female has two pectoral mammae.

Young
Newborn animals are covered with black hair, especially thick on the top of the head. They weigh between 175 and 265 lb and stand at least 3 feet high.

Subspecies
The two varieties of African elephant are the bush elephant (*Loxodonta africana africana*) and the forest elephant (*L. a. cyclotis*). The latter's weight seldom exceeds 4 tons, its height not more than 115 inches. It has five nails on the fore-feet, four on the hind-feet. The ears are rounded and the tusks smaller than those of the bush elephant. This is the largest of land mammals, the male weighing up to 6 tons. It has four nails on the fore-feet, three on the hind feet. The tusks, curving upwards with advancing age, are common to both sexes, the record length for a male being 11 feet 5½ inches. The trunk may be more than 6 feet long.

The all-purpose trunk

The strangest and most useful part of the elephant's anatomy is of course its trunk or proboscis (which lends its name to the order to which the animal belongs). This appendage is far more versatile than the limbs of other mammals, including the human hand.

There have been many scientific attempts to explain the origin of the elephant's trunk, but nobody really knows the circumstances which caused it to evolve by a series of selective and mutational developments over a period lasting some 60 million years. It all began with a grass-eating creature named *Moeritherium*, believed to be the ancestor of the modern elephant, living in the swampy regions of Egypt during the Eocene period. This animal was about the size of a pig and had a muzzle resembling that of a tapir. Four of its teeth were already quite sharp. Later species—about 300 of them, distributed over all the continents with the exception of Australasia—gradually came to look more like the enormous mammals that live today. Earlier examples had long, pointed incisors and a muscular, mobile neck to support a head made heavy by such over developed teeth. At this stage there was no sign of a proboscis and the short lips of the animals were not of much use for rooting up vegetation. An organ capable of gripping and pulling branches and leaves was therefore indispensable for these creatures' welfare. The trunk, formed by the elongation of the upper lip and its fusion with the nose, was to fulfil such functions to perfection, although not in itself a guarantee of a species' survival. The enormous proboscideans of the Pleistocene period, for example, all became extinct.

The trunk, nevertheless, proved a tremendous asset for gathering food and for other purposes. The two species that have survived to this day employ it for a remarkably wide range of activities. It is powerful enough to be used as an extra limb—capable of uprooting bushes and young trees, or of delivering a crippling blow—but can also perform actions demanding great concentration and care. The tip is especially sensitive, and furnished with a finger-like process or 'lip' so that objects as small as leaves and berries can be plucked with delicacy and precision. Tramping across the savannah, the huge animal will use its trunk to snatch up a tuft of tall grass, shaking it vigorously or slapping it against flanks and tusks to remove the dirt and finally introducing the cleaned grass into its mouth. The branches of trees will be carefully sniffed and felt before twigs and leaves are gently broken off, and when the lower boughs are stripped the trunk is used as a tentacle to bring the lateral branches within easy reach.

The appendage plays an important role in respiration, air being conducted through it to the elephant's nostrils. It is also an extension of the animal's smell apparatus—a very highly developed sense. Should an elephant suspect danger it will lift its trunk in the direction of the wind to detect the presence of tell-tale scents. Yet another valuable function of the trunk stems from its amazing absorptive capacity. It can suck up as much as a gallon of water at a time, expelling the contents into the mouth for drinking or spraying it over the body to cleanse itself. Alternatively, the trunk can be filled with dust, which is then sprinkled

over the back and flanks as a double protection against the heat of the sun and the bites of insects.

This storage capacity is of particular importance during the dry season for it enables what little water there is to be used to best advantage. When the river beds are cracked and empty, the elephant can use the trunk to locate water, digging pits with its tusks and sucking up the water that filters thinly through the subsoil. Thus even in periods of severe drought the elephant can usually find enough drinking water to survive until the rainy season returns.

Although the trunk is clearly an all-purpose tool, the surprising fact is that it is not absolutely indispensable for the creature's survival. On the rare occasions when elephants have been mutilated – possibly by poachers' snares – they have been seen to kneel down in order to eat or drink, and even to submerge themselves completely for the latter purpose.

Mere size is not necessarily a passport to survival in the wild, as the great dinosaurs and even the huge prehistoric mammals

The African elephant uses its trunk to spray dust over its body both to get rid of insects and to keep cool. Because of this it tends to take on the colour of the soil of the region which it inhabits.

were to discover. But the African elephant is not a lumbering, useless relic of the past. Despite its enormous size, it has succeeded in coming to terms with its surroundings—something its ancestors apparently failed to do. To achieve this it has had to solve three of the most vital problems of existence in a hot climate —nourishment, locomotion and regulation of body temperature. Unlike most of the large and medium-sized herbivores, it does not need to move far or to bend down in order to feed, simply reaching out for anything it needs, without being forced to change position or to relax its guard. It can even drink and keep its body cool without abandoning its upright stance. The lofty giraffe has similar advantages but is compelled to lower its neck to quench its thirst and occasionally to browse, moments that can prove fatal if a lion is lurking in the neighbourhood. But the elephant has no such fear of being caught off balance or taken unawares by an enemy. It is prudent enough not to allow its more vulnerable calves to stray off on their own and its natural defences are formidable enough to deter the strongest carnivore. This is one animal giant that has found the way to survive—and not at the expense of other living creatures.

Cattle egrets are sometimes seen in the company of elephants. They seldom perch on the backs of the massive pachyderms, however, being driven off by a flick of the trunk.

New teeth for old

The elephant, because of its immense size, requires a vast amount of food every day in order to replace lost energy. Depending on circumstances, the quantity may be in the region of 400–500 lb of mixed vegetable matter daily–equivalent to approximately five or six per cent of its own body weight. The only other creature of comparable bulk–the whale–has a very much simpler nutritional task in its watery environment. All it has to do is to open its massive mouth and sieve out from the water it takes in the plankton which form its main food supply. But the elephant–despite the fact that it enjoys a much more varied diet of grass, branches, bark, leaves, roots, pieces of wood, bulbs and fruit–cannot of course just swallow its food.

During the long course of its evolution the elephant has acquired a set of teeth admirably suited for coping with its vegetarian diet, particularly for crushing and grinding hard substances and for extracting the juices from fibrous stems. Each half of its upper and lower jaw is provided with one functional cheek tooth, about a foot in length and several inches high. In the case of the African elephant these teeth are covered with enamel crowns, which are lozenge-shaped ridges and thus ideal for their work of grinding and pulping. Subjected to continuous use, however, the teeth, although very strong, gradually become worn down. When this occurs, each is immediately replaced by a new tooth.

The first molar tooth appears when the baby elephant is three months old and each of the five permanent teeth is replaced at intervals during the animal's life–when it is three, five, ten, twenty and thirty years old. The new molar does not grow directly below the old one–as is the case with other mammals–but behind it, pushing along horizontally to replace the used tooth when it drops out. The last molar is the largest–about fourteen inches long–and when this is eventually eroded, the elephant, by now about seventy or even as much as eighty-five years old, is no longer able to chew hard vegetable matter. It will be compelled to confine itself to river banks, eating leaves, stems and soft shoots, until it dies–unable to feed at all.

The mastodonts–prehistoric proboscideans which included the mastodon and related species–ranged over the entire globe, with the exception of Australasia, for the best part of 40 million years, the mastodon itself surviving until the Ice Age. The cheek teeth of these huge creatures did not consist of transverse folds of enamel surrounded by cement, as in the modern elephant, but of rounded projections or cusps, which were probably incapable of crushing anything but soft vegetable matter. This type of dentition, typical of the tapir family, was obviously far less flexible and efficient than that of modern elephants and may have been an important cause of their gradual decline and eventual disappearance. The teeth of the African elephant can cope with the abrasive silicates contained in grass, the stringy stalks of acacias and the bark of baobabs.

The age of an elephant can be fairly accurately determined by the examination of its teeth–notably from their general condition and signs of new growth.

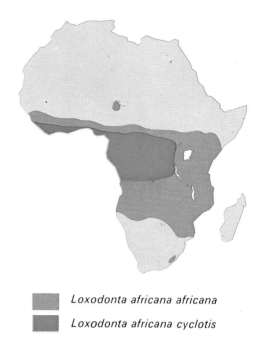

Loxodonta africana africana

Loxodonta africana cyclotis

Geographical distribution of the two subspecies of African elephant.

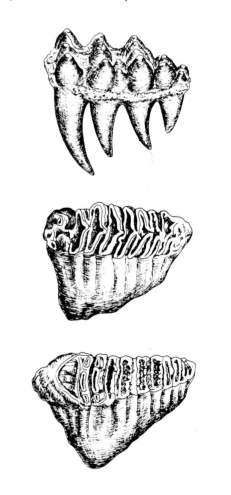

Molar teeth of mastodon *(top)*, Asiatic elephant *(centre)*, mainly a grass-eater, African elephant *(bottom)* mainly a leaf-eater.

Giant on the move

An animal that attains gigantic dimensions is faced with a serious problem when it comes to moving around, for its legs have to become progressively stouter and stronger in order to support the expanding body. In fact, the volume of the body increases in cubic proportions whereas the limbs—which have the responsibility of propping it up—only grow two-dimensionally. According to Clifford Bingham, if the African elephant were for some reason to grow to several times its present size its legs would have to be so enormous in cross-section that they could not be accommodated beneath the body. The modern elephant has therefore reached just about the maximum practical size for a land mammal.

For aquatic and marine mammals the problem of locomotion is more easily resolved. Whales have been able to attain their enormous bulk simply because the sea water which is their natural element frees them from the pull of gravity and lightens their true body weight. This enables them to propel themselves with the aid of flippers, which are activated by powerful muscles. Similarly the sauropods and other great reptiles of the Mesozoic period, although much larger than modern elephants, managed to move about quite easily with relatively short limbs, probably because they kept to swampy regions and not firm ground.

Although the elephant appears heavy and ungainly, its straight, column-like legs are well adapted to support its enormous weight; furthermore, because of their broad area of contact with the ground any possibility of slipping on soft, dangerous terrain is prevented. The five toes, enveloped in fibro-adipose tissue, are, thanks to powerful flexor muscles, comparatively mobile. The soles of the feet are covered with thick epithelial padding which counteracts slipping and deadens sound. The surface of the feet is thus very flexible and sensitive, adapting naturally to any irregularities of the terrain. By this means the elephant is able to move forward silently and with surprising agility.

An elephant is unable to jump or to gallop, so it cannot negotiate an obstacle such as a 6-foot-wide ditch. This is one method of confining the animals in captivity. The animal's normal walking pace is about 5 miles per hour but it can, if hard pressed, break into a run—similar to that of a camel, a giraffe or a bear—in which the two legs on one side of the body are raised and moved in unison, while the other two provide momentary support. If the elephant is in a hurry to find a waterhole or to get across a dangerous patch of ground it may increase its rate to about 10 miles per hour; and over short distances, when charging or panicking, it can reach up to 25 miles per hour.

Contrary to popular belief, however, the elephant is a skilful and confident climber, both on bare rocks and steep inclines. In the Murchison Falls National Park in Uganda, troops of elephants may sometimes be seen picking their way down the rugged slopes that border the Nile in order to feed on the succulent plants growing on the river banks. The precision of their movements and their delicate sense of balance is quite astonishing. At other times they have been seen clambering up a sandy slope, planting the back legs solidly in the soft ground and using the front legs to

Facing page : The African elephant is a strict vegetarian, with a marked preference for branches, leaves, bark and fruit. The trunk is used for uprooting bushes and breaking off branches, as well as for more delicate operations such as picking leaves and berries.

The African elephant's tusks are well-developed incisors of the upper jaw, and are used both as weapons and as tools. Although one tusk is often sufficient for normal activities, the loss of a tusk or a portion of same may handicap the animal when browsing among thickets. Such an injury may be the result of lifting a heavy weight or of a violent fight with a rival.

Facing page : An elephant in the wild needs to eat upwards of 400–500 lb of vegetation every day. Although some of this consists of grass, its main preference is for the branches, leaves and bark of the trees of bush and savannah.

test the terrain and find a suitably secure base to bear their weight. They then shift the balance of the body, thrusting head and trunk forward, putting all the weight on the front legs and slowly dragging the back legs up the incline, almost kneeling.

The elephant is also an adept swimmer, capable of crossing a wide river, holding the trunk clear of the water so that there is no difficulty in breathing.

Although it is amazingly versatile and able to overcome difficulties posed by many different types of terrain, the elephant does not deliberately court trouble and will always choose the easiest possible route. If compelled to climb a hill or a mountain-side it will use considerable ingenuity to pick a path that is comparatively level and free of obstacles; and should it be forced to cross soft, swampy ground – which it generally tries to avoid – it will advance very cautiously indeed, testing the ground with its trunk or with one foot before committing itself.

The elephant's cooling system

Solving the problems of food and locomotion are vital for a creature as massive as the elephant, but there is also a third necessity – that of regulating body temperature. All living organisms generate a certain amount of heat through metabolic action and there must be a balance between heat production and heat loss. The heat production of warm-blooded animals with a constant body temperature is greater than that of cold-blooded creatures, but it tends to decrease as the animal's size increases. The major part of this heat is eliminated by radiation through the exposure of the body surface to the air.

The skin of an elephant is almost an inch thick and its characteristically wrinkled appearance is due to the presence of over-developed soft pimples or papillae. These aid temperature regulation by increasing the area of the skin surface, both for the conduction of heat by the cutaneous blood vessels and for heat elimination. In this way a balance is maintained between heat production – which varies according to the degree of activity of the various tissues – and heat loss – which depends on the animal's relationship to its environment.

The enormous ears of the African elephant also play a significant role in the temperature-regulating process, an extensive network of capillaries augmenting the skin surface area for heat elimination. They are also used as fans during the heat of the day.

Early warning

The largest terrestrial carnivores and most efficient hunters are the lions and tigers. It stands to reason, however, that grass-eating mammals which surpass them dramatically in both size and strength should be more or less immune to their attacks. The only reason why elephant calves and baby rhinoceroses are sometimes preyed upon by these carnivores is that the former have not yet acquired what might be called 'dissuasive weapons', not so much fangs and claws as sheer weight and physical power, coupled with ritual movements and attitudes calculated to warn

off and intimidate an enemy. In the case of the African elephant, these attributes enable it to defend itself without running away (thus wasting no energy) and to protect its young. Should it sense danger, it will neither seek shelter nor take flight. Yet at the same time it will avoid an actual confrontation by assuming any of several aggressive postures which are likely to deter predators.

In the event of a hostile carnivore coming within striking distance, the elephant will confront it, charge, and then come to a halt a few yards from the intruder. It has been confirmed that in nine cases out of ten the elephant will stop before reaching the spot where its enemy is waiting. If—as generally happens—the latter is sufficiently terrified to turn tail and flee, the bloodless conqueror will swing its head several times from side to side.

When an elephant decides to charge, it lifts its head so that the tusks are horizontal, parallel to the ground. The trunk is not thrust forward but lowered to a vertical position in front of the legs. The ears, fully unfurled, make the animal look even larger than it really is—a further deterrent to the enemy. But if the elephant's intention is to intimidate rather than attack, it behaves rather differently. The ears are still spread wide but the head is kept low, with the tusks pointing downward. The animal sways its head and trunk, sometimes breathing or trumpeting noisily. Many hunters who remain convinced that they have killed charging elephants may have mistaken the signs—possibly intended merely to warn them off; but in all fairness, there is not usually time, in such circumstances, to stand still and try to distinguish between a ritual display and a full-scale attack!

It was the Bushmen who first learned, from direct experience, how to interpret the behaviour of an elephant confronted by a potential enemy. They fully understood that, in certain situations, the massive creature—for all its hostile attitude—was not really dangerous. To the great amazement of the Boer colonists who watched them in action, the intrepid hunters stood their ground and then silently slipped away, the elephant making no attempt to follow but resuming its tranquil browsing.

The pair of splendid ivory tusks are not—as is sometimes believed—canines, but incisors growing from the upper jaw, the only ones retained by the adult animal. Those of the adult male bush elephant each weigh 65–90 lb, those of the female seldom exceeding 20 lb. There have been verified reports of immense pairs of tusks weighing as much as 250 lb, but these are quite exceptional. There seems to be no connection between the length and weight of the tusks and the size of the elephant, and the figures vary greatly from one region to another. In some herds the tusks are especially long and powerful, whereas in others—notably among elephants living in parts of Zambia and Mozambique—they are non-existent. This variation may be the result of an hereditary factor but it has not been proved. If it were true, it would be in the scientific interest to protect those animals possessing the finest tusks, since the progeny might be expected to display similar characteristics. Unfortunately, the animals with the most magnificent tusks are invariably picked off by hunters and poachers because of the value placed on the ivory.

The elephant does not only use its tusks as weapons to wound

The elephant's trunk is a remarkable appendage, indispensable for feeding and drinking, and highly sensitive to various stimuli. By means of smell and touch it can be used to pick leaves and berries with the utmost delicacy and precision.

Facing page : The impressive tusks of the African elephant are utilised as tools for a variety of tasks—digging pits, pulling up roots and knocking over obstacles. Each elephant normally makes use of only one tusk, always the same one, so that some are left-handed, others right-handed.

or intimidate enemies or rivals of its own species during the mating season, but employs them as tools for digging pits and removing heavy obstacles. It is interesting to note that in undertaking such peaceful tasks some elephants are right-handed and others left-handed, so that the tusk used more frequently shows all the signs of wear and tear.

It often happens that an elephant loses a tusk or a portion of a tusk in the course of lifting heavy objects or during a fight. Such an accident may have a serious effect on the temperament and behaviour of the injured animal. Gravely handicapped for vital everyday activities, the elephant may even abandon its herd and turn into an aggressive, solitary wanderer. The tusks may also be subject to bad decay and this too can prove detrimental to its food-seeking capacities. One elderly female elephant whose left tusk had been reduced to a mere stump was seen to move backwards through thickets in order to avoid bruising it, and to refrain entirely from eating, except when trees and branches were sufficiently wide apart not to cause it further painful damage.

Skin and parasites

Most mammals spend much of their time grooming their coats or their skins, either by licking or rubbing themselves against the rough bark of trees. Some of them take regular mud baths to get rid of irritating and harmful parasites. For agile, medium-sized creatures such activities pose few problems, but for massive animals such as the rhinoceros and elephant these procedures obviously demand more time and effort.

The rhinos, together with most of the other large African herbivores, find the problem largely solved for them as a result of their give-and-take association with oxpeckers, small birds that feed on the insects lodging in the folds of the animals' skin. But elephants do not play the gracious hosts either to oxpeckers or to cattle egrets—chasing them off their heads and backs with mighty swipes of their heavy trunks.

Cattle egrets frequently collect near the herds but they perform no useful cleansing function, simply feeding on insects that the elephants happen to disturb with their feet. Another bird, however, belonging to the Corvidae, and known as the piapiac (*Ptilostomus afer*), is permitted to perch on the elephant's back and head. But even this bird seems to play little part in ridding the pachyderm of parasites, using the animal's body as a convenient vantage point for catching insects on the wing.

Since birds are not tolerated for this purpose, the trunk assumes added importance in helping to keep the elephant's body clean and healthy. Insects are dislodged by using the trunk to spray water or dust over the body, and this activity becomes an essential and regular routine.

Although the baby African elephant at birth is covered with black hairs, the skin of the adult animal is practically naked, except for a few bristles scattered about the trunk, and two hard, thick, hairy tufts at the tip of the tail. Local tribesmen sometimes use this hair for fashioning into bracelets, which are regarded as good luck charms and sold to appreciative tourists.

The hide of the African elephant is thick and wrinkled. Frequent baths in muddy water and sprinklings of dust help to keep it in good condition and free of parasites.

Facing page : The enormous ears of the African elephant are more important as a heat-regulating mechanism than as organs of hearing. They constitute a broad surface area for heat elimination through the skin and can be used as huge fans to keep the body cool in the hottest period of the day.

The natural colour of the elephant's hide is often completely hidden below a coating of mud after the animal has emerged from a pool. Under normal conditions this skin colour is iron-grey, some animals being darker than others, but when they come out of their muddy bath the colour may be glistening black. Mud and dust in combination often bring about a dramatic alteration in the natural skin colour as well. The elephants of the Tsavo National Park in Kenya, for example, have a brownish appearance, tallying with the colour of the soil, whilst elephants inhabiting areas with volcanic soils are black or ash-coloured.

Some authorities claim that elephants consciously realise the therapeutic benefits of the water or mud in which they immerse themselves, but whether this is true or not, it does appear that their skin is generally more free of parasites than that of rhinoceroses. What does seem to be confirmed is that elephants do not select their bathing places at random, but are drawn again and again to sites which appear to offer no greater amenities than others that are habitually shunned.

In a particularly dry year, water is often difficult to find. The elephant, however, can endure a period of severe drought by digging holes in dried-up river beds with its tusks and trunk until it reaches the level of water in the subsoil. When sufficient water has seeped through to fill the hole, the elephant can quench its thirst.

Sense and intelligence

The elephant's eyesight is very poor, experts claiming that it is quite unable to distinguish a man from a tree at a distance of 30 yards. Nobody seems to know why this should be so, though there has been no shortage of ingenious explanations. Some authorities advance physiological reasons, others believe that it can be attributed just as much to indifference as to any physical deficiency. Whatever the reason, however, the lack is more than compensated by a very highly developed sense of smell, enabling the animal to detect the presence of an intruder at 200 yards, even when there is little wind.

The trunk plays an important role in this scenting capacity, for it can sniff the air at various heights as well as at ground level. It is, in addition, a highly sensitive tactile organ, but it is interesting to note that baby elephants do not seem to use it for touching and feeling until they are several weeks old.

The fact that an elephant can be trained to perform quite a wide range of simple tasks and tricks would seem to confirm that it possesses a fair level of intelligence. The brain, though highly convoluted, is not large in relation to skull size, nor particularly well developed. But there is some truth in the popular assertion that it 'never forgets', in the sense that it retains much of what it has learned either from example or experience.

One characteristic worth bearing in mind when judging the relative intelligence of elephants is that their biological cycle is very similar to that of humans, though—in the wild, at least—rather shorter lived. The calves remain with their family unit until they reach sexual maturity—between twelve and fourteen years of age. After that they become more or less independent, but young males may serve a kind of apprenticeship (he is usually referred to as a 'squire') with an older, more experienced adult. A few of them choose a solitary existence, or may join a group of other young males, but even after leaving the family unit they tend to stay in the vicinity, returning to it from time to time. Only when they are old will they deliberately isolate themselves and perhaps retire to the banks of a river, there to die alone.

A young female elephant will not couple with a male until she is about eighteen years old, and when she gives birth she may be assisted by other females, often her own mother or grandmother. Unlike the male, however, when she reaches an advanced age she stays together with the rest of the herd until she dies.

The daily round

The nucleus of the elephant community is the family unit, consisting of a female, her youngest mature daughter and several youngsters of varying ages. A number of these families will join together to make up a herd, and these in turn may link in order to form an enormous herd of up to a thousand individuals. The older females dominate the herds, directing all the activities.

The movements of the herds are conditioned by the never-ending quest for food—grass, leaves, bark, branches, roots, buds and fruit. The constitution of the diet depends on the natural

A typical family group of elephants may consist of from five to fifteen individuals usually two adult females with their young of various ages.

Following pages : Family groups of elephants often join together to form large herds of several hundred individuals. The herd is a matriarchal organisation, dominated by the older females, and the utmost care and protection is given to the young until they are old enough to fend for themselves.

resources of the region and the time of year. The daily wanderings of the herds continue virtually without interruption. During the dry season, however, the elephants are content to spend the hot daytime hours resting in the shade of trees, fanning themselves with their huge ears and feeding in the immediate vicinity. When it gets cooler they head for the nearest waterhole.

The African elephant does not eat as much grass as its Indian cousin and has a distinct preference for other types of vegetable matter. It is, for example, particularly fond of the soft, juicy wood of the baobab tree, gashing the bark deeply with its tusks and extracting the succulent fibres with its trunk. These slivers are then munched with extreme care and relish, the harder parts being spat out. A troop of elephants will reduce a large tree to fragments in a very short time, and cases have been reported of animals being crushed under the weight of a tree that they have rooted up or snapped in half by leaning against the trunk.

The African elephant also eats vast quantities of leaves and has a liking for the fruits of certain species of palm. The seeds of the latter are not broken down by the digestive juices and are expelled with the excrement, often some distance from the place where they were swallowed. The dung provides a favourable medium for the seeds to germinate and grow, and in certain parts of the continent the paths travelled by elephants are lined with palm-trees, as if someone had deliberately planted them there.

It sometimes happens – for reasons not satisfactorily explained – that an elephant manages to topple a tree by pushing its forehead against it and then applying its full body weight, but then refrains from eating either the bark or the leaves. This apparently misdirected use of natural resources is of some value and importance to smaller animals such as impalas and dik-diks, and to even larger creatures such as black rhinos, bringing within their reach tasty morsels that would otherwise have eluded them.

The loud, dry cracks of trunks and branches being broken by elephants is a familiar sound on the savannah, and in the Serengeti the noise of elephants battering down a tree can be heard for miles. The sound often alerts the wardens to an invasion of elephants from the neighbouring Masai Mara reserve, carrying a threat to the wooded savannah bordering the Seronera river.

As a general rule, elephants show great punctuality in drinking and bathing. When food is relatively plentiful they do not have to wander too far from water to seek it, and will usually be found, when evening comes, on the banks of their favourite pool or river. If, however, a period of drought compels them to make long journeys to obtain food, they may take their opportunities when they can, quenching their thirst and bathing at night or at dawn.

An elephant can go for several days without taking in any liquid, deriving enough from the juices of the vegetation eaten, but this period of abstinence cannot be tolerated for too long. When it does eventually find a plentiful supply of water, it will show its delight by completely immersing its body.

When a troop of elephants approaches a waterhole, other animals that may already be drinking there will give way immediately. The female elephants come on at a fairly brisk pace but display some caution, sniffing the air before taking their place

Facing page : Although the African elephant is found in every kind of habitat, except for desert, it normally seeks out regions where the vegetation is abundant and the water supply plentiful. Bathing is a regular activity and one that affords ample opportunity for fun and games.

The African elephant is an accomplished swimmer, capable of fording a river as wide as the Nile. The trunk is held clear of the surface to permit breathing.

along the bank. The males, on the other hand, show considerably more confidence, taking a good look at the other elephants already enjoying the water or arriving by another route. When they meet, they salute each other by sniffing and then interlocking trunks, pushing with their tusks until their mouths are touching. After this ritual they separate and enter the water to bathe. If it is deep enough, they soak the entire body, keeping the tip of the trunk above the surface so that they can breathe; alternatively, they may stretch out on one side, rubbing their face and ears. When the washing is done, they seek out a corner where they can siphon up dust to sprinkle all over their body. Finally, they make an un-hurried departure from the site and tramp off in search of food.

In some parts of Africa the dry season lasts for an exceptionally long time and for many weeks on end not a drop of rain falls. The waterholes are dry and the flow of the rivers is reduced to a thin trickle. Severe drought brings in its train many difficulties for animals that need a daily drink, but less for those species which can adapt to a shortage of water. Elephants have their own re-markable way of overcoming the problem. With the aid of their tusks and trunk, they dig holes in the river bed until they reach the level of water below the surface of the soil. Like water-diviners, they have an unerring ability to choose precisely the right spots to dig their pits. This ingenious procedure enables them to stay put in a region badly affected by drought and also performs a service for thirsty animals such as black rhinos.

Because of their capacity for adaptation, elephants are found in every type of natural environment in Africa apart from deserts. Their needs are in fact similar to those of buffaloes and the two species are often found together in the parts of East Africa where there is plenty of rainfall and a rich vegetation. The elephant is a tireless traveller, covering great distances in a relatively short time, so that it cannot be considered a territorial animal in the accepted sense.

Bringing up baby

The mating season of elephants may occur at any time of the year. As soon as the female is on heat she breaks away from the herd to follow one of the males. During the next couple of days, when she is responsive to the sexual advances of a mate, other males may gather round; and although there is no initial rivalry between the different contenders, the time sometimes comes when fights flare up, the victor having the right to claim possession of the female. In normal circumstances, the males all come from the same herd and know one another, so that the contests are usually resolved by means of recognised ritual postures. Should matters not be decided in such a painless fashion, the fights that take place may be incredibly violent, as each animal tries to plunge its tusks into the most vulnerable parts of its adversary's body.

A game warden in the Zanda district of Sudan described how he came across the body of a large elephant which had apparently been killed in one such confrontation with a rival male. The winner had not escaped unscathed, for one of its tusks was embedded deeply in the body of its victim. When the ranger extracted the incisor from the corpse, he found that although it was broken in several places, it was a perfectly healthy tusk and the fractures were caused by its own offensive thrusts.

During the courtship and mating period the female and the males accompanying her spend long hours of complete indolence, interspersed with short moments of intense sexual activity. Food is of little interest at such times. Gestation lasts for 22 months, at the end of which one calf, weighing about 250 lb and standing some 3 feet high, is born. Very occasionally, twins are born.

Frank Poppleton, for many years warden of the Murchison Falls National Park, has described how he once watched a baby elephant being born. A troop was quietly browsing when all of a sudden there was a general ripple of excitement. One of the females removed herself a few yards from her companions and was closely followed by a young male, probably her son, and another female, apparently her grandmother. All the other elephants then surrounded the little group, but all facing outwards, waiting expectantly. Then a shining dark object tumbled to the ground – the birth had taken place. Immediately, the young male and elderly female approached and together removed the enveloping fetal sac. The umbilical cord had already been broken in the fall and the mother was busy eating part of the placenta. When the two assistants had completed their cleansing activities, the entire troop gathered round once more to sniff the new arrival with gentle curiosity. After a little while they withdrew to resume their tranquil feeding, and soon afterwards they were joined by

A baby elephant does not learn to make proper use of its trunk until it is several weeks old. Throughout its adult life it relies on the trunk for drinking, scenting, testing and gathering food.

the female elephant, the younger male remaining behind to help the mother get the newborn animal to its feet. It stayed with her for the best part of two hours. Meanwhile, the vultures had collected, eyes fastened greedily on the remains of the placenta, but both elephants refused to allow them to come near until the baby had been removed some distance from the spot where the birth had taken place, the mother protecting it between her front legs. The baby then began to suckle vigorously while the elder brother wandered back to rejoin his companions.

This devoted attention on the part of the mother and the other members of the troop is characteristic, nor is it relaxed during the critical weeks to come. The baby elephant is suckled by its mother for two years. Contrary to what one might think, it does not use its trunk for the purpose but attaches its mouth directly to her teats, which are located between the front legs. To do this it lifts the trunk and rests it against its head, so that it does not get in the way. During the first few days the baby elephant remains almost literally implanted between its mother's legs. When it has acquired sufficient strength and confidence to move around a little, it still sticks close to her while she keeps a continual watch on its movements.

The first days and weeks are dangerous times for most baby animals in the wild, and even a young elephant risks ending up as prey for a prowling hyena or lion. There is also a possibility that it may be killed by a snake-bite. To guard against such contingencies, not only the mother but also other females of the herd will band together to protect the baby; and if, for any reason, it is orphaned, another mother will adopt it, suckling it together with her own offspring.

The female African elephant is capable of giving birth once every five years, even up to an advanced age of 60–65, although there is a significant decline in fertility in her later years.

Whenever the elephant troops cross rivers or are obliged to take a difficult path on their journeys in search of food and water, the adults pay particular attention to the calves, helping them along with their tusks and trunks to prevent them from falling, sinking into soft ground or being swept away by the current. Yet despite all these precautions, fatalities do occur, and it is estimated that during the first year about a third of the newborn elephants die. A mother, however, will continue to lavish affection even on her dead baby. One female was seen carrying the body of her offspring between tusks and trunk for several days, tenderly placing it on the ground whenever the herd paused to feed. It was only when the body was in an advanced state of decay that the mother finally abandoned it, but not before concealing it under a heap of branches and dry grass. Similar affection or loyalty is displayed by the young males when their master dies. They remain with the body for several days, defending it against hyenas and vultures, and sometimes covering it with vegetation before leaving it behind. This type of considerate behaviour is typical. The instinct of co-operation and mutual aid is highly developed, especially towards elephants that are somehow handicapped, either because of youth, sickness or injury. One observer reported seeing a couple of elephants literally pushing along a large male which was

Facing page: The baby elephant suckles for the first two years of its life. It does not use its trunk for the purpose but brings the mouth into direct contact with its mother's teats, located between her front legs.

The ivory tusks of the African elephant are in great demand commercially. Those of the adult male may weigh up to 90 lb, but those of the female rarely exceed 20 lb. Length and weight vary considerably from one region to another and do not seem to bear any direct relationship to the size of the animal.

clearly in agonising pain after being wounded by a hunter.

Although elephants do not demarcate the boundaries of fixed territories, they secrete, from the temporal glands situated between the eyes and ears, a substance which they spray on the branches of trees and over bushes. The odour cannot be detected by a man, but evidently it lingers on for quite some time, helping the elephants to maintain order and cohesion within the herd, however constituted.

The elephant graveyards

The first European explorers who penetrated the interior of the mysterious dark continent returned with dramatic accounts of elephant 'graveyards' – remote places chosen by aged animals for dying in seclusion. Many adventurers, excited by the prospect of finding treasure hordes of ivory, free for the taking, set out in search of these celebrated graveyards. Their quests, however, were as vain as those of the white colonists of South America who trekked through mountain and jungle in the hope of discovering the fabulous kingdom of El Dorado. It is true that the bodies of old elephants are often found in parks and reserves, and since it is their habit to cut themselves off from the herds when they are too feeble to find food, quite a large number of skeletons have been discovered in the vicinity of lakes and rivers. An epidemic might account for an unusually large quantity of bones being found lying side by side. But there is no evidence whatsoever that elephants seek out a particular region in which to end their days, and the stories of elephant graveyards can be rejected as myths.

Too many elephants?

A century ago elephants were to be found living peacefully over most of the African continent south of the Sahara down to the Cape of Good Hope. At that time there must have been over three million of them roaming through the forests and across the savannahs, showing a general preference for wooded regions during the dry season and for open plains at other times of the year. They would often undertake extensive journeys of several hundreds of miles, which might last as much as three years. They were hunted by the pygmy tribes of the Congo, by the Sudanese Arabs and by the Bushmen of the Kalahari Desert, but their numbers were not significantly affected. The white man, however, with his trusty rifle, his lust for ivory and his determination to protect his cultivated fields, altered the natural population balance drastically. As was to prove the case with so many other species, the African elephant was threatened to such a degree that the authorities had to step in to place it under protection.

Today the immense herds have vanished and it is estimated that there are about 300,000 elephants left throughout the continent. There are reckoned to be several hundred thousand in the Congo, most of them concentrated in the heart of primeval forests, 60,000 in Tanzania – which has the highest density of elephants per square mile – and 30,000 in Rhodesia and Zambia (they are well represented in Rhodesia's Wankie National Park

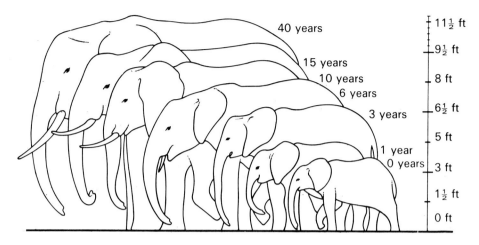

A diagram illustrating the comparative sizes of the African elephant at different ages.

and in Zambia's Luangwa Valley Game Reserve). Uganda has about 45,000 elephants and the population in Sudan was estimated ten years ago at 20,000. Other sizeable elephant herds are still to be found in Angola, Mozambique, Chad, the Central African Republic, Cameroon, Dahomey, Upper Volta, the Ivory Coast and Guinea, but only a few in Ghana and Nigeria.

Yet now that the wholesale massacres are nightmares of the past, and the African elephant is fully protected, a curious situation has arisen. The problem is no longer that of preventing their numbers from diminishing to the point of possible extinction but of finding some way of checking population growth.

Scientific study of the elephant population in the wild has revealed that in a typical well-balanced community, 60 per cent of the animals are adults, 16 per cent babies and young, and 24 per cent individuals that are capable of breeding but have not yet reached their full development. In such herds the mortality rate is 16 per cent and the birth rate 90 per cent. Given these figures, a herd might be expected to increase by 7 per cent each year. Actually, because many animals die before attaining sexual maturity, the increase is nearer 4–5 per cent. Even so, the numbers are likely to double within 20–25 years.

In the Congo's Albert National Park there were 800 elephants in 1931, but by 1950 the numbers had rocketed to 25,000. In the Kruger National Park in South Africa the ten elephants collected together in 1905 founded a herd which today numbers 2,000 animals. In Kenya's Tsavo National Park and in Uganda's Murchison Falls National Park the overpopulation problem is even graver. At one time, when the herds migrated towards the slopes of Mt Kilimanjaro, they used to spend only a very short period in the area now covered by the Tsavo park because the region lacked permanent sources of water. When a railway line was built to connect Uganda with the Kenyan port of Mombasa, wells were dug and many elephants became sedentary in the district. After the creation of the Tsavo National Park, artificial waterholes were provided so that the animals could enjoy a regular supply of drinking water. The consequence was that some 3,000 elephants settled in the region and gradually multiplied until they reached double that number. Nowadays, although the figures tend to fluctuate, it is estimated that the herds of elephants in the park sometimes exceed 10,000!

When the baby elephant is one year old it stands about as high as its mother's belly.

The destructive elephant

The Murchison Falls National Park, situated on the banks of the Nile and founded in 1952, is regarded as a special area of protection for the African elephant. Before it was created, the herds used to collect in the valleys during the dry season to feed on the succulent grass and numerous tender plants. The females regularly gave birth to their young in the forest and woodland groves that bordered the great river. Around March the family groups would begin to break up and disperse, the troops heading for those distant parts where heavy rainfall stimulated the growth of new grass. When the herds returned in November they found the local vegetation once more luxuriant–sufficient to support their numbers for the next five or six months.

Today this migratory ebb and flow has ceased. The elephant herds are strictly confined to the park for the entire year. Their numbers have tripled and the pastures can no longer support them. Hunger and death are commonplace in an area that formerly provided the animals with ideal living conditions. The same sad story has been repeated in many other regions.

A traveller who knew what these splendid grasslands looked like fifty years ago would be incredulous and appalled to see them today. The bush-covered plains have been transformed into arid wastes, and districts that were once well-wooded, especially on the west bank of the Nile, are now empty savannahs, dotted here and there with stunted, skeleton-like trees. The dramatic change

Ironically, the problem facing naturalists where elephants are concerned is not one of safeguarding the existing population but of checking the natural increase in their numbers. Protected in national parks and no longer able to migrate freely according to the cycle of the seasons, the African elephant is destroying its own habitat. Trees are bare and stunted, vegetation sparse and soil impoverished. This dismal landscape in the Murchison Falls National Park is reflected in many other African reserves, too limited in area to support the growing elephant population. The only solution open to the authorities at present is to cull thousands of young females in order to lower the birth rate.

African elephants browse on leaves and the cracking of trunks and branches is one of the most familiar sounds on the savannah. Larger trees are knocked down by the pressure of the elephant's head and body weight.

in the surroundings has been brought about by the elephants themselves. Though content to graze during the rainy season, they do not find the grass sufficiently tempting when the dry season arrives and turn their attentions to the trees. They rip off the branches with their trunks and if the leaves are out of reach knock down the whole tree by leaning against it. If the tree is too large and heavy they peel off the bark near ground level, up to a height of about 10 feet. In these ways they manage to destroy trees and devastate entire forests, damage that often proves irreversible, for the frequent fires that rage in the dry season also burn down young trees and prevent new growth, so that only the grass flourishes where woods and forests once stood.

Deprived of trees and shrubs, the leaf-eating animals such as impalas, gerenuks and black rhinoceroses are gradually disappearing, whereas those species that feed exclusively on grass—zebras, Thomson's gazelles and the like—are becoming ever more widely distributed. Thus the herds of elephants, allowed to roam freely in parks measuring many thousands of square miles in area, have been responsible for drastic alterations to the natural surroundings, which affect many other animal species. If the trend were allowed to continue, they would eventually destroy themselves. To avoid unnecessary suffering, the Ugandan authorities have been compelled to resort to painful methods of controlling the elephant population. In the Murchison Falls park some 2,000 elephants have been killed—mainly young females who would otherwise have swelled the already high birth rate.

It is a sobering thought that only about a hundred years ago this continent of Africa supported a population of three million elephants, whereas today it can sustain barely a tenth of that number. But that was in the days when the forests were not threatened and the great herds could move at will—according to the rhythm of the seasons—from woodland to savannah, fording rivers, climbing mountains and finding ample nourishment on the open plains, on the banks of lakes and rivers, and in the hearts of bush and forest.

Man alone must bear the responsibility for bringing about the abnormal natural conditions that forced the elephants to abandon their traditional ways of life. Deprived of their mobility, they were forced to start destroying the very refuges that should have afforded them absolute security. By a tragic stroke of irony, the people who had been instrumental in gaining protection for the animals were now compelled to slaughter them so that the species could survive. Man, whether he comes bearing ill or good will, seems destined to be the only predatory creature that the elephant has reason to fear. His ancestors once helped to destroy the mastodons and mammoths, and the future fate of the surviving species equally depends on man's decisions and actions.

An uneasy alliance

Although many people refuse to accept the fact, the African elephant, like its Asiatic relative, can be domesticated. History is there to attest to it. The Egyptians were probably the first nation to use huge Nubian elephants in warfare and although the great beasts must have lacked mobility, they would have presented a terrifying sight to an enemy that never dreamed such creatures could exist, and their impact may have been as shattering as that produced by the first tanks at Cambrai during the 1914–18 war.

In the Punic Wars between Carthage and Rome, elephants reinforced the Carthaginian cavalry, helping to defeat the Roman army at the battle of Tunis in 255 B.C. During the Second Punic War, in 218 B.C., the Carthaginian general Hannibal used African elephants to bolster his cavalry in the Pyrenees and then transported his entire army over the Alps. The 38 elephants had been successfully floated over the river Rhone on rafts, but the mountain snow and ice proved too much for the heavy creatures and only a handful survived. Elephants were obviously not very manoeuvrable for such purposes, yet records show that they continued to be used in warfare by the emperors of Ethiopia until the 18th century.

It is reasonable to assume that an animal which can be trained to obey simple instructions in battle would also respond to similar tutelage for more peaceful ends. But if such an idea did occur to those nations or tribes that had some experience of the behaviour of elephants, it was not put to the practical test until comparatively recent times. It was during the 1880's that the Egyptians, French and Belgians turned their minds to the problem. The Egyptians decided to import Asiatic elephants and to introduce them into the Sudan, in the hope of 'educating' the native African species. The French confined themselves to setting up committees to discuss the subject. Only the Belgians seemed interested in carrying the idea through to a logical conclusion. With the encouragement of King Leopold II, training centres were established in various parts of the Belgian Congo and by 1925 there were reported to be about 100 domesticated animals, which were employed for such jobs as hauling logs and removing heavy natural obstacles.

This initiative, though commendable in theory and fairly impressive in practice, was disappointing in that it failed to stimulate similar experiments in other parts of Africa. As time passed, the problems seemed to mount. In the first place, the elephants were competing with machines, which were becoming increasingly efficient for such tasks. Even more decisive, however, was the difficulty of capturing them–both time-consuming and dangerous–and then finding suitable personnel to train them. In India, the position of *mahout* or elephant-driver, would be handed down from father to son for generations. Having spent their lives in the company of elephants there was little they did not know about the creature's habits and behaviour. But in Africa there was no such reservoir of experience.

Long before anyone talked about taming elephants, men had hunted them for their valuable tusks. The use of ivory for carving dates back to the Stone Age and many figurines have been found in Europe, especially in southern France. The Egyptians used the ivory from elephants' tusks to fashion statuettes and toilet articles, as did the Phoenicians, the Etruscans, the Greeks and the Romans. The Oriental craftsmen of China, Japan and India have produced a wealth of ivory treasures both for secular and religious use; and today ivory is used for ornaments, musical instruments and domestic articles.

Young elephants are affectionately tended by their mothers and by the other females in the herd. During the first few days and weeks they rarely stray from their mothers' sides and are thus well protected from the attacks of predators.

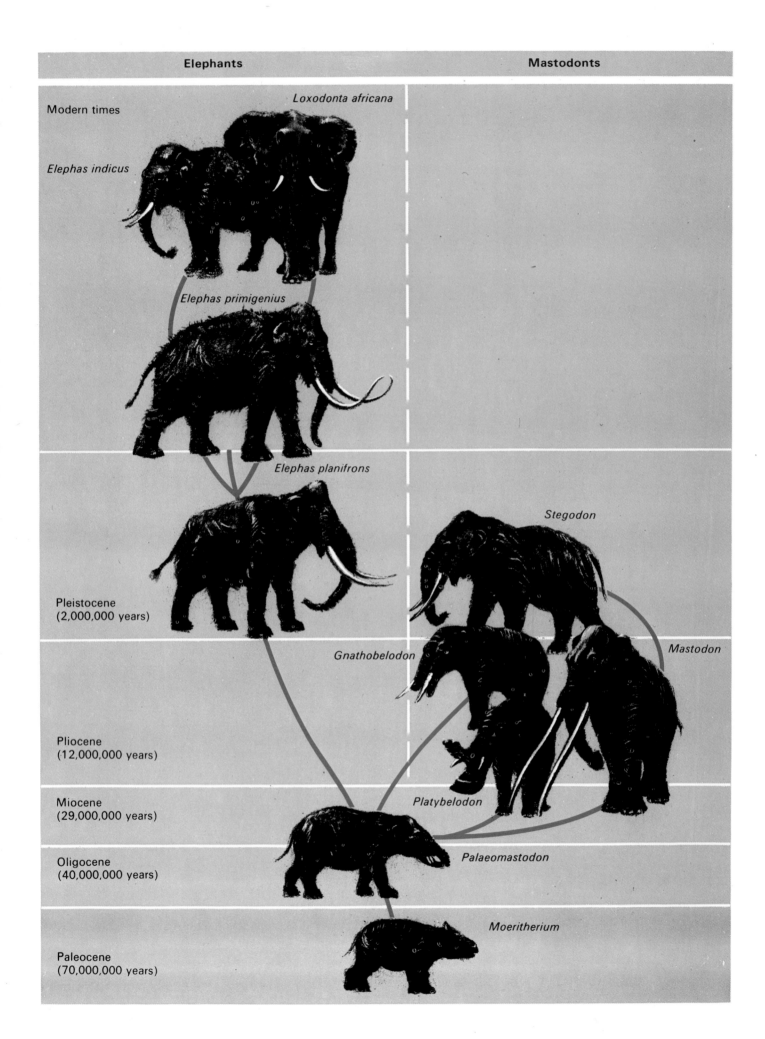

Elephants

Mastodonts

Modern times

Loxodonta africana

Elephas indicus

Elephas primigenius

Elephas planifrons

Stegodon

Pleistocene
(2,000,000 years)

Gnathobelodon

Mastodon

Pliocene
(12,000,000 years)

Miocene
(29,000,000 years)

Platybelodon

Oligocene
(40,000,000 years)

Palaeomastodon

Moeritherium

Paleocene
(70,000,000 years)

ORDER: Proboscidea

About 60 million years ago, at the start of the Tertiary period, the mammals began to usurp the dominant position in the natural order hitherto occupied by the reptiles. During the Upper Eocene a creature called *Moeritherium* was to be found among the lagoons and swamps of the El Fayum region of northern Egypt. The animal was about the size of, and much resembled, a tapir; but, like the modern hippopotamus, it was an amphibian, probably feeding largely on aquatic plants.

This animal did not, of course, have a trunk and looked nothing like a modern elephant; but paleontologists who studied the structure of its molars and the rudimentary elongation of its second pair of incisors were satisfied that it was the ancestor of those mammals known as proboscideans.

As the environment and the climate changed, over millions of years, the various land mammals were forced to adapt themselves to the changes or perish. Some of the descendants of *Moeritherium* were well fitted to survive in new surroundings and conditions. One such creature was *Palaeomastodon*, in the Oligocene, about 40 million years ago, whose fossil remains have also been unearthed in the El Fayum area. Although there were a number of different species—some of which were no larger than *Moeritherium*—the North African animal was fairly big, had sprouted a rudimentary trunk and possessed tusk-like incisors on the outside of the mouth.

It had taken about 20 million years for a trunk and tusks to evolve, but it was to be another 15 million years before a creature emerged that bore a really close physical resemblance to the present-day elephant. Yet the trend is unmistakable. Smaller vertebrates, in order to escape from predators, had to rely on greater mobility to survive. The proboscideans, however, evolved quite differently, gradually growing in size and weight, with a short, strong neck capable of supporting the huge incisors. The trunk—an extension of the upper lip fused with the nose—was a particularly important acquisition, for it enabled the animal to feed without difficulty on grass and leaves, functioning as an additional limb.

Palaeomastodon was a primitive form of mastodon—a group of proboscideans which flourished in the Miocene and Pliocene periods in every part of the world except Australasia, and which became extinct early in the Pleistocene. There were a number of species, all of them larger than *Palaeomastodon*, and with more typically elephant-like bodies. The fossil remains of *Platybelodon*, found in Mongolia, show a creature which had enormously long and flat lower incisors protruding from the elongated jaw—evidently used for digging in soft soil and mud. The lower jaw of *Gnathobelodon* lacked tusks but was concave in shape like a spoon and was doubtless employed for the same purpose. But the most characteristic and celebrated member of the group was *Mastodon*, standing about 9 feet high and with a tremendously long pair of upper incisors. These tusks—usually curving downwards—measured on average 7–8 feet in length. The long trunk was used for both eating and drinking.

Towards the end of the Miocene, another elephant-like creature called *Stegodon* appeared in Asia. The cusps of the mastodons' molars were rounded, with a few ridges, but the separating valleys had no cement. In *Stegodon*, however, there were a greater number of transverse, roof-like ridges, and the areas separating them were filled with cement. The creature therefore represents an intermediate stage between the mastodons and the elephants proper, in which the ridges, even higher and more numerous, are enveloped in cement.

It was a creature very similar to *Stegodon* that is regarded as the true ancestor of the elephant—the mammoth known as *Elephas planifrons*. Fossils show that its range covered the entire globe, with the exception of Australasia and South America. From it stemmed three groups—the extinct mammoths, the African elephants and the Asiatic elephants.

Although the elephant can dispense with water for a short period, its treks to and from waterholes—both for drinking and bathing—are parts of a regular routine.

Facing page : Evolutionary family tree of the proboscideans.

The African elephant differs from its Asiatic relative in several ways. Its forehead is flatter, its ears are much bigger, the trunk is ringed (with two 'lips' instead of one) and it consumes a large proportion of leaves, shoots and bark in addition to grass.

The mammoths were the largest proboscideans ever known, some species being 14 feet high. All had immense curving tusks, were hunted energetically by Stone Age man, and became extinct about 10 thousand years ago. Best known of all was the woolly mammoth (*Elephas primigenius*) of cave-painting fame, an inhabitant of Eurasia and North America, whose fossils have been recovered from frozen ground in Siberia, remarkably well preserved. It stood about 9½ feet high and its long shaggy coat and thick layer of subcutaneous fat minimised heat loss and made it possible for the creature to endure the rigours of an intensely cold climate.

The second group of proboscideans were African species, some of them now extinct. One of the latter was *Elephas recki*, whose fossils have been discovered near sites of primitive human habitation and which show anatomical similarities to the modern African elephant. The two species may be directly related, but the link has not been positively proved.

The third·group included *Elephas antiquus*, an inhabitant of Europe and Asia, with related dwarf species in the islands of the Mediterranean. This creature was probably the ancestor of the present-day Asiatic elephant.

The elephants are classified as a separate order of the animal kingdom, displaying physical characteristics that are found in no other group of mammals. One striking feature of the massive, heavy animal is the large size of the head in relation to the rest of the body. This is true of many mammals when young, but in the elephant it is equally marked in the adult. Surprisingly, however, the head does not weigh as much as might be supposed, because of the diploe, a layer of cancellous bone tissue situated between the inner and outer tables of the skull, which is filled with air-cells and cavities.

The front part of the elephant's body is significantly more sturdy and powerful than are the hindquarters. The long, thick, pillar-like legs support the enormous bulk of the body—as long as it is high—and help to balance it. The knees of the back legs are situated fairly low down. The club-like feet, on superficial examination, do not appear to have toes, but the projecting nails mark their presence. In fact there are five toes on each foot, interlinked by enveloping fatty tissue, and protected by a thick pad which takes the body weight. This posture is neither strictly digitigrade nor plantigrade, but a mixture of both—digiplantigrade.

The skin is tough and wrinkled—naked except for a scattering of hairs on the trunk and a tuft on the tail. Temporal glands located between the eyes and ears secret an odorous substance used for mutual identification.

The normal grey colour of the hide is often modified as a result of regular mud and dust baths, and the variation of skin pigmentation is considerable, depending on the region concerned.

The trunk or proboscis is a multi-purpose appendage—long, muscular and prehensile. It is used for breathing, smelling and feeling, for gathering food, for drinking and for keeping the body clean and parasite-free.

Elephants are strict vegetarians, their diet including grass, leaves, roots, bark and fruit. Evans and Sanderson have reckoned that the Asiatic species consumes at least 100 lb of fodder daily and Jeannin considers that the African elephant eats 25 per cent more. It must be remembered, however, that these statistics apply to animals in captivity and that elephants in the wild, being far more energetic, require even more food.

The teeth are in keeping with the animal's vegetarian diet. In the upper jaw, the first pair of incisors are absent and the second pair usually only temporary, normally falling out before the age of two years, although sometimes remaining permanently. It is the third pair of incisors that develop into tusks. These are basically formed of ivory; the enamel which covers the tips in young elephants is quickly worn down and soon disappears.

The tusks, which grow continuously, may reach a considerable size, those of the African elephant generally being somewhat longer and heavier than those of the Asiatic species, and the females' tusks invariably shorter than those of the males. Size—and colour—vary according to the individual's environment and diet; they may be pure or creamy white, pinkish, yellow or brown. The degree of curvature also varies with age, species and geographical location. Although normally straight and tapering, turning upwards at the tips, they may be spirally twisted or even curved inwards like a ring to encircle the trunk.

There are no canine teeth either in the upper or lower jaw, and there are no lower incisors. Six cheek teeth appear successively in each half of each jaw (three milk teeth, followed by three permanent teeth), but there is usually only a single functional tooth on either side of the jaw at any one time. These molars are worn down with constant use and are replaced from the rear at certain intervals during the animal's life. These continuously growing molars are of the lophodont type–that is, with enamel ridges on the crowns, surrounded by cement. Such heavily ridged teeth are especially designed for grinding and are differently structured according to the species and its diet. Thus the molars of the Asiatic elephant have transverse, almost parallel ridges on their surface (suitable for a largely grass-based diet), while those of the African elephant have fewer ridges and are lozenge-shaped–better suited for grinding up tougher, stringier substances such as bark and foliage.

The dental formula of all species of elephant is therefore

$$\text{I}: \frac{(1)\ 1}{0\ \ 0} \quad \text{C}: \frac{0}{0} \quad \text{M}: \frac{(3)\ 3}{(3)\ 3}$$

the figures in parentheses indicating the milk teeth.

Because of the exceptional development of the incisors, the mouth structure is modified, the trunk being an extension of the upper lip.

In spite of the enormous size of the head, the cranial cavity encloses a brain which is only about four times heavier than that of a human. Of all the senses, the most highly developed is that of smell, this capacity being augmented by the mobility of the trunk. The animal's hearing is unremarkable–despite the dimensions of the ears–and its vision poor. Various reasons have been advanced for this, and the lateral positioning of the eyes, set wide apart from each other, is certainly a contributory cause.

As in tapirs, elephants' lungs adhere to the pleura. There is a simple stomach and a long caecum. The testicles remain inside the abdomen throughout the animal's life.

There are certain differentiating characteristics between the African and Asiatic species of elephant. The African elephant (the bush form) is normally larger, with a hollower back and a flatter forehead. The ears are enormous and the trunk is roughened by ring-like folds which extend down its entire length. At the tip of the trunk are two tactile, prehensile lip-like processes. The African elephant is rather more tolerant of intense heat than is its Asiatic relative. It also frequently sleeps standing up, whereas the latter prefers to lie down.

Both subspecies of African elephant are of the genus *Loxodonta*. The bush elephant (*Loxodonta africana africana*) is the largest land mammal in the world, living in a variety of habitats in most regions south of the Sahara. The forest elephant (*Loxodonta africana cyclotis*)–also known as the pygmy elephant, despite the fact that it is only a couple of feet shorter than the bush elephant–is a creature of the western equatorial rain forests. The two forms have in the past been regarded as distinct species.

The Asiatic elephant (*Elephas maximus*) is smaller and less heavy than the African species, with smaller ears, a domed forehead, convex back and smooth trunk, with only one prehensile 'lip'. Only the males have large tusks. Its range is fairly wide and although authorities do not distinguish any subspecies, they do recognise four separate races–the Indian, Ceylonese, Malayan and Sumatran. Females of the Ceylonese elephant do not have tusks. All Asiatic elephants normally live longer than African elephants.

Albino elephants–light grey, with pink eyes–are sometimes found in Siam and Burma. These are the famous sacred white elephants, never used for work.

Despite their primitive appearance, elephants have gradually adapted themselves to new surroundings and conditions during the millions of years of their evolution. Their gait is part-digitigrade, part-plantigrade and the thick pads on the feet which support the body weight expand and contract as the animal presses down and then raises each foot. This natural adjustment is especially useful when the elephant is crossing soft or swampy ground.

CHAPTER 3

The birds of the savannah

No visitor to East Africa can fail to be impressed and thrilled by the varied spectacle of wildlife on the savannah–the vitality and elegance of the herds of zebras and antelopes, the majestic confidence and strength of the lions, the massive power of the elephants and rhinoceroses. It will be a pity, however, if he does not take note of the drama and beauty offered by the hundreds of species of East African birds–a pageant of continuous and colourful activity that rewards patient and discerning observation. The dawn and dusk flights of flocks of sand-grouse, the courtship dances of the bustards, the strident song of the barbets, the splendid plumage of the starlings and whydahs–these are sights and sounds calculated to divert the attention from the more familiar, conventionally-behaved herbivores and carnivores, richly satisfying for anyone who may be momentarily sated with size, space and grandeur and craves beauty on a more modest scale.

Some of these birds are omnivores, notably the bustards, the thrushes and the barbets, which feed indiscriminately on insects, small vertebrates, grass and seeds. Because of their catholic tastes, such species are able to lead a comparatively sedentary existence. Others, however, such as the larks and weaver-birds, are granivores (grain-eaters), and have to move about in order to find food. The weavers, for example, flock in large numbers to nest on the savannahs after the rains. These nests, shaped like little baskets and suspended between the branches of acacias, are made of miscellaneous materials, including grass, sticks, twigs and seeds.

The vast, empty stretches of plain and savannah are ideal surroundings for most of these birds, whose far-ranging vision enables them to spot natural enemies from a distance. For species that nest and shelter on the ground, exposure brings risks, but eggs and fledglings alike are usually so coloured as to provide

Facing page : The white-bellied bustard (*Eupodotis senegalensis*) is a medium-sized bird, often seen on grassy plains in South Africa, where it feeds on grain and insects.

Facing page : Among the many typical flying birds of the African savannahs are the bustards, the whydahs (or widow-birds), the sand-grouse and the barbets. The large Kori bustard acts as host for the smaller carmine bee-eater (*Merops nubicus*), here seen perched on its back. The bee-eater feeds on the insects disturbed by the bustard, which spends more time on the ground than in the air.

Barbets build their nests in tree-crevices, in sandy banks or on the bare ground. The D'Arnaud's barbet digs a hole in the ground, about 3 feet deep, broadening it at the bottom to form a small pocket in which the eggs are laid and the chicks hatched and reared.

effective natural camouflage. Moreover, the chicks are capable of leaving the nest shortly after being hatched and running about in their parents' company. Such species are called nidifugous, in contrast to nidicolous, birds that are virtually helpless at birth and confined to their nests for several weeks.

Certain species, including wading birds, that live in the unprotected grass of the high plains, have also acquired remarkable survival techniques for deceiving predators. These birds pretend to be injured, either by drooping a wing as if it were broken, by falling to the ground or by leaping around with clumsy, jerking movements. Such ruses are intended to attract the attention of watchful carnivores and guide them away from nest and young.

Open plains are not favourable habitats for the weaver-birds, which are far happier among shrubs and trees. Since their ingenious nests are constructed high up in trees, the chicks are well protected from reptiles and small carnivorous mammals; and by the time the dry season comes they are old enough to fly with their parents to more hospitable climes.

The birds that feed exclusively on insects leave the savannah at the height of the summer. Most of them are true migrants and join with the birds from Europe which spend the winter in Africa to make up a fluctuating bird population, swelling the numbers of sedentary native species.

Ornithologists have been puzzled at the behaviour of some of the migratory species of Europe and Asia that winter on the African plains, wondering why the birds do not all gather together in areas which would seem to offer the best climatic conditions. In fact, the species that halt north of the equator arrive at the peak of the dry season, while those that continue southwards find a profusion of new vegetational growth. The latter consequently nest and breed freely—competing for territory with existing native species—whereas those that remain farther north rarely breed at such times.

Not only each genus but each species has its own ecological requirements, the habitat being largely determined by its feeding preferences. Sometimes these coincide in certain particulars, but only a limited number of species—such as the gregarious weaver-birds—will be found in the same habitat and eating the same type of food. In fact, rivalry between different species is far less common than between members of the same species. Whereas strangers are often tolerated, so that one habitat may be shared by birds with similar regimes but of disparate appearance, the infringement of territory by others of the same species is seldom countenanced. In one survey taken in the Usambara district of Uganda—covering an area of some 700 square miles—it was established that of the 172 species counted, 94 per cent of those belonging to the same genus showed differences either as regards diet, habitat or behaviour.

Many African birds of prey, notably the lanner falcons, great sparrowhawks, Bonelli's eagles, and martial and Verreaux's eagles, feed on smaller species of birds. Generally speaking, such raptors are more widely active in the holarctic zone (North Africa) rather than in the Ethiopian zone south of the Sahara. There is usually enough, however, in the way of reptiles and small vertebrates to supplement the diet of these birds of prey.

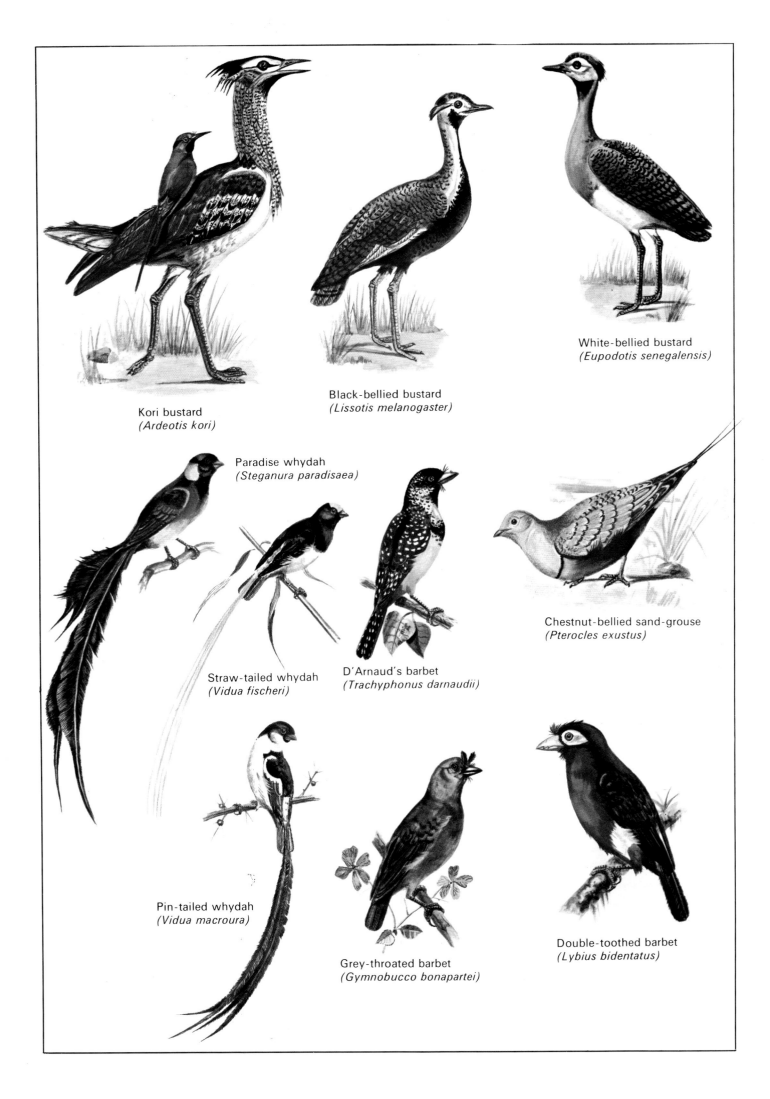

Kori bustard
(Ardeotis kori)

Black-bellied bustard
(Lissotis melanogaster)

White-bellied bustard
(Eupodotis senegalensis)

Paradise whydah
(Steganura paradisaea)

Straw-tailed whydah
(Vidua fischeri)

D'Arnaud's barbet
(Trachyphonus darnaudii)

Chestnut-bellied sand-grouse
(Pterocles exustus)

Pin-tailed whydah
(Vidua macroura)

Grey-throated barbet
(Gymnobucco bonapartei)

Double-toothed barbet
(Lybius bidentatus)

The bustards

The bustards, of the family Otididae, are birds of the grassy plains and savannahs, particularly well represented on the African continent. Their omnivorous diet includes grains, insects and small mammals, and their food requirements can thus be varied according to the seasonal cycle and natural resources.

Bustards are essentially ground birds, walking with a firm, heavy gait, holding the head high and making good use of keen eyesight to scan the treeless expanses for food. If an enemy should threaten, they may take wing, flying in a straight line with head and neck outstretched, beating the air heavily and rhythmically with strong, broad wings. On other occasions they will simply run away from the enemy, generally fast enough to elude a hunter with a gun.

During the mating season the males indulge in magnificent and very elaborately ritualised courtship displays. Such shows are of course common to many species of birds, though their details vary. All would seem to have the same purpose—namely to enable individuals of the same species to recognise one another, the sexual attraction of females often being the main instinct.

The male bustard's courtship display begins with a swelling of the gular pouch—extensible, air-filled sacs situated at the front of the neck. When fully expanded, these may touch the ground. The bird then extends his wings, showing white patches normally concealed by the brown plumage, puffs out the tufts of ornamental feathers and lifts his tail. This makes him look like a fluffy ball, completely transforming his normal appearance. Thus decked out, he rocks his body and struts about, turning in tight circles until his gaze lights upon a possible partner. She does not at first seem at all impressed by this acrobatic behaviour and extraordinary attire, but the show of disinterest does not last long. The male's passion sometimes finds another outlet in aggressive fights with rivals, and this jealously possessive attitude may continue after the female starts to brood, a task undertaken without his aid.

The nest is situated on bare ground. Sometimes it is simply a hole or a depression, but often it is composed of scraps of grass. The female lays from one to four eggs—olive-green and speckled with darker markings. Incubation lasts 20–28 days, according to species, and the young, when hatched, show great liveliness and precocity, the mother caring for them attentively during the first few weeks. They make their initial tentative efforts to fly when they are five to six weeks old, and are already quite expert before they have reached anything like full adult size.

Bustards are found in southern Europe, large parts of Asia, Africa and Australia. Fossil remains indicate that related species date back about 50 million years. There are 16 species in Africa alone, with strong representation in East Africa. Here the most celebrated species is the Kori bustard (*Ardeotis kori*), a very large bird nicknamed 'rubber turkey' by the early Boer settlers because of its apparent craving for the rubbery resin of a species of acacia. Although bustards usually collect together in small flocks, the Kori bustard is a more solitary species, with a rather hesitant manner of walking. While doing so, the soft feathers adorning

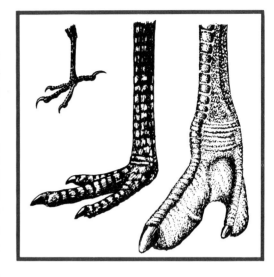

The toe-structure of birds varies according to their style of walking and their environment. The Corvidae, one of the many families belonging to the order Passeriformes, are perching birds, and their feet have four toes, three of which face forwards and one backwards. The bustards, belonging to the Gruiformes, are strong walking birds, and the rear toe has disappeared. The ostriches, of the order Struthioniformes, are powerful runners and have only two toes, both of which are highly developed.

Facing page (above, left): The black-bellied bustard's black and brown plumage serves as perfect natural camouflage in the tall grass.
(*Above, right, and below*) the male Kori bustard is a large bird, solitary in habit and especially imposing in its courtship display.

Facing page : Sand-grouse fly long distances twice daily, at dawn and at dusk, to quench their thirst at waterholes. They drink rapidly, not needing to extend their necks or lift their heads—as do the pigeons, which they greatly resemble. Their feathers retain the water droplets which are carried back to the nests for the young.

AFRICAN BUSTARDS

Class: Aves
Order: Gruiformes
Family: Otidae

These are ground birds, most of them omnivorous, with three toes on each foot. The males are normally larger and more colourful than the females. Incubation of the eggs—one to five, according to species—lasts 20–28 days.

KORI BUSTARD
(Ardeotis kori)

Total length: 30–40 inches (75–100 cm)
Wing-length: Male 25–31 inches (63.5–78 cm)
Female 22–26½ inches (55.5–66.5 cm)

One of the largest flying birds in the world, and certainly the most impressive member of the family. There is a small crest on the head and the plumage of the upper part of the body and the neck has wavy black and grey markings. The soft, loose feathers covering the neck made it look thicker than it really is.

WHITE-BELLIED BUSTARD
(Eupodotis senegalensis)

Total length: 24 inches (60 cm)
Wing-length: 10–11½ inches (26–28.5 cm)

The neck and upper part of the breast are grey-blue, the belly white and the upper part of the body delicately streaked with orange and black marks. There is an inverted V marking on the throat of the male.

BLACK-BELLIED BUSTARD
(Lissotis melanogaster)

Total length: 24 inches (60 cm)
Wing-length: 12½–14½ inches (31–36 cm)

Male and female are sharply differentiated, the former being light auburn, the latter brown, with lighter colouring on the lower part of the body. The female lays one greenish egg on the bare ground.

---

head and neck become erect, clearly displaying their grey and black markings.

Other East African species include Denham's bustard (*Neotis denhami*)—identified by the nut-brown colour of the plumage covering its back—the white-bellied bustard (*Eupodotis senegalensis*), the little brown bustard (*Heterotetrax humilis*), the buff-crested bustard (*Lophotis ruficrista*) and the black-bellied bustard (*Lissotis melanogaster*). The last-named species is only about the size of a chicken, and others range upwards in size, the Kori bustard being as large as a plump turkey.

The water-loving sand-grouse

The many species of African birds, whether they live on the plains and savannahs or in semi-desert regions, are all dependent, to a lesser or greater degree, on water, and this problem becomes particularly acute at certain times of the year. The sedentary species that inhabit very dry or relatively arid zones have adapted to the situation in one of two ways. Some of them—notably the bustards, bitterns and waders—can make do with very little water, deriving a large part of their daily requirement from dew deposited on grass and plants and from the organic liquids in insects and their larvae. Generally speaking, the birds that drink sparingly are fairly thin, walking as much as flying and thus saving energy.

At the other extreme are species such as the sand-grouse, strong, stoutish birds whose powerfully developed pectoral muscles provide the necessary propulsion for rapid, sustained flight. Yet this flying technique is somewhat wasteful of energy. Instead of moving their wings in a slow, measured beat, the birds flutter them rapidly and seemingly laboriously, in the manner of pigeons and ducks. This energetic mode of flight makes it important for sand-grouse to quench their thirst copiously and at regular intervals. Twice daily, therefore, enormous flocks of these birds head for waterholes, often a great distance away, returning repeatedly to the same sites. Because of this capacity for long-range flight, sand-grouse are able to live permanently in areas where there are plenty of seeds and berries, but where they do not have to contend with the competition of other birds.

Naturalists have always had difficulty in classifying the sand-grouse. With its squat body and short legs it strongly resembles other species of grouse—and it is in fact appreciated by hunters as a game bird; but its small head and neck make it look something like a pigeon, though it lacks the pigeon's hard, fleshy cere at the base of its short, pointed bill. The bird's characteristic method of flying also seems to place it midway between a grouse and a pigeon. After lengthy and controversial debate, ornithologists agreed to classify the bird among the Columbiformes rather than the Galliformes. Even so, the sand-grouse differs from other representatives of the order (pigeons and doves) in possessing only three toes on each foot instead of four, and in having a thicker skin. Also, it is a nidifuge, whereas the pigeon is nidicolous.

This last characteristic—namely the capacity for being active and lively immediately after hatching, and thus relatively mobile and independent—shows how successfully a species can adapt

56

AFRICAN SAND-GROUSE

Class: Aves
Order: Columbiformes
Family: Pteroclidae

Ground-nesting birds, with feather-covered toes. All species fly effortlessly. The female lays two or three elongated eggs which are incubated by both sexes, the male by night, the female by day.

CHESTNUT-BELLIED SAND-GROUSE
(Pterocles exustus)

Total length: 12½ inches (31 cm)
Wing-length: 6¾–7½ inches (16.7–18.8 cm)

The head, neck and breast of the male are ochreous, down to the straight black pectoral line. The belly is very dark and the wings sandy-brown. The female is yellowish, with wavy marks all over the plumage except at the throat and the meeting point of breast and belly, where there is a conspicuous band. The central rectrices are long and tapering in both sexes. The species is found in plain and desert regions of Equatorial and East Africa, in North Africa, in the Middle East, and in India.

BLACK-FACED SAND-GROUSE
(Eremialector decoratus)

Total length: 10 inches (25 cm)
Wing-length: 6¼–6¾ inches (15.7–17 cm)

Less gregarious than many other species, and also one of the smallest. The central rectrices are not very long. The male has a black mark on forehead and neck. A characteristic large, light-coloured band separates breast and belly. An inhabitant of East Africa, it joins the chestnut-bellied sand-grouse in seeking out waterholes.

YELLOW-THROATED SAND-GROUSE
(Eremialector gutturalis)

Total length: 13¼ inches (33 cm)
Wing-length: 8¼–9 inches (20.8–22.5 cm)

Largest of East African species of sand-grouse. Central rectrices not tapering as in chestnut-bellied species. Both sexes have a yellowish mark on the throat and upper part of the breast. Otherwise the male is more uniformly coloured than the female, which is boldly speckled. The species is found on grassy plains and savannahs in Central, East and South Africa.

itself to new surroundings and altered circumstances. In the course of its evolution this bird had to acquire a behavioural pattern consistent with building a nest and laying its eggs on bare ground—a procedure that would normally make it, together with its eggs and chicks, especially vulnerable to the attacks of predators both of the land and the air. Inability to move rapidly away from the nest in order to escape enemies, coupled with inordinately bright, conspicuous plumage, would inevitably prove fatal for such a bird. Thanks to its mobility and fairly plain plumage that exactly matches the colour of the terrain, the sand-grouse is well equipped to survive on open ground, without the protection of a carefully constructed nest in a tree. In addition, if real danger threatens, the adults resort to a broken-wing display.

Sand-grouse are tolerant of other species and frequently share the same type of savannah habitat as bustards—open ground and rocky or sandy districts where there is poor, sparse vegetation. They are able to endure these relatively harsh, inhospitable conditions by reason of their tough skin, which is covered with stout contour feathers and beneath which is an insulating layer of fine down. The short legs are also enveloped in feathers to the toes.

Although sand-grouse often display fiercely aggressive tendencies among themselves, they are gregarious birds. A typical flock may consist of more than 100 individuals, which set out twice a day, at sunrise and at dusk, in search of water. They fly by the shortest direct route, twittering loudly as they go. When they arrive at the waterhole, perhaps after a flight of 30–35 miles, they break up into smaller groups, landing about 100 yards from the water's edge, casting wary glances in every direction before advancing any closer. When they drink they plunge their beaks into the water, sucking it up in the manner of pigeons, but unlike other birds they do not lift their heads in the process.

The part of the day not occupied by flying to and from the waterholes is spent searching for food, consisting in the main of leguminous seeds and leafy shoots. The birds often take sand baths, seemingly unaffected by the heat of the sun.

The plumage of the birds blends naturally with their surroundings, and there are slight variations in marking distinguishing the male from the female. The predominant colour is cream or fawn, with darker marks on the back, and a grey or black breast. There are often one or more dark stripes across the neck.

Sand-grouse are monogamous and construct a very simple nest—sometimes little more than a hole scooped in the ground or a natural depression which is then lightly covered with bits of dry grass. The female proceeds to lay two or three eggs, which are of a bright ivory colour, streaked with dark brown or purple markings. Both ends of the egg are the same shape. The incubation period is 22–28 days and both male and female share the responsibility, the hen normally sitting on the eggs during the day and the male, with his rather darker plumage, at night. The young birds are fed with food regurgitated for them by both parents.

One mystery that has fascinated naturalists for some time concerns the way sand-grouse provide their young with water, considering the latter are incapable of accompanying the adults on their twice-daily journeys to distant waterholes. Meinertzhagen, who has bred these birds under laboratory conditions, has pointed out that they normally wade into the water up to breast level and that after they emerge their feathers retain the droplets. Nevertheless, he noted that chicks under his care quenched their thirst by absorbing liquids regurgitated for them by the adult birds. Recent studies in the wild would seem to have resolved the question, having shown that the young sand-grouse definitely suck up the water that the adults carry back to the nest in their plumage.

The plains and grassy savannahs are the homes of the yellow-throated sand-grouse (*Eremialector gutturalis*) and the double-banded sand-grouse (*Eremialector bicinctus*). The chestnut-bellied sand-grouse (*Pterocles exustus*), the spotted sand-grouse (*Pterocles senegallus*) and the black-faced sand-grouse (*Eremialector decoratus*) all prefer semi-arid steppes. Lichtenstein's sand-grouse (*Eremialector lichstensteinii*) and the painted sand-grouse (*Eremialector quadricinctus*) are birds of the desert, and the masked sand-grouse (*Pterocles personatus*) is an aberrant species which lives only on the island of Madagascar.

The dancing whydahs

The Masai—that sturdy nomadic race of East African hunters—claim that their ancestors taught themselves to dance by imitating the ritual courtship display of the male widow-bird or whydah (the latter name is an anglicised form of the port on the coast of Guinea where the bird was first identified). Anyone who has the good fortune to see this extraordinary dance during the mating season in the grasslands of the Masai Mara reserve will surely understand how this belief may have originated.

A typical species is Jackson's whydah (*Euplectes jacksoni*), whose fascinating nuptial ceremony takes place in the small grassy arena which constitutes its territory. The male of the species, a little larger than a sparrow, boasts an unusually long black tail during the mating season. His first act is to tread down and clear a patch of ground encircling a large tuft of grass. He then jumps up and down on this hillock—leaping as high as 5–6 feet in the air—fluttering his wings in an agitated manner and extending his tail to the limit. He comes to a stop and resumes his activity after a few seconds. This performance attracts several females towards the nuptial territory where mating will take place. In similar fashion the male paradise whydah (*Steganura paradisaea*) clears a patch some 30 inches in diameter around the central column of grass, on which he then takes his stand. With his magnificent black tail fully extended, he preens himself, strutting and prancing, while the females gather in a circle, making whistling noises to draw his attention to them. The glistening black tail of the whydah stands out sharply against the bright green of the grass, and this is the main instrument of recognition and sexual attraction, corresponding to the black mane of the lion, the black flank-stripe of the Thomson's gazelle and the dark tone colours of many other animals of the savannah. To see these birds leaping about like miniature ballet dancers is most exhilerating.

The widow-birds or whydahs belong to the very large family of Ploceidae—seed-eaters of Europe, Asia, Africa and Australasia,

AFRICAN WHYDAHS

Class: Aves
Order: Passeriformes
Family: Ploceidae

Small birds, little larger than sparrows. They do not build a nest but lay their eggs in the nests of other species. The males perform remarkable courtship displays.

PIN-TAILED WHYDAH
(Vidua macroura)

Total length: Male 12–13 inches (30–33 cm)
Female 4½ inches (11–12 cm)
Wing-length: Male 2½–3¼ inches (6.6–7.8 cm)
Female 2¼–2¾ inches (6.1–7 cm)

The central rectrices of the male are very long and shining black. The plumage colour of either sex is sharply differentiated, that of the male being black and white, that of the female brown with a large auburn stripe over the eye. Both sexes have a red beak.

STRAW-TAILED WHYDAH
(Vidua fischeri)

Total length: Male 11 inches (27.5 cm)
Female 4 inches (10 cm)
Wing-length: Male 2½–2¾ inches (6.5–7.1 cm)
Female 2¼–2½ inches (6.1–6.5 cm)

The four central rectrices of the male are very long and straw-yellow, this colour also appearing on the front of the head. The breast and wings are black, the belly white and the rump ivory-white. The female is brownish, with yellow on the back and reddish markings on the head. Her breast and belly are white. Both sexes have a pink beak.

PARADISE WHYDAH
(Steganura paradisaea)

Total length: Male 15–16 inches (37.5–40 cm)
Female 5 inches (12.5 cm)
Wing-length: 3–3½ inches (7.3–8.5 cm)

The male is remarkable for the appearance and length of his tail. The central feathers are black, very long and distinctively shaped. The head and throat are black and there is a reddish patch on the breast; the belly and nape are yellow. The lighter-coloured female resembles the pin-tailed whydah, but she is more sturdy and her beak is darker.

which include such a familiar bird as the house sparrow. In Africa they are represented by such showy species as the waxbill finches and the weaver-birds. The latter are divided into four subfamilies, the widow-birds being one of these (Viduinae).

Looking at the magnificent colours and long tail of the male whydah in his courtship attire, it is perhaps difficult to realise that he is a relative of the ordinary European house sparrow; but when he resumes his drabber livery after the mating season he is much less impressive, as is the female with her altogether duller brownish plumage at all seasons.

Apart from their courtship rituals, the notable feature of the whydahs' behaviour is their breeding pattern. This is very similar to that of the cuckoo. Like the latter, they do not construct any nest but lay their eggs directly in the nests of other species. They do not, however, normally emulate the cuckoo in tossing out the eggs or killing the chicks of their hosts. In fact, the young whydahs are reared in the same nest and at the same time as the fledglings of the host species.

The birds selected more frequently than any others for this doubtful honour are the waxbills—birds that also belong to the Ploceidae. The whydahs' eggs are white, almost identical to those of the waxbills. It is interesting to remark that the eggs of other related species are speckled, leading experts to conclude that the loss of pigmentation in such cases is due to an adaptive process. Even more remarkable, however, is the fact that when the whydah chicks are hatched, they look exactly like the young of the host birds, being not only similar in size and shape, but with identically coloured mouths and inner edges of the beak. Thus the foster-parents make no distinction between their own young and those of the intruder species when bringing food back to the nest.

These similarities exist even when the same species of whydah lay their eggs in the nests of different species of waxbill. This seems to indicate that each group of parasitic whydahs is subdivided into races or branches, the young birds of which perfectly imitate the chicks of the host species involved—and no other. Naturally the males and females of these different whydah strains do not mate, because the resultant hybrids would, figuratively speaking, fall between two stools, not exactly resembling any of the waxbill species and therefore unable to survive. Another interesting observation is that both the male and female of these parasite species have the same song as that of the host birds and one that is quite different from that of others of their own kind.

In addition to the already-mentioned Jackson's whydah and paradise whydah, there are several other noteworthy representatives of the genera *Vidua* and *Steganura*. The gregarious pintailed whydah (*Vidua macroura*) lives on fallow ground and in desert regions over most parts of Africa south of the Sahara. The straw-tailed whydah (*Vidua fischeri*) is found all over East Africa, as is the steel-blue whydah (*Vidua hypocherina*), though the latter bird is comparatively rare.

The broad-tailed or Sudan paradise whydah (*Steganura orientalis*) has a more limited range than the related paradise whydah: parts of East Africa and spasmodically farther south, in Mozambique, Angola and South Africa.

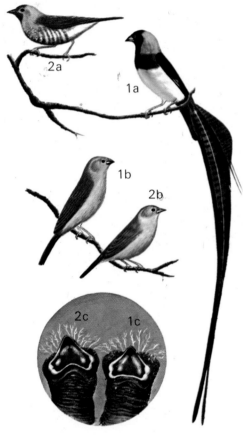

Although the adult paradise whydah (1a) is very different in appearance from the Melba finch (2a), the female lays her eggs in the latter's nest. When hatched, the young whydah (1c) and the young waxbill (2c) are almost indistinguishable, with identical coloration of the mouth and inner edges of the beak, so that both are fed by the host birds. At the age of about one month, the whydah (1b) and waxbill (2b) are still very similar in appearance, although the physical differences are beginning to show.

The courtship display of the male
Jackson's whydah (*left*) is one of the most
remarkable sights of the savannah.
Normally no bigger than a sparrow, he
takes on a spectacular long black tail in the
mating season, leaping and prancing in
acrobatic style to attract the females of the
same species. The male pin-tailed
whydah (*above*) also sports an excessively
long tail at breeding time, which slows up
his flight.

Following page : The D'Arnaud's barbets
are arboreal birds, living alone or in pairs.
Their song is monotonous, composed of
one note only, repeated again and again
without change of rhythm from dawn to
dusk.

The barbets—heralds of the dawn

If you camp out on the East African savannah you will find it almost impossible to sleep late, for as soon as the sun rises nature comes alive and the dawn chorus of the birds begins. On the banks of the Seronera, in the Serengeti National Park, the most energetic—if not exactly the most melodious—songsters are the barbets; and of these the most persistent is without doubt the D'Arnaud's barbet (*Trachyphonus darnaudii*). This spotted bird— brown, yellow and white—is not unlike a woodpecker in general appearance. Both birds in fact belong to the same order Piciformes, but the barbet is a member of the family Capitonidae, whereas the woodpecker is one of the Picidae.

From the higher branches of the acacias, the barbets, usually in pairs, welcome the new day. Male and female huddle closely together, flicking their tails from side to side, and lift their voices in song—something of a euphemism in their case, for their 'song' is a grating metallic note, never varying and continuously repeated by both birds in unison. Local nicknames inspired by this monotonous call are 'blacksmith' and 'coppersmith'. Most of the other barbets emit the same kind of strident, repetitive cry.

Barbets derive their common name from the tufts of bristles which are found at the base of their beaks, faintly resembling beards. All are exclusively arboreal and mainly sedentary birds, tending to live alone or in pairs; some of them are able to climb vertically up tree-trunks, in the manner of the black woodpeckers. Certain groups of barbets, however, roost together on tree-covered savannahs and in fields. Their vegetarian diet consists in the main of fruit and grains, though some species are particularly fond of insects collected among the foliage. The nest may be situated in a small hole, sometimes bored into a dead tree trunk, in earth or sand embankments, or—as in the Serengeti— on the bare ground. The birds often return to the same nesting site year after year.

These little birds are found in tropical forests the world over, except in the Antilles, in Madagascar and on some Pacific islands. They are, however, particularly abundant in the Ethiopian region, with the majority of species inhabiting open savannah.

Barbets are characterised by their stocky build, comparatively large head, heavy beak and short, rounded wings. Most species have gaily-coloured plumage. There are a number of highly colourful African species, in addition to the already-mentioned D'Arnaud's barbet, which is especially abundant in the Serengeti. The double-toothed barbet (*Lybius bidentatus*), for example, ranges far and wide through East Africa, both as a local resident and a partial migrant. The black-collared barbet (*Lybius torquatus*) is found in the Congo, in the western part of Kenya and in the southernmost regions of South Africa. The grey-throated barbet (*Gymnobucco bonapartei*) and the white-eared barbet (*Buccanodon leucotis*) are both residents of East and South Africa, the latter species ranging as far westwards as Angola; and the red and yellow barbet (*Trachyphonus erythrocephalus*) is found both in Kenya and Tanzania. There are in fact 37 recognised species in Africa alone, more than half the total number.

AFRICAN BARBETS

Class: Aves
Order: Piciformes
Family: Capitonidae

These birds derive their common name from the bristles at the base of their strong beaks. Their plumage is generally brightly coloured. Each foot has four toes, two facing forwards and two backwards. They nest in holes, the female laying 2–5 eggs, and both parents take turns to incubate them. The chicks remain for some time in the nest.

DOUBLE-TOOTHED BARBET
(*Lybius bidentatus*)

Total length: 9 inches (22·5 cm)
Wing-length: 4–4½ inches (10–11 cm)

One of the larger barbets, with plumage that is blackish on the back, dark red on the throat, breast and belly, and a whitish lateral mark. A yellow patch surrounds the eyes. A local resident and partial migrant from East Africa, the bird lives in woods and brush.

GREY-THROATED BARBET
(*Gymnobucco bonapartei*)

Total length: 7 inches (17·5 cm)
Wing-length: 3½–4 inches (9–10 cm)

Overall colour dark chestnut-brown, but head, throat and part of neck are ash-grey. Two tufts of bristles grow on either side of the beak. A local species of the East African forests.

D'ARNAUD'S BARBET
(*Trachyphonus darnaudii*)

Total length: 6 inches (15 cm)
Wing-length: 2¾–3 inches (7–7·5 cm)

Smallest and most delicate of all barbets. Back, wings and tail are brown with white spots. Crown black spotted with yellow, sides of face yellow spotted with black. Lower part of body sulphur-yellow, throat and upper part of breast spotted with black; rear part of belly red. In some strains the top of the head, neck and throat are pure black. The bird lives in wooded areas and open plains in north-east Africa.

62

CLASSIFICATION OF PASSERIFORMES

Suborder	Family
Eurylaimi	Eurylaimidae
Tyranni	Dendrocolaptidae
	Furnariidae
	Formicariidae
	Conopophagidae
	Rhinocryptidae
	Cotingidae
	Oxyruncidae
	Pipridae
	Rupicolidae
	Tyrannidae
	Phytotomidae
	Pittidae
	Acanthisittidae
	Philepittidae
Menurae	Menuridae
	Atrichornithidae
Oscines	Alaudidae
	Hirundinidae
	Dicruridae
	Oriolidae
	Corvidae
	Grallinidae
	Ptilonorhynchidae
	Paradisaeidae
	Paridae
	Aegithalidae
	Remizidae
	Cracticidae
	Sittidae
	Certhiidae
	Climacteridae
	Chamaeidae
	Campephagidae
	Pycnonotidae
	Irenidae
	Cinclidae
	Troglodytidae
	Mimidae
	Turdidae
	Sylviidae
	Muscicapidae
	Picathartidae
	Prunellidae
	Motacillidae
	Bombycillidae
	Dulidae
	Artamidae
	Vangidae
	Laniidae
	Cyclarhidae
	Callaeidae
	Sturnidae
	Meliphagidae
	Promeropidae
	Nectariniidae
	Dicaeidae
	Zosteropidae
	Vireonidae
	Coerebidae
	Drepanididae
	Parulidae
	Ploceidae
	Estrildidae
	Icteridae
	Tersinidae
	Thraupidae
	Fringillidae
	Emberizidae

ORDER: Passeriformes

No order in the bird kingdom is as rich and varied in species as that of the Passeriformes or perching birds, and none is more difficult to classify. The problem is that although the order contains many families that display typical characteristics, others depart from the norm to such an extent that their place within the order is debatable. These difficulties have provided ornithologists with so many headaches that they have been led to classify as Passeriformes many birds which simply do not possess sufficiently distinctive features to be listed as members of a separate and new order. Because of this, we find, grouped together as related genera, birds as varied as crows, wagtails, canaries, tits, swallows, dippers and birds of paradise!

The perching birds have beaks that lack a fleshy cere and whose feet are covered with scales. The feet and toe-structure differ slightly according to the genus concerned, but it is due to this characteristic anatomical formation that the birds are able to grip perches and branches. There are four toes of unequal length, three of which face the front and one that points backwards. The latter is not normally reversible and is well developed, its claw generally being longer than those of the other toes. In certain genera the front toes are joined together as far as half-way down. The muscles and tendons of the feet are so arranged that when the bird adopts a normal crouched position, they pull the toes in such a way that they close round the support—rather like a clenched fist—thus preventing the bird from falling.

Many of the Passeriformes, especially those belonging to the suborder Oscines, are song-birds. They are distinguished from other perching birds in possessing a complicated voice-producing structure known as the syrinx or song-box. This organ is situated at the point where the windpipe divides into the two tubes leading to the lungs. The strength of the syringeal muscles determines, to a large extent, the quality of the bird's song.

The wings of perching birds are of the normal type, with 9–10 well-developed remiges and a single set of covert feathers. The tail is usually comprised of 12 rectrices. The colours of the plumage are widely diversified, from dull and sober hues to the most garish, brilliant chromatic blends. Equally variable is the shape of the beak, depending on the food requirements of the particular bird. In the granivores the beak is conical, in the insectivores it is short and deeply-cleft. The birds that suck nectar have slender, curved beaks, while those of the carnivorous species are large and pointed. Furthermore, there is a marked difference in body size and weight among the numerous species, ranging from the diminutive wren to the much larger-than-average crow.

The Passeriformes are found in almost every kind of environment, including deserts and mountains. For many of them, however, the sea—which has to be flown over on their migratory journeys—represents a special hazard. The migratory species follow an orderly and regular flight pattern year after year, but many species are sedentary. Others, especially certain insectivores, tend to move around according to the season between their nesting sites and their winter quarters.

The nests of Passeriformes are constructed in different ways, depending on the surroundings. Whether in a tree hollow, at the tip of a branch or on the ground itself, they are generally built with extreme care and patience, though not always in such an elaborate manner as the mud-plastered nests of the swallows. There are, however, a number of parasitic species which follow the usual pattern of laying their eggs in the nests of others. Just as varied is the actual egg-laying procedure, the number, shape and size of the eggs, the colour of the shells and the frequency of the broods. The young of all species are nevertheless born blind and defenceless, strictly confined to the nest and carefully tended by their parents.

Golden oriole
(*Oriolus oriolus*)

Peruvian cock-of-the-rock
(*Rupicola peruviana*)

Long-tailed broadbill
(*Psarisomus dalhousiae*)

Lyrebird
(*Menura novaehollandiae*)

The Passeriformes are to be found in every part of the world, with the exception of the polar regions and certain far-flung, remotely situated islands. They make up more than half the total number of known bird species, and comprise about one-third of the total list of families.

This very profusion and diversity is the main cause of the problems that face the ornithologists when it comes to classifying them. At one time or another, naturalists have adopted a number of different systems. Some authors have insisted on lumping together into large groups all those families that show some distinct departure from the norm. Others have attempted to allot a separate genus or even family name to every individual which displays a specialised physical characteristic or unusual pattern of behaviour.

The criterion for such classification used to be the shape of the bird's beak, but this proved to be highly misleading. Modern systematics therefore sub-divide the order according to the arrangement of the tendons of the feet, the horny sheath covering the tarsi, the number of flight feathers and, above all, the number of syringeal muscles. Thus most authorities now agree in recog-nising four suborders—the Eurylaimi (broadbills, one family only), the Tyranni (flycatchers and relatives, 14 families), the Menurae (lyrebirds, two families) and the Oscines = Passeres (songbirds, with 52 families).

The Passeriformes are subdivided into four suborders—Eurilaimi, Tyranni, Menurae and Oscines (=Passeres). Although markedly different in appearance and habit, all the above species are related to one another, each representing one of these suborders.

CHAPTER 4

Stone islands in a sea of grass

When the rainy season is over and the savannahs are once again carpeted with fresh green grass, the dying rays of the setting sun cast a red glow on the small rocky outcrops that rise like lonely islands from the surrounding level plains. These steep, gaunt projections – on average about 100 feet high – with their rounded summits, which rear so dramatically above the grasslands are known as kopjes (Afrikaans for 'peaks'). They are constituted of granite – as is the rock basement underlying most of the high plains of East Africa – and they have appeared and acquired their shape as a consequence of slow erosion by the elements and the extremes of day and night temperatures. What is remarkable about them is that they support a distinctive fauna and flora – different from that encountered in the surrounding grasslands.

The reason for this phenomenon is that the environmental conditions of the kopjes are completely at variance with those existing in the flat grassy regions encircling them, even though the two areas lie next to each other. Rain water filters into the rock fissures and is retained there, dew is deposited daily and plentifully on rock and plant surfaces, and consequently, although the area is tightly restricted, the vegetational cover is thick and luxuriant. This in turn helps to attenuate the effects of extreme climatic contrast, keeping the atmosphere humid, and likewise providing a barrier against the devastating fires which frequently rage across the plains. Also, during the rainy season, when much of the surrounding land is flooded, these islands of granite remain unaffected. As a result, therefore, of their moderate climate and abundant vegetational growth, the kopjes are able to support a self-contained, self-sufficient animal community.

At the foot of the kopjes and immediately encircling them grow the wild agave, the aloe and the hibiscus. Shady evergreen

Facing page : The hyrax is the most common of all animals inhabiting the kopjes. Some feed on grass and others, such as this tree hyrax, browse on leaves and shoots.

66

The rocky savannah outcrops known as kopjes harbour an entirely distinctive fauna. As in animal communities ranging over a much wider area, there is a vital inter-dependence among the typical species, with herbivores, predators and super-predators sharing the same habitat. The food chain may be a simple one, as in the case of the leopard feeding on the dik-dik, but it is frequently more complex; thus the grasshopper is eaten by the agama, which is in turn killed by the cobra. The mongoose preys on the cobra and is also one of the many victims of the Verreaux's eagle. The life cycle of this restricted community is no different from that elsewhere in the animal kingdom.

shrubs are dotted around and inside the deep rock fissures and in these pleasant surroundings many animals live secure from the dangers of the outlying savannah and the rigours of the climate. Lizards, snakes, hyraxes, antelopes and birds of prey share this habitat. Rodents and other small vertebrates scurry about at the lower levels and the carnivorous mongooses are never short of food. The acrobatic klipspringers leap from peak to peak, the dainty dik-diks, hardly bigger than hares, hide in the bushes, while on the summit—inaccessible to most of the other creatures—the huge eagles build their nests. As dusk falls, the melancholy screech of a bird of prey may be echoed by the deep roaring of a lion that has wandered in from the plain and is now scrambling up among the rocks to stake its territorial claim. As the shadows deepen, a leopard may also take up silent residence in a sheltered spot; and higher up the kopje a troop of baboons will often turn the sheer slopes into an impregnable fortress. At dead of night, with a rapid, rhythmical beating of broad wings, the sombre-hued nightjars arrive, gleaming eyes on the alert for flying insects. Now only the nocturnal creatures are awake—hunters and hunted—all playing their part in the unending drama of life and death. For even though its living area is circumscribed, this little animal world—complete with plant-eaters, predators and super-predators—has to conform to the rigorous laws of the wild.

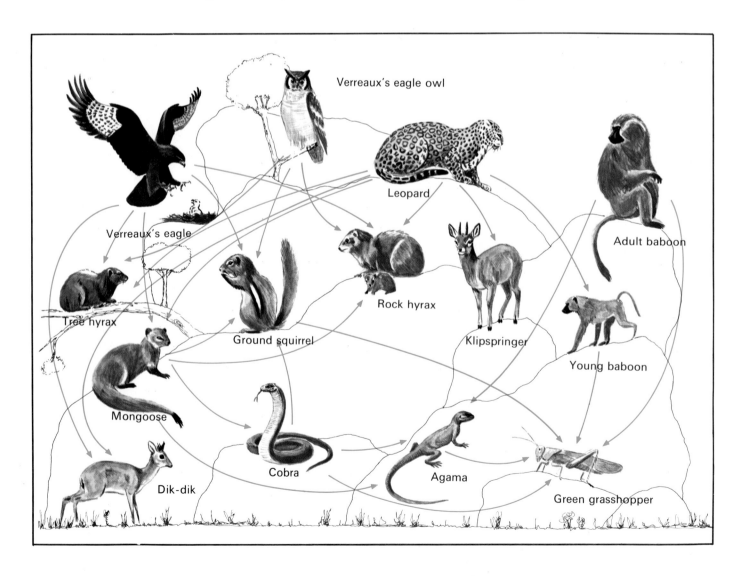

The hyrax

The best known animals of the East African kopjes are the hyraxes or dassies. These squat creatures, with their thick brownish fur, flat heads and stumpy legs, look rather like short-eared rabbits or marmots; but they are actually hoofed mammals, more closely related to the huge elephants and rhinoceroses, with a family tree that dates clearly back some 30 million years!

The hyrax is the 'coney' of the Bible and it belongs to the order Hyracoidea, primitive and long-extinct forms of which were probably larger than surviving pachyderms. But although affinities are admitted to exist between the tiny 9-lb hyrax and the massive 6-ton elephant, zoologists are cautious when it comes to tracing a direct link.

Highly adaptable creatures, the various species of hyrax are found at sea level and at altitudes of over 10,000 feet, on plains, in deserts and in tropical forests. The selected habitat will invariably supply them with all their normal food requirements and afford them protection from their many enemies.

On certain kopjes in the Seronera district of the Serengeti National Park, the hyrax populations have become so accustomed to the presence of naturalists, photographers and tourists that they are untypically tame and trusting. Here both species find ample nourishment, the one grazing on the red oats and millet of the open plain, the other browsing on the foliage of the myrrh and acacia trees of the wooded savannah. Scientists from the Michael Grzimek Memorial Laboratory have, as a result, been able to carry out a series of observations and experiments with both species.

At daybreak the rock hyraxes poke their noses out of the cracks and holes where they have been clustering together for the night. They swarm nimbly up the rock faces and when they have reached a suitable vantage point lie down alongside one another, heads all pointed towards the east so that their temporarily numbed bodies can receive the warmth of the sun's first rays. The young huddle against the adults to absorb their gradually increasing body heat. Then, having paid homage to the sun, they stretch and begin to groom themselves, making their leisurely way towards a rock with vertical walls that serves as urinal for the entire colony. The urine is highly concentrated, due to the fact that the kidneys reabsorb the maximum amount of water, allowing the animal to prosper in the driest of environments. All members of the colony also deposit their excrement in a pile in one particular place. During the 18th and 19th centuries the dried brownish waste matter was said to have been scraped up and rendered into a powder called hyraceum, to be used by pharmacists in treating a variety of disorders.

Considering that the animals are plantigrades, they show extraordinary dexterity in moving over the rough rock surface of their habitat, both vertically and horizontally. The secret of their climbing skill lies in the pads covering the soles of their feet – comparable to the lower surface of a climbing boot. These pads enable them to obtain a firm grip on smooth, slippery rock, even when this is steeply inclined. There are four toes on the

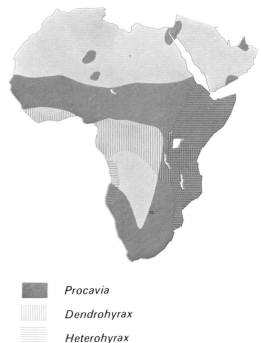

██ *Procavia*

▓▓ *Dendrohyrax*

░░ *Heterohyrax*

Geographical distribution of the three genera of hyrax. The genus *Procavia* is typically represented by the rock hyrax, *Dendrohyrax* by the tree hyrax and *Heterohyrax* by the yellow-spotted hyrax.

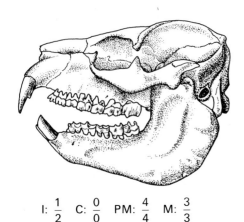

$$I: \frac{1}{2} \quad C: \frac{0}{0} \quad PM: \frac{4}{4} \quad M: \frac{3}{3}$$

Skull and dental formula of the rock hyrax.

ROCK HYRAX
(*Procavia capensis*)

Class: Mammalia
Order: Hyracoidea
Family: Procaviidae

Length of head and body: 16–20 inches
 (40–50 cm)
Weight: 5–9 lb (2–4 kg)
Diet: dry grass, shoots, lichen, bark, fruits, etc.
Gestation: 225 days
Number of young: usually 2–3, but sometimes
 up to 6
Longevity: 6 years in captivity

Adults
The genus *Procavia* includes the largest hyraxes. This species is thickset, with a pointed muzzle and rounded ears. The body is covered with short dark hairs, a lighter mark on the back indicating the presence of the dorsal gland.

Young
At birth, the young are well developed, with eyes open. They begin to nibble vegetation from two days onward, soon becoming very active, but not reaching sexual maturity until the second year.

front paws, linked by skin down to the point where the nails begin. These nails are blunt and hoof-like, but flexible enough for clinging to uneven ground and to the bark of tree trunks. The hyrax's hind limbs have only three toes, two with flat hooves, the middle one with a curved claw. This acts independently of the others and is used for such activities as scratching and grooming the fur.

When they have completed their morning toilet, the rock hyraxes clamber down the rock faces and cautiously begin feeding in the immediate vicinity of the kopje. The tree hyraxes, which normally sleep high up in trees by day, make full use of their large, pointed incisors to scramble down the trunks of their favourite acacias and greedily devour the tender leaves of the topmost branches. The rock hyraxes stray out a little way onto the plain to nibble at the dry grass. Normally they will not wander much farther than some 50 yards from their island refuge, but should they exhaust the available vegetation within this area they may have to be more venturesome. In such a contingency they form a little procession and stick to a well-marked and familiar path. When the leader of the group comes across a suitable spot, he takes a few wary mouthfuls and all the others follow his example, gobbling the grass as rapidly as they can.

As the hyraxes graze, they separate themselves into small bands, each of which forms a compact defensive unit. The animals crouch close to one another in a circle, backs turned inwards so that, as they feed, they can obtain a clear view in every direction. It takes them about 20–30 minutes to complete their meal, after which, if all goes according to plan, they scuttle back to their rocky base and stretch out once more on the flat, shady ledges. When they are taking their ease in this fashion, they are very difficult to see against the granite background, and even their plump, rounded bodies seem to merge inconspicuously with the natural swellings of the rock.

The natural enemies of the hyraxes include snakes, leopards, caracals, servals, jackals and large birds of prey such as Verreaux's eagles and owls. Yet because of the protection afforded by their rocky haunts and the efficiency of their own security system, the little animals have managed to adapt themselves to a hazardous existence and to keep their population level steady. All members of a community are on their guard for enemies, but one in particular is responsible for keeping a special watch for lurking predators whenever the groups are feeding. Should this sentinel sense danger, it utters a piercing cry through half-opened lips (a clear indication of fright), the signal being prolonged in relation to the gravity of the peril. On hearing this, the other hyraxes immediately stop feeding, raising their heads to see what is happening and remaining quite motionless for several seconds. If the danger is imminent, the sentinel giving the alarm darts back to its rocky lair, continuing to emit shrill cries, but now with mouth fully open. The others then lose no time in following. In the ensuing panic one of them may stumble and perhaps fall into a rock cleft where a predator has been waiting. The other hyraxes will then show considerable bravery by facing the enemy, baring their sharp teeth and snarling viciously – a manoeuvre that is often sufficient to frighten it off.

The tree hyrax is sometimes diurnal and found living on a kopje. It is more vulnerable than the rock hyrax to such attacks because it has to come down from its acacia in order to get back to the safety of its lair; but it also enjoys a slight advantage in that its elevated position gives it the opportunity of spotting an enemy more easily, especially a bird of prey.

One morning, during a particularly dry summer, a group of naturalists in the Serengeti were keeping watch on a colony of baboons near the summit of a kopje. The monkeys had come down from their rock fortress and had ventured out onto the surrounding plain, where they had been joined by groups of rock and tree hyraxes, the former grazing in the tall grass, the latter busily browsing in the acacia branches. Suddenly an ear-splitting cry shattered the morning silence. A Verreaux's eagle had been seen alighting high on the granite wall. The hyraxes, looking like small furry balls, were instantly on the move, scurrying about in every direction for shelter, clearly in a state of terrified confusion. The baboons too were apparently equally panic-stricken, the young clutching the adults for protection, the males agitatedly scouring the sky, the entire troop barking madly. Then the huge raptor was seen flapping its broad wings and swooping down at lightning speed, claws extended, right into the centre of the swarming throng of hyraxes. As quickly as it had come, it soared off, clutching in its talons one piteously screaming little ball of fur. The whole performance had lasted a few seconds.

A couple of days previously, the same naturalists had stumbled across a nest of one such Verreaux's eagle and had discovered small piles of hyrax bones strewn all around. This confirmed what they had suspected – that the birds of prey regularly supplemented their diet with these readily available little mammals.

Yet even though they are continually menaced by these and other predators, the hyrax population as a whole does not appear to be seriously endangered. Despite the fact that their birth rate is low in comparison with other small mammals, their numbers remain high. Rock hyraxes, for example, do not attain sexual maturity until they are two years old, and the gestation period of the female lasts more than seven months – exceptionally long for an animal of that modest size. She gives birth to a litter of one to six young (the average number being two or three) and looks after them until they are old enough to leave the lair.

As has been mentioned, the two species of East African hyrax have different feeding habits, one group being herbivores, the other phyllophages or leaf eaters. It is precisely because they have their own specialised tastes that they can live together harmoniously, without competing for food and territory. Thus a large number of animals can occupy a comparatively limited living space, something that would be out of the question were they all to have similar food preferences. Ecologists believe that this rational use of natural resources is not necessarily a recent adaptation but may go back millions of years to the time when the ancestors of modern hyraxes were all forest dwellers. The slow but extreme changes in climatic conditions which resulted in the gradual retreat of the forests necessitated no alteration in

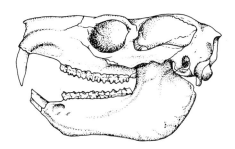

$$I: \frac{1}{2} \quad C: \frac{0}{0} \quad PM: \frac{4}{4} \quad M: \frac{3}{3}$$

Skull and dental formula of the tree hyrax.

TREE HYRAX
(Dendrohyrax arboreus)

Class: Mammalia
Order: Hyracoidea
Family: Procaviidae

Length of head and body: 16 inches (40 cm)
Weight: about 9 lb (about 4 kg)
Diet: leaves, shoots, fruits, etc.
Gestation: 7–8 months
Number of young: 1–2

Adults
Somewhat less sturdy than the rock hyrax, this species has longer, thicker hair. Colour varies from grey to light chestnut-brown. The long upper incisors enable the animal to grip branches firmly while climbing, at which activity it is surprisingly skilful.

Young
Able to move about as soon as it is born, the tree hyrax grows at about the same rate as the rock hyrax.

the life pattern of the tree hyrax, but caused the rock hyrax to adopt a herbivorous diet. Much later, as the areas covered by woods and forests continued to contract, both species confined their habitat to the shrub- and tree-lined rocky outcrops of the savannah. After first seeking refuge in the natural openings of the trees, they eventually took up residence in the rock crevices which nowadays provide them with permanent shelter, though still going their separate ways for food.

The visitor to East Africa, attracted by the stirring spectacle of the immense, ever-moving herds of ungulates and the relaxed grace and power of the feline predators, is likely to overlook the drama and interest provided by the smaller creatures of the savannah. The inconspicuous hyrax, concealed among the clefts of its rocky citadel, is one of many fascinating species generally ignored—a pity, because this unusual little animal is of special interest to the naturalist as a wonderful example of survival in an environment not originally its own, to which it has adapted without undergoing any significant anatomical modification.

The acrobatic klipspringer

The little antelope known as the klipspringer or 'African chamois' (*Oreotragus oreotragus*) is related to the dik-dik, but spends its life in hills and rocky mountains, with a range extending from Ethiopia down to the Cape, and westwards as far as Nigeria. It is a superbly graceful creature, very strong and agile.

The klipspringer's thick coat is made up of bristle-like hairs, basically reddish-yellow but with grey-green overtones—a colour which blends perfectly with the lichen-covered granite rock of its habitat. Furthermore, the dark lines on the animal's large ears, combined with the relatively small head, large black eyes and white eyebrows, all help to make the klipspringer even more inconspicuous when it is standing stock-still among the rocks and foliage. The dark grooves on the inner surface of the ears are similar to the veins of a leaf. Some experts conclude that these may have the effect of increasing receptivity to sound waves, but whether or not this is so, the ears are widely extended and positioned well forward on the head—ever alert to danger. The male may be identified by its short, widely separated horns.

By nature a solitary animal, the klipspringer sometimes gathers in a group of not more than eight individuals. It feeds both on grass and on the leaves of rock plants, never leaving the kopje for the open plains in quest of water. All drinking requirements are satisfied by the rain water that accumulates in the crevices and by the morning dew.

Should the klipspringer find itself in any kind of immediate danger, it emits a soft whistling sound as it makes its escape, leaping with incredible acrobatic skill from rock to rock, and retaining its foothold with the aid of its remarkably small, blunt, cylindrically shaped hooves. What is quite extraordinary, however, is that in addition to climbing towards the summit of a kopje, it will drop down just as effortlessly from the heights to a lower level, sometimes clearing a gap of 15–20 feet in a single leap and almost rebounding from one ledge as it springs down to

Preceding pages : The granite kopjes jut out sharply from the grassy savannahs, with climate and vegetation in clear contrast with conditions in the surrounding level plains. They support a plant and animal population perfectly adapted to such a specialised environment. The hyraxes, not rodents but hoofed mammals, live among the rocks in colonies; and the most characteristic reptiles of the kopjes are the agamas.

another. In this fashion it literally tumbles down the sheer slopes of rock from summit to base, and will then, if necessary, clamber up an equally steep incline to reach safety.

In addition to its phenomenal jumping ability, the klipspringer has another form of natural protection against its foes. The thick, bristly coat—unlike that of any other African antelope —helps it to withstand the scratches of thorny scrub or the jagged edges of rock as it hurtles downhill. What is more, the hair comes away in tufts so that it can escape from the very jaws of a lion or the talons of an eagle, the effect of surprise usually being sufficient to allow it to make a speedy departure to safer ground. The thin patches are soon covered by a thick new growth of hair.

Among the most persistent predators of the agile klipspringer are leopards and such birds of prey as the Verreaux's eagle, the latter sharing the same habitats—kopjes, rocky peaks, steep cliffs and even mountains towering over 14,000 feet—as in the case of Mt Elgon on the border of Uganda and Kenya. If cornered by an enemy, the antelope will remain momentarily frozen to the spot, feet close together, hoping to stay undetected. Compelled to take flight, it will climb or drop down no more than 25 yards before

The klipspringer is an expert rock-climber, able to keep its footing thanks to tiny cylindrical hooves. Its coat and facial markings make it very difficult to detect when standing still in its characteristic natural surroundings, and the thick, bristle-like hairs can be shed in tufts, enabling the animal to escape literally from the jaws of predators.

Geographical distribution of the klipspringer.

stopping to look round at its pursuer. This habit serves it well enough when another animal is after it, for it can keep track of the predator's movements and take appropriate evasive action. But in the case of a man, armed with a rifle, such frequent halts may, and indeed have, proved fatal. At one time, the coat of the klipspringer was much in demand for the stuffing of cushions and riding saddles, and the animals were so ruthlessly hunted that they were exterminated locally and imperilled as a species. Happily, conservation measures have permitted the population figures to revert to normal in most areas.

The colour-changing agama

We are accustomed to associate bright colours with birds but the chances are that we think of most reptiles as rather drab, uninteresting creatures. There are, however, exceptions to the rule, and one of these is a strange little lizard which is frequently seen on the Serengeti kopjes. Not only is the common agama (*Agama agama*) generously endowed by nature in this respect, but it has the even more astonishing ability to change colour at will, according to its mood!

This reptile belongs to the family Agamidae, the Old World equivalents of the iguanas of the New World. When it is especially excited, the male common agama's head takes on a bright rose-red hue, while body, limbs and tail turn cobalt-blue. The tail, incidentally, is cylindrical in shape and rather shorter than that of other lizards; nor is it brittle and capable of being shed and regenerated.

The agama commands attention not only because of its colour changes but also as a result of its unusual reactions when it feels itself being watched. It rears up to confront the intruder, supporting itself on sturdy fore-limbs, and sends the front portion of its body into a kind of rhythmic dance. This exhibition lasts a couple of minutes, after which the animal resumes its search for food—nosing its way into rock fissures to find ants, grasshoppers and other insects, all of which are rapidly and greedily devoured. This efficient feeding procedure is made possible by sharp teeth, diversified into incisors, canines and molars, which are wedged into the free edge of the jaws. The canines of the insectivorous agamids are pointed, whereas those of the grass-eating species have cutting edges.

Although this rainbow-coloured lizard is regularly found on kopjes, it is sufficiently trusting of humans to venture into homes, insinuating itself between loose stones and even basking on window-sills.

The behaviour and the appearance of the common agama are designed to draw attention to itself, but as with other animals possessing bright colours or unusual shapes, the deliberate objects of attraction are not naturalists but other animals of the same species. This is the way it makes itself known to its companions, courts its mate and discourages its rivals. Being a typical territorial creature, its only means of announcing presence and identity at a distance is to assume vivid colours that are completely at variance with the surrounding rocks and vegetation.

Since these are predominantly grey, green and yellow, the reptile's red and blue livery is particularly prominent and distinctive. It will also deliberately turn its head in the direction of the sun so that the rays are reflected by the scales of its body.

As is the case with many other territorial animals, one primary objective is to deter intruders–but not so much strangers of another species, which may be tolerated, as potential rivals of its own kind. Dissuasion is certainly a function of the warning-colour mechanism but in the case of the common agama and related species it has an important additional purpose. The splendid coloration of the male undoubtedly plays a significant role in defining territorial boundaries and keeping rivals at bay, but it has an equally obvious sexual function–offering a clear invitation to the female to draw near with a view to mating. So when the agama glistens jewel-like on a rock, his purpose is two-fold–to attract a mate and to retain her against all comers.

The ritual pattern is continued during the next stage of the

Well concealed among the bare branches and lichen-covered rock of the kopje, the klipspringer must be constantly on the alert for enemies. Fortunately the animal is nowadays protected from the most persistent of its former foes–man–who hunted it for its unusual coat and once threatened the species with extermination.

courtship ceremony—the defence of territory. Should this be disputed, intraspecific contests may occur, the first part of which is the confrontation, intended to intimidate and deter, and the second part being the combat proper. Since a rival will usually not dare to overstep the territorial bounds, such contests are normally fought on the frontiers themselves. The intimidation ritual is begun by the threatened individual turning sideways to his adversary, flattening himself slightly against the ground and swaying his head repeatedly. This procedure may last only a few seconds, after which the two animals take up new postures and begin again. As often as not, the less courageous individual, generally the one that is farther from the centre of his own territory, beats a retreat and the hostilities end there. But should neither be prepared to concede defeat, battle begins in earnest. The rivals grab each other by the throat, trying to throw the opponent off-balance and tumble him to the ground on his back. Firmly supported by their strong limbs, breathing rapidly and

The male agama is able to change the colour of its body at will. During the mating season it takes on particularly bright colours which serve to attract the opposite sex and to warn off potential rivals.

Male agamas in ritual combat.

snapping viciously with their powerful jaws, the two antagonists jerk each other from side to side, using every ounce of energy in a fight which, though dramatic, is rarely fatal. Gradually the teeth relax their grip, whereupon one of the combatants gives in and returns to his own domains.

The territorial defence ritual is similar to the nuptial display ceremony. The male approaches the female and tries to impress her by waving his head to and fro, waiting his moment to grab her neck with his teeth and hold her still with his front paws. Then he draws her nearer and places his tail under hers, the act of copulation lasting little more than a minute. Sometimes the female takes a more positive role in the courtship ritual, enticing the male by moving in a circle round him. As soon as the latter shows signs of responding, she allows herself to be caught. Once they have coupled, no matter which has initiated the act, they separate, each going its own way without regard for the partner.

This use of natural colour in order to provoke a double reaction – positive in a female, negative in a rival – is especially characteristic of other agamids belonging to the genus *Calotes*. The Indian bloodsucker (*Calotes versicolor*) is particularly aggressive during the courtship period, changing its colour from brown to yellow and then to blood-red in extraordinarily rapid succession. The vivid red hue may be restricted to head or shoulders, but may encompass the whole body. Another remarkable characteristic of this creature is that during the contests for defence of territory or for possession of a female, the red coloration becomes progressively deeper in the animal which is gaining the upper hand, whereas the adversary gradually becomes paler, until it is. the same olive-grey colour as the female, which never changes colour.

The agama provides the brightest spot of colour on the grey granite rocks of the kopjes, but it needs a sharp eye to spot this strange little reptile. Other species live in deserts and all are capable of enduring high temperatures and dry climates. Some agamids can also be kept in captivity. During the first few days they are likely to bite anyone who comes close, but as they become accustomed to their new surroundings they grow tamer.

AFRICAN AGAMAS

Class: Reptiles
Order: Squamata
Family: Agamidae

Of the three genera of African agamids, only the genus *Agama* is found in the Ethiopian region. All these reptiles are lizards measuring about 12 inches long, with a more or less triangular-shaped head and often with a double chin. Some species have spines around the ears. The tail is usually longer than the head and body together, narrowing towards the tip.

COMMON AGAMA
(*Agama agama*)

The main characteristic of this agama is its rapid colour changes. An insectivore, it is often seen in built-up areas. The agamas living in equatorial regions have a well-defined breeding cycle. The females give birth only between June and September, several months after the rainy season, when food is abundant. Favourite habitats are rocks and bush country in almost every part of the African continent.

Other representatives of the same genus are the tree or black-necked agama (*Agama cyanogaster*) of South Africa; the desert agama (*Agama mutabilis*) from the dry parts of North Africa; and the hardun or starred lizard (*Agama stellio*), very common in the Nile delta.

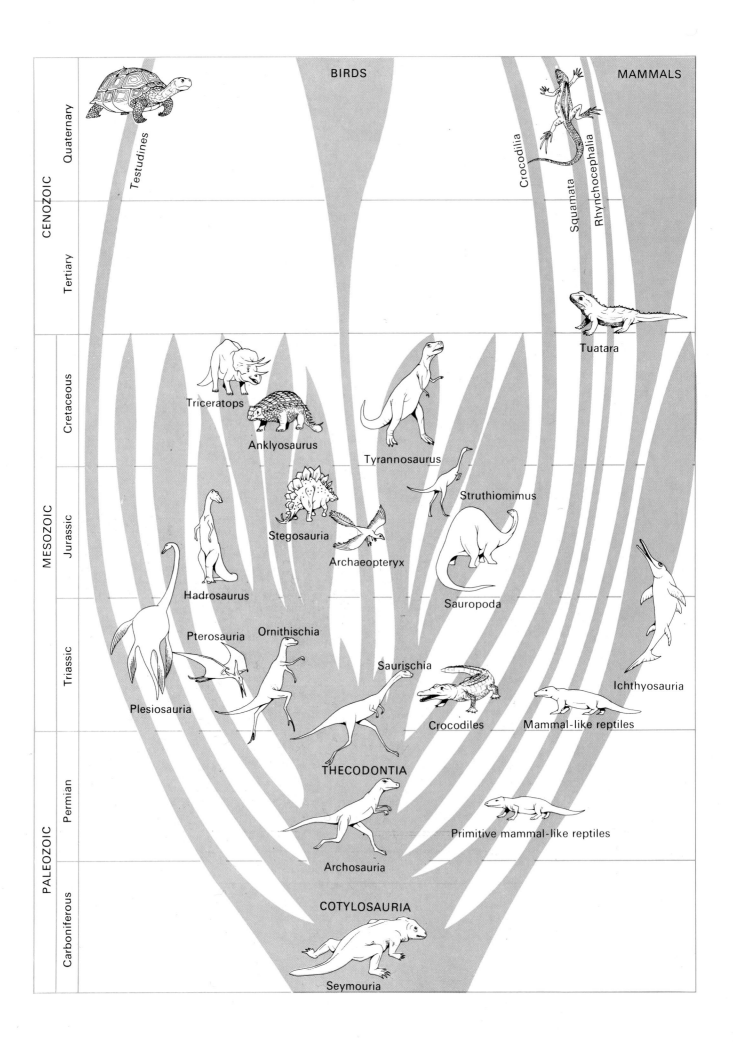

BIRDS

MAMMALS

CENOZOIC

Quaternary

Tertiary

MESOZOIC

Cretaceous

Jurassic

Triassic

PALEOZOIC

Permian

Carboniferous

Testudines

Crocodilia

Squamata

Rhynchocephalia

Tuatara

Triceratops

Anklyosaurus

Tyrannosaurus

Struthiomimus

Stegosauria

Archaeopteryx

Hadrosaurus

Sauropoda

Pterosauria

Ornithischia

Plesiosauria

Saurischia

Ichthyosauria

Crocodiles

Mammal-like reptiles

THECODONTIA

Primitive mammal-like reptiles

Archosauria

COTYLOSAURIA

Seymouria

CLASS: Reptilia

In the long history of the animal kingdom the first vertebrates to break completely free from their watery environment were the reptiles. The amphibians which preceded them by some 25 million years already possessed lungs that enabled them to spend the major part of their lives out of water, but they were inextricably bound to it during the early stages of their development. The main reason why the reptiles were capable of surviving on land was that their eggs were quite different in structure from those of the amphibians – having undergone a remarkable evolutionary modification. In the so-called amniotic eggs of the reptiles the developing embryo is wrapped in a thin sac filled with a watery fluid (amniotic fluid), which protects it from drying out and from suffering external damage.

The history of the reptiles began towards the end of the Paleozoic era, in Carboniferous and Permian times, about 300 million years ago. At that time the earth's flora was largely composed of tree-like ferns and conifers, and the land area divided into two enormous continental masses, known as North America and Gondwanaland. It was probably in North America that the first transitional forms between amphibians and reptiles evolved. The Stegocephali (amphibians with armoured heads) were the ancestors of the slender fish-eating amphibians known as Embolomeri. From this latter group were derived the seymouriamorphs, considered by some, though not all, experts as the distant ancestors of the reptiles proper.

According to the American paleontologist Henry Fairfield Osborn, the first reptiles made their appearance on earth at a time when the climate was semi-arid and comparatively hot. As they adapted themselves to new conditions on land, these creatures underwent a number of external and internal physical changes (development of the amnion, a perfected nervous system, the formation of an exoskeleton, acquisition of a secondary bony palate, partition of the cardiac cavities, etc). Thanks to these and other anatomical modifications, they gradually conquered the land.

The second stage in reptilian evolution began approximately 230 million years ago with the Cotylosauria or stem reptiles, believed by the majority of paleontologists to be the true precursors of modern reptiles. This class saw its greatest distribution and diversification during the Mesozoic era – commonly known as the Age of Reptiles – and especially in the Jurassic, some 150 million years ago. Fossils of cotylosaurs have been found in North America, Europe, Asia and Africa and they apparently flourished in every environment – on land, in fresh water, in the sea and in the air.

The Cotylosauria formed the main trunk of the reptile family tree, but there were several side branches. One of these was the order Testudines (turtles and tortoises), which made its appearance towards the end of the Carboniferous and whose present-day representatives have scarcely displayed any evolutionary modification since the Permian. The various aquatic reptiles later became widely differentiated during the Triassic. Among the groups of these creatures, whose representatives now possessed swim-paddles or flippers instead of limbs, were the Ichthyosauria and Sauropterygia. The former were highly specialised and had the overall appearance of modern dolphins, although the shape of their tails was more like that of the present-day sharks. The second order, typically represented by the Plesiosauria, had bodies that were similar to those of tortoises, but with huge necks and paddle-like limbs.

Two other distinctive reptile orders were the Sauropsida and Therapsida. Most paleontologists suggest that the former group were the ancestors of the large reptiles as well as of the birds, and the latter – which later formed an independent evolutionary line – of the mammals. The Rhynchocephalia were a branch of the Sauropsida and there is still a surviving representative in one of the most primitive creatures on earth – the tuatara (*Sphenodon punctatum*)

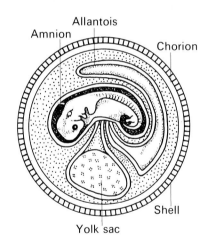

The special structure of reptiles' eggs enabled them to go a step further than the amphibians and to establish their dominance on dry land 300 million years ago. The embryo is protected and develops in the fluid contained in the amnion, and the allantois, provided with blood-vessels, functions as a respiratory organ. The yolk sac provides nutrition and the chorion an outer membranous covering adjoining the shell.

Facing page : Evolutionary family tree of the reptiles.

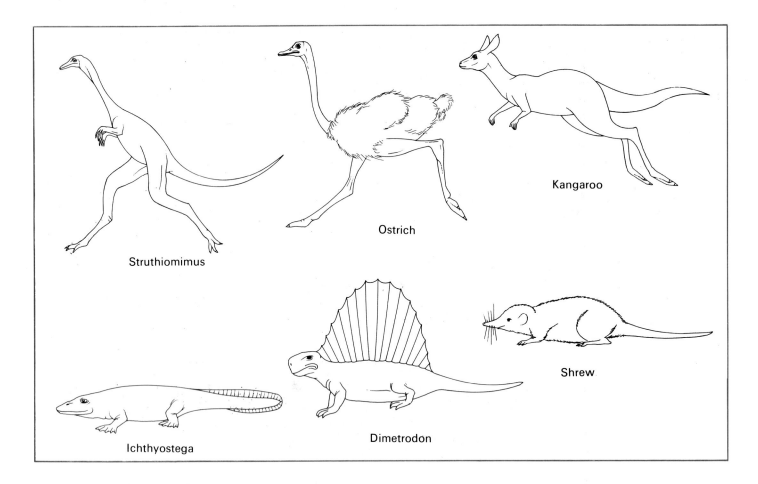

The shapes of animals are more indicative of their way of life than of their actual ancestry. Animals that need to cover considerable distances in a short time have long legs, and examples of this are found in some extinct reptiles, birds and present-day mammals. Those more static in their habitats have short legs, as illustrated here by two extinct reptiles and a present-day shrew.

of New Zealand. This reptile has hardly changed since the Triassic. From the Sauropsida also stems the order Squamata, (lizards and snakes).

In the Mesozoic era, however, the most widely distributed reptile order was the Archosauria, or 'ruling reptiles', with anatomical characteristics which are nowadays found only in the Crocodilia. Linked with the archosaurians were the Pterosauria or flying reptiles, with massive wing membrants.

Closely related to the Archosauria were the two-arched reptiles or Thecodontia, considered by many authors to have branched out in two directions – one leading to the birds and the other to the huge reptiles commonly known as dinosaurs. The latter branch was made up of the Saurischia and Ornithischia. The former were reptile-like dinosaurs and were subdivided into the Sauropoda and Theropoda. The sauropods appeared in the Jurassic and included the largest known terrestrial animals, quadrupeds feeding on grass and foliage and leading an amphibious existence. Among typical representatives were *Brontosaurus*, *Diplocodus* and *Brachiosaurus*. The theropods came later, at the start of the Triassic, and most of them were smaller and more primitive in structure than the sauropods. They were bipeds, able to run and jump, with a carnivorous diet. Among their larger representatives was the enormous *Tyrannosaurus*, measuring about 50 feet long and 20 feet high.

The Ornithischia were bird-like reptiles with a vegetarian diet, more highly evolved than the Saurischia. From them stemmed three suborders – the Ornithopoda (including the well-known *Iguanodon* and other so-called duck-billed dinosaurs), the Stegosauria (armour-plated dinosaurs) and the Ceratopsia or horned dinosaurs.

Another branch of the Cotylosauria was the order Pelycosauria, dating from the Permian – large reptiles with strange shapes. They were carnivores, with numerous well-developed teeth, important because they were situated in the direct line of mammalian evolution. One of the many representatives of this order was *Dimetrodon*, which had a huge dorsal fin that may have played some part in the regulation of body temperature.

The massive dinosaurs which ruled the earth during the Mesozoic era had all vanished by the end of the Cretaceous period, for reasons which still baffle the scientists. Some authors claim that the chief cause must have been climatic change, with warmth and humidity giving way to colder, drier conditions and transforming the vegetational cover to such an extent that the plant-eating dinosaurs simply died from lack of food. The carnivorous dinosaurs, accustomed to feeding on the vegetarians, would eventually have disappeared as a direct consequence. Others maintain that the extinction of the reptiles was due to the appearance and successful competition of the first mammals, which would also have eaten their eggs. One detailed survey of dinosaurs' eggs has led to the conclusion that because of the intense cold they would have been retained too long in the maternal oviduct, growing so large and thick-shelled as to preclude their hatching; and among other theories, disease and parasites, and (most recently) the effects of a cosmic explosion causing a rapid lowering of temperature on the earth's surface.

All present-day reptiles possess an exoskeleton that is furnished with epidermal scales that may overlap to give the appearance of a mosaic or to form a kind of plate-armour. In addition to these scales, the crocodiles and tortoises have dermal bones that are linked to the inner skeleton. The vertebral column is joined to the skull by a single occipital condyle (two in the tuatara and crocodiles), as in the birds.

The Serpentes (snakes) have a large number of flexible ribs and their belly is covered with overlapping plates which follow the movements of the ribs and enable the reptiles to move. The suppleness of the ribs is also one of the important factors of the digestive process, making it possible for snakes to swallow creatures that are even larger than themselves. Turtles and tortoises, on the other hand, have fixed, immovable ribs which are attached to the carapace or body-shell.

Most reptiles are four-legged, apart from the Serpentes which, with a few exceptions, are limbless. The limbs of lizards, for example, usually terminate in three to five toes which in some cases have long claws and in others are adapted for swimming. The geckos have short toes with claws which are generally dilated and provided with suction-like plates enabling the animals to cling to smooth surfaces. Chameleons possess toes that are joined down to the nails and arranged in two groups to form pincers.

Reptiles' teeth are usually long, conical and all alike, neatly arranged in two rows, implanted in alveoli (small sockets) and linked with the dentary bone. The teeth are not really intended for chewing and are essentially instruments for grasping and maintaining a firm hold on objects. Snakes have fewer teeth than do the lizards, and these display some differentiation. In the groups of venomous snakes, for example, two of the teeth are generally transformed into hooks, which are linked with the venom sacs. Turtles and tortoises, however, have no teeth at all, but horny jaws with jagged edges.

Not all the reptilian senses are equally well developed. Vision, however, is particularly important and the characteristics of the eye differ according to the degree of the reptile's activity. In the diurnal species, for example, the pupil is generally rounded, whereas it is vertical in those reptiles with nocturnal habits. There is considerable variation in the structure of the lids. In the Serpentes these are joined so as to form a transparent, immovable membrane. Other reptiles have separate, opaque and mobile lids, and some, such as the solitary tuatara and the crocodiles, possess a third eyelid (or nictitating membrane), which moves sideways across the eye, protecting and cleansing the cornea.

Reptiles were the first vertebrates to acquire an inner ear with a differentiated cochlear canal, but, contrary to what might be supposed, their hearing is not usually very acute. Taste and smell, however, are highly developed senses, largely due to the presence of a special structure known as Jacobson's organ. This is linked with the nasal cavity and the mouth, and in the opinion of many authors plays a vital role in locating food, partly by smell, partly by

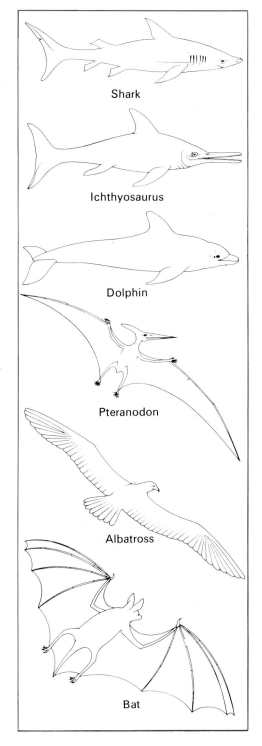

Shark

Ichthyosaurus

Dolphin

Pteranodon

Albatross

Bat

The limbs of primitive reptiles were in some species modified into swim-paddles and wings, enabling them to live in water and to take to the air. Some of the largest of modern fishes, such as the shark, and marine mammals, such as the dolphin, retain the body shapes of their prehistoric ancestors; so too do large birds, such as the albatross, and the numerous species of bats.

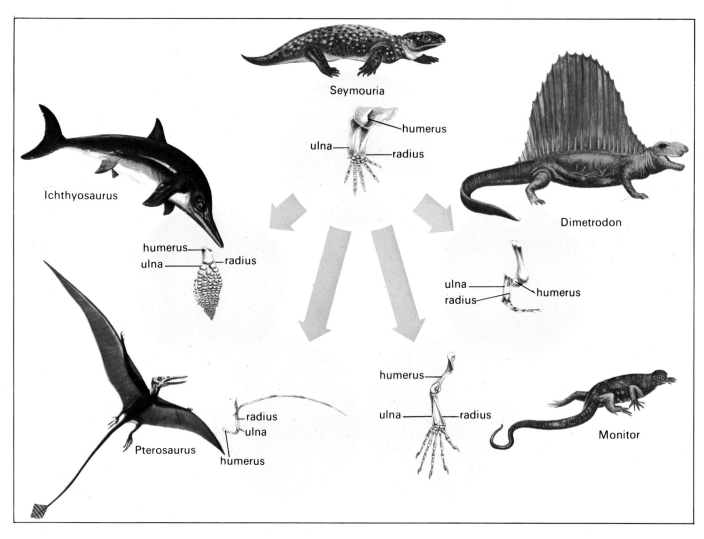

The fore-limbs of reptiles are widely
differentiated, depending on their method
of locomotion. Whether they are in the
form of feet with separate toes or claws—
suitable for progressing over dry land—
flippers for swimming or wings for flying,
they are all perfectly adapted for life in a
particular environment. They are not very
different in structure from the limbs of
Seymouria, thought by many authorities
to be the ancestor of all modern reptiles.

taste. In addition, the tongue, with its taste buds, is highly specialised. That
of the crocodile is provided with flaps which close off the rear of the oral
cavity and prevent the creature from swallowing any water while it is feeding.
The retractile tongue of the chameleon is tubular at the base, and special
muscles provide the propulsive power necessary for catching insects on the
wing. The snake's tongue is forked, protractile and furnished with sensory
papillae.

All reptiles breathe by lungs. In the snakes, the right lung is very long while
the left one is atrophied—a characteristic which conforms to the shape of the
creature's body. Chameleons have air-sacs branching from the lungs,
situated between the internal organs.

Reptiles are poikilotherms—animals with a variable body temperature—
but their internal regulating mechanism is such that they are unable to withstand extremes of heat and cold.

The sexes are separate and fertilisation is internal. The male organs may be
single—as in the crocodiles and tortoises—or double, as in the lizards and
snakes. Most reptiles are oviparous (egg-laying), but some are ovoviparous
(eggs hatched inside body). Only a few of them are viviparous (giving birth
to live young). The eggs have large yolks and the shells are normally brittle
and parchment-like. They are laid in natural depressions or in holes dug by
the female and are then often abandoned, incubation being effected by the
natural warmth of the ground, heated by the sun.

Present-day reptiles are subdivided into four orders. The Testudines
include the turtles and tortoises; the Rhynchocephalia are represented by only
one species—the tuatara. The Crocodilia consist of crocodiles, alligators and
caymans; and the Squamata are further subdivided into two suborders—the
Sauria (lizards) and the Serpentes (snakes).

ORDER: Squamata

The order Squamata is broken down into the lizards and the snakes. Although experts in paleontology are not in agreement as to how these vertebrates actually evolved, it is to this science that we have to turn in order to learn about their probable origin and development.

According to some authors, the first signs of a structural adaptation consistent with that of the Squamata are to be found in the Paleozoic era, the ancestors of the order being animals of the *Youngina* type, judging from fossils discovered in the Upper Permian beds of the Karoo in South Africa. The strongest evidence for a direct ancestral link is a creature called *Prolacerta*, which was similar in appearance to modern lizards.

Other paleontologists dispute this theory, and there has been so much controversy that perhaps the only safe statement to make is that the first representatives of the Squamata flourished in the Triassic period, at the beginning of the Mesozoic era. This group gradually became differentiated, and it was during the Cretaceous, about 50 million years after the appearance of the first saurians, that the snakes arrived on the scene. This period also saw the emergence and development of a group related to the Squamata, known as Mosasauridae–marine animals with a serpent-like body and limbs that were transformed into flippers. The most typical of these was *Mosasaurus* (or Meuse lizard), which was over 30 feet long. All members of this group were extinct by the end of the Cretaceous.

The lizards and snakes of the order Squamata make up about 95 per cent of living reptiles and are widely differentiated. They are found all over the world, with the exception of the polar regions, and have established themselves in every type of environment. Their common characteristic is a body covering of scales, which may be rough or smooth, sometimes small and granular, often overlapping like bony plates. They form a protective film which can, in many species, be sloughed off, with new skin replacing the old.

The most important feature, however, in the definition and classification of the order is the structure of the skull. The position of the temporal fossae and the mobile quality of the quadrate bone are the two characteristics that differentiate these creatures from other reptiles. The wide angle of the lower jaw in lizards is due to the loose articulation between the quadrate bone and the skull; in the snakes this characteristic is even more marked, the link between the bones of the skull and the ligaments of the lower jaw being so flexible that the potential gape of the mouth is huge, enabling the reptile to swallow all kinds of prey in a single gulp.

The Serpentes are limbless, as are a few of the Sauria–notably certain species of Anguidae (blindworm), Anniellidae and Amphisbaenidae. The Scincidae may be regarded as transitional forms, some of which are limbless and some with four legs.

Many lizards possess an anatomical peculiarity which functions as a defensive measure. They are able to shed their tail in certain circumstances. If one grabs hold of the caudal appendage of a typical lizard, there is a violent muscular contraction which may result in its partial or total rupture. This is apparently due to the presence of blocks of linking tissue, very fragile, covering the muscles and scales. When the tail becomes detached from the rest of the body, there is no bleeding because the veins twist back on themselves and the arterial sphincters contract. The missing portion later grows again but the second tail is different in structure. Should it break for the second time it cannot be regenerated.

The teeth are not in themselves remarkable, usually simple and peg-like in the insectivorous lizards but stronger and sharper in the omnivorous agamids and iguanas. Snakes' teeth are inclined in a backward direction in such a way that it is almost impossible for prey to prise themselves free.

In certain species of venomous snake two of the teeth are quite different in structure from the others, being long, mobile and virtually transformed into grooved, canine-type hooks. They are situated in the upper jaw and are

CLASSIFICATION OF SQUAMATA

Suborder	Family
Sauria	Gekkonidae
	Iguanidae
	Agamidae
	Chamaeleontidae
	Xantusiidae
	Scincidae
	Dibamidae
	Lacertidae
	Teiidae
	Amphisbaenidae
	Lanthanotidae
	Varanidae
	Pygopodidae
	Helodermatidae
	Anguidae
	Xenosauridae
	Anniellidae
	Cordylidae
	Feyliniidae
Serpentes	Typhlopidae
	Anomalepidae
	Leptotyphlopidae
	Aniliidae
	Uropeltidae
	Xenopeltidae
	Boidae
	Acrochordidae
	Colubridae
	Dipsadidae
	Elapidae
	Viperidae

linked with the venom sacs—modified salivary glands—behind the eyes. These snakes are subdivided into four groups depending on the way the poison mechanism is constructed and how it functions. In simplest terms, however, what happens is that when the snake opens its mouth to capture its prey, the tooth becomes erect, the anterior temporal muscles press against the venom sac, and the poison is ejected into the wound.

The only venomous lizard is the Gila monster (*Heloderma suspectum*), an inhabitant of several of the southern states of the U.S.A.

As in the majority of reptiles, reproduction is either oviparous or ovoviparous. Only in a few rare cases does a reptile give birth to live young. The eggs are normally incubated by the heat from the sun and although parental attention is uncommon, pythons tend to care for their offspring by the simple expedient of wrapping their bodies around the eggs until the moment of hatching.

The suborder Sauria comprises the world's lizards—muscular reptiles, usually of medium size, with feet and toes—which are further subdivided into 19 families. They include the Gekkonidae (geckos), Agamidae (agamids), Iguanidae (iguanas), Chamaeleontidae (chameleons), Scincidae (skinks), Lacertidae (lizards of the Old World), Anguidae (including the limbless blindworm), Varanidae (monitors—largest of living lizards, including the enormous Komodo dragon of the East Indies), and the worm-like Amphisbaenidae. These last are limbless, subterranean creatures whose name is derived from the fact that the head is virtually indistinguishable from the tail and that they can move both backwards and forwards.

The suborder Serpentes is subdivided into 12 families. Among them are the Typhlopidae (blind snakes), Leptotyphlopidae (thread snakes), Boidae (including the well-known boas, pythons and anacondas), Colubridae (a large family including many common snakes, tree snakes, sand snakes, water snakes, chicken snakes, rat snakes and so forth), Viperidae (vipers, pit vipers and rattlesnakes), and Elapidae (many poisonous species, including the cobras and mambas).

Two representatives of the order Squamata. The gecko (*left*) is a member of the family Gekkonidae, one of the saurians or lizards. The grass-snake (*right*) is one of the Serpentes, belonging to the family Colubridae. It is here seen swallowing a salamander, which is not a lizard but an amphibian.

ORDER: Hyracoidea

Experts have not always agreed about the classification of the small hoofed mammals known as hyraxes, mainly because they have been uncertain as to which of the animals' distinctive physical features should be regarded as of primary importance. At one time they were all classified as pachyderms – to which they are probably related – and later among the perissodactyls. It was Thomas Huxley, in 1869, who finally placed them in the separate order of Hyracoidea. Yet although they are of primitive stock, no fully satisfactory explanation has been provided as to their origin.

The living representatives of this order are dumpy creatures, about the size of hares (but lacking tails), with a short, thick neck and small ears. In general appearance they somewhat resemble marmots, and in common with the latter they possess one well-developed pair of upper incisors, curving in a forward direction and continuously growing. The lower jaw, with its high ascending ramus, has two pairs of incisors. There are no canine teeth in either jaw but there is a complete set of cheek teeth (seven in each half of each jaw). However, some of the premolars – the first, second and often the third – may drop out comparatively early in life. The grinding teeth are similar in structure to those of rhinoceroses, separated from the incisors by a wide diastema or gap. This is a characteristic of many animals with a vegetarian diet, hyraxes feeding on leaves, shoots and grass.

The upper lip is cleft and twelve long vibrissae surround the snout; three or four other hairs are present on either cheek and there is another tuft of hair above the eyes.

A cutaneous gland on the animal's back is covered with hair which is of a lighter colour than that of the rest of the body, but there are no sweat or anal glands.

All species of hyrax emit piercing cries, possibly due to the lining of the Eustachian tubes between pharynx and ear, acting as a sound-box.

Hyraxes are plantigrades, the front feet having four toes, all joined by skin, and the back feet three toes, of which the two outer ones are linked down to the phalange. The pads on the soles of the feet enable the animals to cling to rocks or bark. The nails are black and flattened, only the nail of the inner toe of the back foot being sharply pointed like a claw.

The main characteristic of the skeleton is the absence of a clavicle and the broad outward bulge along the back of the vertebral column.

The brain is not highly convoluted, though this apparently varies with subject and species. The sense of smell is especially well developed.

In addition to a normal large caecum, the digestive system contains a second, supplementary caecum; the liver is made up of two large, subdivided lobes, and there is no bile duct.

Hyraxes live in plains, savannahs, forests and rocky regions south of the Sahara, as well as in the Middle East, making their homes either in rocks or in trees. All of them are grouped together in the family Procavidiae, which is subdivided into three genera – *Dendrohyrax*, *Procavia* and *Heterohyrax*. The genus *Dendrohyrax* is typically represented by the tree hyrax, an animal with a rough, thick coat, which lives in holes in trees and which is a particularly agile, sure-footed climber. There are three species of tree hyrax, with a broad range of distribution through the African continent. The genus *Procavia* comprises the rock hyraxes – best known of all – which are subdivided into four species. These are all somewhat larger than their arboreal relatives and are also adept climbers, living in rock fissures and usually found in small colonies. Their distribution extends through much of Africa and parts of western Asia. The genus *Heterohyrax* contains two species of yellow-spotted hyrax, found in eastern and southern parts of Africa – generally inhabiting open plains but also often found in forest and mountain regions.

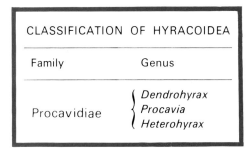

CLASSIFICATION OF HYRACOIDEA	
Family	Genus
Procavidiae	*Dendrohyrax* *Procavia* *Heterohyrax*

CHAPTER 5

Baboons: inheritors of the earth

During the Miocene period, which lasted about 13 million years, almost the entire African continent was covered by impenetrable forests that stretched uninterruptedly as far as India and Southeast Asia. The warm, humid climate encouraged this luxuriant growth of trees, some of which were of enormous height and girth, affording food for a wide range of arboreal creatures (in the form of leaves, bark, shoots and fruit) and sheltering them effectively from the many predators that prowled on the ground below. It was a virtual paradise for such creatures as the primates, which were physically adapted to this kind of life and had to contend with very few rivals for a place of honour in these lofty, shaded regions. The eyes of these monkeys were placed in the front of the head, giving them far-ranging, stereoscopic vision which enabled them to gauge distances with great accuracy – vitally important when it came to leaping from branch to branch. On each of their four limbs were five fingers with fleshy tips and flat nails, so that they could grip surfaces firmly and hook their feet to the slenderest of boughs. Their keen sense of hearing was also of inestimable value in guarding against enemies. Thus the primates managed to become both numerous and diversified.

At the beginning of the Pliocene, about 12 million years ago, the climate became drier, with rainfall less frequent, so that the immense mass of tropical and subtropical forest slowly began to retreat. As time passed, the forest area contracted until it retained its former luxuriance only in the mountainous regions of East Africa, in the Congo basin and along the banks of other rivers in Central and East Africa. Many primates, unable to abandon an arboreal life, were ever more tightly constricted in their traditional habitats; but others, already accustomed to spending only a part of their life in trees and the rest on the ground – particularly

Facing page : Baboons often form protective associations with impalas which, thanks to their subtle sense of smell, can immediately detect the presence of a leopard or a lion in the undergrowth. The baboons, in turn, make use of their keen eyesight and lofty position in trees to give their own alarm signal. Both species thus have plenty of time to take appropriate evasive action.

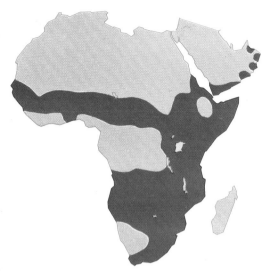

Geographical distribution of baboons.

Facing page : Although they have long dog-like faces, baboons use their hands – complete with thumb and four fingers – to gather their food and carry it to their mouth. The acquisition of hands with flexible fingers was a vital stage in the evolution of primates when they abandoned life in the trees for a terrestrial existence.

ANUBIS BABOON
(Papio anubis)

Class: Mammalia
Order: Primates
Family: Cercopithecidae
Length of head and body: 32–38 inches (80–95 cm)
Length of tail: 18 inches (45 cm)
Weight: male 72 lb (33 kg), female 37 lb (17 kg)
Diet: fruit, grains and other vegetable matter, insects, small invertebrates and vertebrates
Gestation: 183 days
Number of young: one, sometimes two
Longevity: about 10 years

Adults
A short, stocky animal with grey-brown or olive fur. Adult males, larger than females, have a well-developed mane. Long canines and elongated, dog-like face. Tail held in inverted 'U' shape when walking. Ischial callosities flesh-coloured, particularly prominent in female when on heat.

Young
Face and ears pink at birth, body covered with black hair. At four months the face becomes darker, taking on the same appearance as the adult at ten months. Sexual maturity is attained at the age of four years.

on the fringes of forest-galleries – gradually adapted themselves to an entirely new mode of existence on the plains and savannahs. Survival was considerably more difficult than it had been in the forests, not only because food was much scarcer, but also because they were now exposed to strong, implacable predators. The Felidae, Canidae and Hyaenidae, already experienced hunters of fleet-footed, self-defending ungulates, found the newcomers much easier prey. Among those first monkeys venturing into a new environment there must have been many that fell victim to carnivores or were forced back to their ancient habitats. But as a result of mutation and natural selection over a lengthy period, some species of primates made good use of their better-developed physical and mental attributes to come to terms with their surroundings. Among these favourably endowed groups were our own hominid ancestors; and since it is reasonable to suppose that the mode of life and behaviour of terrestrial monkeys is similar in some respects to that of primitive man, zoologists and paleontologists have an interest in studying monkeys in the wild.

Among those primates capable of surviving away from forest regions, the baboons, geladas, macaques and mandrills are especially strong, aggressive creatures, owing their successful adaptation to an environment that did not naturally favour them to qualities such as audacity, discipline and co-operation. The vervet or green monkey is an explorer, despite the fact that it rarely strays far from its wooded retreats; for it selects its habitat and is sufficiently adaptable to follow a way of life midway between that of the belligerent baboons and that of the shy patas or hussar monkeys. The latter form the last group of terrestrial primates and are without doubt the most independent, being equally happy in trees or among rocks. But instead of adopting communal techniques of attack and defence when confronted by predators these monkeys resort to sudden, rapid flight, group dispersal and immobilisation on the ground – a philosophy of 'each for himself'.

The disciplined baboons

As the horizon turns red and the first rays of the rising sun light up the savannah, there is still complete silence among the branches of the huge acacia where a troop of baboons has passed the night. The outlines of the monkeys, huddled in the foliage, stand out sharply against the brightening sky. The largest and strongest animals have their niches in the most spacious and comfortable forks of the tree, while the smaller, less robust individuals have to make do where they can.

These primates have an intense, irrational fear of darkness, for this is the time when the leopard, their most determined enemy, customarily prowls. The baboons therefore take nightly refuge in a tree which is high enough to elude the predator. Often they spend hour after hour completely motionless in the branches, apparently not in the least inconvenienced by the roughness of the bark. The adult males may weigh as much as 70–80 lb, yet even they have no difficulty in maintaining their unvarying position. The answer to their secret is that the ischial portion of their anatomy (or backside) is well protected by prominent callosities.

With the arrival of daylight this unreasoning fear of the shadows subsides and the baboons begin to go about their normal everyday activities. The young, who have slept without relaxing their hold on the hairs of their mothers' chests, now take themselves off a little way to join their companions in boisterous games; and all the other members of the troop – solemn patriarchs, mothers with babes in their arms, and males and females of less important status – start to scratch themselves and to yawn, opening their mouths to show their huge canine teeth.

The first to clamber down from the tree and touch the ground are the young males. Glancing warily from side to side, they hang like acrobats from the branches, then grasp the trunk and slide straight down. When all the members of the troop are safely on the ground, they set out for the savannah. This is no casual dawn ramble, however, but a strictly organised expedition – almost a military manoeuvre. In the van, going ahead as scouts, are the strongest of the young male baboons, together with adults belonging to the lower social order of the rigidly hierarchical society. Other young males patrol the flanks of the column and bring up the rear, mingling with the females that are either very

The limbs of all terrestrial monkeys, including baboons, are perfectly adapted for movement over every type of terrain. The thumb, set some way apart from the other fingers, is an ideal instrument for gripping branches and a variety of small objects.

young, do not carry babies or are not currently on heat. In the centre of the group, protected on every side by these sentries, are the strongest dominant males, forming an inner ring of security for the mothers with families. The latter carry their young on their rumps or, in the case of a newborn baby, tightly clasped to their breasts. As the baboons move forward, with calm, determined gait, they snatch at tender stalks of grass, prise up roots and bulbs, grab handfuls of fruit, catch stray lizards or wandering fledglings, and filch birds' eggs. When they reach an appropriate spot they all come to a halt, then disperse in various directions to make a serious search for food.

Although baboons have elongated, dog-like faces, they do not eat like dogs but make use of their hands to obtain their favourite food. Each hand is equipped with a thumb and four fingers, supple and flexible enough to seize hold of any object, no matter how small. It was largely due to this prehensile capacity that the species became so successful in coping with conditions on the ground once they had descended from the trees. Other anatomical features, such as the structure of the skull with its long, pointed, male canine teeth, and certain behaviour patterns, which will be described later, are of paramount interest in showing how the species adapted to their terrestrial way of life. Primitive man may well have been confronted by problems of survival similar to those facing the Primates whose ancesters were tree-dwellers.

The baboon overlords

After they have finished their breakfast the baboon troop spends a few minutes relaxing in the sunshine, prudently keeping within striking distance of a nearby kopje, which will serve them as a place of refuge in the event of an attack by lions. When they have digested their morning meal they turn their attention to the daily mutual-grooming routine. As with all highly disciplined animals, this is in the nature of a social ritual. Each animal devotes itself to cleaning the skin of another, the adult males and females with very young babies receiving especially meticulous attention. Two females, for example, may be seen rummaging in the fur of one massive male reclining blissfully against a tree trunk, his eyes closed. They go about their cleansing task with the utmost delicacy, removing with their fingers any impurities that may have lodged in the hairs, and sometimes plunging their incisors deep into the fur of their lord and master in order to kill an insect. After some ten minutes of patient work, the complaisant male opens his eyes, gets to his feet and condescendingly takes his turn to perform a similar service for the older of the females.

This grooming procedure is of particular importance in the baboon community. Compared with the coat of a lion or indeed any other animal sharing the same habitat – full of ticks and spots of dirt – the baboon's fur is absolutely clean. Furthermore, this daily habit serves to relax the rigidity of the group organisation, allowing individuals of every social rank to mingle freely with others and maintaining mutual confidence and cohesion.

The baboon community is especially noteworthy for its rigid and many-tiered social structure. The aristocrats are indisputably

The baboon, like other primates, normally gives birth to only one young at a time, providing it with maternal care and affection during the first weeks of its life. During this time the baby clings to the hair of its mother's chest, day and night. In the animal kingdom a single offspring, attentively supervised by its mother, has a better chance of survival than a larger litter or brood which must inevitably be left to their own devices at certain times during the first vital days and weeks.

According to the zoologist Irven de Vore, the skin and coat colour of young baboons has an important bearing on the behaviour of the mothers and other members of the troop. The baby (A) is born with pink face and ears, and black hair all over its body. This colour scheme evidently stimulates the maternal instincts. At four months (B) the face becomes darker and the fur turns brown. These changes coincide with a lessening of maternal attention and the development of the youngster's instinct for independence. At ten months (C) the animal has taken on the typical adult coloration and is ready to join companions of its own age.

the dominant males. These are powerful, fully grown individuals which have risen to such an eminent position by a combination of physical strength, intelligence and self-confidence. They are the élite—a compact little group that governs the rest of the troop. It is their right to lay claim to the most attractive females, the most comfortable 'beds' in the trees and the choicest morsels of food. Next in rank to these privileged creatures are what might be termed the 'second-class citizens', which, although they enjoy certain rights over younger animals, still have to acknowledge the supremacy of the troop leaders. They are, in fact, content simply to be left alone by the dominant males. On the fringes of this social hierarchy live the young and adolescent baboons. These spend the greater part of their time playing in small groups but are not without ambition of some day succeeding their elders to the elevated ranks of the ruling class. For the moment, however, they have to mingle with their sisters and male companions.

The females too belong to different social ranks but their status depends on their breeding pattern. When a female gives birth she automatically joins the inner circle of dominant males and enjoys their protection at all times. But a female that is neither expecting nor rearing a baby is consigned to the ordinary outer margins of society. When she is on heat she has to satisfy her sexual appetite with one of the young or 'second-class' males, these animals being permitted to couple with her during the days preceding the moment of maximum receptivity. At that point one of the dominant males steps in to claim her and carries her off without further ceremony or argument. The pair will then perform the sexual act in the presence of the other members of the troop and will remain together for several hours or sometimes several days.

Although this behaviour may appear to be unjust and tyrannical, it can be justified when one considers it from the point of view of the troop's welfare and future. The dominant males are, after all, the best-endowed individuals, both physically and mentally. They are able to recognise with unerring precision the moment when the female is most likely to conceive, the degree of her sexual response being clearly indicated by her ischial callosities and the bright purple colour of the soft epithelial tissue of her perianal region. The dominant male will therefore mate with such a female at the exact moment that ovulation occurs, virtually ensuring that pregnancy will result and that the species will be provided with an offspring worthy of its father.

Pretenders and heirs

Many groups of Primates, such as the patas monkeys and sacred baboons, as well as most of the wild ungulates, are governed by a single dominant male, this individual bearing the sole responsibility for directing the affairs of the herd, troop or pack. This is not the way things are done in the baboon community, where a group of older, experienced males make all the communal decisions and monopolise the most desirable females and the choicest portions of territory. There is a mutually observed hierarchy within this dominant clan and each male comes to the aid of any other who may be challenged by a rival of lower social status. Such a system makes it almost impossible for an outsider to usurp power and protects the entire troop from internal disputes.

The advantage can be seen when one compares this structure of government with that of gorilla family groups, each with a single dominant male. Should this individual be killed by a hunter the entire group falls into disorder, the other adult males often failing to survive because of their inexperience in taking the initiative and commanding the obedience of the rest of the group; and when the leader dies of old age, bloodthirsty feuds follow.

Human history has shown only too often that dictatorial coups are risky and sometimes catastrophic adventures. Without drawing too close a parallel, it is clear that the emergence of a ruling caste within the baboon community was a striking evolutionary step forward. If a dominant male is killed, perhaps by a leopard, anarchy never results, for the other leaders promptly take up the reins of command until the vacant position is filled by the best qualified of the surviving dominant males.

The frontier that separates the élite from the 'second-class citizens' cannot be lightly crossed. Woe betide any individual that fails to show proper regard and respect for one of its overlords. Should such an animal omit to lower its eyes and give its master precedence, the latter will punish the offender by giving chase and biting its neck, just hard enough to show who gives the orders.

The 'rat-race'—if we are permitted to mix our species—begins almost as soon as a baboon is born. Even the females are not exempted and those that belong to the lowest rank of society are frequently teased and tormented by their companions. Their abject, timorous temperament is often reflected in their offspring, the latter soon learning to adopt the same kind of submissive gestures and postures that their mothers use to calm the wrath of

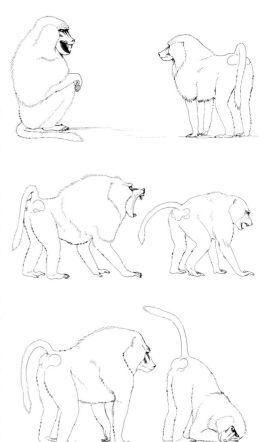

Baboons generally go through an elaborate ritual of threat, intimidation and self-abasement in order to avoid actual combat. A dominant male will snarl angrily at a potential rival of lower social rank and force him into submission. This consists of stooping low to present the hindquarters in the posture of a sexually receptive female. The leader will then sometimes simulate the act of copulation before allowing the other animal to rejoin the troop. The ritual may have to be repeated at intervals whenever the two baboons meet, until honour is fully satisfied.

The young baboon has a bland, carefree expression on its face but as it grows will gradually take on the rather pained, frowning look of the adult which, with its powerful, elongated face and jaws, might be taken for an entirely different species.

Facing page : The daily exercise of mutual grooming is important for the health and security of the baboon troop. The mother continues to search the fur of her baby for parasites even when it is old enough to leave her side and engage in youthful games. Previously it has been carried close to her breast but now that it is older it often prefers to ride on her back.

higher-ranking females. The sons of these 'upper-class' mothers also seem to follow the parental example, showing a lofty arrogance in their youthful games and giving clear notice, by their proud and confident bearing, of their future intentions.

This class distinction is evident from the earliest childhood days, so much so that there seems to be no way of later avoiding either social responsibility or anonymity. As soon as the young baboons are free of maternal attention their future status can be read in their recreational behaviour. In these apparently carefree jousts it is invariably the fearful, undisciplined, irresolute animals that come off second best, finding it hard to accommodate themselves to the confident, organised play-pattern of their companions; and from the latter ranks come tomorrow's leaders.

When an adult baboon of inferior social rank decides to challenge one of the dominant males he can show his defiance in several ways, either by failing to step out of his way or refusing to lower his eyes. If he is particularly audacious he may venture into the centre of the group where the lord holds court with his chosen female. The latter will immediately fix the pretender with a steady, frowning gaze; if unable to outstare him he will then open his mouth wide to show his formidable long fangs. This threat should be sufficient to deter the upstart but if the latter continues to hold his ground the infuriated lord will spring into action, trying to plant his sharp teeth in his rival's neck. If it reaches this stage the other members of the ruling caste will rush to their colleague's aid and present a solid front, forcing the younger animal to abandon his grandiose ideas and plans.

The intruder can only avoid retribution in future by adopting a ritual pattern of behaviour signifying submission and self-abasement, which inhibits the aggressive intentions of the affronted male. He must turn his back and offer himself to his master, in exactly the same position as that of a sexually aroused female. The overlord then simulates the act of copulation with the terrified animal which meanwhile has to keep his face pressed to the ground. When this rite of pacification is concluded the humiliated creature is allowed to rejoin the troop; but in the next few days, every time he comes face to face with his insulted lord he must repeat the identical ritual or risk a vicious bite in the neck.

Disputes are not always so easily settled and in the natural course of events old leaders disappear and are replaced. But it would seem that mutual assistance within the dominant clan, coupled with their own self-confidence, enables ageing individuals to retain their position of power for some time, even when they have lost canine teeth, whether by decay or in combat.

Priority and privilege

Life in a community of baboons is not a round of violent quarrels and fights. On the contrary, such episodes are few and far between. So long as the social structure is not upset by the death of a dominant male or the sudden aggressive behaviour of a pretender, life goes on in an untroubled and orderly fashion. One of the main responsibilities of the leaders is to instil a sense of respect and understanding in the young and adolescent baboons for the social

virtues of tolerance and discipline. It often happens that youthful games spill over into violence and that a hard-pressed participant is forced to utter piercing cries for help. The dominant male nearest to the scene of action at once intervenes, handing out slaps and bites until calm is restored, while the animal which has sent out the alarm finds refuge with its mother or special friends.

The attentive attitude of the adult baboons towards the young also helps to maintain solidarity and good relations within the troop. As soon as a female seats herself, babe in arms, she is immediately surrounded by her companions, who try to take it from her in order to clean and fondle it. The males, young and old alike, also appear to enjoy being in contact with the baby baboons, as if aware of their protective responsibilities towards these defenceless creatures. When a troop is on the move and a mother with offspring finds herself temporarily cut off from her companions, she is quickly rescued by one of the leaders who will not leave her side until she is safely restored to the group. On the other hand, should a male or a female without young prove unable to keep up with the troop, either as a result of sickness or injury, they will in all likelihood be left to their fate, the other baboons not pausing in the course of their implacable forward advance.

The little central group made up of the leaders and the females with progeny serves as a rallying point for the rest of the troop. Each baboon knows that it is courting danger to lose sight of the others or to wander too far away from them.

Facing the enemy

Whenever the baboons are out in the open and suspect the presence of an enemy their ranks close and strict 'army' discipline is imposed. The vigorous young males at the front, in the rear and on the flanks redouble their wariness and as soon as they sight a carnivore begin to bark loudly. If the enemy is a cheetah, jackal or other relatively innocuous creature, a few intrepid baboons advance in its direction. But should a leopard launch one of its sudden characteristic attacks the 'second-class citizens' on the fringes of the troop stay where they are, barking furiously in unison. This is the occasion for the dominant males to set an example and confront the traditional foe. Close study of baboon behaviour in such a situation, both in the wild and using captive animals for controlled experiments, reveals the same unvaried reaction. In many cases such a bold confrontation is tantamount to suicide, especially if one of the baboons is isolated from the others and cornered by the leopard. But the primates are equally capable of launching such a ferocious concerted attack that it may be the predator that is literally ripped to shreds. While this bloodthirsty battle is going on the females with young, accompanied by the younger and lower-ranking animals, make for the nearest acacia or kopje to await the outcome.

It is not entirely fanciful to compare the band of dominant males with the élite corps of an army. In just such a way did the ancient Greek champions and knights of the Middle Ages go out to do battle on behalf of the weaker members of the community, as a matter of privilege and duty.

Baboons show extreme caution when approaching a waterhole to drink. Seated on a branch or on top of an anthill, they will keep a close watch on the activities of giraffes, zebras and antelopes before venturing down to the water themselves. They will then drink rapidly so as not to spend more time than necessary in a position where they are exposed to predators.

The appearance of a pride of lions on the savannah will provoke an entirely different group reaction. The baboons begin to bark, but there is a less aggressive note to it. The females and young make straight for the trees while the dominant males bring up the rear. There is no attempt to stand and fight. The whole company perch themselves on the highest branches and wait for the lions to depart, refusing to come down so long as the slightest risk remains. It is interesting to note, however, that if the immediate cause for concern is a man armed with a rifle the baboons react first of all by seeking shelter among the branches, but soon return to ground level to disperse one by one through the undergrowth. This difference in behaviour implies a deliberate adaptation of defensive methods to suit the circumstances, the baboons making a distinction between a predator killing at close quarters and one inflicting death from a distance.

Being constantly exposed to danger on the open plains, baboons make use of every natural weapon in their armoury to escape enemies. One of their most effective security measures is to associate with a group of ungulates, most frequently with impalas. One member of the baboon troop is permanently stationed at the top of an acacia or anthill and uses its excellent vision to scour the surrounding plains. The impalas, for their part, have remarkable scenting ability and will invariably pick up an intruder which may have escaped the notice of the baboon sentinel. Each group supplements the other, the antelopes recognising the alarm barks of the monkeys, which in turn take evasive action the moment they hear the characteristic cry of fear uttered by the impalas. Probably the antelopes derive greater benefit from the association, thanks in part to the baboons' natural aggressiveness. Some naturalists once watched a cheetah stalking a small

When a troop of baboons ventures out onto the open plain where there is little tree cover (1), strict military-style discipline is observed. The females (F) with young and those that are on heat group themselves in the centre, together with the dominant males (D). Around them are the juveniles (J) and the other females, while in the van and in the rear, as well as on the flanks, are the social inferiors (I), males that have the responsibility of sounding the barking alarm and advancing to the attack should a predator such as a cheetah or jackal put in an appearance. If, however, a leopard launches an attack (2) it is the dominant males who advance to the front and try to keep the enemy at bay, giving the other members of the troop time to scamper away to safety.

herd of impalas when suddenly half a dozen young baboons hurled themselves, barking furiously, at the predator which made off at all possible speed. If impalas are not available, bushbucks, with their subtle sense of smell, make acceptable substitutes.

Before approaching a waterhole to drink, the baboons will carefully look around at the assembled ungulates to satisfy themselves that the coast is clear. If a clearing of cracked mud separates the trees from the waterhole, the monkeys will sit themselves down on the borders of the wood and wait patiently until the giraffes, zebras or gazelles put in an appearance. These herbivores are ever on the alert for lions lurking in the tall grass and will never approach a waterhole without first sniffing the air to make sure all is well. The baboons continue to wait and watch until the ungulates have quenched their thirst and only then do they begin to move forward, slowly and cautiously in military file, sometimes under the very feet of the retreating giraffes and antelopes. Lining the bank, they drink hastily, returning soon to shelter.

Baboons show no apparent uneasiness in the company of larger animals such as elephants, rhinoceroses and buffaloes. They simply give them right of way or discreetly withdraw in as dignified a manner as possible, depending on the degree of risk involved.

Terror of the unknown

The baboon troops live in fixed territories, passed on from generation to generation, from which they rarely stray. In the Amboseli game reserve the American zoologist Irven de Vore carried out a survey of fifteen groups of baboons, comprising in all some 2,300 animals. The number of individuals in a single troop varied from as few as thirteen to as many as 185, and the area of their domain ranged from four to seven square miles. The monkeys roamed freely over the whole territory for food and water; but within the territorial confines there were special sites—well furnished with trees and rocks—which were more frequently used than others and which served as sleeping quarters for the troop.

It was precisely because they were familiar with every inch of their kingdom and had complete confidence in the security afforded by their nightly resting places that the baboons were so successful in warding off predators. This knowledge and assurance was clearly transmitted by the elders to the young.

It is at night that the danger from snakes and leopards is accentuated. Normally the higher branches of a tree furnish sufficient protection for the sleeping baboons and thanks to their ischial callosities they are not in much danger of losing their balance. But it does sometimes happen that a baboon tumbles from a branch while asleep and if a predator is on the prowl below there is little chance of the monkey clambering up again to safety. The possibility of this kind of accident may be at the root of that ancestral fear of the dark and terror of falling into empty space that seems to afflict all primates, man himself included.

In certain districts the baboons' territories overlap, but when there is plenty of food and water there is rarely any need for one group to infringe upon another's rights. When, however, as in Amboseli at the end of the dry season, there are only isolated pools

Facing page : The leopard is the baboon's most terrible enemy. Although it is rare for the feline to attack a powerful adult male baboon in broad daylight, it may single out one of the younger members of the troop, given a suitable opportunity. These dramatic photographs show the methods adopted by the carnivore to kill a baboon without coming within range of its sharp teeth.

to be found, several troops may share the same drinking place, both for quenching their thirst and for feeding on the surrounding vegetation. De Vore and his colleagues spent some time in these areas studying the relationship between the different troops and their attitude to other animals using the same waterholes. At one time they counted more than 400 animals gathered around the same spot. Although the baboons seemed at first glance to belong to the same troop, further observation showed that they were made up of three groups whose members came and went but never mingled with one another. At times some of the younger baboons would approach those of another group but their games were never of long duration and they quickly rejoined their own little clan. When the different groups met, the dominant males pretended to ignore one another but there was never any conflict. The naturalists noticed that the smaller groups usually gave way to the larger ones. There were also examples of baboons that seemed to be resentful of the dominance of their own leaders and who hung about on the fringes of the group, waiting a chance to make an approach to another. These 'deserters' were unquestioningly accepted by the adult members of the second group and eventually became fully-fledged members of their new community, sometimes rising to a higher social rank than the one formerly occupied in the troop into which they had been born!

Natural aggressiveness usually turns to passivity and indifference when baboons meet to stake out rival claims for territory, and the boundaries are generally fixed without any resort to violence. The animals are, in fact, only completely at ease within the secure bounds of their own territory. Outside is the great unknown, into which they dare not stray. Zoologists have often tried to tempt baboons away from their domain with food baits, but without much success. Should a young baboon be rash enough to wander a few hundred yards into foreign territory the rest of the troop will watch horrified from the top of their trees and ant-hills until the straggler realises its mistake and scampers back.

Within each portion of territory there are well-trodden paths which the baboons use for their daily comings and goings, normally involving them in a journey of two to three miles every day. There are also favourite trees, rocks, glades and thickets that provide immediate refuge in the event of a predator's attack.

The baboons will steer well clear of spots regularly frequented by prides of lions, though they appear quite contented to feed among the trees at a safe distance. In the Murchison Falls National Park a group of naturalists watched a dozen lions basking in the shade of a large tamarind in which a troop of baboons were perched. It was about ten o'clock in the morning and the lions had perhaps stationed themselves on this spot in the knowledge that it was shortly after dawn that the monkeys regularly clambered down from the branches to file out for their food. On this occasion the baboons had no alternative but to endure their hunger pangs, seeing that it would be suicidal to abandon the safety of their tree. The mothers clasped their babies to their breasts while the males barked angrily at the lions. The carnivores, evidently replete, showed not the slightest signs of moving. It was not until late in the afternoon that they strolled off and ended the siege.

Safety in numbers

The earliest studies of the behaviour of terrestrial Primates were conducted in zoological gardens. Although researchers recognised that cage conditions were abnormal, they were able to arrive at some important conclusions, thought to be equally applicable to the same animals in the wild. It was their opinion that the strength and solidarity of the group depended above all else on mutual sexual attraction. There is no doubt that the sexual instinct does play a significant role in the social life of monkeys. We have already seen how, in contests of wills that take place between two males over questions of social status, the loser adopts a posture identical to that of a female prior to sexual intercourse; also how, in all animal communities in which there is a close relationship between the parents and their young, such attitudes of submission become a routine procedure at an early age. Thus a wolf that wishes to appease a victorious enemy or rival will crouch down, place the tail between the hind legs, stretch itself flat on its back and perhaps urinate–all postures and actions performed by wolf cubs. In the same way a baboon will present its hindquarters to its vanquisher, raising the tail and lowering its head.

Subsequent surveys of the behaviour of baboons and other monkeys in the wild revealed, however, that there was rather more involved to community life than simple sexual appetite. The mating of baboons in fact depends on the hormone cycle of the

Preceding page (above) : The canine teeth of the adult male baboon are especially well-developed, ideally adapted for a terrestrial way of life and of particular value for defending females and young and maintaining order within the troop. (*Below*) Baboons are naturally aggressive creatures and the males often fight with each other, especially over matters relating to social status.

Although baboons feed chiefly on vegetable matter they will, if hungry, kill small mammals. These two have captured and bitten to death a young gazelle and now share the feast.

female, who ovulates during one week of each month. But since a female which is too young to breed, is pregnant or is suckling a baby, holds out no attraction for the male, it is comparatively rare for her to be on heat. When that time comes she temporarily forsakes her young (which will by that time be fairly grown-up) as well as her chosen group of female companions, and seeks out the males, coupling first with the younger and lower-ranking animals and later with the leaders of the troop. Once this mating interlude is over (lasting a few hours or days) she is of no further interest to the males, who either seek new partners or go off to find food and busy themselves in maintaining and asserting their social rights. But in whatever condition she happens to be, the female never leaves the group. Even in troops consisting of only a few individuals, when several months may elapse without any female being on heat or engaging in sexual activity, all the members live together in perfect harmony.

It cannot therefore be sex alone that is responsible for keeping the baboon communities compact and united. Irven de Vore believes that there are several types of behaviour pattern testifying to this inherent gregariousness, each reinforcing the other and binding the members of the troop together. The social links between the various individuals in the community change as the animals grow older but they are powerful from the very first days of a baboon's life. There are obvious bonds between the mother and her baby, between the young baboon and its companions and between a mother and an adult male. There are equally close ties among the various females of a troop, between a male and a female in the mating period and among members of the dominant clan.

The baboons and patas, though both ground-dwelling Primates, organise their lives very differently. The typical baboon troop (*left*) contains several dominant males (D) who form an aristocratic clique, responsible for defending and protecting the troop, and generally maintaining discipline. The patas troop (*right*) is much more loosely organised, with only one dominant male in general charge, surveying territory and creating diversionary tactics rather than directly confronting an enemy. In both cases the social structure and behaviour accords with the temperament and capacity of the species concerned.

COMPARATIVE CHART, BASED ON WORK OF PROFESSOR K. R. L. HALL, SHOWING PRINCIPAL CHARACTERISTICS OF PATAS MONKEYS AND BABOONS IN EAST AND SOUTH AFRICA

	Patas	Baboons
Physical attributes	Lightly built, moving very rapidly on ground. Male weighs 30 lb, female 15 lb.	Powerfully built, tall, expert rock-climber. Male weighs 72 lb, female 37 lb.
Breeding habits	Female cycle about 30 days; fixed season for mating and births; gestation 160–170 days.	Female cycle about 30 days; swelling in genital region; season for births variable; gestation 180 days.
Habitat	Plains and savannahs, forest fringes and copses, well away from streams and rivers.	Mountains, savannahs, sometimes forests, but not virgin forests.
Territory and travel	Territories sometimes overlap; for a group of 30, area up to 20 square miles, without 'retreats'. Distance travelled, from $\frac{1}{2}$ mile to 8 miles daily.	Territory averages 5 square miles in area, with 'retreats' for security and food. Distance travelled, up to 5 miles daily.
Activity and rest	Two meal periods, separated by two to three-hour rest period. Group dispersal at dusk, with different sleeping site every night. No regrouping in morning.	Major part of day spent feeding, without fixed rest periods. Regroup at dusk and dawn. Same sleeping sites used repeatedly.
Size of troop	Between 6 and 30, averaging 15; one dominant male, several females and adolescents.	Up to 200, averaging 25–30; several dominant males, females, adolescents.
Outside troop	Single males or groups of males.	Single males, but not exclusive groups of males.
Food	Mostly vegetation, but also insects, lizards, etc; rarely drink, never in streams and rivers.	Mostly vegetation, but also small mammals; in general a more varied diet than patas; drink stagnant water, sometimes running water.
Relations with other animals	Hunted by leopards, cheetahs and hunting dogs; give way to baboons.	Dominant males confront leopards but troop flees from lions.
Sexual behaviour	Mating rarely observed; females invite males; harem system with single dominant male.	Mating often observed; couples change partners; no harem system.
Social relations	Frequent grooming, especially by female; clue to social status.	Similar to patas; also certain ritual greeting patterns.
Play	Frequent towards mid-morning, usually in full heat of sun.	Usually early and late in day, near to rocks and trees.
Fights	Rare, short and silent; few physical contacts; dominant male not aggressive.	Frequent, violent and noisy; dominant males aggressive.
Mother–baby relationship	Baby carried against mother's belly; not 'loaned' to other females or protected by male.	Baby carried close to breast and later on back of mother; both protected in centre of troop.
Vocal range	Voice sparingly used, silent communication; male only 'speaks' to subordinates.	Large range of sounds, frequently used, including when humans present.
Social structure	Dominant male responsible for reproduction, guard duties and diversionary tactics; females direct troop activities; male often removes self from troop.	Several males responsible for reproduction and defence, remaining in centre of troop with females and young; other males on troop fringes.

The gregarious instinct which is a feature, to a lesser or greater degree, of almost every group of Primates was originally the result of the pressure exerted on them by the predatory carnivores. The solid, firmly-knit structure of the baboon troop is consequently of vital importance to them when called upon to defend themselves against their natural enemies. Those individuals which lack the normal social instincts, or which for one reason or another abandon the troop, tend to fall easy prey to leopards and lions. The offspring of such 'mavericks' tend to inherit the individualistic qualities of their parents and rarely manage to adapt to the group spirit which is typical of the species. For the majority the 'safety in numbers' rule unquestionably applies.

The baboon troop spends the greater part of its day foraging for food, always preserving tight 'military' formation and giving enemies few chances to pick them off individually. When dusk falls the noisy throng flocks back to the safety of its tree. All the animals exude an air of complete confidence – the youngsters as they tumble about, screeching with excitement, the warrior males as they peer around for predators, the mothers proudly carrying babies at their breasts or perched on their backs, the arrogant leaders pacing steadily ahead in the centre of the troop.

Thanks in large measure to their adaptive capacity, the cunning, intelligent baboons have done more than simply survive. They have extended their range of distribution to cover large parts of the African continent south of the Sahara, as well as Arabia.

The distinctive coat colour of the patas, varying considerably among different individuals, serves to dissuade predators. The adult male, with his white mane, is especially prominent and can easily be recognised both by friend and foe.

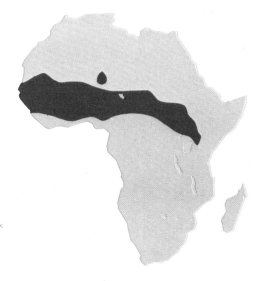

Geographical distribution of patas.

PATAS OR RED MONKEY
(*Erythrocebus patas*)

Class: Mammalia
Order: Primates
Family: Cercopithecidae

Length of head and body: 20–23 inches
   (50–58 cm)
Length of tail: 22–26 inches (55–65 cm)
Weight: Male 22–28 lb (10–13 kg)
       Female 11–14 lb (5–6.5 kg)
Diet: Vegetation, insects, lizards, etc
Gestation: 160–170 days
Number of young: one

Adults
Males are larger than females, but both sexes
have slender bodies and long limbs. Coat colour
varies according to individual's age and sex,
from brick-red to grey on upper part of body to
light brown or pure white below. Adult male has
a mane and well-developed canine teeth. Although overall colour varies greatly from one
individual to another, all have white markings on
face and eyebrows.

Young
Dark brown at birth, there is a gradual change in
colour to light grey-brown at the age of about
three months. Female fully developed at three
and a half years, male at five years, though latter
sexually mature at four years.

The timid patas

The coherent group structure of the baboons is an exception to the rule on the African savannahs and plains. It is true that some of the larger and more powerful ungulates such as buffaloes and elephants will join together to present a common front against a predator, but smaller animals generally resort to individual defensive techniques, depending on their natural endowments. Thus some will run away while others stand stock-still and try to avoid detection. Many of them combine both methods, their subdued colours enabling them to conceal themselves in the surrounding vegetation and their speed carrying them out of range of pursuers. Both attributes are possessed by the shy patas or red monkeys, which are distant relatives of the baboons but very dissimilar to their more aggressive cousins both in appearance and behaviour.

The patas are not to any large extent dependent on water and roam much more freely than baboons over the plains of equatorial Africa south of the Sahara, their range of distribution bounded only by the dense forests. Within their traditional habitat isolated groups are sometimes found – often in steep, inaccessible rocky terrain – but this is exceptional. Professor K. R. L. Hall of Bristol University, who has carefully studied these monkeys in the Murchison Falls National Park, has found them gathered in largest numbers on grassy and wooded savannahs and among the forest-galleries bordering the Nile. In these parts the most familiar trees are acacias, tamarinds and candelabra-like euphorbias. During the rainy season, from April to October, the grass may stand as high as 8–10 feet, which makes close study of all small- and medium-sized animals somewhat difficult. This is an even trickier task with the patas, which are particularly timid creatures. So whatever the habitat and time of year, the naturalist studying this species needs a great deal of patience and wariness.

The most important members of the troop – which averages up to 30 animals – are the single dominant male and the 12–14 females. The rest of the group consists of babies and young. In certain troops there may be another solitary adult male which is singled out by the leader for special torment. Rarer still are the instances of three or four 'bachelors' forming solitary groups.

This type of organisation is perfectly in keeping with the needs and capabilities of the species, for survival in their case depends on rapid and silent flight, followed by concealment. The presence of several dominant males would be of no advantage when confronted by danger and would also compel the troop to spend more time looking for a larger quantity of food.

The dominant male patas thus has the double responsibility of being both reproducer and sentinel; but he leaves it to the females to direct the normal everyday comings and goings of the troop. It is the latter who are the first to be on the move after the siesta period and as soon as they begin trekking across the open plain all the others follow. If the leader of the group, however, shows no inclination to join them, they stop, not letting him out of their sight; and should he or any other individual decide to branch out along a different path to the one selected by the females, it is the latter who will change direction and bow to the will of the rest.

The dominant male is not normally a fighter though he may display aggressive tendencies during the mating period. Surprisingly, it is the adult females that give vent to the most violent outbursts of passion and violence, disputes frequently arising over matters of precedence and rank. These rivalries seem to release a kind of chain reaction of angry feeling as one female is attacked by another of superior station and promptly works out her hostile feelings on a third female of lower status.

These aggressive feelings find their natural outlet in a range of ritual attitudes and expressions. Sometimes, though not often, the monkeys will utter sharp cries which are only audible at close quarters. More frequently the contests will take place in complete silence. Even youthful games are played without a single sound being emitted. This is not because the patas are incapable of using their voices; in fact observation of the species in captivity shows that they have a wide range of vocal sounds and tones. It is simply a characteristic feature of their general behaviour. From the moment they are born they are trained to use their voices sparingly. A young baboon will give clear notice of its pain or displeasure by emitting not just one but a series of piercing howls, which will almost certainly bring its mother or one of the troop leaders to the rescue. Not so the young patas which, like its elders, is quite capable of communicating with others of its species without making a great performance of it and without signalling its presence to predators.

The patas' territorial limits are only vaguely defined and they range far more widely than baboons. In fact they never sleep two nights in succession in the same place. Their daily journeys vary according to season, sometimes up to six miles but usually one or two. They may, however, spend several successive days in the same district until they have exhausted the available vegetation. Their quest for food continues as long as the light lasts, with only a brief pause in the middle of the day. Any spare time is devoted to mutual grooming or, in the case of the young, to fun and games.

The grooming ritual may take place on the top of an anthill or in the branches of a dead tree. Once again the females set an example to the others, the whole business being very formal and stereotyped. One female will approach another of superior social rank, waving her head from side to side and avoiding the other's eyes. Having thus obtained permission to proceed, she gently grasps the hair of her companion's head in order to reach the neck. The female on the receiving end shows her evident satisfaction and enjoyment by reclining in a relaxed position, raising her arms and then stretching out so that every part of the body can be carefully scrutinised and properly cleaned. The females of course give special treatment to the dominant male who, for his part, does not demean himself by reciprocating their favours.

The patas are leaf-eaters but supplement their diet with fruit (especially of the tamarind tree), seeds and insects. Sometimes they catch small reptiles, gobble eggs and even swallow mud. Except on these latter occasions and when they are licking up ants they use their hands to carry food to the mouth, picking up seeds and grains with their supple fingers and reaching up into the branches to pluck a tasty shoot or piece of fruit. If the food they

Patas use their hands to carry food to their mouths but crouch down to drink, lapping the water like other animal species.

are eating happens to be dirty they will rub it vigorously between the palms of their hands before putting it in their mouth. One especially dainty titbit is a toadstool and should any patas be fortunate enough to find one it will eat it greedily. A young monkey may be able to save such a treasure from the dominant male or an adult female by running off with it, while even the babies will collect round a female and try to snatch a piece or two.

Because they are not greatly reliant on water and can make do with the liquid content of vegetation, dew and drops of rain falling on the grass, patas are quite happy to live in dry areas that would not suit baboons. Nor do they need to find refuge in high trees for their nightly sleep. Isolated shrubs and bushes are quite sufficient for shelter. When they do decide to go looking for water they proceed to their destination in exactly the same way as when they are setting out to explore unknown territory. The male plays the part of both scout and leader, going on ahead and sometimes climbing to the summit of an anthill or to the top of a tree to make a careful survey of the surroundings. When he is satisfied that all is well he leads his troop towards the waterhole, each monkey quickly quenching its thirst in a matter of seconds. Like the baboons, they refuse to stay in such exposed parts for a moment longer than is necessary. When water accumulates in tree hollows the patas may plunge their fingers inside and then lick the water off them.

Siesta and sleep

The hottest part of the day will generally be spent resting and this siesta period may vary in duration according to the local availability of food. If the vegetation is comparatively sparse and a long distance has to be covered to find nourishment, the patas' rest period begins later and is correspondingly shorter. But in the normal course of events they will climb the branches of a convenient tree – usually a tamarind – shortly after midday, and bask in the shade for several hours. If the tree trunk is more or less vertical they clamber up with considerable agility, using any small projections as footholds. They come down in the same manner, using hands and feet for support and jumping off when they near the ground, with body inclined forward and with arms stretched wide. If the trunk is nearer to the horizontal they simply run up and down, curling their tails round boughs to brake and to keep their balance as they dart in and out of the branches. But since they are better adapted to ground conditions it is only the younger monkeys that sometimes swing from the branches by their arms, the adults showing greater prudence. Once up a tree, the patas settle themselves down in a fork, legs stretched out along one branch and back reclining against another. Alternatively, they may straddle a branch and hang their legs down on either side, or they may crouch with head lowered on the knees. This siesta interlude provides the females with an opportunity to suckle their young and clean each other's fur.

It is only when they are resting in the heat of the day that the patas display the gregarious instinct that characterises troops of baboons all round the clock. At other times they engage in frenzied activity independently of one another and do not even group

Facing page (above) : The patas are terrestrial monkeys, spending most of the day looking for food on the ground, but making use of trees for resting and sleeping. (*Below*) A patas strips a grass stem with its supple fingers, prior to eating the juiciest part.

closely together, in the manner of baboons, when dusk approaches. In fact they show little apparent sign of fear or unease as the shadows lengthen. Instead of closing ranks for common protection when night falls, the patas disperse and go their own ways, heading for any isolated clumps of trees that may be dotted about an otherwise empty plain. Not that they proceed without some caution, however, for the dominant male will make a close inspection of the surrounding terrain beforehand. The females then lead the way in clambering up into the branches where once again they go through the laborious procedure of coat-grooming and settle down to suckle their babies. But every member of the troop will seek out a different tree, often some distance from another, and it is rare for more than two or three to shelter for the night in the branches of the same tree.

It may seem surprising that such naturally shy and unaggressive creatures should abandon one another's company precisely at the time when many of the most terrifying of savannah predators are on the prowl. But in fact this very dispersal affords the species as a whole some measure of protection. Should a nocturnal hunter manage to detect them, it may succeed in trapping and killing two or three, but rarely more. If a larger number were to seek shelter in a single tree they would all be sitting targets.

Games and lessons

Baby patas are born during the dry months of December, January and February, after a gestation period of 160 days. They are carried everywhere by their mothers, clutching the hairs of her belly, their heads facing to the front. Whether the females are climbing trees or are seated among the branches or on the ground, the babies never have to be abandoned even for a brief moment; and as with the baboons, the position that will later be occupied in the social scale by the individual is largely determined by the status of its mother, from whom it will learn the appropriate way of behaving towards the other members of the troop.

At about the age of three months, while it is still suckling, the baby will begin to take solid foods. It is around this time too that it will be allowed to leave its mother's side and venture out to play with its companions.

Zoologists who make detailed studies of animal behaviour often use play patterns as points of reference, and many of them consider that games provide an important clue to the mental evolution of the species concerned. The timid patas, perfectly adapted to a terrestrial way of life, are as playful as other species. The young monkeys chase one another about and engage in mock battles, but not a sound do they utter as they romp and wrestle in the tall grass. These games take place most frequently in the cool hours of early morning and their duration depends on the type of terrain.

The play period may be initiated by one young monkey inviting another to join in a game. The invitation consists of the first monkey jumping up and down on the spot, limbs stiff and body balanced alternately on hands and feet. Then it darts off, followed closely by its chosen playmate. Another method of attracting attention is for the first patas simply to run off and make a sideways

Although the patas are not mute for physiological reasons, they rarely make use of their voices, uttering single cries perhaps twice daily but nevertheless communicating with one another quite efficiently.

leap into a small bush. It then sits quite still, as if momentarily stunned, while the second monkey goes through the same playful antics. In due course the other young patas are drawn into the game until they are all leaping about with carefree abandon. One will chase another some distance away from the main group, then both animals will return to base and face each other in a warrior-like posture. Rearing themselves up on their hind legs they will then proceed to grapple with each other until both tumble to the ground in a heap. This wrestling is never very seriously intended and there is usually no need for an adult to intervene. Sometimes, however, a mother may be called upon to come to the rescue of a youngster that is being mauled by a particularly rough companion, a feeble cry on the former's part being sufficient to summon her. Fully-grown females may occasionally join in the youthful rough and tumble but will not engage in similar lighthearted games among themselves. As for the dominant male, he will certainly consider it beneath his dignity to take part in such nonsense.

Although all the mothers in the troop tend to stick closely to one another, none will allow a stranger to touch her child. This is another feature of behaviour consonant with the security of the group and the survival of the species. The dominant male has the ultimate responsibility of defending the troop, making use of a

The patas take to the branches of trees for their daily noon siesta, making themselves comfortable either by squatting down or stretching out, sometimes with their backs resting against the trunk.

Baboons, patas and vervets all have different reactions when faced by an enemy. Baboons will directly confront all predators except lions and humans, snarling and showing their fangs. Patas will use their speed and make for a hiding place in the grass and undergrowth, while vervets will climb to the top of the nearest tree.

variety of distracting and dissembling manoeuvres to do so; and since the safety rule is 'everyone for himself', babies that might have been loaned temporarily to another female could easily find themselves abandoned and left to the mercies of predators.

The male patas is sexually mature at the age of four years. He is then left to his own devices, the choice being either to remain with the group and try to usurp the position of leader, or to abandon the troop in order to lead a solitary existence or join a group of males in the same situation. Competition being what it is, he will usually opt for one or other of the latter solutions.

The patas' normal attitude towards the larger mammals of the savannah, such as elephants, rhinoceroses and buffaloes, is one of strict neutrality. If they come across them they simply yield them right of way. They are sometimes attacked by certain species of antelope and are also occasionally preyed upon by some species of birds, notably drongos, ground hornbills and grey kestrels, perhaps in retaliation for the monkeys' own habit of eating eggs and fledglings.

The virtues of discretion

Baboons and patas have both been successful in mastering their terrestrial environment but they have achieved it in different ways, according to their specific temperaments and capacities. Baboons have no hesitation in facing predators, seeking to deter them by their aggressive, confident bearing. This can only happen as a consequence of the rigid, universally accepted social hierarchy within the troop itself, in which the strong and experienced leaders enjoy all the privileges. Thus when danger threatens they close ranks and co-operate, each in a predetermined manner, defending the weakest members of the troop with a concerted display of audacity, but always tempered by prudence. If need be they retreat to the safety of a tree. Such animals can therefore roam freely over their little territory without the need for concealment, having nothing to fear from any but the most powerful carnivores. The young are noisy and demonstrative, and although their cries may reach the ears of predators, the adult male baboons are always on the alert.

The patas, much more retiring by nature, have learned to survive by diametrically opposed methods. Faced by an enemy, the troop, figuratively speaking, melts away. Each animal is responsible for its own safety, whether by running away as fast as it can or by hiding in the bushes and undergrowth. Silent when they play, cautious in all their movements, the peaceful patas show no inclination to band together in warding off an enemy. Only the leader of the troop shows any sense of social responsibility, creating a diversion should this be practicable, generally in the form of a headlong flight across the plain rather than a direct, obviously suicidal, confrontation.

These widely contrasted reactions in the face of an enemy have influenced the community structure and behaviour of both species and have to some extent determined their ecological needs. It is interesting to note that patas display none of the inhibitory attitudes and movements that characterise the baboons. This is in keeping with the general rule that only animals possessing effective natural weapons and thus capable of harming others of their own species need to adopt ritual behaviour designed to appease the anger of a stronger, superior individual. The various submissive postures—the symbolic white flag of surrender—provide each member of such a community with a built-in mechanism of self-defence and self-protection. Animals that lack such weapons have no need for this kind of instinctive behaviour.

The opportunistic vervets

The best known and most popular of all the Primates in the East African parks and reserves are the vervets or green monkeys—agile little creatures with olive-coloured fur, black faces, large and sparkling eyes, long tails and slender bodies with well-proportioned limbs. Since they have long been accustomed to the presence of visitors, zoologists can study them in tranquil conditions.

As soon as they are born the baby vervets attach themselves closely to their mothers, clutching the fur near the teats from which they suckle. For tourists the sight of a mother monkey feeding her baby has an immediate appeal but the significant point about this tender scene is that it represents one of the most important adaptations conducive to the survival of the Primates—the simple fact that a female gives birth to only one baby at a time.

It is worth pausing to wonder what might have happened to the Primates during the long course of their evolution if nature had decreed that the females should give birth to several babies at once. The mother would have been hopelessly handicapped in keeping up with the rest of the troop as they swung and clambered their way through the treetops. She would have been compelled to abandon her offspring in a nest or a tree cavity, thus leaving them to be picked off at will by predators. One baby, however, could easily be transported and cared for at all times. This evolutionary advance—important as it was for creatures that were exclusively arboreal—was of even greater significance when they descended to the ground, with its graver attendant perils.

People are often astonished to see what a remarkable appetite these green monkeys have—and for any kind of food. They snatch sweets from the hands of tourists, readily accept ham or roast beef sandwiches, and are quite happy to guzzle coffee or fizzy drinks. This is dramatic proof of the ability of certain groups of Primates to adapt themselves to a diet which is not only omnivorous but opportunistic—taken as and when available.

The vervets have another secret which helps to explain their apparently insatiable appetite. The seeds and fruit which they collect in the course of their wanderings and the tasty titbits which they accept from visitors are not just swallowed on the spot. Nor are they chewed and hastily ingested, to be regurgitated at leisure in the fashion of the ungulates. They are simply stored in expandable cheek-pouches, rather in the manner of squirrels, to be put aside or carried about and enjoyed at a later stage.

This is not just a matter of whim or pure chance. When we looked at the ungulates we saw that their characteristic manner of feeding—taking in large quantities of food very rapidly and then

The baby vervet is closely protected by its mother until it is strong and experienced enough to venture out on its own. When adult, it must be constantly on the alert for predators, including baboons. Vervets are less shy than patas and well used to the presence of humans in parks and reserves.

Geographical distribution of vervets.

Facing page : The vervets are adaptable creatures, living partly on the ground and partly in trees. The latter provide refuge when danger threatens, for the monkeys possess neither the aggressive instincts of baboons nor the speed of patas.

VERVET (GREEN MONKEY)
(Cercopithecus aethiops)

Class: Mammalia
Order: Primates
Family: Cercopithecidae

Length of head and body: 22–28 inches
 (55–70 cm)
Length of tail: 26–32 inches (65–80 cm)
Weight: 11 lb (5 kg)
Diet: Vegetation, insects, occasionally small
 vertebrates
Gestation: 7 months
Number of young: one

Adults
Greenish coat, black face and white tufts on cheeks and above eyes, the long tail tipped with black. Very large cheek-pouches; small, blue scrotum, red ischial callosities separated by fringes of hair.

Young
Baby at first clutches mother's breast, later perches on her back, its tail entwined with hers.

---

chewing and digesting very slowly, well away from the exposed feeding sites where predators might surprise them—was a protective adaptation. These roomy cheek-pouches of the green monkeys perform a somewhat similar function. The species, living on the ground, is ever at the mercy of carnivores, and this anatomical peculiarity enables it and species that are similarly endowed to minimise this risk. The food can be hastily stored away and carried up into the branches of a tree, there to be thoroughly chewed, softened with saliva and digested without fear of disturbance.

Living in troops, the green monkeys' social pattern is midway between that of the fierce baboons and the retiring patas. From the anatomical point of view they are more primitive than either species, their relatively small size being typical of many Primates that are exclusively tree-dwellers. In fact they are opportunistic animals, generally found at points where forest and savannah meet, having no hesitation in venturing out several hundreds of yards into the open plain where food is plentiful yet always keeping within handy range of the trees which afford them security in case of sudden danger.

In East Africa the vervets are found in greatest numbers in the Amboseli game reserve, particularly among the vegetation that grows around springs and pools fed by the waters trickling down from Mt Kilimanjaro. There are usually ten to fifteen individuals in a troop, with a roughly equal proportion of males and females, in addition to immature animals. The size of the territory occupied depends not so much on the number of monkeys in the troop as on the food potential of the area. Provided there are enough trees and shrubs the territory will be of limited size, but if vegetation is scarce the territorial bounds are correspondingly extended.

At nightfall the green monkeys divide into small groups and each animal makes for its favourite tree. They resemble baboons in preferring to stick to the same tree night after night, though they do not congregate in such numbers. They are familiar with every twist and turn of their refuge, which puts them at an advantage should they have to make a sudden dash for safety in the face of an attack by a nocturnal prowler.

During the day the vervets roam the fringes of the savannah in search of food but do not generally travel such great distances as the baboons and patas. Their diet is comprised in the main of vegetation but they also feed on invertebrates and sometimes on eggs and fledglings. They eat only the tenderest portions of the tall grass—near the base of the stems—snatching it up with both hands and picking off the leaves with their teeth. In their quest for insects and grains they may forage in bits of wood and sometimes make a close inspection of the dried excrement of elephants. But they are discriminating in their selection of insects. The adults know that certain kinds of grasshopper have a particularly unpleasant taste so they leave them alone. The less knowledgeable youngsters sometimes catch these insects but spit them out as soon as they place them experimentally in their mouths.

In their drinking habits the vervets follow the same pattern as many herbivores, making their trek to the waterholes shortly after

noon, during the scorching hours when the majority of carnivores can be counted on to be taking their siestas.

The green monkeys are not short of enemies, including servals, lions and leopards, baboons, Verreaux's owls, and crowned and martial eagles. Elephants are competitors rather than enemies. In the dry season the huge pachyderms collect around stagnant pools and denude the surrounding area of all vegetation. By knocking down the trees and stripping them of bark and foliage they deprive the little monkeys both of food and nightly shelter. But a more serious threat to the species comes from man himself, who hunts them, not in this case for sport or commercial gain, but in the cause of science. Several thousands of these monkeys are caught and exported every month to be used for laboratory research in many parts of the world.

Vervets also form mutually protective associations with other animals, their closest allies being the yellow-necked spurfowl. When the birds utter their shrill alarm cry the monkeys scamper for safety into a tree. They do not, however, perform a reciprocal service for the birds but raid their nests and devour their chicks.

Although the green monkeys have much in common with baboons, the relationship between the two species is rather unpredictable and complicated. Both keep well out of the way of predators such as lions and leopards; and very often they may sleep in the same tree and share the same waterholes. But the baboons frequently use their superior strength, numbers and cunning to drive the smaller monkeys away from feeding grounds and it is not uncommon for the vervets to be killed and devoured by hungry baboons.

Part-time hunters

Zoologists who choose monkey behaviour as their special field of study need an enormous fund of patience. Research on one species may take months or even years, for it is important that the animals should become so accustomed to human presence as not to alter their normal life pattern. Several naturalists have made a special survey of the predatory instincts of such Primates as baboons, vervets and chimpanzees. They have pointed out, for example, that baboons are especially proficient in capturing newborn gazelles, searching out their hiding places in patches of tall grass. Having located their victim, they kill it with their teeth and share out its flesh among one another. Baboons also prey on the more vulnerable vervets, but are in their turn sometimes killed by chimpanzees.

Such examples of predatory behaviour are, however, exceptional and do not mean that Primates are true hunters. Most of them are vegetarians but the fact that some have carnivorous instincts is of interest to scientists studying the evolution of man. In South Africa, where fossil remains have been found of what are probably the most primitive hominids, some paleontologists distinguish between the genus *Paranthropus*, believed to be a vegetarian, and *Australopithecus*, who certainly included meat in his diet, relying to a large extent on his hunting prowess for survival.

In all Primates the positioning of the teats on the female's breast facilitates suckling and conveniently allows the mother to keep her baby under constant surveillance. Clutching the hair of her belly, the young monkey can be prevented from falling out of the branches of the trees where so much of its life is spent.

Facing page (Above) : Like other Primates, the green monkeys spend much of their time high in the branches of a tree. (*Below*) A sub-adult grooms the fur of the dominant male. This is a practical hygienic measure and an important social ritual.

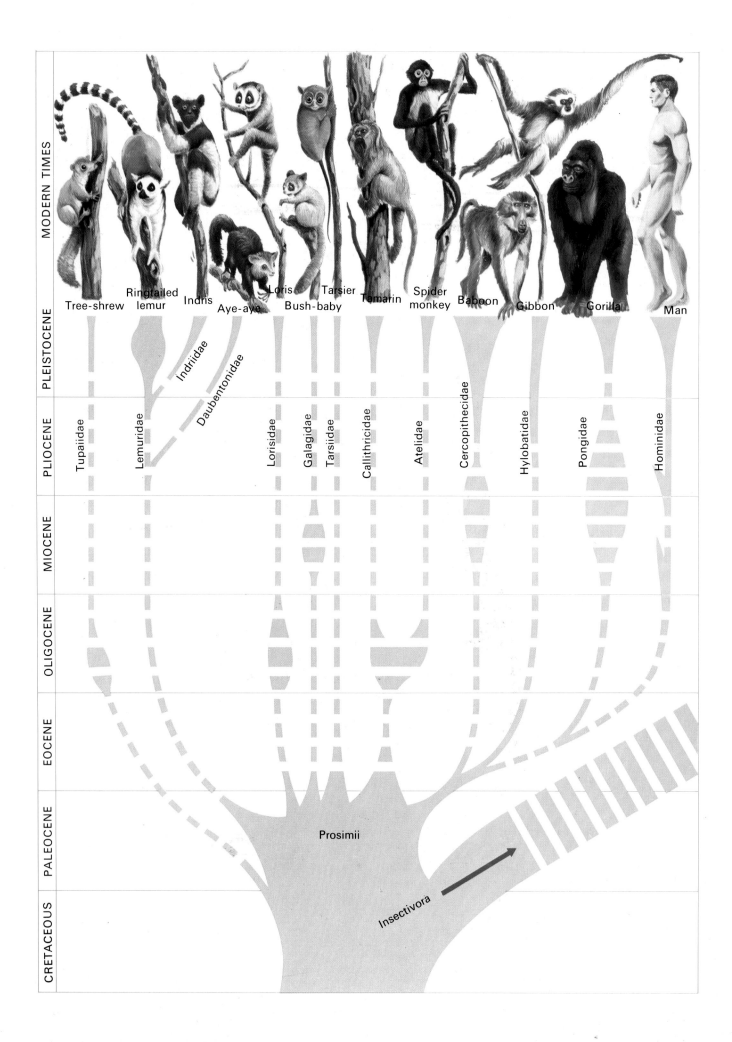

Tree-shrew | Ringtailed lemur | Indris | Aye-aye | Loris | Bush-baby | Tarsier | Tamarin | Spider monkey | Baboon | Gibbon | Gorilla | Man

MODERN TIMES

PLEISTOCENE

Indriidae

Daubentonidae

PLIOCENE

Tupaiidae | Lemuridae | Lorisidae | Galagidae | Tarsiidae | Callithricidae | Atelidae | Cercopithecidae | Hylobatidae | Pongidae | Hominidae

MIOCENE

OLIGOCENE

EOCENE

PALEOCENE

Prosimii

Insectivora

CRETACEOUS

ORDER: Primates

In a sense, the study of living Primates – which include tree-shrews, lemurs, monkeys, apes and man – is the story of evolution itself. As Thomas Huxley pointed out in one of his essays on *Man's Place in Nature* (1863): 'Perhaps no order of mammals presents us with so extraordinary a series of gradations as this . . .' In fact, within this order today we can find animals – from the most primitive to the most advanced – representing every step of the evolutionary ladder.

Unlike other orders of mammals, there is no fundamental, specialised feature of the Primates which automatically leads the various members of the order to be classified under a single heading. Indeed, according to the anthropologist W. E. Le Gros Clark, what distinguishes the Primates is precisely their lack of specialisation. If this is true it is largely explained by the fact that Primates are directly descended from a branch of insect-eating, tree-dwelling mammals; but because they themselves remained in a forest environment they did not need to undergo any significant anatomical modification in order to adapt themselves to new conditions of life.

The principal characteristics of the order – sketchily outlined in the most primitive of its representatives, the tree-shrews, but clearly marked in the later species, such as the monkeys and apes – are directly related to the arboreal way of life which most of them have traditionally led and still lead today. Thus they possess five fingers on each of their limbs, usually with a thumb opposable to the other four, making it easier for them to take hold of branches and other miscellaneous objects, and to move about in the trees. They also have a collar-bone which helps to support the lateral movements of their arms – vitally important for tree-dwelling animals.

The structure of their teeth is closely linked with the feeding habits of each species. The molars of insect-eating Primates have sharp cusps, whereas those of the fruit-eating species have rounded tubercles. But since there is such a wide choice of food for arboreal mammals (leaves, fruit, seeds, insects, eggs, etc) the animals that are higher up the evolutionary scale have tended to become less dependent on one particular type of food or on a rigidly defined habitat. The trend has therefore been towards an omnivorous diet, culminating in the enormously varied food habits of man himself.

With only a few exceptions, the Primates are not equipped with any natural weapons of offence or defence; most of them have flat, rounded nails rather than sharp claws. This apparent lack is of course also related to the pattern of their tree-dwelling life. For them survival depends not on aggression and deterrence but on agility and cunning. The need for quick, instinctive (or intelligent) reactions when danger threatens was an important factor in the evolution of the brain, which gradually increased in size and complexity.

The comparative development of the different senses has also been determined by the requirements of an arboreal existence. Terrestrial mammals need a subtle sense of smell in order to detect prey and enemy alike; but for animals living high up in trees this is less important than keen vision. The eyes of Primates are positioned not at the sides but near the front of the head, allowing them to gauge distances with accuracy so that they can run and jump – many of them in acrobatic style – with the utmost ease and assurance.

All these and other acquisitions – notably the perfection of the reproductive system, the increased size of the brain and volume of the cranial cavity (and the corresponding reduction in the dimensions of face and head) – present to some extent in certain monkeys and apes, have reached their acme of development in the family Hominidae, to which only man belongs. In modern man the evolutionary process has attained an unprecedented level. For man's upright, two-legged stance has freed his fore-limbs for a multitude of other activities, including the handling of tools and weapons.

CLASSIFICATION OF PRIMATES	
Suborder	Family
Prosimii	Tupaiidae Lemuridae Indriidae Daubentonidae Lorisidae Galagidae Tarsiidae
Anthropoidea	Callithricidae Cebidae Atelidae Cercopithecidae Hylobatidae Pongidae Hominidae

Facing page : Evolutionary family tree of the Primates. Recent research has suggested that the tree-shrew may not be as closely related to the Primates as was hitherto thought. The principle of the two diagrams is, however, unaffected.

Ringtailed lemur

Spider monkey

Baboon

Chimpanzee

The Lemuridae and their relatives, represented here by the ringtailed lemur, have many monkey-like characteristics, many monkey-like characteristics, consistent with their arboreal habits. The spider monkey, one of the numerous New World species, uses its tail as a fifth limb for hanging from branches and leaving hands and feet free for leaping. The baboon, one of the Old World Primates, has callosities on its rump which enable it to sit for hours on rough or sharp surfaces. The man-like Primates, of which the best known is the intelligent chimpanzee, use their arms for swinging from branch to branch and keeping their balance.

Zoologists and anthropologists have always had difficulty in classifying the Primates and there are hardly two authors in the field who are in complete agreement as to how they should be subdivided. Most authorities, however, accept a scheme which divides the order into two suborders–the Prosimii (primitive Primates) and the Anthropoidea (man-like Primates). The former, made up of seven families, include the Tupaiidae or tree-shrews, most primitive of living mammals (earliest representatives date back to the Eocene some 50 million years ago), which were for some time classified among the Insectivora. About five million years later came the first Lemuriformes, including lemurs, aye-ayes, lorises, bush-babies and the like; and the Tarsiidae or tarsiers, represented today by a single genus from Indonesia and Malaysia.

The Anthropoidea comprise the Ceboidea (New World or platyrrhine monkeys) and Cercopithecoidea (Old World or catarrhine monkeys)–roughly distinguished and so-named because of the positioning of their nostrils. The former go back about 30 million years and are made up of three families, the Callithricidae (marmosets and tamarins), the Cebidae (capuchins, howlers, douroucoulis) and the Atelidae (spider monkeys). The Old World monkeys consist of the Cercopithecidae (macaques, baboons, guenons), the Hylobatidae (gibbons) and the Pongidae (gorilla, chimpanzee, orang-utan). Finally there is man himself, who because of certain features that distinguish him from the next-highest group of apes, is classified in the family Hominidae.

FAMILY: Cercopithecidae

The Cercopithecidae are the so-called catarrhine monkeys of the Old World (characterised by nasal openings which are close together and by the fact that their tails, when present at all, are never prehensile). Fossil remains of some of the earliest members of the family, dating from the Miocene period, suggest that they must have looked much like modern Primates, though the exact evolutionary line of descent has not been traced. In contrast with the man-like apes (gibbons, gorillas, orang-utans and chimpanzees) the catarrhine monkeys are quadrupeds, their arms being the same length or rather shorter than their hind legs. The front legs of the apes, however, are far better developed than the hind legs and are used for hanging from the branches and for leaping from one to another. The Cercopithecidae are also tree-dwellers but altogether less acrobatic. In addition the methods of walking of the two groups are different. The catarrhine monkeys walk on the palms of the hands and the soles of the feet, whereas the apes walk on the soles of the hind feet only, supporting themselves on the knuckles of the fingers of their hands.

The buttocks of the catarrhine monkeys are often characterised by fleshy ischial callosities or naked areas of skin which have a cushioning effect when the animals sit on or astride a tree stump or branch. In some cases the prominent colour of the callosities in the female indicate her degree of sexual receptivity during the mating season. Certain authorities suggest that these protuberances are already present in the fetus of the Cercopithecidae, whereas they appear only at birth in gibbons and around puberty in chimpanzees and gorillas. The fact that they are not present at any stage of human development is an example, according to W. E. le Gros Clark, of the abandonment of a specialised feature in the course of evolution.

The Cercopithecidae are usually further divided by taxonomists into two subfamilies, based on their respective food preferences and digestive mechanisms – Colobinae and Cercopithecinae. The former group feed on leaves and have a large stomach in the shape of an elongated sac, which looks something like a colon. The latter group are virtually omnivorous, with a simple stomach and expandable cheek-pouches in which they store food.

The teeth of all these monkeys are in some degree specialised, according to their particular diet, generally with flat incisors and well-developed canines. The upper canines of male baboons, for example, jut out to form fearsome and effective defensive weapons. The premolars are always strong and the cusps of the molars are joined by pairs of transverse ridges. The dental formula is the same as for human teeth –

$$I: \frac{2}{2} \quad C: \frac{1}{1} \quad PM: \frac{2}{2} \quad M: \frac{3}{3}$$

but certain species have a diastema. The power of the jaws is correlated with the ample development of the facial muscles, particularly marked in the case of the baboons with their dog-like heads.

The convolutions of the brain in the Cercopithecidae already herald the structure of the human brain but the frontal lobes are of less importance than the temporal and occipital lobes. All the senses are well developed, the eye-structure being closely similar to that of man (it is claimed that these monkeys can distinguish colours) and their sense of smell being sharper than that of any other group of Primates.

The Cercopithecidae all have some degree of organised social life and behaviour, being naturally gregarious creatures. Most of them come together in polygamous family groups, which may in turn make up troops of up to one hundred individuals, under the leadership of one or more older dominant males.

The reproductive system of the catarrhine monkeys is also highly perfected,

Vervet or
green monkey

Abyssinian guereza

The Cercopithecidae are divided into two subfamilies, the Cercopithecinae and the Colobinae – here represented respectively by the vervet (*Cercopithecus aethiops*) and the Abyssinian guereza (*Colobus abyssinicus*).

Mandrill
(*Mandrillus sphinx*)

Greater white-nosed monkey
(*Cercopithecus nictitans*)

Barbary ape
(*Macaca sylvanus*)

Guinea baboon
(*Papio papio*)

Black ape of Celebes
(*Cynopithecus niger*)

Grey-cheeked mangabey
(*Cercocebus albigena*)

Gelada
(*Theropithecus gelada*)

Patas or red monkey
(*Erythrocebus patas*)

the females menstruating–depending on species–once every 28–40 days. The sexual appetite of the males does not seem to vary much from one season to another.

The first subfamily–Colobinae–are exclusively tree-dwelling monkeys, with slender bodies, long tails and front legs which are shorter than the back ones. The thumb is either reduced in size or absent altogether. The stomach is elongated and divided into several compartments. Apart from the genus *Colobus*, none of these animals has cheek-pouches. Other genera, beside the guerezas (*Colobus*), are the langurs (*Presbytis* and *Rhinopithecus*) and the proboscis monkeys (*Nasalis*).

The Ceropithecinae have more robust bodies and the fore and hind limbs are of equal length. They have cheek-pouches and a simple stomach capable of coping with an omnivorous diet. Although most are African genera, the subfamily are well represented in Asia. The most important are the guenons (*Cercopithecus*), the macaques (*Macaca*), the baboons (*Papio*), the mandrills (*Mandrillus*), the mangabeys (*Cercocebus*) and the geladas (*Theropithecus*).

A mother green monkey with her young.

Facing page : These monkeys each represent one of the eight genera of the subfamily Cercopithecinae.

CHAPTER 6

The bush: a dry and thorny land

The shrub- and tree-covered steppes commonly known as the 'bush' display a form of vegetation that is ideally suited to a very dry climate. On the African continent the bush extends from Mozambique in the east to Angola in the west, with a more limited zone in eastern Kenya. It is characterised by an abundance of thorny shrubs and trees of varying size–most of them belonging to the subfamily Mimosoideae (mimosas). Some species are enormous trees which stand up to 60 feet high, their branches spanning up to 100 feet. Other species are dwarf-type shrubs, prominent among which are the characteristic dwarf acacias of the Kenyan bush, with sharp thorns capable of inflicting nasty grazes and cuts. These little acacias have rough, grey bark which assumes metallic reflections in the full glare of the sun and can therefore be extremely wearing on the eye.

The African bush is for the most part a harsh, savage and inhospitable region into which man has often penetrated but where he has understandably seldom chosen to settle. Native African tribes describe the terrain as *nyika*, wild country and desert.

Because of the very sparse rainfall in these parts the vegetation is of a type that is especially structured to make the most economical use of available water. Thus the roots of the acacias are deeply entrenched in the ground, spreading out radially in such a way as to take the greatest possible advantage of the surrounding humidity. Their thick, impermeable bark acts as a virtual barrier to water evaporation. The small leaves make their appearance several days before the rains are due, apparently stimulated by a rise in the temperature. The longer arid conditions last, the more they wither, but despite this they retain much nutritive content.

The immense, monotonous stretches of bush are normally dotted only with dwarf acacias and myrrh, but at intervals huge

Facing page : A typical African bush or *nyika* landscape – similar in appearance to the open steppes of Europe and Asia. The bush is characterised by its hot, arid climate but the thorny shrubs and trees that dot it are perfectly adapted to the meagre, irregular rainfall.

The acacias are armed with sharp thorns and ant-infested galls; these tend to prevent excessive damage being caused by voracious leaf-eating animals. Nevertheless, the giraffes consume the foliage, thorns and all, with relish.

baobabs rear grotesquely up against the skyline. This strange tree (*Adansonia digitata*) belongs to the family Bombacaceae and is instantly recognisable by its thick barrel-like trunk and sparse growth of slender, wispy branches. Sometimes known as the 'upside-down' tree because these branches look more like inverted roots, there are specimens believed to be as much as 2,000 years old. When the rainy season arrives the tree is soon covered with green foliage and shortly afterwards wax-coloured flowers, each about five inches in diameter, appear hanging down from the branches. At dusk the corollas open up to be pollinated by bats and bush-babies and after about twenty-four hours the blossoms drop to the ground.

The baobab bears an enormous, oval-shaped fruit, about the size of a pumpkin, with a greenish or yellowish skin and a firm, slightly acid but edible pulp—only eaten, however, in its country of origin. The tree is one of the largest in the world and is capable of storing vast quantities of water.

In most areas the grass of the bush is scattered and not very abundant, but the various species are perfectly adapted to the extremely dry environment. When the first rain of the season falls the grass grows rapidly, the seeds being remarkably tough and lying on the sandy soil for several months, to germinate in the following rainy season.

It is not only the climatic conditions and the geological formation of the terrain which have given the bush its characteristic appearance and constitution. The many plant-eating animals which have made it their home have also played their part. Here, where grass is relatively scarce and shrubs and trees plentiful, it is natural that many animals should have turned to leaves as their main source of food.

In order to avoid dying in the excessive heat and prolonged periods of drought, the characteristic plants of the bush have acquired a special kind of structure which protects them against the animals feeding so ravenously at their expense. Their foliage stretches wide to provide welcome shade, yet the branches support the minimum growth of leaves necessary for respiration and photosynthesis. In addition they sprout sharp thorns which provide a defensive wall against many leaf-eating mammals.

The animals, for their part, have also adapted themselves to these special conditions, many of their anatomical modifications arising as a result of the changed structure of the trees and shrubs. Thus vegetable and animal species alike have made the most rational use possible of the natural resources afforded by the terrain—indispensable for their survival. The long neck of the giraffe enables it to feed at high levels where there is no fear of serious competition. The gerenuk has succeeded in rearing itself up on its hind legs so as to nibble the leaves some ten feet from ground level—again with little likelihood of rivalry; and the small antelope known as the dik-dik concentrates on the leaves and shoots lower down the tree which are difficult for the larger animals to reach. Likewise, with the aid of prehensile lips and a long protrusible tongue, the black rhinoceros manages to withstand the thorny deterrents presented by the acacias and other plant species. The reason why this ecological balance is still

relatively undisturbed is that man, who has meddled so disastrously with the environment elsewhere, has not yet established himself in the bush or tried to exploit its natural resources.

There are two wet seasons in the bush, one in August, the other in November. The landscape at such times changes in spectacular fashion. From one day to the next the grey trees are covered with tiny green leaves and then the acacia flowers appear, scenting the air and attracting swarms of bees. In the previously dry, sandy beds of the rivers there are now raging torrents. But the rainy period is short and soon the bush reverts to normal.

In the region extending from south-west Angola to the Transvaal there is another type of vegetational growth, known as the veld, with a flora and fauna which are similar but not exactly the same as those of the bush proper. Nevertheless the two zones have developed in parallel ways, both having been subjected to the same dry, torrid climatic conditions for some 20,000 years. The rainfall incidence, however, differs from that of the bush, with one long rainy season instead of two short ones, lasting from November until May. The veld winter is also drier and colder.

South Africa's famous Kruger National Park is in the veld and is in itself a complete ecological unit where animals can live all the year round without having to depart on seasonal migrations.

The two areas of bush in the east and veld in the south are separated by a region known as *miombo* forest or tree-steppe – vast stretches of plain where the climatic conditions are fairly similar to those of the more northerly savannahs but where the chronological sequence of the seasons is different.

One of the typical inhabitants of the bush is the impala which, during the brief rainy season, finds ideal food conditions here.

Animals of the bush

In certain parts of the Tsavo National Park and in the Samburu game reserve of northern Kenya the bush can be seen in its most savage and impenetrable form. Elsewhere, however, there is a gradual progression from open steppe or prairie—with its variable cover of vegetation consisting of short grass and thorny trees and shrubs—to the subdesert steppe of the *nyika* type. The open tree-covered steppes, considered by botanists to represent transitional zones, support a flourishing animal population with widely selective food habits, eating either grass or leaves according to the season and the local availability.

One of the most remarkable and abundant of animals inhabiting this transitional zone is the impala, a particularly graceful and handsome member of the antelope family. Grant's gazelle is also frequently encountered in these parts, as are many other medium-sized ruminants that derive sustenance from the more nutritious species of grass and leaves—animals such as the eland, the roan and sable antelopes, the oryx and the greater and lesser kudus. Since these creatures do not have a strictly specialised leaf-eating diet they tend to congregate in the more open sections of bush rather than penetrate the densely wooded parts where for much of the year there is no grass. Such partial or exclusive grass-eaters lead a more or less nomadic existence for they are wholly reliant on seasonal rainfall for the fresh growth of grass on which

The immense baobab is one of the most easily recognisable trees of the African bush. Its barrel-shaped trunk and spreading branches (somewhat resembling roots) have earned it the nickname of the 'upside-down tree'. Bearing delicate flowers and large edible fruits, it is capable of storing water in quantity and thus well suited for survival in periods of severe drought.

survival depends. On the fringes of the bush live such animals as the giraffe and the black rhinoceros, both feeding on leaves and shoots, but not venturing deeper into the thickly wooded areas where they would find movement difficult. It is essential for these larger creatures to enjoy plenty of room for their browsing.

Elephants often make incursions into the bush during the course of their seasonal wanderings, tearing off the acacia branches with their trunks and devouring the tenderest shoots and leaves near the tops of the trees—delicacies normally reserved exclusively for the giraffes. In those regions where the ecological balance has not been unduly disturbed by man, elephants abandon the bush during the driest, hottest times of year; but where they are artificially hemmed in by parks and reserves—as in Tsavo—the depredations of the herds have a seriously impoverishing effect on the natural vegetation of the enclosed bush.

In the heart of the bush, amid a dense entanglement of thorny trees and shrubs, live those ruminants that are perfectly adapted to the most arid conditions and which enjoy a highly specialised leafy diet. Foremost among these animals are the gerenuk and the dik-dik—antelopes which are not only capable of threading their way unharmed through the thick labyrinth of thorns but are equally content to remain in these well-sheltered parts when, after a particularly dry spell, all the natural sources of water have run dry. The Grévy's zebra too is well adapted to the harsh conditions of the bush and able to dispense with water for lengthy periods, though not as abstemious as the gerenuk and dik-dik and therefore preferring to stay fairly close to waterholes.

It is obvious that such a large and varied population of grass- and leaf-eating animals must inevitably run the gauntlet of the customary range of predators. But the carnivores that prey on the herbivores of the bush also have to be tough and adaptable in order to cope with heat, drought and impenetrable undergrowth. Not many of them will venture deep into the bush. Lions, for example, confine themselves to the more open parts where there are waterholes, such conditions providing them with the best opportunities of ambushing their favourite prey. In the dry season most of the herbivores have no alternative but to make a daily journey down to one or other of the few available waterholes where the chances are that a pride of lions is standing guard. It is near such sites that the patient photographer may be rewarded with some really dramatic pictures of lions stalking and killing their prey. The zebras and antelopes make it quite clear from their wary approach and nervous behaviour that they are conscious of being particularly vulnerable at such times to the attacks of their traditional enemies.

Far better suited than the lion to hunting in the bush is the leopard. It too has to drink copiously in order to survive but because it is a smaller, stealthier creature its range is that much wider; it can stalk its prey among the spiny thickets of dwarf acacias— areas rarely explored by the lion. Another predator of the African bush, though seldom found in large numbers, is the caracal—a skilful hunter relying on the surprise of ambush to trap its prey and an animal that also has the advantage of being

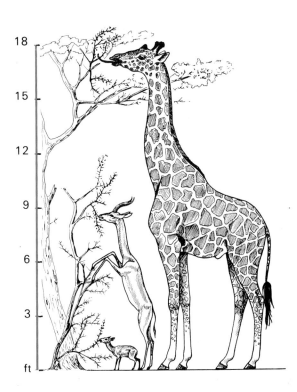

The giraffe, the gerenuk and the dik-dik all feed on the same leaves and shoots but since they browse at levels compatible with their varying heights there is no rivalry between them.

Following pages : The giraffe is the tallest living land animal. These two are seen in the type of open bush country which suits them best, providing them with their favourite vegetation and ample opportunity for keeping a watch on the movements of predators.

able to do without water for unbelievably long periods.

The small, less conspicuous hunters are no less busy in their quiet way. Mongooses, genets, civets and jackals prey voraciously on the many rodents, reptiles and insects of the bush. But the typical carrion eaters, including the jackals and vultures, that normally tag along in the wake of the predators, are not nearly as abundant in these inhospitable parts as they are in the more easily accessible open steppes and savannahs.

The African bush is a veritable paradise for birds. As soon as the rains stimulate a new growth of grass the weaver-birds start to busy themselves collecting the bits and pieces of straw, grass and twigs needed for the construction of their intricate nests in the acacias, as well as the special food required for their young the moment they hatch. The branches of the acacias, looking like huge opened umbrellas, are black with the hanging nests of these cheerful birds, which flutter and swoop everywhere in their quest for tasty larvae and insects for the fledglings and for the seeds that form the basic food requirements of the young when they are ready to embark upon their first flight. But there is no such merry, bustling activity in these same parts when the dry season is at its height. The spreading branches of the acacias are stark and bare, for the weavers have long since flocked southward in their tens of thousands, probably to make an unwelcome descent on cultivated fields in their unremitting search for food.

The weavers, however, are only some of the many bird species of the bush. Others include francolins, guinea fowl, hornbills, shrikes and bee-eaters. Then too there are the birds of prey—the great sparrowhawk, swift-flying hunter of francolins and turtle-doves; and the martial eagle, most powerful of all predatory birds in these parts. From the top of an acacia this fierce-looking raptor keeps patient watch hour after hour, ready to swoop down on a dik-dik, a young antelope or a Guinea fowl.

The monotonous stretches of open bush are broken here and there by termitaria—mounds topped by little towers of dried red mud, sometimes reaching an overall height of 10–12 feet. The termites responsible for building these edifices feed on the dry wood of the surrounding trees and shrubs and play their indispensable role in the life-cycle of the region by transforming assorted waste vegetable matter into substances that can be assimilated by the soil. At the foot of these mounds grow certain types of plant which are especially appreciated by some species of antelope; and it is the ants and termites themselves that provide the staple diet of such curious and specialised mammals as the aardvark (earth pig) and aardwolf. Here, as in other environments, there is a close, indeed vital, interdependence between the different animal species, large and small.

For many months on end the African bush is an inhospitable place both for the casual visitor and for the many animal species that make it their home. One of the few touches of light relief is provided by the tiny, agile ground squirrels that rear themselves up on their hind legs to make a cheeky survey of the passing scene. But when the rains return to freshen the grass and the foliage, the bush is suddenly and miraculously transformed into a wonderland of sights, scents and sound—a naturalist's paradise.

Facing page : In the short rainy season the branches of the umbrella-shaped acacia trees are crowded with the hanging nests of the weaver-birds.

CHAPTER 7

The tall world of the giraffes

The giraffe, tallest of all living land animals, is the better-known member of the family Giraffidae, which also includes the rare okapi. It is generally considered to belong to the single species *Giraffa camelopardalis*. Until quite recently taxonomists distinguished thirteen subspecies but they have now whittled the number down to eight. Distributed over much of the African continent from the Sahara down to the Cape, the different races of giraffe are distinguished chiefly by their coat patterns.

The most handsome member of the species is without doubt the reticulated giraffe (*G. c. reticulata*) which lives in the open bush of Kenya, Ethiopia and Somalia. Its richly coloured coat is made up of large, almost rectangular, dark brown blotches separated by a network of white lines. The coats of the other subspecies are similarly spotted or blotched, normally against a light brown ground colour. Although magnificent to look at, the coat colours and patterns of all giraffes have a practical function, for in the shifting half-lights and shadows of the acacia thickets, the mesh of fine white lines against the darker background makes the animals nearly invisible.

Whatever the subspecies concerned, giraffes are creatures of well-wooded regions, though not of dense forests. They are found in greatest number in open bush country and tall-grass savannah. Groups are occasionally encountered on the fringes of mountain forests, at an altitude of about 7,000 feet.

The males have a marked preference for those areas where the vegetation cover is fairly thick whereas the females and young normally stick to more exposed regions. Both sexes often journey across completely treeless ground but never linger there. Males either keep to themselves or band together in herds of between two and twelve individuals. One or two males will also usually be

Facing page : The elegant giraffes blend well with their natural surroundings in the African bush. Although they often come together to form small groups the herds are not permanent and individuals wander freely in search of food and water. Since acacias and other trees and shrubs provide them with ample food they are sedentary creatures with a wide distribution through central, eastern and southern parts of the African continent.

Geographical distribution of the giraffe.

GIRAFFE
(Giraffa camelopardalis)

Class: Mammalia
Order: Artiodactyla
Family: Giraffidae

Total length: 144–160 inches (360–400 cm)
Length of tail: 36–44 inches (90–110 cm)
Total height: 200–244 inches (500–610 cm)
Height to shoulder: 108–132 inches (270-330 cm)
Weight: 2,100–2,900 lb (950–1,300 kg)
Diet: leaves, shoots and bark of trees and bushes
Gestation: 420–468 days
Number of young: one
Longevity: up to 28 years in captivity

Adults
The giraffe has a very long neck, front legs which are longer than the hind ones and a tail ending in a dark hairy tuft. There is a mane from neck to shoulder. The head, with its pointed ears, has 2–5 horns—a central one on the forehead, two frontal ones and often two behind these, all with a terminal tuft of hair which is absent in aged individuals. The male is larger than the female.

Young
The animal weighs 100–150 lb at birth and is about 4–6 feet tall. In other respects it is like the adult, reaching sexual maturity at 3–4 years.

Subspecies
Classification is controversial but the 8 subspecies are distinguished by coat colour and pattern. One of the handsomest is the reticulated giraffe (*G. c. reticulata*).

Facing page : The handsome reticulated giraffe is protected in Kenya's national parks and is also found in the wilder parts' of Ethiopia and Somalia.

---

found in small herds otherwise composed of females and their offspring. In some parts larger herds of up to forty giraffes may be seen but it is never possible to determine whether these consist of one compact group or are made up of several smaller groups which have converged from different directions. In any event the herd's population is constantly shifting and it is rare for the same animals to remain together for two days in succession. Although they are not migratory in the manner of other ungulates, they are for ever on the move; but during these continuous comings and goings they keep in close touch with one another by reason of their remarkably acute eyesight—a faculty reinforced by the unique position of their head at the end of an incredibly elongated neck. If we can use the term 'sea of grass' to describe the level surface of the savannah it is merely extending a metaphor to say that the giraffes are 'living periscopes' in that sea!

The large, expressive eyes of giraffes, bordered by long, thick lashes, are undeniably beautiful but, as in the case of their coat, nature's intention was not an aesthetic one. This is yet another example of a singularly successful evolutionary process which has enabled these stately creatures to survive in an environment where danger is always lurking.

It is, above all, thanks to its wonderful vision that the giraffe is able to defend itself so effectively against its natural enemies. From its elevated vantage point it can make a leisurely survey of the terrain for miles around, trying to spot a lurking predator. By gathering together in small groups, with each animal facing in a different direction, there is hardly an inch of ground that does not come under close scrutiny. The sense of smell, though far less developed, is nevertheless a good second line of defence, scents wafted on the breeze conveying messages of an unwelcome presence that may have eluded even its remarkable eyes.

The giraffe is a silent creature which seldom emits any sound; but although local natives allege it to be mute, its vocal organs show normal signs of development and on the basis of studies made in various zoos it is clear that the animal is capable of a fair variety of noises. In the wild, however, it is content to give out the odd snort when alarmed or a series of harsh coughs and grunts in the course of a combat with a rival male. Some naturalists are of the opinion—probably rightly—that the animal makes contact with another by ultrasonics, beyond human hearing capacity.

The suggestion that these creatures somehow communicate among themselves by means of gestures was also put forward by an animal photographer at the turn of the last century. The poor man was derisively howled down by the experts but time has proved him correct. Scientists who have made surveys of the giraffe's behaviour have confirmed that it frequently conveys its mood and intention by adopting attitudes and postures that are always the same in certain situations. Thus when a giraffe nervously flicks its flanks with its tail or walks stiffly with neck extended and head held high, this is a clear signal to its companions that a predator is around.

The giraffe's typical gait is an amble—in other words, it lifts the two legs on one side of the body and then the pair on the

opposite side. This characteristic manner of moving is slow, deliberate and remarkably graceful, almost as if the actions were filmed in slow motion. Yet when it is necessary the leisurely gait can be accelerated into a sustained gallop, at a speed of around 30 miles per hour. At such times it progresses in a series of long leaps, still with each pair of legs moving in unison. The tail is curled back over the rump and the long neck sways backwards and forwards with the same rhythm as the rest of the body. Whether moving at an amble or a gallop, however, the body is perfectly balanced in order to avoid a dangerous and perhaps fatal fall. The vertebral column and long legs are of course particularly vulnerable.

Life at the top

The giraffe is a ruminant with a highly specialised diet consisting of leaves, twigs and thorns, most of which are to be found on the diverse species of acacia that grow in the African bush. The animal's range of distribution, however, is not exclusively conditioned by the absence or presence of acacias because it is content to browse on the foliage of other shrubs and trees as well.

The disproportionate length of the neck enables the giraffe to feed at levels varying from 6–18 feet from the ground, so that the trees often end up shaped like hour-glasses.

The giraffe's only competitor at the lower levels is the gerenuk, while higher up only the elephant, with its long, coiling trunk, can get anywhere near the same topmost branches. The ability to reach the summit of a tree gives the giraffe a tremendous advantage over other leaf-eating mammals. Not only are these branches more abundantly covered with leaves but they are also more nutritious, receiving more sunlight than the foliage at the lower levels. This is probably why, in times of severe drought, the tall giraffe manages to look sleek and well fed in comparison with other animals such as the black rhinoceros, which often appears to be thin and undernourished at such seasons. This seems to afford clear proof that the giraffe derives a double benefit from its unusual physique, enjoying quality as well as quantity.

The giraffe's extraordinarily long, flexible and prehensile tongue (it extends to about 16 inches) can curl itself around branches, drawing them close to the mouth with its well-developed, mobile lips and tearing off leaves, shoots, twigs and fruit with consummate ease.

The giraffe's favourite tree is the acacia and it is quite astonishing to watch how the animal browses on the foliage, swallowing the hard, sharply pointed, two-inch-long thorns that protect the leaves as if they were the most succulent shoots, and paying not the slightest attention to the colonies of ants that cluster in the galls of the tree trunk—these insects normally attacking without mercy any animal or person unwise enough to touch them.

Because it is a typical ruminant the food ingested by the giraffe is brought back into the mouth to be rechewed and softened with saliva, in exactly the same manner as in the case of a gnu or a sheep. But although it is a very large animal it does not lie down during this phase of the digestive process as do the majority of

The giraffe uses its long, curling, prehensile tongue to reach the tasty topmost branches of the acacia – impervious to the tree's barrier of thorns and to the bites of the *Crematogaster* ants that infest the trunk.

Facing page (above) : The normal movements of the giraffe are graceful and leisurely but if alarmed it can gallop at up to 30 miles per hour. (*Below*) The giraffe makes good use of its long neck, flexible tongue and mobile lips to browse on the highest leaves of a tree which, being more exposed to sunlight, are especially nutritious.

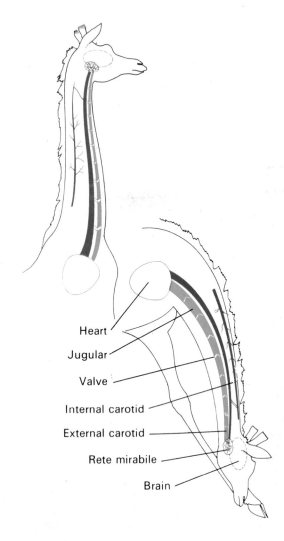

Heart

Jugular

Valve

Internal carotid

External carotid

Rete mirabile

Brain

The giraffe's circulatory system is extremely ingenious, a special arrangement of valves keeping pressure constant in the blood vessels of the brain both when the animal is in an upright position – with the brain above the level of the heart – and when it stoops to drink – at which times the brain is lower than the heart.

Bovidae. Instead it remains on its feet, slowly grinding up the vegetable mass by moving its jaw from side to side. It is mainly for protective reasons that the animal stays in a standing position while ruminating. To lie down at the very time when bodily movements tend to be most relaxed and the senses somewhat dulled would be to abandon the natural advantages of height and vision that normally afford the giraffe its best means of self-defence. In fact the animal will very seldom stretch itself out on the ground, even when resting, the only exception being when it feels completely secure. At all other times it sleeps or dozes in an upright position, solidly planted on all four legs. Lying down and getting up are in any event laborious manoeuvres for such a streamlined animal, involving a gradual and complicated un-folding process, with the neck having to move from front to rear in order to provide a counterbalance to the weight of the body. On those occasions when the head has to be lowered to ground level, either to drink or to browse on low-lying shrubs, the giraffe takes every precaution to make sure that there is no enemy about to take advantage of this temporary awkwardness.

Although in theory the neck should be long enough not only to reach the lowest branches of a tree but also to bring the lips down to the level of the water, the giraffe is compelled to open its front legs at a wide angle in order to get its head down to the ground. The reason is that during the natural growth process it is not only the neck that gets longer but also the front legs, which grow to a greater length than the hind legs. The disproportionate structure of the animal is very evident when it is standing, with the line of the vertebral column descending from shoulder to root of tail.

Problems of circulation

The giraffe is a real prodigy of adaptation, and for physiologists perhaps the most interesting feature of its anatomy is the way in which the blood circulates. The heart of this enormous creature weighs about 24 lb, measuring 24 inches long, with walls 3 inches thick. It is not surprising to learn that the propulsive power of the organ is three times that of the human heart – as indeed it must be in order to pump blood through an arterial system which is the longest of any living land mammal.

The most astonishing characteristic of this circulatory mechanism is the way in which it regulates pressure in the delicate blood vessels of the brain. In its normal upright position, when browsing on leaves at the top of a tree, the giraffe's brain is some 9 feet above the heart, whereas when the animal bends down to drink or collect plants at ground level the brain is more than 6 feet *below* the level of the heart. With these conditions con-tinually changing, the problem is to ensure that constant blood pressure is maintained which will allow normal oxygenisation and not lead to congestion of the arteries of the brain. This is made possible by means of a wonderful vascular system known as the rete mirabile, a multiple transmission mechanism, located at the base of the brain, which stabilises the pressure in the cerebral blood vessels by causing the arterioles (small arteries) to expand.

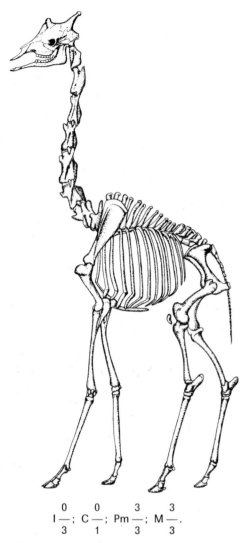

$$I\frac{0}{3}; C\frac{0}{1}; Pm\frac{3}{3}; M\frac{3}{3}.$$

Skeleton and dental formula of the giraffe.

Preceding page : The horns of the giraffe, partially or totally covered with rough hair, are not for defence but are used by the males in their ritual combat during the mating season.
Facing page : Even while her baby suckles the female giraffe keeps a careful watch for possible predators hidden in the tall grass.

The carotid artery, composed of layers of elastic fibres and muscular tissue, is the principal vessel conveying blood to the brain. At the point where it reaches the level of the brain it divides into two branches—the external and internal carotids. The former branch is the one that, strictly speaking, feeds the brain but it too has been subdivided several times to form the rete mirabile. The internal carotid does not lead to the brain but passes under the base of the skull.

When the giraffe lowers its head part of the strongly flowing blood is diverted towards the internal carotid while part travels through the rete mirabile whose elastic walls become distended to allow a decrease in pressure. The delicate blood vessels of the brain are thus relieved and suffer no damage. When the animal raises its head the rete mirabile retains a quantity of blood sufficient to provide a constant supply of oxygen to the brain. After traversing and irrigating the brain the blood then returns to the heart by way of the jugular vein, which measures about an inch across and contains a series of valves that prevent the blood flowing back when the giraffe bends its neck.

It is worth pointing out that the unusual length of the neck, which gives rise to all these special problems of blood pressure regulation, has not resulted, as might be supposed, in an increased number of cervical vertebrae but rather to exceptional elongation of these spinal bones. In fact, like most mammals, including mice, elephants and man, giraffes have seven cervical vertebrae. The only difference between animals of short stature and those with longer necks is that the latter possess a far longer vertebral column. In the case of the giraffe each bone in the neck measures about eleven inches in length.

The six-foot baby

Although the male giraffe does not put on an elaborate display to woo his mate he does go through a sequence of prescribed ritual postures prior to actually coupling with her. His first action is to sniff her anal region, lick her tail and gently rub his head against her rump. The chief object of this exercise is to induce the female to pass urine, which he then proceeds to taste, so determining whether she is sexually receptive. At the same time he lifts his head and opens his mouth wide to reveal the incisors. When satisfied that the female is ready to receive his favours he follows her indefatigably for hours on end, never moving far from her side. If necessary he goes through the same ritual movements at intervals until she eventually permits him to mount her.

The female's gestation period varies between 420 and 468 days, at the end of which the baby giraffe—already standing almost six feet high and weighing 100-150 lb—is born, the forelegs making their appearance first, followed by the head. The baby's first encounter with the outside world must come as a bit of a shock because the mother remains in an upright position from start to finish, so that her offspring literally tumbles straight onto the ground. An hour or so later it staggers to its feet and after a little while begins to suckle.

The female giraffe does not give the impression of being as

attentive a mother as other ruminants. It is quite common to see a young giraffe wandering about in the midst of a group of adult females, none of which claims it as her own. The mother has in fact probably left the herd to browse in isolation some distance away, without unduly worrying about her offspring's welfare. At other times small groups consisting entirely of young giraffes will be found living together without adults, perhaps for several days on end, but this independent behaviour only occurs in regions where there is virtually no menace from predators. At the first sign of danger the young giraffe normally seeks the protection of its mother, squeezing itself beneath her belly and turning sideways so that she is not prevented from using her front legs or from turning round to meet the enemy head-on.

At a week old the baby giraffe is able to start nibbling grass, and at four months it is capable of browsing on foliage, adult-fashion, though continuing to suckle until it is nine or ten months old. During its first year it will grow approximately three feet.

The female giraffe is likely to be on heat again and ready to couple with another male before her first baby is weaned, and some seventeen to twenty months may elapse between two

In order to browse on low shrubs or to drink from a waterhole the giraffe is compelled to spread its forelegs wide. As it lowers its long neck to concentrate on feeding or drinking an opportunity is provided for a quick-moving predator to catch it unawares.

successive births. The young animals are sexually mature at three or four years of age and at this point the males are forced to leave the circle in which they have been reared to join another 'bachelor' group living in more thickly wooded areas. Here they will remain until they are fully adult, when they will elect either to live on their own or to join a few companions in following the herds composed almost entirely of females.

The battling males

Adult male giraffes living in the same region seem to spend their days in an endless succession of quarrels and fights, all of which are to decide which of them is to assume leadership of the herd. The trouble is that since these herds are forever changing their personnel there must inevitably be continual struggles for supremacy, and hardly a day goes by without a temporarily dominant male having to defend his status against a rival.

These fights begin with both contenders unhurriedly taking up positions alongside each other, facing in the same or opposite directions, and then pushing with the full weight of their bodies.

Male giraffes engaging in combat plant their forelegs apart for balance and proceed to butt each other with head and horns. Such fights are generally ritualised with neither animal sustaining injury, the weaker of the two ultimately conceding victory.

The giraffe's horns vary in number according to the subspecies concerned and from one individual to another. When the animal is young (A) there is generally a small central growth in front of the usual pair, the latter being covered with hair. As the giraffe grows (B) so does this frontal protuberance, while a smaller pair of horns often appears behind the first pair—now bald at the tips.

Although they are capable of lashing out with hefty kicks neither animal makes use of its legs on these occasions, storing up the deadly power in their hooves for predators alone. In these bouts of rivalry only the head and horns serve as offensive weapons. There are up to five such small bony horns, covered with hair at the base but bald and slightly pointed at the tip. Both animals plant their forelegs wide so as to keep their balance and exert the strongest possible pressure, then swing their necks rhythmically and clash heads, striking with the front pair of horns for the opponent's most vulnerable spots. The impact may be so violent as to break the spinal column but in the normal way no such serious injury is either intended or sustained, most of the blows failing to land or being successfully parried. Once the contestants begin swaying their necks they are unable to take precise aim and it is relatively simple for evasive action to be taken. One of the rivals usually surrenders before any great damage is done, the victor not normally giving chase.

Height and its handicaps

Sheer size is generally a reasonable guarantee against carnivores, the latter seldom risking a clash with an animal weighing more than a ton. Since an adult giraffe may weigh up to 2,900 lb a predator must consider carefully before tackling it, but a young animal presents more of a temptation. Any baby giraffe abandoned, even for a short period, by its mother risks ending up as the victim of a hyena, a leopard or a hunting dog; in most cases, however, the herd will scent the predator and once the alarm is given the females will rally round to defend their offspring with their powerful hooves.

Nevertheless, if conditions are favourable, lions will attack even a healthy, full-grown giraffe, choosing the moment when the animal stoops to browse on a low-lying bush, thereby throwing away its most valuable protective asset—unimpeded vision. A hungry pride of lions fortunate enough to find a giraffe thus occupied will make careful plans. Invisible in the tall, dry savannah grass, and making sure to remain downwind of their prey, one male or perhaps an elderly female will track the unsuspecting giraffe until within striking distance. From a range of a few yards it then pounces on its victim, planting the claws in its neck and sinking the fangs into its muzzle. The leap, with a 400-lb body weight behind it, is generally enough to knock the giraffe off balance and send it sprawling to the ground. Now it is helpless and certainly doomed. The other waiting lions close in and quickly deliver the finishing touches. Sometimes reinforcements may not even be necessary, for the attacker is quite capable of breaking the giraffe's neck or strangling it with its powerful jaws.

Lions and other carnivores have never really been an influential factor in the fortunes of the giraffe population as a whole. Once again it is man alone who has figured as the animal's most deadly enemy, responsible for the dwindling numbers of certain subspecies. Local African tribes may be forgiven for hunting the enormous beast with bow and arrow, regarding it simply as food; but the white man, with his rifle, has never pretended to treat the

exercise as anything else but sport. Fortunately the craze seems to have passed its zenith and the giraffe as a species is now safe.

Although some giraffes have lived more than 25 years in captivity studies indicate that it is rare for the animals to reach such an advanced age in the wild. Older animals often succumb to crippling arthritis or other diseases which enfeeble them to such an extent that they are easy prey for lions. Others may die accidentally. Doctor Grzimek, for example, once found a dead giraffe hanging from an acacia in the Serengeti. It had apparently been browsing on the highest leaves of this tree which was standing on the bank of a river. Suddenly losing its balance, it must have slipped and caught its neck in the fork of a branch. Others have been found drowned in muddy pools. In the normal way a giraffe will test out soft, dangerous terrain with its hooves before settling down to drink, but if it makes a mistake and starts sinking into muddy ground, no amount of struggling will free it and once the legs are deeply entrenched the animal's fate is sealed.

Fortunately, now that professional hunting expeditions are largely memories, giraffes can be found in reasonably large number not only in parks and reserves but also in unprotected bush and savannah regions.

Two splendid reticulated giraffes in the bush of northern Kenya. The male, as can be seen, is considerably taller than the female.

Reticulated giraffe (*G. c. reticulata*)   Rothschild's giraffe (*G. c. rothschildi*)   Masai giraffe (*G. c. tippelskirchi*)

FAMILY: Giraffidae

The family Giraffidae belongs to the order Artiodactyla and to the suborder Pecora (= Ruminantia). It consists of two genera, *Giraffa* and *Okapia*, both of which are taller-than they are long, with a pronounced tendency towards elongation of the cervical column. This is especially marked in the giraffes which are also provided with a thick fatty layer in the subcutaneous tissue of the neck. The abnormal length of the spinal column is not due to an extra number of vertebrae – there are only seven, as in the majority of mammals – but to their exceptional size. This means that the neck is comparatively rigid and inflexible.

The head is relatively small and slender, the muzzle flat and the eyes large and prominent. The lips are thin and mobile, the nostrils longitudinal slits. There are no tear ducts. The ears are large and the hearing good. The senses of smell and vision are also exceptionally sharp so that it is rare for these animals to be taken unawares.

Horns are present in the male okapi and in both sexes of the giraffe. These are of a special type, quite unlike the hollow horns of the Bovidae or the solid antlers of the Cervidae. In fact they are really bony knobs joined to the frontal bones. Each horn is covered with rough skin and in the young giraffe is topped by a tuft of hair. In the okapi the two short horns are no more than rudimentary sheaths. The giraffe always has typically a front pair but some individuals have an additional smaller pair behind and, invariably, a fifth bony boss on the forehead.

Apart from the long neck, the striking feature of the giraffe's anatomy is the slope of the back from shoulder to rump, the front legs being longer than the back pair. There are two toes on each foot, with no trace of lateral toes, the phalanges being almost perpendicular to the ground and the hooves short.

The giraffe feeds mainly on the leaves of high trees and large shrubs but also has a liking for the foliage of certain smaller plants. To reach the latter and in order to drink, the animal is forced to lower its head to ground level and spread its forelegs wide apart, a position which is not only inconvenient but which also exposes it to the attacks of predators.

The tongue, particularly that of the okapi, is long, protrusible and prehensile – used, together with the flexible lips, for plucking leaves and shoots off the branches.

The dental formula of the Giraffidae is

$$\text{I}: \frac{0}{3} \quad \text{C}: \frac{0}{1} \quad \text{PM}: \frac{3}{3} \quad \text{M}: \frac{3}{3}$$

The canine teeth have a furrowed crown which gives them a bilobed appearance and the cheek teeth are of the brachydont type, that is, with low crowns.

The digestive mechanism is in keeping with that of ruminants in general but the Giraffidae lack a bile duct.

The colour and pattern of the giraffe's coat varies with the subspecies; basically it is made up of brown patches, either rectangular or irregular in shape, superimposed on a much paler brown background (white in the reticulated giraffe). The okapi's coat is rich chestnut-brown, the male being darker than the female, and both sexes having alternate black and white horizontal rings on the upper part of the legs. Giraffes and young okapis have a short, stiff mane running down the back of the neck to the shoulders. The giraffes have a tail extending down to the hocks, ending in a hairy tuft.

All the Giraffidae are exclusively African. The giraffe (*Giraffa camelopardalis*) lives in open, wooded savannah and thorny bush country, usually in shifting herds. The much rarer okapi (*Okapia johnstoni*), not discovered by scientists until the beginning of the present century, is solitary, confined to the dense forests of the Congo.

Facing page (above): There are eight recognised subspecies of giraffe, each showing differences in height, coat colour and pattern and number of horns. Three are illustrated here – the superb reticulated giraffe (*Giraffa camelopardalis reticulata*) from northern Kenya, Somalia and southern Ethiopia; the five-horned Rothschild's giraffe (*G. c. rothschildi*) from western Kenya, Uganda and Sudan; and the Masai giraffe (*G. c. tippelskirchi*), its markings with jagged outlines, from Tanzania and southern Kenya. The others are the Nubian giraffe (*G. c. camelopardalis*), pale in colour, with an almost reticulated pattern; the Kordofan giraffe (*G. c. antiquorum*), with reddish markings, from north-western Sudan; the Niger giraffe (*G. c. peralta*), also reddish and in danger of becoming extinct; the Angola giraffe (*G. c. angolensis*), with irregular fawn marks; and the Cape giraffe (*G. c. giraffa*), light in colour, and not very abundant. (*Below*) The rare okapi (*Okapia johnstoni*) is related to the giraffe and lives in a different habitat, in dense forests.

CHAPTER 8

The antelopes of the bush

On the open savannah the herds of wild ungulates can be seen from afar, peacefully grazing, but in bush country the inhabitants are more cautious and secretive, and none more so than the graceful antelopes. One of the most typical members of the family, roaming the edges of the bush where the grasslands gradually give way to thorn and shrub, is the impala, a graceful creature with a beautiful sleek coat and lyrate horns. The latter, found in the male only, are admittedly not quite as dramatic in size or shape as those of the greater kudu; nor is the impala as massive as the eland or as strikingly handsome as the sable antelope. Nevertheless, it is elegantly built, magnificently proportioned and noteworthy above all for its extraordinary athleticism. There is hardly an ounce of excess fat on its body, its slim legs are not too long and its slender neck is stronger than that of the gerenuk. This splendid animal is indeed well equipped to deal with its natural enemies. Like other species of antelope, vision, hearing and scenting powers are remarkable but what particularly distinguishes the impala is its fantastic leaping ability.

Both the male and female impala have a rich reddish-brown coat which is somewhat lighter on the flanks and turns to white on the belly and hindquarters. Prominent on the rump are two vertical black lines which serve as recognition marks. The overall colour of the coat merges to perfection with the dappled light of the background vegetation, camouflaging the animal from predators, the sharply-etched black streaks being part of an intraspecific signalling system. When an impala senses danger it uses special muscles to ripple the bands on the rump, the rest of the herd then making off by leaps and bounds.

The impala enjoy a mixed diet of vegetation and are therefore happiest among trees and shrubs, where they browse on leaves,

Facing page : The impala is one of the most handsome of all African antelopes. The male bears ringed, lyre-shaped horns— useful weapons in fights against rivals in the mating season.

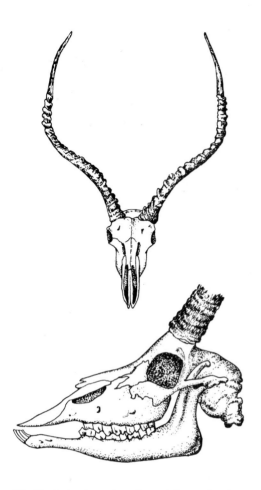

Skull of the impala, viewed from the front and in profile.

Facing page (above) : The most usual type of impala herd consists of females and their young, with a single dominant male, easily distinguished by his horns. It is his responsibility to prevent the females from straying and to ward off incursions by members of all-male herds. (*Below*) Young male impala unable to form their own harems group together but often attempt to penetrate the larger female herds, especially during the mating season. Here such a group prepares to take flight from an intruder.

interspersed with clearings of open grassland. They stick as closely as possible to water and never venture either into the thick forest or out onto the open plains. Since the areas affording them ideal food conditions are somewhat restricted, their range is narrow and their population somewhat scattered; but in those parts that offer them exactly the correct balance of vegetation and shelter they are found in reasonable numbers.

Much of the latest information about the social behaviour of impala is due to the intensive work of Rudolf Schenkel of Nairobi University, who has studied them in their natural habitats. Detailed surveys of these fascinating antelopes are justified by the fact that whereas Thomson's gazelles are typical creatures of the open savannah and the gerenuks characteristic inhabitants of the bush, the habitat of the impala represents a transitional zone linking the two forms of terrain.

High-jumpers of the bush

Impala are markedly gregarious animals which normally make up herds of two distinct types. The more compact and organised of the two is that containing up to one hundred individuals, consisting of numerous females with their young and a single dominant male. The other comprises 'bachelor' males only, all less than a year old, of which there may be as many as sixty. Two herds of females may occasionally come together to graze or spend several hours feeding alongside a group of males, but eventually the different groups will separate and go their own ways.

In the female herds overall direction of activities does not, as might be expected, devolve on the dominant male but on an elderly female who takes her place at the head of the column, the others following in Indian file, with the male bringing up the rear. The leading female makes frequent halts, remaining absolutely still for some seconds, head erect and ears twitching to catch the faintest sound of alien movement. Those behind her, nibbling leaves and grass as they go, seem to rely on her to perform all guard duties; and when, during the most intense heat of the day, they all lie down to ruminate in the shade of the acacias, it is she alone who is impelled to stay on her feet to keep watch.

Within a large herd there are smaller, distinct subdivisions—groups made up of an older female, her daughters (of different ages) and their offspring. These family groups are at all times closely knit, feeding, drinking and resting together, so that the herd is really comprised of a number of compact little units, each virtually autonomous.

The dominant male has the arduous responsibility of keeping all his females together and rounding them up whenever they stray too far from the herd or make a deliberate escape bid. In either event the male darts off and ushers the guilty female back by nudging her with his head. He does not offer any violence but pushes her determinedly in the right direction, taking care not to touch her with his sharp horns. In this way he asserts his authority firmly enough to persuade her to rejoin her companions. At the same time, however, in the manner of a dog gathering

stray sheep, the male impala cannot afford to let his attention to the rest of the herd lapse, and although he may have to chase the culprit for some considerable distance he keeps on casting anxious glances at the other animals to make sure that there are no more defectors while he is thus occupied.

On no account will the dominant male permit other adult males to infiltrate or even remain inside the herd. As soon as the young males are a year old he drives them out, forcing them to seek a group of similarly-aged bachelors. The newcomers are then obliged to keep to themselves, occupying a lower social position than those already in the group. Yet there are compensating advantages for these 'exiles'. Within the new herd they have more freedom of action than the females they have left behind, for there is no omnipotent leader to harry them or force them back into the group should they decide to seek their fortune elsewhere.

It frequently happens that a wandering female finds temporary refuge in one of these bachelor groups, causing a great deal of disturbance and confusion. Not unnaturally, the young males pay

There are frequent fights among the members of the all-male 'bachelor' groups of impala, but they are not usually very violent or protracted. The contests begin with each animal taking up a defiant attitude from a short distance (1) and then, if not too aggressively inclined, turning away again (2). Alternatively, they may approach and encircle each other (3), often making diversionary movements in order to lower the tense atmosphere. When battle proper commences each animal attempts to twist the other's neck (4). They may lock horns for twenty minutes or more, until the loser surrenders (5), leaving the victor to try his fortune with the females. When he is a few yards from his intended mate he rears up on his forelegs (6) and totters towards her, then resumes his normal position.

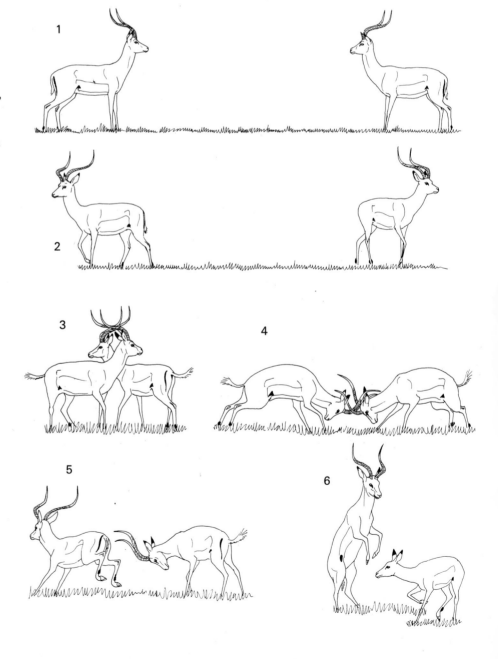

court to the intruder and dispute violently with one another for her possession. Calm only returns when the stray female is guided back, as is invariably the case, to the security of her own herd. Even without the presence of a strange female, however, there seems to be a compulsion to let off steam at regular intervals and the vigorous young impala use up a vast amount of energy in fighting. Two animals will clash horns, swinging their heads from side to side or backwards and forwards. There is never any bloodshed in these ritual encounters, which stop as suddenly as they begin, both animals unconcernedly resuming their tranquil feeding.

The impala herds go out in quest of food in the early morning and late afternoon. Soon after it gets light they spread out over the pastures, showing no signs of haste, groups of males and females sometimes intermingling without intervention on the part of the dominant male. Those on the fringes of the group may interrupt their grazing or browsing from time to time, showing signs of nervousness; but the animals in the centre of the herd feed quietly, almost continuously. Sometimes an impala will raise its head and quickly rebury it in the grass, evidently reassured that there is no danger; but this is a ruse, for the animal in question is on the alert and will look up again a few moments later. The precaution is especially against a predator such as a cheetah which makes a habit of stalking an antelope, crouching motionless in the grass until the latter resumes grazing, all suspicions lulled. In the case of the impala it is often the hunter which is forced to break cover and reveal itself. The daily journey to river or waterhole also necessitates one animal being detailed to stand guard while the others drink.

As the morning goes on and the impala become replete, the dominant male shows increasing signs of agitation, keeping a close watch on the females which form groups well out of reach of the other males. All his movements betray unease and anxiety and he does not relax until his rivals have moved away. No longer tolerant, he stations himself in the centre of his harem and gives out a series of loud snorts as a warning not to break ranks or even as much as cast an amorous glance at the potentially disruptive males.

Should a carnivore surprise adjacent groups of females and young males, a complicated situation may arise. The normal reaction of impala in an emergency is to panic and make off in different directions. Once the danger is past little groups of males will, as like as not, find themselves mixed with stray females and will naturally try to take advantage of the fact. The unfortunate dominant male is now faced with the unenviable task of regathering the stragglers and his fury and aggressive instincts are unbounded. He dashes madly from side to side, desperately trying to sort out his females, butting the unwelcome males with his horns and uttering sharp cries, rather like fretful coughs. As order is gradually restored he takes up a commanding position in 'no man's land', midway between the two groups, ready to intercept any young male still ardent enough to try breaking into the female camp. By this time the almost exhausted male's worries are over and he can turn once more to asserting his authority.

Geographical distribution of impala.

IMPALA
(Aepyceros melampus)

Class: Mammalia
Order: Artiodactyla
Family: Bovidae

Length of head and body: 52–72 inches (130–180 cm)
Length of tail: 10–17 inches (25–42 cm)
Height to shoulder: 36–40 inches (90–100 cm)
Weight: 145–155 lb (65–70 kg). Large males weigh up to 200 lb (90 kg)
Diet: vegetarian (leaves and seeds of acacias, grass)
Gestation: 180–210 days
Number of young: one

Adults
The body is slender and graceful, with long legs. The stronger male has a pair of ringed, lyrate horns that may be up to 33 inches in length. The eyes are large and dark, the ears pointed, light brown and black at the tip. The reddish coat becomes lighter on the flanks and almost white on the belly. The white hindquarters are bordered on either side by a black line, and a dark line runs centrally down the tail which terminates in a white tuft. The scent-secreting glands, located in the upper part of the hind legs, above the hooves, are surrounded by tufts of dark hair.

Young
Growth is rapid and the horns, not yet curved, appear in the males at the age of two months.

The illustrations above and on the facing page show three stages in the courtship behaviour and coupling of impala. The male begins by sniffing the genital region of the female to ascertain whether she is yet sexually receptive, then stretching his upper lip to show his teeth. The sexual act itself is of brief duration. Although the male impala shows great gentleness and consideration for his mate he is especially aggressive at such times towards rivals threatening to disrupt his harem.

Stretching out his neck and head, he lifts his upper lip to show a protruding tip of tongue, then takes a few steps in the direction of one of the females. Suddenly he veers off to confront another, repeating the head and lip movements, turning his attention to each female in turn. Occasionally he stops dead and assumes a threatening posture, not intended for the now-submissive females but for any remaining rival, real or imagined. At no stage does he show any disposition to copulate, this ritual being quite unlike that adopted for sexual purposes. Such behaviour simply has the effect of bolstering his own confidence and reaffirming his privileged status after the period of temporary disorder.

The female impala is not by temperament aggressive but it may happen that she will compel another female to yield a few square feet of pasture or relinquish a tasty branch. This kind of unsociable behaviour is generally more noticeable among females accompanied by offspring and does not necessarily hinge upon superior size and weight.

Contests between rival males, whether between two masters of a harem or between a dominant male and an aspiring bachelor (perhaps especially emboldened by the approach of the traditional mating season), usually follow a pattern but their intensity will depend on how aggressive the herd leader shows himself to be and how far he succeeds in intimidating his opponent. A young male which has already managed to seduce one or more females before the dominant male arrives on the scene will probably be brimming over with confidence and put up a good fight. Even if the intruder has failed to attain his objective, however, and been driven off repeatedly with butts and prods, he will not necessarily be deterred from making one last desperate attempt.

As the mating season draws near the herds' daily activities seem to take on added momentum, the males fighting more frequently and showing their obvious interest in the opposite sex. But

The impala is noted for its remarkable leaping powers, the most certain means of escaping from a predator. These high jumps over pools and bushes alert other impalas to the danger and the clearly etched black lines on the white rump serve as a directional guide for the herd.

Facing page : This baby impala is less than an hour old, not quite steady on its legs and, like all other baby antelopes, especially vulnerable to the attacks of carnivores. It will stay concealed in the undergrowth for a couple of days before being guided by its mother back to the safety of the herd.

whereas among many species of territorial antelope contests between males are preludes to the conquest and defence of nuptial ground (the Uganda kob is a good example), the impala, roaming freely over extensive and undefined pastures, is only concerned with simple possession of his mate. Although details vary, the breeding ritual usually begins with the male selecting a female and vigorously pursuing her. From a gentle trot both animals soon break into a gallop, stopping abruptly to make their way slowly back towards the rest of the herd. It is at this point that the brief act of copulation takes place; when it is over the male heads for the centre of the herd, still looking fierce as if intending to rout imaginary competitors.

The pregnant females later form small groups or wander off on their own. After a gestation period of 180–200 days they hide behind a convenient clump of bushes and give birth. The new-born impala, unable to follow its mother, remains concealed in the undergrowth for a while but the female is careful not to move too far away, mounting guard, often in company with her previous offspring. When the baby is able to get about on its own she guides it back to the herd and rejoins the other females that have given birth at about the same time.

When ready to suckle or when alarmed and in need of comfort and reassurance, the baby goes out in search of its mother, not vice versa. It grips the teat firmly, resting its head against the maternal belly and waving its tail. Meanwhile the mother gently sniffs at her baby as it drinks. It makes a charming picture of motherly affection and juvenile trust.

Leaping to safety

The impala of the bush, like the gazelles of the savannah, are surrounded by implacable enemies, including large birds of prey and jackals (these concentrating especially on the babies), leopards, lions, cheetahs, hunting dogs and hyenas.

The pressures exerted by these many predators has resulted

in the impala reaching a high pitch of physical perfection and has also set in train a sequence of varied defensive manoeuvres on its part. For example, there is the close protective alliance formed with baboons. The monkeys, from their vantage points in trees, use their remarkable vision to spot predators and sound a noisy alarm; additionally, they form a kind of bodyguard around the impala herds, keeping carnivores at a safe distance. The antelopes, like other ruminants, use their own excellent eyesight, hearing and sense of smell to return the service and provide a second line of security.

Such precautions may not be enough to keep the more persistent predators, such as leopards, at bay, in which case the impala scatter in all directions with a succession of prodigious leaps. Each jump may cover as much as 30 feet and take them 10 feet into the air. They leap with surprising grace over the thorny bushes, their feet barely seeming to touch the ground. As they bound up and down, briefly vanishing from view and then reappearing, the predator has to make a rapid decision as to which animal to pursue, for the very unpredictability of these acrobatic feats makes it impossible to choose a victim in advance. As they go, the black streaks on their white hindquarters provide extra warning to other impalas in their path, enabling these in turn to make their own leaps to safety.

Of course the predators living in and around the bush have kept pace with their prey, acquiring and perfecting hunting techniques designed to counterbalance and foil the most skilful of defensive manoeuvres. The scales are weighted fairly evenly and in accordance with nature's laws advantage and victory will go by turns to the hunter and the hunted.

The impala, like all other members of the animal community of the bush, plays its part in helping to maintain the ecological equilibrium, underlining yet again the wonderful way in which animals and plants depend, to a lesser or greater degree, upon one another for survival. Among the leaves especially favoured by the impala are those of the abundant acacia species *Acacia tortilis*. The seeds are moistened in the course of their journey through the animal's digestive tract and this facilitates their germination after they are deposited on the ground in the excreta. From these seeds grow more acacias which provide nourishment for animals such as the giraffe. When the trees die they are food for the innumerable termites which are in their turn devoured by the aardvark and the aardwolf.

This interdependence of plants and animals takes other forms. At the summit of many termite mounds grows a grass of the genus *Cynodon* which is eaten by the impala in the dry season; and the impala itself is preyed upon by many carnivores, particularly the leopard. In fact there is not one animal or vegetable species in the bush that is not in some way linked with another at some point of this unending life cycle, although intensive research is often required to determine the precise nature of such relationships. Here, as throughout the wild, the ecological balance is so delicate that what may at first sight appear to be an insignificant alteration of circumstances can only too often turn out to have fateful consequences.

The kudus

It needs the trained eye of an expert – one of the native guides of Tsavo, for example – to pick out from the tangled growth of dry acacias an animal that might well be called the 'phantom' of the bush. This shadowy creature flitting through a labyrinth of thorns is the lesser kudu (*Tragelaphus imberbis*), a beautiful antelope with a coat that ranges in colour from ash-grey to light brown, broken vertically by a number of thin white lines – a pattern that makes it virtually invisible in the thick undergrowth. An elegant animal with a proud bearing, the lesser kudu is unfortunately becoming rare. Poachers, traffickers and trophy collectors have mercilessly hounded it to the point of near-extermination for the sake of its magnificent spiralling horns, so that nowadays it is found only in national parks and reserves.

The greater kudu (*Tragelaphus strepsiceros*), an equally hand-some animal, is built on a more massive scale and since it has adapted itself to a number of contrasting habitats it is not simi-larly endangered by illicit hunters and poachers. Its delicately striped grey-brown coat also provides an effective form of natural camouflage amid dense vegetation. Much more widely distribu-ted than the lesser kudu, it may be found living in all parts of the African bush, in the Ethiopian massif, in the *miombo* tree-steppe regions, in Chad, Sudan, and – most typically – in the Kruger National Park of the South African veld.

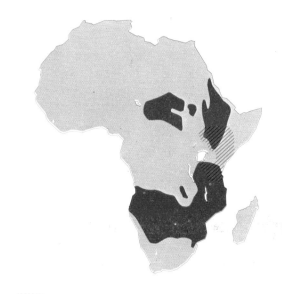

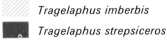

/// *Tragelaphus imberbis*

■ *Tragelaphus strepsiceros*

Geographical distribution of lesser kudu (*Tragelaphus imberbis*) and greater kudu (*Tragelaphus strepsiceros*).

The vertical white stripes adorning the coat of the greater kudu help to break the animal's outline and increase the effectiveness of its natural camouflage in the undergrowth.

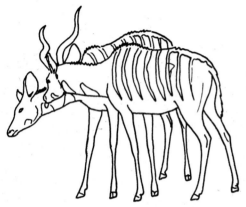

Prior to coupling the female lesser kudu invites the male to lick certain parts of her body by adopting recognisable ritual postures. It is thought that her behaviour on such occasions is designed to inhibit the naturally aggressive tendencies of the male.

Facing page : Only the male kudu possesses horns, which have been highly prized by big game hunters, thereby leading to massacres and near-extermination in some areas. Numbers are creeping back to former levels thanks to protective measures and kudus are nowadays a familiar sight in many national parks and reserves.

Like the majority of antelopes inhabiting wooded terrain neither species of kudu is a particularly proficient runner, for superior speed is not the method it usually chooses for protection against predators. On the contrary, its immediate reaction when confronted by danger of any kind is to stay absolutely still. The slightest rustle or quiver and it is immediately on the alert, 'freezing' in exactly the same fashion as a pointer when it scents game. As long as the animal remains quite motionless it is fairly safe, its outline practically indistinguishable from the ever-shifting light and shade of the undergrowth; but once it moves, the kudu's presence may be betrayed by the vertical marks on the back, the white hindquarters and the light facial patches.

The largest herds of kudu are made up of males, females and young in varying numbers, but all under the leadership of a single, experienced male. More typical, however, are the smaller herds consisting of five or six antelopes, all of the same sex. Bulls tend to be solitary.

Both the lesser and the greater kudu are leaf eaters but during the rainy season they also feed on grass, buds and young shoots. An important part of their diet consists of the dry seeds of acacias, which they either take directly from the trees or collect from the ground after they have fallen. Another tree that especially attracts them is the sausage tree (*Kigelia*), which blossoms almost all the year round. To reach the succulent leaves of this tree the kudus rear up on their hind legs, leaning either against the trunk or against the rump of a companion.

The antelopes of the bush all modify their feeding habits to some extent in accordance with the cycle of the seasons. Scientists examining the stomach contents of several kudus killed in a population control exercise in northern Rhodesia found leaves of the great gourd, stalks and leaves of maize, bamboo foliage, down from guinea fowl fledglings, scraps of tobacco and pieces of *Tilapia*–edible fishes of the cichlid family–apparently filched from a local drying-shed.

Life in the heart of a kudu herd is comparatively tranquil and serious fights are infrequent. Two males confronting each other may entwine horns and press their heads together but there is seldom any indication of real aggressiveness or hostility. The females also fight among themselves and even attack the males occasionally, the latter responding with menacing attitudes.

The favoured breeding season varies slightly according to the geographical situation. The herds north of the equator tend to come together at the beginning of the year, those south of the equator around the end of the year. Nevertheless, mating may occur at irregular intervals at any season. The gestation period is about 212 days so that the chances are the baby will be born at the time when annual vegetational growth is at its peak. The newborn kudu is thus well hidden and protected by the tall grass, the cinnamon hue of its coat blending with the surroundings, provided it makes no attempt to move. Predators are also kept at bay by the mother who, by swallowing the excrement of her baby, eliminates any odours that might betray its presence. By the time it is two weeks old the baby is capable of following its mother, and when the dry season arrives, with its serious risk of bush and

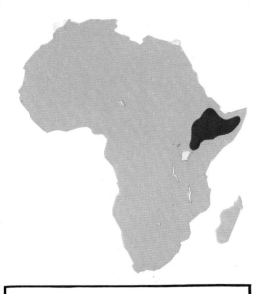

GERENUK
(Litocranius walleri)

Class: Mammalia
Order: Artiodactyla
Family: Bovidae
Length of head and body: 56–64 inches (140–160 cm)
Length of tail: 10–14 inches (25–35 cm)
Height to shoulder: 36–42 inches (90–105 cm)
Weight: 100–120 lb (45–55 kg)
Diet: leaves
Number of young: one

Adults
Small head, very long legs and neck. Only the male has short, cylindrical and completely ringed horns, curving backwards and then forwards at the tips. Coat reddish-brown with a darker band along the back. Belly white. Surrounds of the eyes and interior of ears both light brown. Tail terminating in tuft of black hairs.

Young
Newly-born animal looks very much like the adult with unusually long limbs and neck. Horns of the male resemble inward-pointing stumps.

Facing page (*above*) : The long-necked gerenuk reaches tasty leaves and shoots by standing on its hind legs and balancing itself against the branches, its powerful muscles enabling it to hold this position for some considerable period. (*Below*) horns are found only in the male gerenuk but both sexes have a similar coat colour, the hair being short. It is ideally suited to withstand extreme heat and drought.

forest fires, the young antelope is strong and agile enough to find refuge in areas beyond the reach of the flames.

The kudu must always be on the alert for natural predators such as leopards, hunting dogs and lions, while danger from the air – particularly when there is a baby in the vicinity – may come from lappet-faced vultures.

The lesser kudu, with its very much more restricted range, is most frequently seen in relatively dry regions where there is plenty of tree cover. Small groups of two or three individuals will be content to browse on level plains or on hillsides provided there is sufficient nourishing foliage. Their already meagre numbers are further reduced periodically by certain diseases to which they appear to be highly susceptible.

The gerenuk

The gerenuk or Waller's gazelle (*Litocranius walleri*) is a medium-sized antelope which is marvellously adapted to the harsh conditions of life in the African bush, sometimes solitary by habit but usually found in small groups of from three to ten animals. A voracious leaf eater, especially of the dwarf acacia, the gerenuk is capable of enduring extremely high temperatures and is in addition very resistant to thirst. Furthermore, with its abnormally long neck, slender limbs, enormous eyes and satiny coat, it bears no close resemblance to any other antelope, except the dibatag. Not for nothing has this interesting creature earned itself the nickname of 'gazelle-giraffe'.

In the stifling heat of the dry season most of the other ruminants of the bush gratefully abandon these inhospitable climes to seek food and water elsewhere. The lower branches of the acacias are practically denuded of edible leaves and only the tattered remains of suspended nests mark the sites where only a few months previously the colonies of weaver-birds flocked to rear their broods. But in this wilderness, now almost empty of animal life, the gerenuk is completely at home. For nature has endowed this strange antelope with the ability to stand erect on its hind legs, gently rest its small front hooves against the thorny acacia branches and stretch its neck so as to reach the leaves and shoots unattainable to the other leaf-eating animals of the bush. In fact the only other creature capable of competing with the gerenuk at the same level is the giraffe itself, and this rivalry is not serious in view of the fact that the larger animal seldom risks delving too deeply into the heart of the bush.

Because of its ability to go without water for considerable periods, the gerenuk is also relieved of the need to compete with other animals for standing room on the banks of rivers, streams or waterholes, and thereby also escapes the attention of the many carnivores that choose these sites for tracking and ambushing their favourite prey. Admittedly the gerenuk will not pass up the opportunity to drink should water be easily available, but it can supply most of its liquid requirements from juicy vegetation and is further aided by the fact that its kidney mechanism re-utilises water to the maximum extent. Studies in the Frankfurt zoo have also revealed that in captivity at any rate gerenuks often drink one

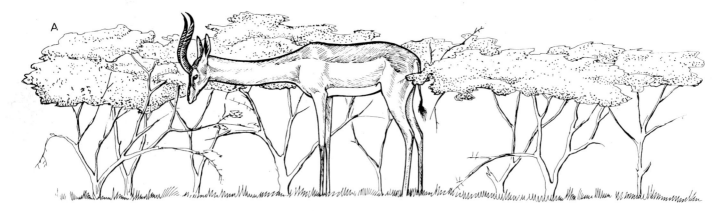

In its normal resting position (A) the gerenuk extends its neck and head to form a horizontal line with the back. When it stands motionless, the shape and colour of the animal merge wonderfully with its typical surroundings of dwarf acacias. Like many other antelopes the gerenuk has preorbital glands that secrete an odorous substance; this is deposited on branches (B) to signify the limits of its territory. The male gerenuk begins his courtship of the female by touching one of her hind legs with his front leg (C), a ritual action designed to determine whether she is sexually responsive. If startled by a predator or intruder the gerenuk pursues a zigzag course through the bush, pushing the thorns aside with its head (D) so that the neck does not get scratched or otherwise injured.

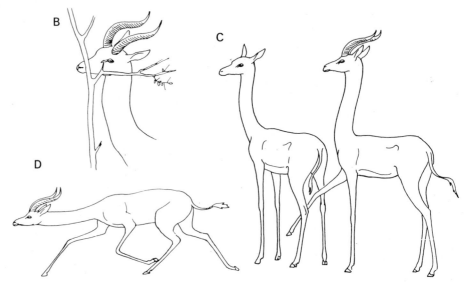

Facing page : The charming little dik-dik, about the size of a hare, is a typical bush-dweller. Because of its diminutive stature it is able to browse on low-lying foliage which is normally inaccessible to larger ruminants.

another's urine. In the severe droughts that are common in the wild it is quite possible that they act in the same manner.

For the greater part of the day the gerenuk prefers to confine itself to the shelter of the enclosed bush, taking up the characteristic stance that helps to make it almost invisible even at close quarters. Standing upright on its four feet, completely motionless, with neck stretched rigidly forwards, it tends to merge imperceptibly with the surroundings. Even the slender legs look like the miniature trunks of the dwarf acacias, and the flat, unbroken outline of head, shoulders and rump is often completely hidden behind the low-lying foliage of the thorny undergrowth.

In the event of the gerenuk being suddenly startled by a human intruder or a predator, it will dart off, neck still held stiffly out, almost as if it intended to use its head as a kind of battering-ram to tear a path through the tangled thickets. This is in fact a deliberate manoeuvre, permitting inconspicuous movement and preventing the neck being scratched by the sharp thorns. It does not, however, venture very far, stopping every few yards to lift its head and to twitch its large ears in order to pick up the sounds of its pursuer and then if necessary resume its course, zigzagging from side to side.

The male gerenuk possesses a pair of extremely solid, prominently ringed horns which are thick at the base and then curve backwards and up at the tips. It is in fact this hard and thick bony casing which originally led scientists to give it the generic name of *Lit(h)ocranius* – 'stony head'.

The dik-dik

When the first white hunters came crashing through the bush in quest of big game their prospects of a successful day's shooting were sometimes unexpectedly ruined by the intervention of a tiny creature, hardly larger than a lamb. The sportsmen might have sighted a herd of grazing antelopes and be ready to move in for the kill when the silence would be broken by a series of piercing cries, loud enough to send the animals careering off in all directions. The alarm signal would be traceable to a little antelope, just over a foot high, known to science as *Madoqua* and more commonly, because of this characteristic cry, as the dik-dik.

The dik-dik is a dainty creature, living on its own, in pairs or in small family groups, and spending the hottest part of the day concealed in the thickets. If surprised by a predator or disturbed by a stranger it plunges deeper into the undergrowth, not by a direct route but making a wide, circuitous detour in an attempt to shake the pursuer off. This manoeuvre is not always successful for the little antelope marks its territory with heaps of excrement.

As dusk falls the dik-dik becomes bolder and before it is fully dark it will be busy searching for food, chiefly in the form of leaves and shoots, interspersed with a little grass.

Like the gerenuk, the dik-dik is a resilient animal, able to exist comfortably in the hottest, driest regions and capable of spending long periods without drinking.

Although the dik-dik is periodically hunted by leopards, jackals, caracals, cheetahs and many birds of prey, such predators have had very little damaging effect on the population as a whole. When the wild animal massacres were in progress, however, man the hunter was largely responsible for a sharp decline in its numbers. Using dogs to track the tiny antelope, man persecuted it for no obvious sporting or commercial purpose—its skin can be used to make leather articles, though of very poor quality—but simply because of the inoffensive creature's nuisance value.

There are several species of dik-dik, all of which look fairly similar, but some being smaller than others and some with a tuft of hair that may cover the short, ringed horns of the males. Individual behaviour does not vary much from one group to another. Thanks to protective measures the various species are once again fairly abundant, the population being concentrated in two major areas, one in East Africa, the other in South-west Africa. Identification is sometimes made difficult by the fact that the habitats of the different species tend to overlap.

The 'horse-goats'

The fringes of the bush and open woodland are the favourite habitats of the extremely beautiful antelopes belonging to the subfamily Hippotraginae. The name is derived from two Greek words literally meaning 'horse-goat' and it is easy to understand how 19th-century naturalists fell into the error of believing that in these creatures they had discovered something to be classified midway between the Equidae and the Bovidae. What misled them was the curvature of the neck, the shape of the back and

---

DIK-DIK

Class: Mammalia
Order: Artiodactyla
Family: Bovidae
Diet: leaves, sometimes grass

There are two genera and six or seven species of dik-dik. All are small antelopes with very large eyes, elongated face and slender limbs. Only one baby is born, extremely small, but with the same prominent eyes.

GUENTHER'S LONG-SNOUTED DIK-DIK
(Rhynchotragus guentheri)

Height to shoulder: 14–16 inches (35–40 cm)
Weight: 10–11 lb (4.5–5 kg)

The elongated muzzle is slightly curved, almost like a trunk. The male has small horns (about $3\frac{1}{2}$ inches long). The eyes and ears are large. A tuft of hairs on the crown of the head sometimes comes down over the eyes. The coat colour is greyish and the lower part of the legs reddish-brown.

PHILLIPS' DIK-DIK
(Madoqua phillipsi)

Height to shoulder: 12 inches (30 cm)
Weight: maximum $7\frac{3}{4}$ lb (3.5 kg)

Even smaller than the preceding species, this antelope has a greyish coat with strong reddish overtones on the flanks. In some individuals the coat has a silvery sheen.

rump, and the structure of the legs—all of which in combination give the animals a horse-like appearance. What should have given the true secret away—and the error was indeed later corrected though the generic name was retained—were the cleft hooves and the presence of horns, indicating that the splendid creatures were unmistakably antelopes, full members of the family Bovidae.

At one time these antelopes roamed at will over many parts of the continent but this distribution range was drastically narrowed as a result of insensate hunting, the chief objective being the magnificent, scimitar-shaped horns of the typical species—roan and sable antelopes. Nowadays these species are often found feeding together on the South African veld.

The roan antelope

One of the most characteristic sights of the veld is a small herd of ten or twelve roan antelopes (*Hippotragus equinus*) trotting along at a brisk pace, muscles rippling under the skin, their movements astonishingly similar to those of wild horses—a resemblance remarked by those who first gave them their specific name. Only the long, curving, ringed horns betray their true relationship.

The roan antelope is appropriately named for many colours go to make up its distinctive pelage, with grey and fawn predominating. The head, however, presents an even more extraordinary appearance. The thick hair of forehead and cheeks is black, contrasting sharply with the whitish markings of the muzzle and lip surrounds. The animal in fact looks as if it were wearing a kind of medieval knight's visor.

Before the white hunter made his unwelcome appearance in Africa there were many thousands of these antelopes; today there are probably more stuffed heads and pairs of horns hanging on the walls of museums and private mansions than there are living survivors of those wholesale massacres. The remaining representatives of the species are to be found in the more inaccessible parts of their traditional habitats in West, East and South Africa.

In the Upemba National Park, part of the Congo Republic, roan antelopes mingle in superb natural surroundings with elands, bastard hartebeeste, oribis, duikers and other species of antelope, for in this area shrub- and tree-covered plains merge with the last traces of the Congolese tropical forest. Because there is such a varied combination of vegetational growth the park provides exceptional conditions for zoological study, as has been attempted with notable success by the Belgian naturalist R. Verheyen.

The roan antelope is an extremely shy creature, standing about five feet at the shoulder and weighing over 400 lb. It is a territorial animal, restlessly on the move within its own domains. A typical herd may consist of one adult male in charge of a variable number of females and their offspring. It is this dominant male who protects his little group by bringing up the rear whenever the antelopes make their way from pasture to drinking place and back again to the sheltered spots where they customarily pass the night. But on the occasions when it is necessary for him to assert his authority—perhaps to prevent a member of the herd from straying

Geographical distribution of the dik-dik.

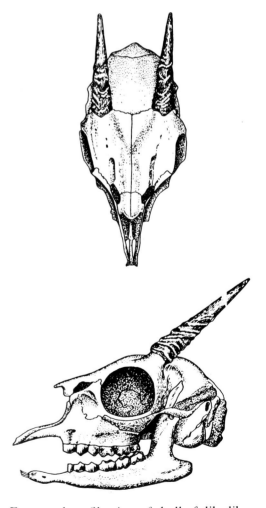

Front and profile view of skull of dik-dik.

too far in the wrong direction—he will make a quick dash to the head of the column, making threatening gestures that usually succeed in restoring order.

During the dry season, when most of the waterholes and streams are bone-dry, or when predators such as hunting dogs compel the roan antelopes to abandon their wooded refuges, the territorial males become noticeably more co-operative and tolerant towards their fellows. At such times it is not unusual to see up to 50 antelopes grouped together and sharing the same territory, under the leadership of four or five dominant males. Yet each leader remains responsible for the security of his own females and young, keeping anxious watch over them and persuading them to return to their own delimited zone at nightfall.

This happy and harmonious situation will change abruptly, however, as the mating season draws near. The first female to show clear signs of being on heat immediately attracts the attention of the dominant male, so much so that he has no eyes except for her and completely neglects his duties towards the rest of his herd. Deprived of his guidance, the other females and young promptly wander off to seek the protection of another adult male or the company of a group of young males.

It is during this mating period that the destiny of the previous year's offspring is decided. A male that couples with a particular female on nuptial territory will countenance the presence of her daughters but not her sons. The latter are unceremoniously banished from the herd, so that it is not uncommon to come across groups of unattached, stray young males which may perhaps acquire their own domains, though without a chief, hopeful of attracting into their midst females that have broken away from a herd temporarily deprived of a leader.

The courtship rites of roan antelopes are deliberate and painstaking. Verheyen has described how the male moves slowly, with hesitant steps, around his partner, trying to touch her rump, while she follows him with her eyes. Eventually her suitor manages to rub a hind leg against one of her front legs. After that he places his head on her hindquarters and rears up on his hind legs preparatory to mounting her, she immediately taking a few steps forward, momentarily frustrating his attempts. Nothing deterred, the ardent male resumes his courtship and each animal sniffs the other until the female, by raising her head, opening the hind legs and lifting her tail, signifies her consent.

For several days after coupling first takes place both antelopes stay together, the male keeping a close watch on the surroundings and on the movements of his companions. The honeymoon is terminated when the female refuses all further advances on his part. They then part company though remaining on communal territory, perhaps 200–300 yards apart. The female becomes noticeably more restless and nervous as the weeks pass and eventually both animals set out on a long journey, heading for the high grassy plains and then for the bush, where they pause long enough to enjoy the fresh vegetation. After a few days they press onward by way of deep valleys and rock-strewn hillsides, descending from the heights to lower altitudes. In due course they settle in a convenient spot where there is plenty of succulent food.

Facing page : The strongly-muscled body of the roan antelopes and their characteristic trotting gait once led scientists to classify them as creatures midway between horses and goats. The horns, however, present in both sexes, label these animals unmistakably as typical antelopes of the family Bovidae.

HIPPOTRAGINAE

Class: Mammalia
Order: Artiodactyla
Family: Bovidae
Length of head and body: 75–107 inches (188–267 cm)
Length of tail: 15–30 inches (37–76 cm)
Diet: leaves, shoots, grass
Gestation: 270–280 days
Number of young: one

ROAN ANTELOPE
(Hippotragus equinus)

Height to shoulder: up to 64 inches (160 cm)
Weight: up to 595 lb (270 kg)

Adults
Long, pointed ears. The strong, closely placed horns, ringed for four-fifths of their length, may measure over 3 feet, but the average is 26–30 inches. The coat colour is grey to fawn. There is a ridge of tough, stiff bristles below and above the neck. Head dark brown, muzzle and area between eyes and forehead white; ears tipped with black hairs. The female is slightly paler in colour than the male and her horns are shorter.

Young
Coat colour light-chestnut. Long ears with short tufts of hair. Facial 'mask' similar to adults.

172

Hippotragus niger
Hippotragus equinus

Geographical distribution of the sable antelope (*Hippotragus niger*) and roan antelope (*Hippotragus equinus*).

SABLE ANTELOPE
(Hippotragus niger)

Height to shoulder: up to 60 inches (150 cm)
Weight: up to 550 lb (250 kg)

Adults
Large head, long, pointed ears. Cylindrical, scimitar-shaped horns, ringed for almost the entire length. In the giant sable antelope of Angola they may be over 5 feet long. The hair is short all over the body apart from the throat and nape of neck which have long bristles. The coat is black on the upper part of the body, white on the belly, knees and the section of face from eyes to tip of muzzle. The females are smaller than the males and their coat dark brown with black reflections.

Young
Coat colour dark brown, the males acquiring the adult male black hue when sexually mature.

During the entire course of their travels the male seems to follow the female half-heartedly some distance behind, almost as if he were being dragged along in her wake. In Verheyen's opinion, this unusual behaviour may be a deliberate manoeuvre designed to protect her from danger.

When the time arrives for her to give birth the female plunges deeper into the woods to hunt for a suitable spot, allowing no other female of the species to disturb her. His duties over, the male now abandons her and wends his way back to his domains on the high plateau, either alone or in the company of other males in a similar situation.

Shortly after giving birth the mother loses her territorial instinct, running at random anywhere, followed by her baby and seeking the company of other females and their young. The little groups so formed remain together for several days only.

The newly-born roan antelope adopts a strange position for suckling, folding its front legs and kneeling down, then stretching out its neck to seize the teats. A little later, when the baby begins to browse, it kneels in exactly the same manner; and the identical attitude is assumed when it is old enough to join its companions in youthful games and simulated fights. In fact the young roan antelope has a pretty busy and energetic upbringing, for as soon as the horns show signs of sprouting, passivity gives way to almost incessant action, much of the day being devoted to half-playful, half-serious confrontations with its fellows. In the course of such 'fights' the rivals plant themselves solidly in front of each other, lowering their heads and making the best possible use of their tiny horns in attempts to twist their opponent's neck. Victory goes to the individual who first topples his rival and forces him to submit, the result often deciding which is to occupy a higher place in the social hierarchy. Later, when the horns are fully developed, these ritual combats reach a more violent and potentially dangerous pitch, with each contender striking at the other's heart. Wounds can be serious, though seldom mortal. Verheyen, nevertheless, has witnessed two fights to the death.

The denser parts of the bush are abandoned very soon after the newborn antelope commences to suckle, with the little groups of females that have recently given birth returning to their previous living quarters. The return journey may last anywhere from two weeks to three months, for since it entails much arduous travel across difficult terrain on the part of the babies it invariably proceeds in a series of very short stages.

While the females are slowly making their way home with their offspring the males await them with impatience. While their mates have been absent they have had to conquer new portions of territory or to expend energy defending old ones. If a group of females now strays into these private domains the owner goes through the same kind of ritual that he normally adopts during the mating season. Should any female be on heat she unhesitatingly accepts his advances, cutting herself off from the rest of her companions. But if no member of the group proves sexually responsive the dominant male takes charge and delays them on his territory until he eventually finds a willing partner.

In the Upemba National Park mating of the roan antelopes

may take place at virtually any time of year although the most favoured period is from the beginning of May until the end of August. Gestation lasts about nine months so that the majority of births occur between February and March.

Among the most dangerous enemies of the roan antelope are lions, leopards, cheetahs, hunting dogs and Nile crocodiles. The last have their greatest measure of success during the dry season when the antelopes come down to the river banks to drink.

The sable antelope, with its velvety black coat, white underparts and curious facial markings, is one of the most handsome of all African animals. Ruthlessly hunted in the past for its splendid ringed horns, the sable antelope will not hesitate to use them in self-defence.

The sable antelope

The sable antelope (*Hippotragus niger*) is an animal of stately build with a glistening black coat, a bristly mane on the neck and a magnificent pair of ringed, scimitar-like horns. Together with the related giant sable antelope (*Hippotragus niger varians*) it has a strong claim to be the most beautiful of all antelopes.

It is an exceptionally shy, nervous creature, the least rustle of leaves or snap of twigs being enough to send it scampering off into the thickets. It has good reason to be suspicious of intruders for in the eyes of many a hunter this handsome creature has ever been one of the most cherished prizes on the African continent, and the fact that it is notoriously difficult to stalk and capture is merely an added incentive and challenge. As a result the sable antelope has been mercilessly hunted and entire herds wiped out in many areas. Nowadays this indiscriminate hunting is severely restricted and every effort made to protect the survivors and encourage them to breed so that the species can continue to flourish.

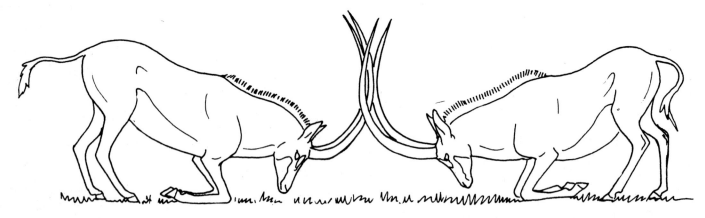

Two male sable antelopes may do battle to decide which of them shall be the leader of the herd. Both animals adopt the ritual kneeling position going back to earliest babyhood when first beginning to suckle. This attitude enables them to measure each other's strength without exposing either of them to the risk of injury, as might occur were they to charge in an upright position.

Facing page : Sable antelopes, often accompanied by oxpeckers, make regular journeys to streams and waterholes to quench their thirst. Circumstances permitting, however, they do not usually stray too far from their territories.

In need of even greater protection is the giant sable antelope, a splendid animal, similar in colour to the sable antelope but with larger horns, these sometimes measuring more than five feet in length. Hunting and poaching have brought this race to the very brink of extinction. A pair of horns belonging to the giant sable antelope is considered a very rare trophy indeed, and 'rare' is nowadays the operative word, the last few representatives of the once-abundant subspecies being confined to the game reserves of Luando and Cangandala in Angola.

The beautiful curving horns of the sable antelope may, in the collector's opinion, be no more than ornamental, but for the hunted animal itself they may be the difference between life and death. It is not only predators that have learned from experience to treat these impressive weapons with respect. An antelope wounded by a tribesman's assagai or a hunter's bullet will resist to the last drop of blood, waiting with head lowered for its enemy to come into range; and when two territorial males meet in ritualised battle, kneeling on their front legs, the clash of their tremendous horns can be heard for miles. Such fights may be incredibly violent for the male sable antelope is a powerful creature, weighing almost a quarter of a ton.

Typical herds of sable antelope are made up of a single male, three or four females and six or seven young of either sex and of varying ages. Each little group stations itself within its own piece of territory, often with natural boundaries such as two river tributaries or two hills. The animals move about incessantly inside their kingdom, always making use of the same paths in their comings and goings so that the whole area is crisscrossed with their well-worn tracks. In the rainy season, when torrential downpours erase all the footprints and the familiar scents, the animals continue to follow the identical routes every few days, which suggests an unusually clear visual memory.

In the course of the sable antelopes' everyday wanderings or in the event of an emergency which may send them streaming through valleys and across mountain ridges, the dominant male of the herd always brings up the rear; but whenever the group comes to a halt and begins to browse peacefully on leaves, shoots or fresh grass, he takes up a central position so that he can keep a careful watch on their movements and the surroundings in general. If, despite his precautions, the group is caught unawares by a predator, with no possibility of headlong flight, the leader bravely faces the foe, perhaps assisted by a couple of younger males,

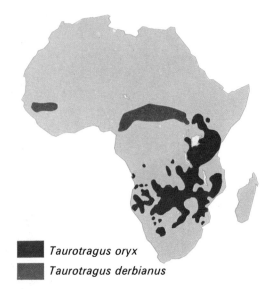

■ *Taurotragus oryx*

■ *Taurotragus derbianus*

Geographical distribution of the common eland (*Taurotragus oryx*) and giant or Lord Derby's eland (*Taurotragus derbianus*).

The eland (*above and facing page*) is the largest of all antelopes, distinguishable from other species by its size and the dewlap hanging from its chin. Elands live in herds, moving across open and wooded terrain in Indian file. Although both sexes have spiralled horns—much sought as trophies—they are peaceful, unaggressive creatures and have been domesticated in many areas.

creating a sufficiently long delay or effective diversion to enable the females and babies to gallop off to safety.

The coat colour of the young males, prior to their becoming sexually mature, is dark brown, like that of the adult females. But when they are fully developed the animals' coats take on the wonderful velvety black sheen that gives the species its name. Now that they are recognisably adult there is no further place for the males inside the group and they are promptly expelled. This does not necessarily pass without a protest but it is usually enough for the dominant male to adopt ritual attitudes of intimidation to ensure the instant departure of those who now feature as his most bitter rivals.

The moment the first female in the herd comes on heat the leader lays claim to her, going through the same programme of courtship as the male roan antelope. Once her consent is won and the two animals couple, they go off together, leaving the rest of the herd leaderless and the territory undefended. The other antelopes do not, however, straggle away but await the arrival of the first available adult male, who is immediately accepted as the new chief. It is very rare for the herd to abandon its territory unless alarmed and then only for a few days.

After a honeymoon period of a few weeks the female, now pregnant, returns to the herd and her companions. The former leader may by this time find his place usurped by a newcomer and will perhaps challenge him to open combat. Alternatively, he may decide to accept the situation and go off to find another compliant group of females, temporarily deprived of their own chief. Thus a herd may well see a change of leadership several times in the course of a season, a process made all the more probable by the continual movements to and fro of small groups of males and solitary individuals. These frequent fluctuations of fortune are of advantage to the health of the species as a whole, providing the maximum possible number of males capable of reproducing and avoiding genetic problems from excessive inbreeding.

When all the females are pregnant the males seem to lose all interest in the herd and often form nomadic groups of four or five individuals, leaving their mates and their previous year's offspring where they are. The new batch of births normally takes place, after a nine-month gestation period, during the rainy season, each female isolating herself from her companions. When the newborn antelopes are about two months old the dominant males return to take charge until the females are again ready to mate.

The elands

The eland (*Taurotragus*) is the largest antelope in the world and certainly the one that most resembles domestic cattle. Heavily built, with a short sand-coloured coat and a muscular neck with double dewlap, this powerful creature can nevertheless leap with something of the grace and ease of an impala; and unlike other typical cattle it is an astonishingly rapid runner, trotting across open plain and savannah with long strides—far lighter on its feet than the buffalo which, after all, is about the same weight. Over a short distance it can move at around 25 miles per hour.

ELANDS

Class: Mammalia
Order: Artiodactyla
Family: Bovidae
Length of head and body: 92–138 inches (230–
345 cm)
Length of tail: 20–36 inches (50–90 cm)
Diet: leaves
Gestation: 255–270 days
Number of young: one

COMMON ELAND
(Taurotragus oryx)

Height to shoulder: 76 inches (190 cm)
Weight: up to 1750 lb (800 kg)

Adults
Heavy and robust in build with a dewlap below
chin. Both sexes have horns, the lower half being
spirally shaped. Those of the female are longer
(44 inches). The hair is short and pale brown, the
coat displaying 5–6 vertical white stripes; there is
a dark band on the back of each of the front legs.

Young
Head rounder than that of adult; coat redder and
vertical lines less conspicuous.

GIANT OR LORD DERBY'S ELAND
(Taurotragus derbianus)

Height to shoulder: up to 80 inches (200 cm)
Weight: up to 2,200 lb (1,000 kg)

Adults
Larger than the common eland, with 13–14 white
stripes on pale brown coat. There is a large white
band at the base of the neck and the male's dewlap is dark brown.

Young
Same characteristics as common eland.

The two species of African eland are the common eland (*Tauro-tragus oryx*) and the giant or Lord Derby's eland (*Taurotragus derbianus*). The latter is the larger and heavier of the two, weighing almost a ton, with a reddish coat vertically broken by thirteen or fourteen white lines and with huge horns, well over three feet long, which are almost straight but spiralled at the base. The horns of the male are longer than those of the female and his coat colour is darker.

At one time the giant elands were numerous and well distributed in many regions of wooded savannah; but hunters in quest of trophies took their customary tragic toll and soon managed to reduce their numbers sufficiently to have them classified as rareties, nowadays confined to localised regions in Senegal and parts of Central Africa eastwards to Sudan and Uganda. Fully protected, herds consist of not more than five to ten animals.

The common eland, with a more southerly range, is less massively built and lighter in colour, the coat being streaked with five or six vertical white lines. The horns too are slightly smaller, though still just over three feet in length, and those of the female are in fact better developed than those of the male. The common eland too has been ruthlessly hunted in the past, both for the sake of its horns and its skin (which provides high-quality leather), and although more abundant than its larger relative is comparatively rare in many parts of its traditional haunts.

The common eland is a docile and intelligent animal, attempts to domesticate it having met with some success. Scientists have reported cases of hybridisation with domestic cattle and kudus.

In the wild, however, its notorious shyness and restlessness have made it difficult to study for any length of time. Much of our recent information about its behaviour is a result of Verheyen's researches in the Upemba National Park; and studies of the movements and habits of the giant eland have shown that the two species show close similarities in behaviour.

Elands normally congregate in herds which, when they are on the move, string out in single file, headed by a leader, generally the largest male. Each animal, however, appears to be continually on the alert for strange movements and sounds in the surrounding undergrowth. At the first hint of peril the elands break into a determined trot, their speed being such that the pregnant females and offspring are often left some way behind. In such a situation the leader returns to round them up and to urge them to move faster, but should repeated efforts prove unavailing he has no hesitation in abandoning them. All the signs are that he is more concerned with the protection of the herd as a unit, together with its healthy members, than with any single individual.

Despite their size and strength elands do not often engage in the spectacular and violent fights that are so frequently seen among other antelope species. In the mating season a male will pay court to a female in the midst of a mixed herd and will not even show any particular resentment should another male with similar intentions approach his chosen partner. In the exceptional cases of two male elands electing to do battle the opponents kneel down on their front legs and attempt to hook horns and twist necks. These quarrels, however, do not last long for they are peaceful by nature – a factor which has facilitated their domestication.

Courtship ritual is likewise of short duration and unspectacular. The male stretches his neck, extends his head and tentatively approaches the female who takes a few steps, jumps to one side and instinctively repulses him. He then circles her slowly, sniffing her and trying to rest his head against her rump. Although she refuses him repeatedly he continues to follow her, preventing her from feeding. Eventually, worn out by the chase, she gives in.

Once the females have mated they form separate groups with their previous year's young while the males, who remain in a state of sexual excitement for some time, wander off in search of other females, with whom they eventually couple.

In the Upemba park most of the births take place in June and July, after a gestation period of 260 days. The baby eland is alert and active as soon as it is born and within several hours is capable of trotting along behind its mother, already showing an instinctive grasp of the herd's normal Indian file formation.

Although elands clearly possess excellent hearing and scenting powers their eyesight is comparatively poor. This deficiency is one reason why they choose well-wooded terrain in which to conceal themselves when necessary.

Apart from man, who has persecuted them ruthlessly since early colonial days, the natural enemies of elands in the wild include lions, leopards, hyenas and hunting dogs.

The oribi

The oribis (*Ourebia ourebi*) are very small antelopes, barely more than two feet in height, widely distributed over the continent south of the Sahara and still fairly abundant.

These graceful creatures normally live in family groups of two or three, consisting of male, female and newborn offspring. Each such group has its own square mile or so of territory, the bounds of which are clearly marked by the male who deposits on branches and leaves an odorous substance secreted by his preorbital glands. Similar glands located between his hooves serve to taint the excreta of the female so that she can recognise his presence.

Confronted by an enemy, the oribis employ one of several rather unusual defensive ploys – rarely the same, even in identical situations. Sometimes they scamper away headlong through the tall grass but at other times, especially after a fire which may have scorched the grass of their normal habitat, they stretch themselves out on the ground, necks extended and ears flattened. The general effect, as they lie completely motionless, is to blend the sandy colour of their pelage with the yellows and browns of the burnt stubble and dust. Another tactic, when they suspect the hidden presence of a hunting dog or leopard, is to seek the immediate protection of a herd of antelopes larger and stronger than themselves.

When they are at full gallop, interspersing their run with a series of enormous leaps that may take them five feet off the ground, oribis may attain a speed of about 30 miles per hour. These high jumps above the level of the grass help to pinpoint a pursuing animal, but since they adopt exactly the same procedure when the grass is razed to ground level it is likely that such acro-

Geographical distribution of the oribi.

ORIBI
(Ourebia ourebi)

Class: Mammalia
Order: Artiodactyla
Family: Bovidae
Length of head and body: 37–44 inches (92–110 cm)
Length of tail: 2½–4¼ inches (6–10.5 cm)
Height to shoulder: 20–30 inches (50–60 cm)
Weight: up to 40 lb (18 kg)
Diet: leaves and grass
Gestation: 210 days
Number of young: one

Adults
Coat colour reddish with yellow reflections. Belly, inside of the ears, chin, lips and eye surrounds white. There is a circular bald patch below the ear. The male alone has horns, about 4½ inches long. Preorbital glands well developed.

Young
The coat provides effective camouflage when the animal is stretched on the ground. Growth is rapid and weight doubled within three weeks.

The oribi, a small antelope which may be distinguished by the black marks below the ears, prefers those parts of the bush where it can feed on both grass and shrubs.

batics are designed to attract the attention of the recumbent female and to warn her of impending danger.

The male courts the female, when she is on heat, by delicately touching her hind foot with one of his front feet, in a similar fashion to other antelopes on such occasions. From time to time he raises himself onto his hind legs and supports his body against his partner's rump; but although she may lift her tail, indicating that she is in principle ready to accept his advances, she continues to move steadily forwards so that he is unable to make proper contact. After twenty minutes or so of this foreplay the male stretches out his head and sniffs the female's genital organs, at which stage she permits him to mount her.

After a seven-month gestation period the baby oribi is born, usually between September and January. Any serious threat to her offspring is warded off by the male who attempts diversionary measures, the female and baby flattening themselves on the ground.

The recent sudden decrease in the oribi population cannot be blamed entirely on the activities of hunters and poachers. Maurice Burton believes that the powerful territorial instinct of the species may itself be a contributory cause, the antelopes invariably returning to their familiar domains even if the predator causing their departure happens to be still in the vicinity.

SUBDESERT STEPPE

BUSH

TREE-STEPPE

Dibatag

Soemmering's gazelle

Springbok

Wild ass

Oryx

Grévy's zebra

Cheetah

Beira

Gerenuk

Impala

Dik-dik

Black rhinoceros

Greater kudu

Baboon

Lion

Hyena

Jackal

Leopard

Elephant

Giraffe

Warthog

Buffalo

Gnu

Eland

Common zebra

Hunting dog

Sable antelope

CHAPTER 9

The black rhino: a timorous killer

Many wild animals have the reputation of being uncontrollably savage and dangerous, especially when they are hungry, when cornered by an enemy or when fighting to defend the lives of their young. Objective study usually reveals that such stories, even though purporting to be based on personal experience, are greatly exaggerated. Indeed, one of the most surprising characteristics of most of the animals of the African wild is their passivity and tolerance in all but the most abnormal situations.

The black rhinoceros (*Diceros bicornis*) has been singled out by generations of zoologists, sportsmen and story-tellers as possibly the most unpredictably short-tempered and violent of all African animals. If appearance were the sole criterion this would be quite credible, for it is a massive, ugly-looking beast and its huge horns hardly seem designed for peaceful purposes. Nor can its reputation for aggressiveness and blind obstinacy be entirely the product of make-believe. If such stories are so universally believed and widely disseminated in books and on the cinema screen, it is only logical to assume that there is a grain of truth to them. How then could this villainous reputation have been gained?

In its long course of evolution the black rhinoceros has had to overcome many hardships in order to survive. Because of its huge bulk it represents, both for predators and man alike, a source of rich food value. For this and other reasons it has been mercilessly hunted; but as a result of the creature's exceptionally poor eyesight it has never proved a real match for its enemies. Consequently it has developed into an unusually timid and suspicious animal; and rather than relying on headlong flight it meets danger with a face-to-face confrontation of its foe.

There is no proof whatsoever that when this enormous pachyderm lowers its head and charges it does so with any seriously

Preceding page : Subdesert steppe, bush and 'miombo' tree-steppe have their distinctive and varied growth of grasses, shrubs and trees, attracting animals with different feeding habits. Thus the more open regions are inhabited mainly by herbivores whereas the leaf eaters are naturally drawn to areas where there is abundant tree cover. The predators, in their turn, have adapted themselves to the conditions imposed by the various types of terrain.

Facing page : Although the black rhinoceros has the reputation of being a fierce, bad-tempered animal, it is not as dangerous as is generally believed. Its charge is as often as not a manoeuvre designed to dissuade an enemy rather than attack it, especially in the case of a female defending her young.

Black rhinoceros

White rhinoceros

The black and white rhinoceroses are slightly different in colour, though both are basically grey. Both have two horns but the upper lip of the black rhino is finger-like, suitable for grasping and tearing off leaves, whereas that of the white rhino is flat, consistent with the animal's grass-eating habits.

aggressive intention. On the contrary, as in the case of the African elephant, this is more likely to be a simple, instinctive act of dissuasion. Felix Rodriguez de la Fuente has described how he was once on the receiving end of an attack by a female rhino, though fortunately protected behind the steering-wheel of a Landrover. The furious animal, concerned for the safety of her youngster, ran full-tilt into the vehicle, her front horn smashing into its side and almost overturning it. But in three subsequent charges she came to a complete halt only a few yards from the truck, then turned and ambled quietly away, apparently satisfied that her demonstration had sufficiently frightened the strange predator for her to be left in peace. Certainly her noisy breathing, the heavy thudding of her sturdy feet across the dry plain and the menace of her massive head and murderous-looking horns should have been enough to deter the boldest of enemies.

The dedicated sportsmen, however, may have neither the will nor the time to make such a fine distinction between inhibition and naked aggression. An animal that weighs close on two tons and comes hurtling towards you at something like 30 miles per hour may well seem to be hell-bent on destruction. It is perhaps natural – and highly flattering to self-esteem – to view the situation as a critical matter of life and death; how admirably courageous in such circumstances to stand your ground and bring the rabid monster crashing to earth with a coolly placed bullet in the brain!

The truth is, however, that for anyone capable of handling a rifle, killing this lumbering, short-sighted creature is almost child's play, as statistics testify and as many an honest hunter will readily admit. Guided only by its sense of smell, the myopic rhino charges in a straight line towards an ill-defined target, usually allowing its antagonist plenty of time to leap out of its path and let it go plunging blindly on. Not that it is wise to be over-confident, for Dr Colb, credited with killing some 150 black rhinos, was once trampled by a badly wounded male.

Human nature being what it is, however, what more satisfying experience can there be for a red-blooded sportsman than to delude himself that he has risked life and limb to acquire such a highly prized trophy? After all, the photographic evidence is there for all to see – the bold hunter with his boot planted firmly on the head of his ferocious-looking victim – and how should his friends know that the enormous creature is really one of the most gentle, shy and vulnerable animals in Africa?

Despite the fact that the black rhino has been – and unfortunately still is – such a frequent victim of spear and gun (the Europeans are by no means the sole culprits), its range of distribution is still much wider than that of the related white rhinoceros and it is in fact found in many different types of terrain, including savannah, bush and wooded mountain regions. In some areas, such as the Hluhluwe game reserve in Natal, the habitats of the two species overlap but in general they are seldom found together, for the white rhino is a grass-eater whereas the black rhino is a leaf eater. This essential fact explains their distinguishing anatomical feature, namely the formation of the upper lip. In the white rhinoceros this is large and completely straight (suitable for cropping grass) but in the black species it is pointed, mobile and finger-shaped, ideal for grasping and tearing off leaves and small branches.

The sedentary habits of the black rhinoceros have increased its degree of vulnerability, for experienced hunters and poachers make themselves familiar with the animal's food requirements, favourite haunts and regularly trampled paths. Yet the very predictability of its routine has also made it possible for small groups to survive in sheltered, well protected sites close to cultivated land.

The behavioural pattern of the black rhino is at last being properly studied and recorded and a much-maligned animal seen for what it really is. The Canadian biologist John Goddard takes much of the credit for the most recent detailed information on the black rhino's life and habits, after his survey in Tanzania.

The cautious rhino

The black rhinoceros has adapted itself pretty well to life in hot, dry regions and though compelled to drink at frequent intervals it is not migratory in the accepted sense. The seasonal cycles dictate its meanderings within its own territory. When the rains come, for example, it is content to roam the open plain and savannah whereas in the dry season it finds its food in the neighbourhood of swamps and brush with enough tree cover to provide shade in the hottest hours of the day.

It is certainly more territorial than the white rhinoceros but even so boundaries are vague and ill-defined, with the living space of one rhinoceros frequently overlapping that of a neighbour.

The adult black rhinoceros can hardly be described as sociable, even towards its fellows, and shows a marked preference for a solitary mode of life. The reverse is true during babyhood and adolescence when it is closely dependent on the protection of its mother and the company of others of similar age. The female encourages its later independence by rejecting her offspring as soon as she discovers that she is expecting another. Should one meet a young rhinoceros on its own, when only a short while previously it was being carefully tended by its mother, this is an almost infallible sign that she is again pregnant. Her youngster is not necessarily condemned to solitude, however, for the chances are that it will soon team up with another animal in a similar situation or even find another female who will accept its presence. The search for a companion or foster-mother may nevertheless take some time and entail numerous rebuffs, the animal being forced to cover a considerable area of territory before eventually settling down.

John Goddard, who has made a study of the behaviour of black rhinos in Ngorongoro Crater and in the neighbourhood of the Olduvai Gorge, concludes that the female's apparently callous treatment of her young at a certain age and the fact that the latter is forced to journey far and wide may in fact be beneficial for the species as a whole, helping to spread the range of distribution and to avoid the risks of inbreeding.

Despite their solitary nature the adult males sometimes form small groups, although their social pattern is extremely variable.

Geographical distribution of the black rhinoceros.

BLACK RHINOCEROS
(*Diceros bicornis*)

Class: Mammalia
Order: Perissodactyla
Family: Rhinocerotidae

Length of head and body: 120–148 inches (300–370 cm)
Length of tail: 28 inches (70 cm)
Height to shoulder: male 68 inches (170 cm)
female 58 inches (145 cm)
Weight: 2,200–4,400 lb (1,000–2,000 kg)
Diet: vegetation (branches, leaves, roots)
Gestation: 450–480 days
Number of young: one

Adults
Normally less massive than the white rhinoceros. There are two horns in the nasal region, the first averaging 24 inches though sometimes up to 44 inches long, the second averaging about 10 inches, exceptionally up to 22 inches. The upper lip is furnished with a prehensile, digitiform appendage. The ears are rounded and mobile, the eyes small, the nostrils opening wide at the tip of the muzzle. The tail ends in a hairy tuft.

Young
The baby, weighing 75–90 lb at birth, grows rapidly and within a year is over 3 feet high.

Two rhinoceroses may establish what amounts to a more or less permanent relationship, while another animal chooses a different set of companions every day. Goddard never saw more than thirteen rhinos grouped together during the entire time he was studying their behaviour and they did not stay together very long.

Such mutual tolerance cannot always be guaranteed and it is not uncommon for a meeting between adult males to end in a quarrel, especially if they happen to be strangers. On the whole, however, considering that territorial boundaries are shifting and loosely demarcated, relationships within a community are reasonably tranquil, and animals that come into continual contact with one another do not display overt hostility. Two males, for example, may demonstrate their goodwill by rubbing heads together or against each other's flanks, and may end up by stretching out side by side in the dust, unsheltered and apparently unheeding of the searing heat of the sun, despite the fact that an acacia offers them refreshing shade only a few yards away. The two of them will lie completely motionless on their bellies and from a distance their bodies might well be mistaken for rocks. At intervals they will rise slowly to their feet for a good stretch and then resume their siesta. Such a display of cameraderie may last for several hours, ending only when one of the rhinos, for no evident reason, wanders away, leaving the other completely indifferent to his departure.

Despite such displays of neighbourly trust no meeting between adult males takes place without a great show of wariness, even diffidence on either side. The same caution is seen in encounters between the two sexes. The male approaches the female with short, hesitant steps, swaying his head or tossing his horn and emitting low rumbling noises. He stops from time to time to nibble the odd branch, while his chosen mate replies with similar sounds. Sometimes she charges her suitor and he is forced to dodge smartly out of her way. He then resumes his wary courtship until she abandons her aggressive behaviour. Should she be accompanied by a youngster the male may push it violently away, but the baby's urgent squeals will immediately bring the mother galloping up to defend it.

The black rhinoceros will be far less tolerant and peacefully inclined towards a strange rhino from another area. The rhinos that make their home on the wooded slopes of Ngorongoro, for example, are compelled to make long journeys to the swamps and salt-pans on the crater floor, where they come into contact with other rhino communities and receive a very hostile reception indeed. The intruder venturing into alien territory must expect to be subjected to violent assault, the incumbent male lowering his head and charging madly, uttering sharp, angry cries. In all probability the stranger will choose to remain silent and simply try to avoid the jabbing thrusts of his opponent's horns, eventually beating a retreat, followed for some distance by the victor.

The black rhinoceros, though not strictly a nocturnal creature, is most active by night and this is the time generally chosen to go out in quest of food. As day breaks a few individuals may still be engaged in this activity but by mid-morning all but the most energetic animals are at rest. The latter will be the exceptions to

Facing page (*above*): The black rhinoceros spends much of the hotter part of the day immersed in a muddy pool, this being one effective way of shaking off insects. (*Below*) Oxpeckers perched on back and rump also help to get rid of ticks and insect larvae that may have lodged on the rhino's skin.

The enormous head of the black rhinoceros is characterised by small eyes, two sharp horns and large, extremely mobile ears. These last, trumpet-shaped and bordered with stiff hairs, are often mutilated.

the rule who have spent the entire night asleep. The others prefer to rest during the heat of the day. John Goddard watched one rhino stretched out for ten successive hours, breaking its rest once every 90 minutes or so to exercise its limbs.

Towards late afternoon the rhinos indulge in their favourite recreation – mud-bathing. This, as we have seen, is not just a game, its function being to rid themselves of parasites, but they evidently derive a great deal of pleasure from the activity. It is amusing to see the enormous creatures cavorting in the mire, sometimes even rolling on their backs and waving their legs in the air. Then, as the sun sinks towards the horizon and the heat becomes less intense, they emerge from the pool, rub the mud and dust off against the trunk of a tree and waddle away to find their next meal, browsing in leisurely fashion until the morning.

Although they eat small quantities of grass during the rainy season, black rhinoceroses are essentially phyllophages, greedily devouring the foliage of all kinds of shrubs and small trees, apparently unbothered by the sharpness of their thorns. They are especially partial to the leaves of the whistling acacia and the proliferation of these trees in many parts of East Africa may be directly related to the gradual disappearance of the black rhino populations in those areas. Another favourite is the euphorbia, not really an African tree but one originally imported from India. The leaves of this tree furnish up to 25 per cent of the total food requirements of the animals in certain districts during the rainy season, and because of the large liquid content this figure may rise to as high as 65 per cent in the dry season. So greedy are the rhinos for these delicacies that after devouring everything within easy reach, including the bark, they rear up to grip the trunk with their front legs and rip the higher branches away between their horns.

Water is virtually non-existent during the dry season in many parts of the bush but the black rhinos are often indebted to the elephants at such times, for the latter, as already mentioned, dig deep pits with their tusks to tap the ground water under dried-up rivers and streams. On other occasions the elephants perform less of a service. In the Tsavo National Park in 1961 a severe period of drought was abnormally prolonged and the seasonal flow of the Athi river was reduced to a thin trickle. All the elephants in the park gathered on the river banks and virtually destroyed the vegetation. Starved and thirsty, some 200 black rhinos suffered a slow and painful death. A few were found still alive around one or other of the rare waterholes in the district but others had evidently drowned, lacking strength to climb out of the soft mud.

Problems of communication

If the vision of an African elephant is poor by the normal standards of the wild, the eyesight of the rhinoceros is even more feeble. It can in fact distinguish no object with any degree of detail unless it is very close to it indeed. Anything in the middle or far distance is in all probability no more than a blur. So the animal has to rely almost entirely on its excellent powers of smell to find its way around and to distinguish friend from foe.

John Goddard carried out an experiment to test this scenting faculty by collecting some samples of the dung of several rhinos and dragging a sackful along on a rope behind his Landrover. About 60 per cent of the animals involved in the survey recognised their own excrement and followed the traces, half of them defecating again on a pile of dung that Goddard had deliberately placed in their path. A similar number of animals followed the Landrover when the sack was filled with the droppings of rhinoceroses from neighbouring territory but only one in five stopped to defecate on the heap. When the excrement originated from rhinos with whom the control group had had no contact whatsoever, including some that lived a considerable distance from the home territory, only 30 per cent followed the trail and about the same number added their contributions to the pile.

The reader may be puzzled to understand why the Canadian naturalist decided to conduct this type of experiment. As we have seen in the case of the white rhinoceros, these creatures appear to be stimulated by the odour of the dung dropped by others of their species, so much so that they are driven to defecate on exactly the same spots, the heaps of excrement being recognisable guides to their everyday comings and goings. At one time scientists were of

The cattle egret or buff-backed heron uses its rhino host as a method of transportation, often fluttering about under its feet to catch insects disturbed by the huge creature as it moves around. It is not uncommon for oxpeckers and cattle egrets to share the same vantage point, the former spending more time pecking away at the rhino's skin and ears to dislodge parasites.

the opinion that these piles of dung were intended to mark the animals' territorial boundaries, but this was subsequently disproved. Had this been the intention the heaps would doubtless have been deposited around the fringes of the rhinos' domains and not, as in the majority of cases, inside the territorial bounds.

When a rhinoceros draws near to one of these dunghills it sniffs at it for a while and sometimes pokes it gently with a horn. It may even lie down on top of it and smear its belly with the dung. Then after defecating on the pile it will trample it and kick out with its hind feet. This is the way the creature labels the heap with its personal odour, enabling companions to identify the trail all over its territory. The same method is adopted by solitary rhinos wishing to maintain contact with their fellows, since they are unable to identify them visually at more than about 100 yards.

Such experiments prove quite conclusively that each rhinoceros has its individual scent which is recognised by its companions just as a dog is able to identify its master in a crowd, even in pitch darkness. The information conveyed to the brain by the olfactory stimuli is comparable to that which we receive by visual means.

The rhinoceros can, however, communicate vocally as well, with a range of sounds varying from soft and almost inaudible mewings to ear-splitting screams reminiscent of pigs being slaughtered. These noises all convey a distinct and recognisable message—of pleasure, anger or alarm—depending on tone and volume.

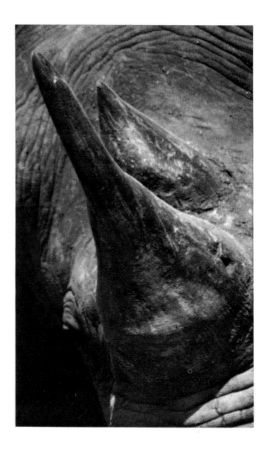

Birth of a legend

The rhinoceros is not faithful to a single mate. A male will couple with more than one female and conversely a female will mate with a number of different males. Rivalry over possession of a particular female will sometimes lead to violent feuds and when the victor eventually takes his leave with the partner of his choice the others often continue fighting fiercely among themselves.

Mating may take place at all seasons and the initiative seems to be taken by the female. The male follows her hesitantly for a considerable distance, frequently sniffing her urine to determine her degree of sexual responsiveness and diffidently approaching her, dragging one foot. The two animals then come close together, rubbing heads and hooking horns. Sometimes the male tramples the ground between the female's feet or stirs up the soil with his front horn and upper lip. After the sexual act itself, which may last a half-hour or more, the two rhinos often stay together for several months; alternatively they may part and go their own ways almost immediately or after a few days. Their behaviour at such times is in fact variable and quite unpredictable.

The gestation period lasts between 450 and 480 days. A month after giving birth the female may be on heat again but will not in fact be impregnated for at least a year later. Thus the minimum intervals between two successive births will be about 27 months, though Goddard's observations have revealed that the average is only one birth every four years. His conclusion is that this low birth rate is an adaptation consistent with the equally low mortality rate among the young of the species.

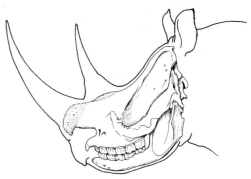

The horns of the rhinoceros are fibrous, with a keratin content, and have no bony core, being merely supported on the thickened sections of the nasal bones.

Facing page : Sixteen months after the prolonged act of copulation the female black rhinoceros gives birth to a single baby. She rears it with great care and affection for about two years, then banishes it when she again becomes pregnant.

The strong beak of the yellow-billed oxpecker is ideal for jabbing at the rhinoceros's thick hide and dislodging ticks as well as eliminating pustules.

Yellow-billed oxpecker
(*Buphagus africanus*)

Red-billed oxpecker
(*Buphagus erythrorhynchus*)

The baby rhinoceros lives with its mother and is jealously protected by her until she is ready to give birth once more. At this stage she not only shuns its further presence but actively chases her offspring away.

The characteristic behaviour of rhinoceroses when they mate has been the indirect cause of their own suffering. Because the sexual act may last for more than a half-hour a legend was built up in the Orient, without any sound foundation whatsoever, to the effect that their horns possessed aphrodisiac properties. As a result of this superstition the international traffic in rhinos' horns assumed unbelievable proportions and prices soared to ridiculous levels. The insatiable demand by dealers encouraged poaching on such a scale that in many regions the unfortunate animals were massacred almost to the verge of extermination. Official protection was not the complete answer for despite strict patrolling and severe penalties there was still sufficient profit at stake for poachers to risk breaking into national parks and reserves in search of these magically-endowed trophies. The problem remains unresolved so long as the demand continues.

For centuries past wealthy Orientals have paid exorbitant prices for the rhino horns which are seriously believed to prolong virility and restore sexual powers in old age. Until quite recently Mombasa and other ports in Africa would be swarming with merchants ready to pay almost anything for the miraculous commodity that would allegedly confer new life and vigour to ageing Indian and Chinese males. The phallic shape of the rhino horn and the apparently inexhaustible sexual prowess of the animals themselves provided all the evidence that was needed; and even if the middlemen themselves had some doubts as to the truth of the legend, which of them would be so foolish or selfless as to try to explain to an Oriental magnate, who had already spent a small fortune to acquire the stuff, that this drink consisting of ground keratin flavoured with wine possessed no power apart from its inherent alcohol content?

Oriental customs and beliefs, however strange they may appear to Western eyes, have had strange repercussions in the animal world. Cows and macaques, regarded as sacred, roam freely through the gardens, markets and temples of India, whereas the Indian, Javan, Sumatran and African white rhinoceroses have been hunted and all but wiped out as a result of this absurd superstition. In the past fifty years even the black rhino population has been alarmingly decimated. The naturalist C. A. W. Guggisberg, who lives in Kenya, has written a fascinating book entitled *S.O.S. Rhino*, drawing urgent attention to the massacres by professional hunters, themselves employed by unscrupulous dealers. In Oubangui-Chari one trader from Goa was finally arrested and charged with having hired native poachers to kill nearly 600 black rhinos for their horns, while another merchant was caught with a cargo of two tons of rhino horns in a single shipment.

The rhinoceros is normally well able to defend itself against any enemy that ventures really close. With its powerful horns, its natural speed and, above all, its habit of never turning its back on a foe, the huge creature is well-nigh invulnerable as far as ordinary predators are concerned. It is true that there have been instances of lions killing rhinoceroses but the victims have either been young or sick individuals. Hyenas too score an occasional success with a baby rhino, especially if the mother has had little experience in defensive measures. But man, with his specialised hunting techniques and commercial ambitions, takes advantage of the animal's wretched vision to kill it at long range. He is the only really dangerous enemy.

Winged allies of the rhinoceros

The black rhinoceros has friends as well as enemies in the wild, notably two species of birds that spend a large part of their lives perched on the pachyderm's back or hindquarters. The birds concerned are the oxpeckers and the cattle egrets, who perform a double function in helping to get rid of parasites and giving early warning of enemies that may be approaching against the wind and thus beyond the scenting range of their animal host. The cattle egrets do not perform the delousing, cleansing operation as efficiently as the oxpeckers, using the rhinoceros as a kind of mobile perch and as an ally in their hunt for insects.

The term 'symbiosis' is applied to those animals or plants that are attached to and dependent upon one another for survival. In the case of the oxpecker of the genus *Buphagus* and various African ungulates, including the rhinoceros, the relationship is not one of true symbiosis but more accurately 'commensalism' or simple food sharing.

Distributed all over the plains and savannahs, these birds live in flocks of six to ten individuals, perching together on the same anatomical portion of the host animal. The hosts include the larger herbivores—rhinos, giraffes, buffaloes, roan and sable antelopes—as well as many smaller ones such as impala and gazelles. All these animals appear to accept the birds' presence with a degree of indifference, despite the fact that the latter feed on the parasites lodging on their skin and play an important role in the animals' defence. In the case of the short-sighted rhino, for example, one or more of these birds may almost always be seen standing on its back or rump, flying off as soon as they spot danger and thus providing ample warning to their host—to the dismay and annoyance of many a poacher. The link between the bird and the huge beast is exceptionally strong, so much so that groups of oxpeckers will often stay for some hours in the neighbourhood even when the rhinoceros has been killed.

The oxpeckers are short-legged birds and their toes are furnished with strong hook-like claws, the middle one being shorter than the others—an unusual feature in the bird world. The broad, thick beak is very powerful and the lower jaw is almost as large as the upper. The dark wings and tail are long and pointed, permitting rapid flight.

Oxpeckers belong to the Buphaginae, a subfamily of the Sturnidae (starlings), which are in turn part of the order Passeriformes. The only two species are the yellow-billed oxpecker (*Buphagus africanus*) and the red-billed oxpecker (*Buphagus erythrorhynchus*). Both nest in the forks of trees, fairly high up, laying from

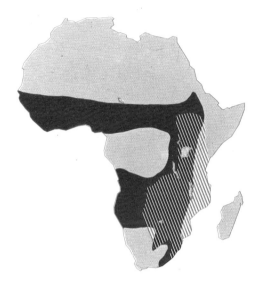

Buphagus erythrorhynchus
Buphagus africanus

Geographical distribution of the red-billed oxpecker (*Buphagus erythrorhynchus*) and the yellow-billed oxpecker (*Buphagus africanus*).

Class: Aves
Order: Passeriformes
Family: Sturnidae

RED-BILLED OXPECKER
(*Buphagus erythrorhynchus*)

Total length: 7 inches (18 cm)
Wing-length: $4\frac{1}{4}$–$5\frac{1}{4}$ inches (10.7–13 cm)
Diet: insects
Number of eggs: 3–5

Plumage predominantly brownish, belly yellowish, beak red. A circle of bare skin surrounds the eye. Strong tail.

YELLOW-BILLED OXPECKER
(*Buphagus africanus*)

Total length: 9 inches (22 cm)
Wing-length: $4\frac{1}{2}$–$5\frac{1}{4}$ inches (11.3–13.3 cm)
Diet: insects
Number of eggs: 3–5

Very similar to the red-billed oxpecker but slightly larger and with a stronger, yellow beak, tipped with red. No circle of skin around the eye.

Facing page : Oxpeckers make use of herbivores as hosts. These two yellow-billed oxpeckers have accompanied a roan antelope to a waterhole and take the opportunity to quench their own thirst.

three to five eggs. Those of the former species are bluish-white, those of the latter chestnut-blotched on a pink ground.

The red-billed oxpeckers have a truly astonishing method of getting rid of the ticks and blood-sucking insects that plague their host. With the persistence of woodpeckers they jab away at the rhino's skin, opening small wounds. The animal, though not appearing to be unduly concerned, reacts to the pecks with a gentle trembling. The blood serves as an irresistible bait for flies, mosquitoes and other tiny winged insects that form the bird's staple diet. It is doubtless this habit which has given rise to the widely held native belief that oxpeckers actually suck the blood of the host animal.

The cattle egret, otherwise known as the buff-backed heron (*Bubulcus ibis*), belongs to the family Ardeidae, part of the order Ciconiiformes. It is a larger bird than the oxpecker, slender and long-legged, though considerably smaller than other representatives of the heron family.

The cattle egret is also less aquatic in habit than most herons and is easily distinguished by its white plumage, buff or salmon-pink on the back (the head-crest has a clearly ornamental function during the breeding season), the naked legs and the slightly curved, pinkish-yellow beak.

This bird is a notable opportunist. Not content to sit on the back of its animal host and feed on ticks lodging on the skin, it hops busily around between the feet of the largest herbivores, missing no chance of snatching up any insect disturbed by the animals as they move (grasshoppers are particular favourites), as well as those that swarm about the heaps of excrement. In many regions the cattle egrets are valuable allies of farmers, helping to keep the domestic herds insect-free and healthy.

At breeding time the cattle egrets flock in their thousands to more temperate climes, making for swamps, rivers, streams and lakes to form enormous colonies. They build their huge nests, made up of innumerable twigs and branches, in trees. Dozens of them may often be counted, row after row, in the same tree.

Each bird lays four or five pale blue eggs. The chicks are entirely covered with down and are nidicolous. Several weeks after being hatched they are capable of independent flight.

The cattle egrets are migratory birds, the European population flying south in vast numbers to spend the winter in the eastern and southern parts of the African continent. In South Africa more than 10,000 nests have been counted in a single district and in Sudan and Ethiopia the population is even denser. The species continues to grow steadily in number and its area of distribution is becoming ever wider. At the end of the 19th century cattle egrets crossed the South Atlantic from Africa and reached the New World, following the coast northwards until they arrived in Canada or heading in the opposite direction down to the southernmost tip of South America. Their first landfall is believed to have been in Guyana and around the Gulf of Maracaibo, where large colonies are still to be found. From there many birds continued their migration westwards across the Pacific until they eventually reached Australia and New Guinea, a well documented example of a species extending its range naturally.

CATTLE EGRET OR BUFF-BACKED HERON
(*Bubulcus ibis*)

Class: Aves
Order: Ciconiiformes
Family: Ardeidae
Total length: 20 inches (50 cm)
Wing-length: 9–10½ inches (22.7–25.6 cm)
Diet: insects
Number of eggs: 4–5
Incubation: 23–25 days

Adults
From a distance the colour appears white, but at close hand, especially in spring and summer, the feathers of head, throat and back are buff or salmon-pink. In the breeding season the beak is yellow, red at the base, and the feet pink; in winter the beak and the feet are darker.

Young
They lack the head-crest; the beak is yellow and the feet greenish.

Distribution
Throughout Africa, with the exception of a part of Somalia. Found also in southern Europe, western Asia, south-western Arabia and the Seychelles, Comoro Islands and Mauritius. At the end of the 19th century colonies migrated to North and South America and thence to New Guinea and Australia.

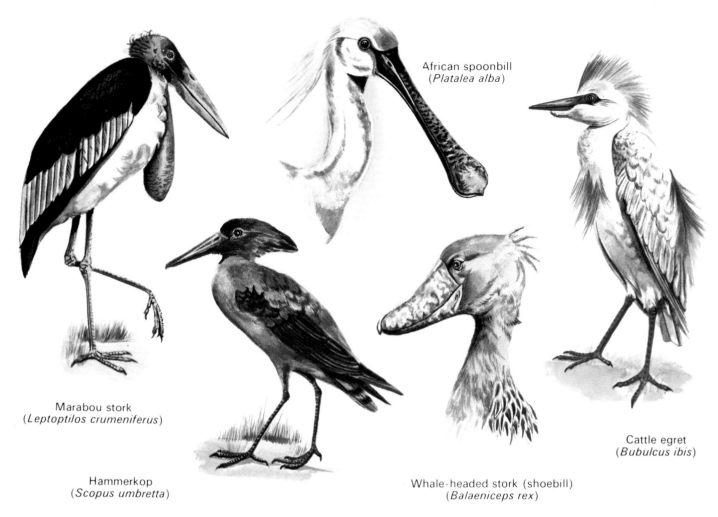

Marabou stork
(*Leptoptilos crumeniferus*)

African spoonbill
(*Platalea alba*)

Hammerkop
(*Scopus umbretta*)

Whale-headed stork (shoebill)
(*Balaeniceps rex*)

Cattle egret
(*Bubulcus ibis*)

ORDER: Ciconiiformes

The birds that belong to the order Ciconiiformes are medium- or large-sized wading birds. Despite the fact that they are fairly strong fliers they are equally capable of walking, thanks to their long, naked legs which terminate in four spreading toes. Although they are not typical water birds all have semi-aquatic habits, living in the neighbourhood of lakes, lagoons, swamps and rivers, where there is sufficient vegetation to provide them both with food and suitable places of concealment.

The order contains seven families which include birds with beaks of many different shapes and sizes, most of them long, straight and pointed, others broad, curving or spatulate. In every case the beak is ideally suited for capturing the type of food favoured by the species concerned, whether it be fish, frogs, lizards, snakes, insects or small mammals. Food gathering is also made simpler by the probing movements of the long, flexible neck, which is folded into an S-shape when the bird is at rest.

Although their flight is not remarkably rapid many of the Ciconiiformes are migratory birds, their large, rounded wings carrying them great distances in the course of their seasonal journeys, often at considerable altitudes.

Many members of the order, particularly those species belonging to the family Ardeidae (herons and bitterns), show closely-packed patches of so-called powder-down under the feathers of breast, flanks and rump. These are special feathers that grow continuously throughout the bird's life and are never shed. The tips are frayed, crumbling into a kind of powder which can be removed with the beak and used for brushing over the rest of the plumage and over any oily or greasy substances smeared in the course of feeding. The claw of the middle toe, which is equipped with a comb-like structure, is then employed for scratching and smoothing the other feathers and for removing the fatty globules soaked up by the powder-down. The number and position of the patches of powder-down are features used for classifying the Ardeidae into a number of distinct groups.

It is often difficult to tell the sexes apart but variations do occur according to season. The egrets, for example, are notable for their 'aigrettes' or ornamental plumes, which appear on the back, shoulders, head or breast during the breeding period. These beautiful thread-like feathers were much in demand by fashion houses at the beginning of the century and the craze led to widespread slaughter of the birds in many countries.

Most Ciconiiformes are gregarious birds which may form colonies of several thousand individuals. Their nests are generally large constructions, built in trees. The hammerkop, for example, chooses the fork of a strong branch for its enormous dome-shaped nest, which is divided into several compartments. This elaborate bowl of sticks and mud may be up to 6 feet in diameter and weigh about 170 lb. Other species prefer to build their nests on the bare ground, often among reeds.

The eggs of the various Ciconiiformes are usually uniformly coloured and are incubated by both parents for 25–30 days, depending on the species. The chicks, when hatched, are covered with down and are extremely voracious. All the fledglings are nidicolous.

Some representatives of the order are very large birds, such as the marabou or adjutant stork of Africa, which is over 4 feet in length. By contrast, the little zigzag heron is about the size of a thrush.

Most authors today subdivide the Ciconiiformes into seven families. The Ardeidae include the herons, bitterns and egrets. The Cochlearidae include the boatbill. The hammerkop belongs to the Scopidae and the shoebill to the Balaenicipitidae. Among the Ciconiidae are the storks, including the marabou and the jabiru; and the Threskiornithidae comprise the ibises and the spoonbills. The Phoenicopteridae include the flamingos.

Facing page (*above*): Typical representatives of the main families making up the order Ciconiiformes – marabou stork (Ciconiidae), hammerkop (Scopidae), African spoonbill (Threskiornithidae), shoebill (Balaenicipitidae) and cattle egret (Ardeidae). (*Below*) A group of cattle egrets or buff-backed herons in a tree – insect-eating birds that act as sentinels for many animals of the African bush and savannah.

CHAPTER 10

The underworld of termites and ants

A visitor from another planet completely devoid of insect life, who happened to make a landing in the East African bush, would be greatly perplexed at the sight of a miniature tower of tightly-packed red earth rearing 12–15 feet above the tangled, thorny undergrowth, and quite incredulous were he informed that this mound was constructed solely by tiny, hard-working insects known as termites.

We who live in temperate regions are familiar with various types of insects and may know something of termites by reputation; but since they are mainly tropical creatures it is probable that few of us have seen them in large colonies. It is therefore difficult even for us to accept the fact that these tall chimney-like structures could have been built by hordes of minute insects. To say that a termite bears the same relationship to the termitarium it has helped to build as a man does to the Empire State Building provides a rough idea of comparative size; but in terms of endeavour and achievement one would have to look back at the Egyptian pyramids, built almost entirely by bare human hands, for a closer analogy.

Although we sometimes call these mounds anthills, termites are not true ants (though confusingly and erroneously known as 'white ants'). They belong to the order Isoptera whereas ants are members of the order Hymenoptera. Distributed over all five continents, the origin of termites is uncertain but some species are believed to have existed as long as 300 million years ago.

Because they are underground creatures, rarely emerging into the sunlight except for nuptial flights in the breeding season, termites have been largely neglected by naturalists. It has long been known, of course, that they are capable of doing widespread damage to wood, paper and even metal; and many aboriginal

Facing page : This high, compact mound of red earth was built by a colony of termites – remarkable subterranean insects that play an important role in the ecological balance of plain and savannah.

In many of the national parks of Africa elephants have transformed the surroundings in the course of their seasonal wanderings by uprooting trees or denuding them of foliage. In these now-desolate regions the grass has sprouted with renewed vigour and grass eaters have to a large measure replaced the leaf eaters. The rhinoceroses at first benefited from the process, feeding on the leaves of broken branches and uprooted trees; but having exhausted the available foliage they were compelled to leave these inhospitable parts and seek areas where trees and shrubs were secure from the depredations of elephants. The dry wood abandoned by the animals is, however, utilised by termites which play a vital part in the life-cycle of the wild.

African tribes have for centuries recognised their edible qualities—not perhaps to everyone's taste. Apart from these superficial facts, however, there has been little enough interest shown in their activities or credit given to their complex social organisation, to their remarkable architectural skills or to the importance of the role they play in the natural life cycle of the wild.

It is thanks to termites, for example, that the soil is able to retain its fertility year after year, as a result of their continually stirring it up and permitting air and water to penetrate it without difficulty. In the world's temperate regions this vital work is performed in the main by earthworms; but in the tropics and subtropics it is the termites, ants and subterranean rodents which dig and aerate the upper layers of the soil. In addition, the accumulation of organic vegetable matter deposited by the termites inside their nests provides favourable rooting conditions for many species of trees.

The larger termites, known as Macrotermes, are responsible for the spectacular mounds that act as convenient landmarks on the savannah and in the bush; but most termites—and there are about 2,000 known species—construct nests which protrude very slightly above ground level or are completely concealed, though often of considerable depth and extent. One eminent entomologist has stated that in any part of the African continent, excepting desert regions, even if there is no external sign of a mound, a few spadefuls of earth taken at random will almost certainly turn up a teeming termite colony.

Inside a termite citadel

The mounds of earth that mark the sites of termites' nests are of many different shapes and sizes but they are nowhere so massive or numerous as in the African savannah and bush, particularly in those regions where elephants, in their search for food, have demolished most of the tree cover. Nothing is left in these parts save stripped trunks and branches yet none of this dead wood is allowed to go to waste. It provides food for millions of termites.

The only scientific way of examining a termite colony is to open up one of their mounds by hacking away with a pickaxe at the hard outer crust of mud. It is a delicate and painstaking process and some who have attempted it admit to feeling rather like explorers profaning the temple of some ancient tribe which has for centuries guarded its secrets from the prying eyes of the outside world. In a sense it is an unwarranted invasion of privacy to expose this shadowy empire to the sudden glare of artificial lights and the cold eye of the camera, its lens fixed on the trembling, swollen body of the termite queen, disturbing the busily scurrying workers and driving the soldiers into a state of suicidal frenzy.

A team of naturalists engaged in an investigation of this kind described how, as they began to attack the mound with their pickaxes, they heard strange echoing thuds from deep down which they could only liken to the sounds of individual grains of corn dropping onto a table top (and which they later identified as the impact of the hard heads of innumerable soldier termites against the walls of their galleries). The scientists continued to scrape away at the termite fortress and when they had removed a layer several inches thick found what they had been looking for – an enormous, teeming colony of insects. Some, almost pure white in colour, dashed madly from side to side, trying desperately to seal up the opening in the mound; a second group, amber coloured and equipped with strong jaws and sharp teeth, ranged themselves in formations that were distinctly aggressive; and a third type, of a deeper shade of brown, had iridescent wings.

The scientists delved deeper to the base of the mound and eventually uncovered the royal apartment – a small chamber housing a monstrous creature measuring some six inches long and over an inch thick. This was evidently the queen, looking like an enormous white worm, lying motionless while an army of diminutive servants bustled around her swollen abdomen. Nearby, her royal spouse, larger than the other termites but appreciably smaller than the queen, made clumsy attempts to escape. There was room for him to move about the cell but no way out through the very narrow galleries used by the ordinary members of the colony. The royal pair were in fact forever imprisoned inside the chamber walls.

The naturalists took careful measurements of the king and queen – the only members of the colony capable of reproducing – and photographed the complex layout of the miniature fortress, noting the prolific growth of fungi in certain places. They then removed their equipment, placing a moist piece of cloth over the breach they had previously made in the walls of the termitarium. When they took off this covering on the following morning they

Some termitaria are tall and prominent, others invisible below ground level. The latter are often built below those that protrude above the surface, as in this diagram, based on the work of Pierre Grassé, showing nests of various species in cross-section.

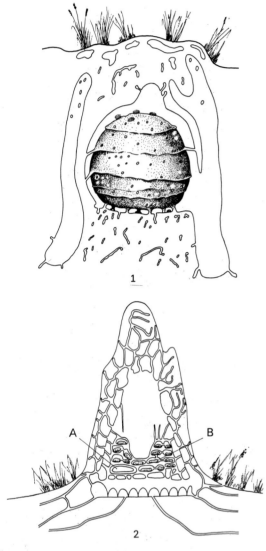

During the first phase in the life of a new colony of *Bellicositermes natalensis*, the nest is subterranean (1). As the colony develops, the mound grows larger and higher (2). Near the base of the termitarium is the royal apartment (A) and the underground 'gardens' (B) where nutritious fungi grow on the accumulated balls of chewed wood.

Facing page: There are about 2,000 known species of termite and the mounds in which the colonies live assume a wide variety of strange shapes and sizes, three examples of which are illustrated here.

were amazed to see that the gap had been almost completely repaired during the brief interval. The broad gash made by the pickaxes was now sealed by a new wall of earth, firm and still slightly damp. A week later there was hardly a sign that the mound had ever been disturbed.

In the short duration of their survey the scientists had been able to obtain a marvellous insight into the structure and constitution of a typical termite colony. They had seen the workers, soft and almost transparent, the soldiers responsible for the defence of the fortress, the immature nymphs later to embark on their nuptial flights, and finally the royal couple or reproductives – all playing a vital role in the remarkable caste system of this vast insect community. They noted with particular interest that the temperature inside the walls of the termite castle was quite unrelated to that of the outside world. Here, where not a ray of light normally enters and where there is not the slightest ripple of air, the temperature in fact remains absolutely constant twenty four hours a day, year after year. There is a greater percentage of carbon dioxide here than in the outside atmosphere and the humidity content is also very high, although in order to maintain this level the termites have to delve deep – perhaps several feet – into the phreatic zone below the water-table.

It is hardly surprising that such hard-working and fascinating insects should have commanded the attention of so many scientists and provided subject matter for a wide range of articles and books. The French biologist Pierre Paul Grassé made an especially valuable contribution to this field of knowledge as a result of his long years of research both in his Paris laboratory and in the wild.

Architects unparalleled

Termites are indisputably the most remarkable builders in the animal kingdom, and among some 2,000 different species it is not surprising to find an almost unlimited variation in the shape, structure and complexity of their nests. The termites of the genus *Bellicositermes* are responsible for enormous mounds up to 20 feet high and about 100 feet in diameter at the base, inside which there may be several millions of individuals. Other species – and by far the majority – construct much more modest edifices, some of them barely appearing above ground level and housing only a few hundred insects; and there are extreme instances of certain species which dig galleries that lack all semblance of order and planning, the termites having apparently lost the ability to work in a coordinated fashion.

As a general rule the termitarium may contain four types of chamber. In the centre is the cell occupied by the king and queen, founders of the colony, where eggs are guarded and some scraps of food kept, alongside pellets of chewed wood on which fungi sprout. From this royal apartment a maze of galleries leads directly to the 'larders' where most of the food is stored. The third type of chamber is not always present nor is it used with any regularity except as a kind of corridor, for it consists simply of an empty space around the nest, isolating it from the supporting

external walls. Finally, in certain structures, there are little tunnels which punctuate but do not actually bore right through the walls themselves.

The most perfectly constructed nests are certainly those that belong to the insects of the genus *Apicotermes*. These are dug below ground level and since there is no external sign of the sites they are difficult to locate. They are about the same size and shape as an ostrich egg and are divided into a series of horizontal compartments, supported by pillars. Along the main axis each level is open, with a ramp leading from one to another. A circular gallery connects the various chambers with the outside wall of the nest. There are smaller linking paths in this network of communications so that the termites can move freely from level to level or through any of the compartments, without needing to take a central route; and additional tunnels snake out to link the entire construction with others of identical form, all of which combine to make up a miniature city.

The underground gardens

A notable feature of the central chamber in many termitaria, especially of the subfamily Macrotermitinae, is the presence of balls of masticated wood which stimulate the growth of certain forms of fungi. These globules are darkish in colour, of a spongy texture and sometimes as large as a human head. For some time their nature and function were incorrectly identified, for they were believed to be mere accumulations of excrement. Closer study later revealed them to be closely packed balls of pulped wood, joined together to make up a single mass of material.

Soon after a new termite colony is established, the workers set about constructing these balls by patiently chewing slivers of dead wood until they have reduced them all to a rounded mass of pulp. These are then placed side by side until they form one continuously growing heap. In the warm, humid atmosphere of the nest they provide ideal germinating conditions for the fungi. The latter do not appear to be consumed in any but small quantities but are believed to furnish an important source of vitamins and thus to play a part in termite growth. In addition, these subterranean 'gardens' help to keep the interior temperature constant (about 30°C or 86°F) by absorbing and releasing moisture.

Workers and soldiers

One of the most fascinating characteristics of a termite community is its elaborate caste system in which the various individuals not only perform distinct tasks but also look completely different, so much so that an unskilled observer might mistake them for separate species. The survival of any species in fact depends upon each individual undertaking the work for which it is best equipped. Such a division of labour is strongly in evidence among social insects–termites, ants, wasps and bees. In the termite empire there are three distinct castes–the inexhaustible reproductives, the versatile workers and the aggressive soldiers. The first are directly responsible for providing the colony with

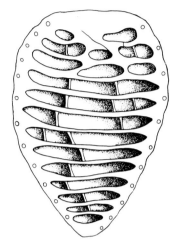

The nests of the genus *Apicotermes* are miniature marvels of town planning. About the size and shape of an ostrich egg, each is made up of interlinking compartments, ramps and galleries, permitting the termites to move about at will. The nests are joined together by tunnels to make up a single termitarium.

Facing page : In many of Africa's national parks elephants in quest of food have destroyed large tracts of woodland and forest. Termites flourish on the dry dead wood and their huge mounds are characteristic features of the scorched plains and savannahs.

Geographical distribution of termites.

The typical worker termite is a white, soft-bodied, transparent insect, without wings.

new members, the second with essential building and feeding duties, the third with defending the fortress against intruders.

The workers have soft white bodies and do not possess wings. It is they who construct the nest, look after the eggs and larvae, and supply food for the reproductives and soldiers. Yet although they themselves have a larval appearance, their powerful jaws, so important for chewing food, are also useful supplementary weapons for the common defence of the colony.

In contrast to many other insect communities, both male and female forms are found among the workers, though the genital organs are much reduced and are not used for reproductive purposes. Because of this it is very difficult to tell the sexes apart. The eyes are either very simple or entirely absent—a common characteristic of animals that live permanently, or for extended periods, in darkness.

A worker meeting another member of the colony, whether it be one of its own caste, a soldier or a reproductive, will lick the other insect's body for quite some time. This is not a ceremonial ritual or a matter of hygiene, as was once believed, but is connected with the maintenance of the caste-structure (see page 214).

The soldier caste too includes both males and females, and in their case the task of differentiating the sexes is even harder. They are, however, easily distinguished from the workers both in colour and anatomical structure, and are additionally aggressive and quick-tempered. Although their powerful jaws are apparently not enough to frighten off an aardvark or an aardwolf (these mammals devour as many insects as are available, without seeming to pay the least heed to the furious offensives of the soldiers), they are sometimes effective against their most ferocious enemies—the army ants.

The members of the soldier caste have a particularly well-developed head which in some individuals may be larger than the rest of the body. In an emergency a soldier termite may thus be able to block up the entrance through which invading ants are swarming. The dark head covering is also unusually tough and solid, and it is the knocking of thousands of tiny heads against the gallery walls that produces the peculiar sound remarked upon by the naturalists digging their way into the mound. It would be tempting to interpret this as an alarm signal but apparently such is not the case, since other members of the community seem to behave in exactly the same manner. Because of their hard armour-casing, however, it is only the soldiers that produce an audible sound in the process.

Conventional and unconventional

All the soldiers, whatever their species, are equal in rank. They differ slightly in structure from species to species. The more distantly they are related the more they differ anatomically. But in general there are two types of soldier, the first furnished with what might be termed conventional weapons—such as many animals possess—the second, known as nasutes, endowed with something more unusual. The former make use of their jaws and teeth, some peg-like, others as sharp as blades or serrated like saws. In the nasutes, however, the jaws are reduced but the front part of the head is elongated into a kind of trunk, with a highly-developed frontal gland at the tip. The termite equipped in this manner resorts to a type of chemical warfare, squirting out a viscous fluid for a distance of several inches which is capable of killing the most ferocious ants. Such a lethal natural weapon is a tremendous protective asset for a social insect such as the termite, for it enables the creature to kill without coming into actual physical contact with the adversary and thus to run no risk of being wounded. In the wild a serious injury represents a dire handicap for any animal, large or small, but for termites a wound is invariably fatal for if it is not killed by the enemy it is promptly devoured by its own companions.

The physical equipment possessed by the soldiers qualifies them for the specialised duty of defending the colony against enemies but it prevents them from undertaking any other responsibilities whatsoever. They are therefore obliged to rely on the worker caste for their sustenance and survival. The soldiers lack any food-gathering instincts and are incapable of chewing wood. If a soldier termite is isolated from its fellows – even if artificially provided with food – it will quickly die, making not the slightest effort to feed itself. Such inaction seems to spring from sheer apathy rather than physical incapacity. When a soldier decides that it wants to eat, it rubs the head of a worker with its antennae or cheeks, these movements evidently stimulating the other insect to regurgitate tiny morsels of food into the hungry soldier's mouth. Alternatively, the soldier may use its antennae or front feet to caress the tip of the worker's abdomen, which will likewise cause the latter to eject particles of food from the digestive tract through the anus.

In certain species the soldiers cannot even be counted on to perform their own defensive duties efficiently. One reason for this is that they may be relatively few in number compared with the workers, and another that their aggressive instincts are exceptionally poorly developed.

The winged reproductives

The termites which are capable of breeding are known as reproductives. Whereas the community is always well provided with workers and soldiers, the winged reproductives are not in evidence at all seasons for they leave the nest shortly after they are born. They swarm out together in short dispersal or nuptial flights, then separate into pairs, each of which goes on to found a new colony.

The insects do not copulate during actual flight but only when they have once more alighted on the ground. During the sexual act the two pairs of wings split close to the base and then drop off. The first activity of the reproductive couple is to construct the royal apartment in which they are destined to spend their lives. This may take 24–48 hours. Both insects then enter an inactive phase, in the course of which they lose their antennae.

In contrast to other social insects, termites continue to fertilise and be fertilised many times throughout their life cycle. Prior

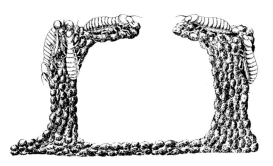

Termite mounds are constructed with the utmost care and precision. Since the insects cannot see what they are doing, however, the way in which they achieve their architectural results is a complete mystery.

The soldier termites, with head the same size as the rest of the body, are indolent creatures – sometimes inefficient even in their designated role of defence – and wholly dependent for their food on the workers.

The queen spends almost her entire life confined to her apartment in the base of the termitarium.

Facing page : The queen, who lays eggs at the unbelievable rate of 8,000-10,000 a day, is an enormous creature with a hugely distended abdomen which prevents her from moving. She is surrounded by a horde of workers responsible for providing her with food and removing the eggs as soon as they are laid.

to each act of sexual union they caress and lick each other's body, especially the head. The two insects then bring their abdomens together, the male lying on his back beneath the female.

The male, although nominally king of the new colony, is not nearly so imposing a creature as his mate. Apart from his testes, no other part of his body is substantially different from that of an ordinary worker, nor does he increase in size. The queen, however, soon shows phenomenal growth, her abdomen swelling as a result of the over-developed ovaries. In the *Bellicositermes natalensis* species, for example, the queen expands from a modest inch or so to the enormous length of ten inches.

On the first occasion only a limited number of eggs are laid, but after that the queen becomes converted into what can only be described as an automatic egg-laying machine, producing the incredible number of 8,000–10,000 eggs *every day*–almost one per second, or over a quarter of a million each month!

A certain proportion of the first batch of eggs is sometimes devoured by the royal couple. The rest, after a period which, in temperate regions, varies from 30–90 days, break open in the form of a T-crack under the internal pressure of the larvae, and in this way the new members of the termite community are born.

At a later stage a team of workers surround the queen and remain in constant attendance. By this time she is so enormous that she can do nothing but lie without moving and wait for the obedient workers to tend to her needs. Some of them place protein-rich droplets of saliva in her mouth so that she can keep up her dizzy round of egg-laying. Others roam around her distended belly, licking the clear fluid which is emitted from her anus and which moistens the eggs the moment they are laid. The latter group of workers also carry the eggs between their jaws into other chambers of the nest. Whenever they see larvae struggling to break the egg membranes they hurry towards them and begin to lick them; then they take up the larvae in their mouths to deposit them in yet another corner of the nest.

The king is permitted to live close to the queen and is provided with the same type of food, although in smaller quantities. His sole duty is to fertilise the queen at periodic intervals, but nobody knows how often this activity is undertaken or how much time elapses between each union.

Termites, like all insects, are invertebrates whose body is encased in a chitinous layer or exoskeleton made up of segments which are articulated to permit the insects to move but do not allow them to develop. In order to grow they have to go through a series of moults in the course of which they gradually take on their adult appearance. During these various phases of skin-shedding they spend several days on end without feeding, lying on their sides, sometimes with folded legs. Eventually the exoskeleton cracks in a T-shape from the back of the head right down the middle of the abdomen. From this opening in the old skin emerges an insect provided with a new skin. This takes several days to harden and during that time becomes stretched to accommodate to the new dimensions of the animal.

The final stage of development may last for some hours, the legs and antennae being the last parts to emerge from the old

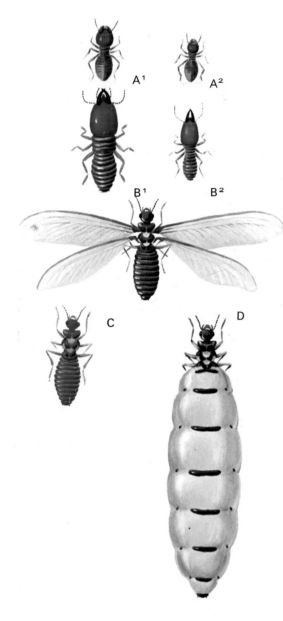

Three distinct types of insects make up the complex caste system in a termite colony. The male and female workers (A¹, A²) and soldiers (B¹, B²) are sterile and the sexes difficult to tell apart. The king (C) and queen (D) are the reproductives, provided with wings that drop off after the nuptial flight. The king remains about the same size as a soldier, but the queen grows to vast proportions.

enveloping cover. Before the new layer becomes solid the termite can only move about clumsily and is repeatedly licked by its companions. The discarded skin is in the meantime seized upon by workers, who promptly eat it.

The mystery of the caste system

Among certain types of social insect, such as bees, the caste to which each individual belongs is fixed from the moment of birth. It used to be assumed that this was also true of termites but it has now proved not to be the case. Scientists do not really know how some individuals develop into workers while others become soldiers or reproductives, but the caste system (otherwise known as social polymorphism) seems to depend, in their case, upon differences in diet.

The termite community is made up of distinct castes which vary in total number but which appear to be linked to one another in more or less fixed proportions. In the event of the numerical balance being radically altered (by the deaths, for example, of a large body of soldiers or workers), the equilibrium is soon corrected. Many insects that have not attained adult form (the nymphs) somehow undergo a modification in development so that they take on the typical characteristics of the caste which is temporarily in short supply.

This extraordinary ability of the termite colony to replace its personnel is not confined to workers and soldiers, for if the king or queen (or both together) should accidentally disappear, other individuals attain sexual maturity very rapidly, whilst still retaining external juvenile characteristics. This phenomenon, known as neotony, is not an exclusive feature of termites but is also found in higher orders of animals.

These replacement or secondary reproductives are at first still able to feed themselves and to chew wood, but in due course they too end up by becoming utterly dependent for their sustenance on their retinue of workers. Like their predecessors, the new reproductives seem to exercise inhibitory authority over their rivals so that there is never more than one secondary reproductive pair to a nest. It is not known how this regulating mechanism works. Sometimes more replacements than are necessary are produced. In these circumstances certain species show themselves to be more tolerant than others. The latter accept the presence of only one potential new king and queen, killing and eating the supernumeraries.

The great adventure

No event in the life of termites presents a greater challenge than the foundation of a new colony. Apart from certain species that venture out by night or in dull weather to look for food, the great majority of these insects never abandon their shadowy subterranean world except to form new communities.

During the days immediately preceding the dispersal flight, the future kings and queens shed their final layer of skin and appear with two pairs of wings. Simultaneously, the workers and soldiers

enter a phase of frenzied activity in preparation for the critical moment when the walls of the termitarium are to be pierced in order to allow the winged reproductives to make their departure. The hard-working members of the colony busy themselves in digging tunnels and are at all times surrounded by the soldiers, some of which go outside into the corridors to mount guard. Those termites which have gone through the final stage of their metamorphosis show no sign of movement until the very last moment, when they bestir themselves for their great adventure.

Eventually the advance guard head for the openings in the nest and swarm out in tight formation, with males and females present in more or less equal number. Since, under the stimulation of climatic factors, this event occurs at exactly the same time in all the termite nests of a particular region, the air is often black with clouds of flying insects. Nevertheless, the different groups of termites do not mingle, nor does their nuptial flight take them more than a couple of dozen yards. While some termites are still swarming out of their fortresses, others have already descended to the ground. It may be two or three hours before the whole flight is completed.

As soon as they touch the ground the reproductives run frantically from side to side and whirl around in circles, with wings outspread. The moment the wings come into contact with a blade of grass, a stone or some other obstacle, they drop off. Some of the females perch on a stem, heads down, nervously fluttering their wings until they are discovered by a male; those of other species stay in the same position but with wings open and unmoving.

Small, wingless worker termites, ever busy, surround a winged reproductive.

The first task of the mated male and female, now wingless, is to construct the royal chamber in which they will spend the rest of their lives. Sometimes more than one male follows her into the ground.

When two individuals of the opposite sex meet, they touch each other with their antennae and rub heads until the female, by describing a semi-circle, signifies her readiness to embark on the long journey with her mate. The pair of termites may then wander for some hours or even several days, the male keeping his mouth close to the female's abdomen at all times. The male eventually digs a small cavity and it is here that their union takes place.

Not all termites behave precisely in this manner. Those of the genus *Pseudacanthotermes*, for example, direct their dispersal flight towards the setting sun. While they are still aloft the male attaches himself to the abdomen of his mate, sheds his wings and spends the rest of the journey tightly clasped to her body.

Other species choose a completely different method of founding a new colony. A long column of workers, carrying in their mouths eggs and larvae, flanked by soldiers and sometimes accompanied by winged termites (and even including the incumbent king and queen), leave the citadel in broad daylight. They wander about at random and as the great army advances the insects split up into smaller groups, each of which eventually creates a new colony.

The amazing feature of this once-in-a-lifetime event is the way in which the different communities synchronise their flights, seeming to know instinctively from deep inside their dark fortresses that conditions outside – temperature, light and humidity – are exactly right. This clairvoyance still baffles the scientists.

The most dangerous moment in the termites' lives is when they leave the nest to embark on their dispersal flights. These often take place shortly before a storm and a sudden downpour may take the winged insects unawares and prove fatal for many of them.

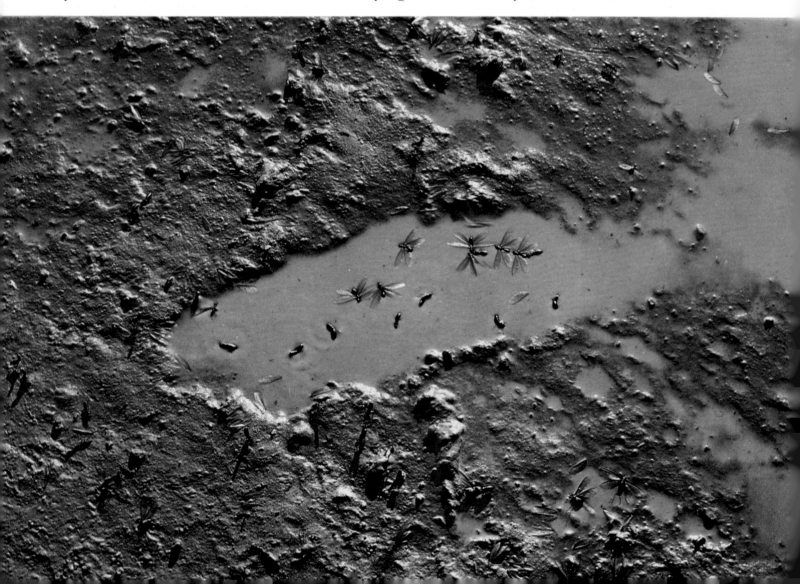

A collective stomach

The king and queen, the soldiers and the larvae, are wholly dependent upon the workers for their food. As Maurice Maeterlinck wrote in *La Vie des Termites* (1926): 'Only the workers know how to eat and digest; they act as a kind of collective stomach and intestines for the community.' This continuous process of transferring food from mouth to mouth is called trophallaxis and whereas it is practised by other social insects, it is among the termites that it is most highly developed.

Although it is the workers alone that nibble away at dead wood, they are incapable of digesting it unaided. This is done by colonies of specialised Protozoa, single-celled animals living in a pocket in the hind-gut, which break down the cellulose into simple, easily assimilable elements. These micro-organisms are not present in their bodies at birth but appear as soon as the termites begin to feed. The king and queen, being unable to provide themselves with food, lack these intestinal Protozoa.

This continual food-exchanging activity, in which all members of the colony share, creates a vital link between the various castes and transforms the termitarium into one large, highly efficient social unit.

Termites, like ants and bees, have the reputation of being untiring and determined workers, as has been attested both by direct observation and in countless stories and legends. It is therefore interesting to learn that scientists who have watched termites building their fortresses under laboratory conditions suggest that the insects do not in fact work quite as hard as is

Although impala and termites are apparently unrelated they are linked in the ecological system of the bush. The impala (preyed on by the leopard) eats acacia leaves and the seeds found in its excrement germinate to form new trees on which giraffes browse. The dead wood provides food for the termites which are in turn eaten by aardvarks.

The exchange of food – known as trophallaxis – is of vital importance in keeping a termite community healthy.

The ferocious army ants feed on small vertebrates and invertebrates and few creatures can withstand the concerted attacks of these nomadic hordes. Termite colonies are sometimes destroyed in their relentless search for food and in the upper picture victorious ants carry away a dead termite in their powerful jaws.

generally believed. They seem to spend a good deal of their time licking each other and exchanging 'kisses', bringing their mouths close together. When entomologists first watched termites engaging in these long, apparently ecstatic bouts of bodily contact, they assumed it was all a matter of simple hygiene. It was only later that they realised that the insects were licking the secretions on each other's bodies or that in the kissing process one was regurgitating and the other ingesting part of their stomach contents. The process was also seen to be essential for maintaining the caste-balance within the colony.

The king and queen, so long as they remain healthy and vigorous, are now known to secrete substances which prevent the developing larvae from becoming fully-fledged reproductives. These secretions also have their equivalent among the workers and soldiers, the latter castes having similar methods of controlling their numbers so that the correct proportions are preserved.

The substances that play such an important role in keeping the termite population properly balanced are called pheromones. In the event of the king and queen disappearing from the nest this hormone no longer circulates through the community by means of normal food exchange and the developing nymphs become winged reproductives. Similarly, if a large number of soldiers are killed in an engagement against army ants, the hormone concentration within the caste is reduced and more soldiers are created.

Five thousand species of ants

Ants, like termites, are social insects and can more than match them in number and range of distribution. They too have a highly complex social organisation but their nests consist of a king and a queen, soldiers, and both male and female workers. Their community is a virtual matriarchy in which the males have no other function but to fertilise the females.

In a typical ant colony there may be one or more fertile queens and numerous workers of varying size that are normally sterile. Once or twice a year winged ants of both sexes swarm out in nuptial flights and drop to the ground where each female proceeds to mate with several males. These queens live for some years and preside over the formation of new colonies, whereas the males die after a couple of days. Some months after the new community is founded the first workers are born. They are responsible for all manner of duties and their life-span too is short, never more than three or four months.

With over 5,000 known species, ants naturally display considerable variation in appearance, size, behaviour and social organisation. Some are extremely primitive–ground-dwelling creatures that hunt and devour other insects; the more highly developed species live in trees and feed on substances secreted by greenflies, cochineal insects and other parasites, while intermediate groups are omnivores and granivores.

The terrible army ants

From the point of view of their relationship with termites, the most interesting types of ant are those belonging to the subfamilies Ponerinae and Dorylinae, commonly known as army ants. The former are sedentary insects that build fairly uncomplicated subterranean nests and live in colonies of a several hundred individuals. The latter are the only known nomadic social insects, also called safari ants. Groups wander far afield in search of food which consists of small vertebrates and invertebrates. The columns never call a halt to their relentless onward advance except to lay their eggs and hatch their larvae. The workers then take up the newborn ants in their mouths and the march continues.

In the event of a column of safari ants coming across a colony of termites which may have abandoned their refuge under cover of darkness, the former launch a fierce attack and quickly exterminate the termites before the soldiers of the rival camp have time to marshal their defences. The bite of these terrible ants is extremely painful, even for humans, and once their jaws have snapped shut around their prey, nothing can shake them loose.

A concerted onslaught by army ants against a termite colony is a dramatic and bloodthirsty affair. The invaders swarm in by the openings used by the reproductives for their nuptial flight or those excavated by the workers venturing out in quest of food. Once the ants are inside the subterranean fortress a merciless battle ensues in the darkness. The better organised and far stronger ants emerge as victors nearly always.

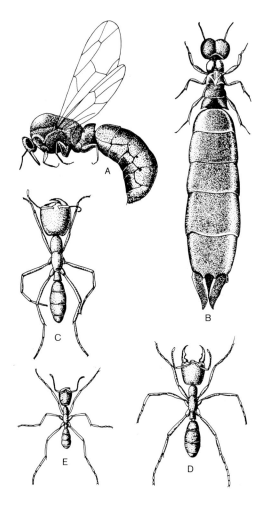

The typical ant community is a matriarchy, in which the role of the male (A) is simply to fertilise the female, shortly after which he dies. The fertilised female loses her wings (B) and lays eggs from which are hatched females of different sizes (C, D, E). These will become part of the worker caste.

CHAPTER 11

Hunters of insects

The earliest explorers of the African continent carried away many unforgettable memories, pleasant and unpleasant. They suffered from the stifling heat, they were incessantly plagued by insects and they were often laid low by diseases, such as malaria, transmitted by these pestilential tiny creatures.

Modern science has now found the partial solution to insect-borne disease in the tropics, waging an unending war against flies, mosquitoes, beetles, termites, ants and locusts across plain and savannah and through swamp and forest.

Man has allies in the numerous predators—especially birds, ranging from the enormous marabou stork to the minute carmine bee-eater—which from time to time kill and devour insects. Many such birds feed on winged termites and ants. Some animals too are specialised hunters of insects. Among the reptiles, for example, the chameleon, with its long sticky tongue, catches flies at a speed undetectable to the human eye; and in the mammal realm, the aardvark's sharp claws and viscous tongue are highly effective tools for capturing termites.

The astonishing bird known as the honey-guide uses an ingenious variety of methods to attract the attention of honey-eating animals—and even humans—and then leads them to the nests of wild bees, taking its commission in the form of scraps of wax and honey left behind when the hives have been pillaged.

The curious earth-pig

The aardvark or earth-pig (*Orycteropus afer*) is not exactly a handsome animal. In fact, with its long, cylinder-shaped head, enormous ears, almost hairless skin, strong claws, out-of-proportion hindquarters and tail nearly half the length of its

Facing page : The chameleon is coloured like its surroundings, and its eyes can swivel independently of each other to give both monocular and binocular vision. This reptile, with a wide distribution range through Africa, feeds on insects which it captures by lightning-like thrusts of its long, sticky tongue.

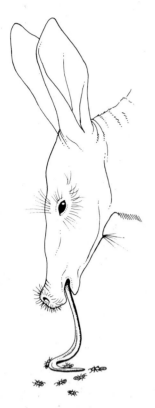

The aardvark feeds mainly on termites which are scooped up with its foot-long tongue. It prefers to catch the insects whenever they leave the refuge of their nest, usually at night, but will if necessary, invade the termitarium itself, digging away the earth with its feet.

Facing page : The aardvark or earth-pig digs burrows with its sharp claws and powerful feet. The tapering body-shape of the animal is well suited to its subterranean habits. Because of its nomadic way of life these burrows are often abandoned and used by other animals.

body (on which, kangaroo-like, it supports itself), the aardvark is a pretty grotesque-looking creature.

As we have remarked, however, beauty in the wild is of no inherent value or importance, and the shape or structure of an animal's body is invariably related to its manner of living and means of obtaining food in order to survive. This ill-favoured mammal is in fact an expert earth-excavator. Curling the tail under its body, it scrapes busily at the hard, dry soil with the front feet and then uses its back legs to kick away the dislodged earth. This digging operation is carried out at top speed, so much so that if danger threatens while the aardvark is some distance from its regular burrow it prefers to dig a new refuge rather than turn tail and flee.

The aardvark normally confines itself to bare ground, free of rocks and stones, so that digging can be unimpeded. The four large, powerful claws on each front foot function as natural spades, and the sturdy hind legs and thick tail as efficient shovels for scooping out heaps of soil. The tapering head and tail and the tough, smooth skin also facilitate movement underground.

This strange animal does not dig a hole simply to escape from an enemy but uses its cool subterranean tunnel as a resting place during the heat of the day. The burrow may extend 7–12 feet under the ground, ending in a chamber large enough to allow the animal to turn about—essential in view of the fact that it enters head first and that there is only one exit.

Aardvark burrows are prominent and easily identified; consequently they tend to be invaded by many other kinds of animal that use them for protection and security. Since the aardvark is basically nomadic, its burrows are frequently left empty. Occasional residents include servals, hyenas, hunting dogs and even leopards. Other creatures such as the aardwolf, porcupine, python, ratel and some species of mongoose take up more regular occupation; but no animal makes better use of a deserted burrow than the warthog. The Belgian naturalist R. Verheyen has pointed out that in fact the range of distribution of the two animals overlaps so closely that it is probable that warthogs will not populate a new region unless they can be certain that the hard-working earth-pigs are already there to make life bearable.

The aardvark, after spending the day relaxed inside its lair, bestirs itself at nightfall. Cautiously emerging into the open, it crouches motionless for a few minutes, huge ears pricked to catch the faintest sound, and nostrils sniffing the air. If all seems safe, it bounds off, pausing when it is about ten yards from the burrow to make a closer inspection of its surroundings. Then, reassured, it scurries around, still listening and sniffing warily. Eventually it calms down and trots off to look for termites.

A meal of termites

Some termites have the habit of streaming out of their citadel at night and sometimes, during and after a storm when the visibility is poor, by day. The aardvark, which, in the view of many experts, feeds on little else, is perfectly familiar with the termites' behaviour, preferring to hunt them by night, possibly guided by its

Geographical distribution of aardvarks.

AARDVARK
(Orycteropus afer)

Class: Mammalia
Order: Tubulidentata
Family: Orycteropodidae
Length of head and body: 60 inches (150 cm)
Length of tail: 24 inches (60 cm)
Height to shoulder: 24 inches (60 cm)
Weight: 110–155 lb (50–70 kg)
Diet: insects (termites, ants)
Number of young: one
Longevity: up to 10 years

Adults
The long, cylindrical head terminates in a kind of snout, similar to that of wild and domestic pigs. The ears are large and tubular, the eyes small. The body is almost hairless and the sturdy feet have toes with long, sharp claws. The muscular tail tapers towards the tip. The tough, thick skin is light brown with reddist tints.

Young
The baby is completely hairless at birth and very awkward and clumsy.

Subspecies
Up to fifteen subspecies have been distinguished, three of them particularly well defined—*Oryctero-pus afer aethiopicus* from East Africa, *O. a. senegalensis* from West Africa, and *O. a. capensis* from South Africa.

---

remarkably keen hearing. Assuming it is able to surprise the insects in the open, it proceeds to scoop them up adroitly with its sticky, foot-long tongue. This appears to be its favourite hunting technique, for although it can use its claws to demolish a termite mound in broad daylight, this calls for much more effort and may not have such predictably successful results. But if the aardvark is really hungry and finds itself face-to-face with a termitarium, it will have no hesitation in tearing it to shreds and devouring the insects as they scuttle through their underground galleries.

The aardvark is known to feed also on certain species of ant, though not in nearly so great a quantity; nor does it touch the enormous red ant which is the only type capable of piercing the mammal's thick hide in self-defence. Many naturalists believe that the animal occasionally eats fruit as well, though opinion is divided. Verheyen cites the interesting case of one individual whose small intestine was found to contain seeds of a species of gourd known to grow only in the areas where aardvarks deposit their excrement. The Belgian naturalist also describes how the animal buries its droppings, digging a hole some four inches deep and then neatly covering it again.

The aardvark's family life

The female aardvark gives birth to one baby (twins do occur, but are rare) which then remains in the security of the burrow for a couple of weeks, the mother not troubling to provide it with any kind of bed made of grass or straw. The little animal is naked and unsteady on its feet but at the beginning of the third week is ready to accompany its mother on her nocturnal forays. The chances are that it will have to get accustomed to a new home, for as soon as the baby is old enough to walk the female abandons the burrow altogether and digs a fresh one.

By the end of a month mother and baby are changing their hunting ground virtually every week, with as many alterations of burrow. When it is about six months old the young aardvark is capable of digging its own holes in the ground and will live separately from its mother, although the two burrows are normally not more than some fifty yards apart.

When, a short while later, the female is once more on heat and courted by several males, the fast-growing youngster, especially if itself a male, may wander off on its own; it is more usual, however, for it to remain close to its mother for it does not reach sexual maturity until nearly two years of age.

The pregnant female does not normally leave her fixed abode until she is ready to give birth, and then only at the last moment. As for the adult males, they are nomadic by habit but considering that they spend hardly any time looking for partners it is possible –Verheyen believes it more than likely–that they are polygamous.

The flesh of the aardvark is edible, that of the young being especially tasty, so they are often hunted by man. Other enemies include lions and leopards but they are not easy prey, for they immediately seek the refuge of their narrow lair and when cornered lie on their backs, curling themselves into a ball, and lashing out at their attackers with sharp claws.

The honey-eating ratel

The ratel is one of the Mustelidae and looks rather like the common badger of Europe and Asia. It is in fact sometimes called the honey badger. The body is covered with long thick hair, black on the underparts and silver-grey on the back. Like other members of the family its front feet are furnished with strong, curving claws, ideal for burrowing, but the claws of the hind feet are reduced. Although there is only one species, *Mellivora capensis*, a number of races have been distinguished, not only in Africa but also in parts of western Asia, Iran and India.

Wherever it lives, on steppes or savannahs, in forest galleries, on rocky slopes or on kopjes, the ratel digs a small burrow in the dry season, after the brush has been devastated by fire, or simply takes over the abandoned lair of an aardvark. In the rainy season, however, when the vegetational growth is again luxuriant, high enough to provide concealment and protection, the ratel may often be discovered lying in the open, against a heap of stones, amid tall grass or near a small tree. It has generally been assumed that the creature has nocturnal habits but there are sufficient variations from this norm to suggest that it ventures out by day as well, alternating its periods of activity and repose.

The ratel is an extremely aggressive animal and the male has strong territorial instincts, tolerating the presence of no rival on its hunting grounds. Nor, in the opinion of some naturalists, will he quail before carnivores larger than himself, boldly challenging human intruders into the bargain.

The female, after a gestation period lasting about six months, gives birth – generally during the rainy season – to two, three or even four babies. Their abode is a hole excavated among stones or in the ground, where both parents will have prepared a bed of leaves and dry grains. Here the offspring remain for a month and a half but only during the first week of their life are they fed exclusively on their mother's milk. The family group stays together for about six months, when the female may again be on heat.

Few medium-sized animals are able to hold their own against the fierce ratel, birds and large insects being equally acceptable as food. Verheyen has pointed out that among the habitual prey of the animal are rodents, shrews, ground-based fledglings, grasshoppers, crickets, beetles, termites and also newly-born antelopes, especially oribis and bubal hartebeeste. But the scientific name of the ratel provides a clue to its favourite type of food – honey. The voracious carnivore not only devours the sweet honeycombs but also the wax and the wild bee larvae.

A cooperative venture

The ratel will sometimes spend several hours squatting on a stone or on the trunk of a dead tree, watching the comings and goings of a swarm of bees before launching an attack on their nest. But occasionally such patience is unnecessary. Verheyen, as a result of his many researches on African fauna, especially in the Congo,

---

RATEL
(*Mellivora capensis*)

Class: Mammalia
Order: Carnivora
Family: Mustelidae
Length of head and body: 28 inches (70 cm)
Length of tail: 10 inches (25 cm)
Height to shoulder: up to 12 inches (30 cm)
Weight: up to 24 lb (11 kg)
Diet: small animals, carrion, honey
Gestation: about 6 months
Number of young: 2

Adults
Looks somewhat like the European badger and similarly has longer, stronger claws on the front feet than on the hind feet. The head is more or less pointed, the eyes very small and the ears barely visible. The face and the lower half of the body are black, separated from the silver-grey upper parts by a near-white band.

Young
The back is rust-coloured and there is no white dividing line.

Distribution
Throughout Africa south of the Sahara, including the Ituri forest in the Congo, where black individuals are found. Ratels also range through Asia, from Arabia to India.

was the first naturalist to provide scientific confirmation that certain birds, about the size of starlings, had the habit of leading various interested animals to the sites of bees' nests, in the expectation of dining on the remains. These birds are known as honey-guides and among the creatures attracted by their tail movements and distinctive call are ratels, antelopes, buffaloes, monkeys and mongooses. Even native hunters take advantage of the honey-guides' signals, which are repeated regularly every twenty yards or so until the entrance to the hive is revealed.

When a ratel discovers a beehive on the ground it uses its sharp claws to delve down, often as much as six feet, to make a meal of honey, wax, larvae and even adult bees. The stings of the angry occupants seem to make little impression on its hair-covered body. Although more difficult to reach, it will also plunder nests constructed in trees, scraping away at rotted wood to thrust in a paw and scoop out the honeycombs. When it has satisfied its appetite and left the site, the patient honey-guide swoops down and carries off anything that is left – honey, wax, insects and all – an unusual assortment of food for any bird, but a diet which seems to be easily assimilated.

Obviously this coincidence of tastes and active food-finding association has benefits both for the animal and the bird. The ratel needs the honey-guide's assistance in locating the nest in the first place while the bird, because of the shape of its beak, would find it impossible to procure its favourite meal were it not for the preparatory work done by the carnivore.

The honey-guides

Honey-guides are members of the order Piciformes and are closely related to the barbets, though they bear little resemblance to the latter either in looks or habits, apart from having the normal number of four toes on each foot, two facing backwards, two forwards. They are divided into four genera (*Prodotiscus, Melignomon, Melichneutes* and *Indicator*) and twelve species, with a range covering the whole of Africa south of the Sahara, apart from Madagascar. Their song is harsh and strident and they are basically insect-eating birds, living alone or in pairs. The largest is the black-throated honey-guide (*Indicator indicator*).

Little is known of the honey-guides' breeding habits except for the fact that they are parasites, laying their white eggs (one at a time) in the nests of other birds, usually in a hole or among rocks. The sharp-billed or Wahlberg's honey-guide (*Prodotiscus insignis*), one of the smallest species, shelters its fledglings in the exposed nests of the white-eyes of the genus *Zosterops*. Scientists believe that the guide-duties performed by these parasitic birds must be entirely instinctive in view of the fact that they can give no instruction to their young, which are reared by foster-parents.

Recent studies in regions where ratels are seldom found and where the local peoples rarely collect the honey of wild bees, have revealed that the honey-guides there spend more of their time hunting insects on the wing, having evidently lost their aptitude for raiding hives.

The honey-guide is an African bird which helps the ratel and other animals to find bees' nests by flying from branch to branch and giving out piercing cries. After the hive has been plundered the honey-guide claims its share in the form of honey, wax and larvae. It is a parasitic bird, laying its eggs in the nests of others.

Facing page : The ratel, African counterpart of the wolverine, is a powerful, aggressive animal, with an omnivorous diet. It has a special fondness for honey and the larvae of wild bees. The sharp claws of the front feet are ideal for burrowing.

The aardwolf

The aardwolf (*Proteles cristatus*) is a strange creature, looking in some respects like a dog and in others like a striped hyena. It belongs in fact to the family Hyaenidae but differs from its relatives chiefly by reason of its unusual tooth structure. Though it possesses the usual canines and incisors of a carnivore, the cheek teeth – twelve premolars and four molars – are two fewer than those of other representatives of the hyena family. They are also astonishingly small and weak, quite unsuitable for cracking or grinding bones, necessitating a specialised diet.

The aardwolf is much smaller than the striped hyena, weighing about 30 lb, and is further distinguished by its large ears and the five toes on each front foot. The resemblance to a domestic dog also turns out to be no more than superficial when one sees the sloping back with its bristling mane, the thick body hair, the black transverse stripes and the dark muzzle.

This animal is found in parts of East and South Africa, its range extending northwards as far as Somalia. The population is most dense in the Kalahari Desert, for in addition to shrub-covered plains the creature has a liking for sandy regions. Nocturnal by habit, the aardwolf spends the day deep in a burrow, usually consisting of two or more galleries up to ten yards long and ending in a circular retreat about one yard in diameter. This is where the animal sleeps and where the female gives birth to and rears her young. Although it sometimes digs its own lair, the aardwolf often takes advantage of a deserted aardvark burrow. Normally it will be found on its own but several females with their young may sometimes occupy a communal burrow.

Termites are by far the favourite item of food, despite the fact that the aardwolf lacks the natural advantages of the aardvark for obtaining its requirements. Nevertheless, the tongue, though not sticky, is sufficiently mobile to be able literally to sweep up the crowds of termites as they scurry to and fro in the darkness. Maurice Burton quotes the example of one animal whose stomach was found to contain some 40,000 termites, evidently gathered in less than three hours!

When termites are in short supply the aardwolf catches rodents, small birds and fledglings; it also steals eggs from nests on the ground and may even feed on carrion. With its long canines, the creature would have no difficulty in killing larger prey, but it would find it almost impossible to tear it up and chew it, and in captivity it refuses to eat meat.

Not very much is known about the reproductive behaviour of the aardwolf. The female is believed to be on heat in August, the ensuing gestation period lasting about three months, at least in the south, so that births normally occur in November or December. Between two and four babies are born (five or six are exceptional), their eyes closed.

When the aardwolf is threatened it defends itself with its canine teeth and excretes a nauseous-smelling substance from its anal glands. Apart from man, who has for a long time waged relentless war against it, its most determined enemies are pythons, lions and leopards.

AARDWOLF
(*Proteles cristatus*)

Class: Mammalia
Order: Carnivora
Family: Hyaenidae
Length of head and body: 38 inches (95 cm)
Length of tail: 14 inches (35 cm)
Height to shoulder: up to 20 inches (50 cm)
Weight: about 30 lb (14 kg)
Diet: termites and ants, occasionally small mammals, chickens, eggs, carrion
Gestation: 90–110 days
Number of young: 2–4, exceptionally 5 or 6

Adults
Somewhat resembles a small hyena, with short, stiff, whitish hairs on body, especially thick on tail. The back is covered by a bristly mane. Muzzle and tips of hairs on mane and tail are dark. Upper part of body is reddish-grey or yellow and lower part somewhat lighter. There are also black stripes on both body and legs.

Young
Very delicate and defenceless at birth, with eyes closed.

Distribution
Tree-covered or subdesert plains of East and South Africa, ranging northwards to Somalia.

The true insectivores

Although they feed regularly on termites and other insects, the aardvark, aardwolf and ratel are not insectivores in the real sense, for the first belongs to the order Tubulidentata and the other two are true carnivores. But there are many African animals of different types which are genuine insect-eaters, even though some of them supplement this diet with molluscs, worms and small vertebrates.

One homogeneous group is represented by the elephant- or jumping-shrews of the family Macroscelididae. These animals are about the size of rats and have very long snouts and large eyes. Their hind legs are particularly well developed, making them expert jumpers. They inhabit tree-covered savannah regions but seldom move far from their lairs, although they are agile over the ground. They neither dig burrows nor climb trees, preferring to take up residence in an abandoned hole, beneath a stone or among rocks. The traces of their tiny footsteps can often be seen weaving out in all directions over the area selected as a hunting ground. Naturalists have even seen the creatures picking up and tossing aside leaves and bits of grass that may have fallen across their path, thus keeping the way clear.

Related to the hyena, the aardwolf is nocturnal, spending the daytime in a burrow, often that of an aardvark. Although a true carnivore, it has weak teeth which are incapable of tearing meat or grinding bones, and feeds on insects, especially termites.

The elephant-shrews feed on termites, grasshoppers and scarab beetles. The females give birth, once a year, to one or two babies, which come into the world with their eyes open and spend not more than three or four days in the nest.

These little insectivores are related to the tupaias or tree-shrews, though the latter have caused scientific controversy in the field of systematics, being originally classified as primitive Primates but now admitted to be more closely related to the Insectivora. The elephant-shrews appear to have strong family ties and according to Verheyen it is not uncommon for several generations to live together in the same burrow.

Africa is also the home of a large number of other kinds of shrew and hedgehog, not differing to any great extent from their better-known European relatives.

The versatile chameleon

In East Africa chameleons have the unenviable reputation of being bringers of bad luck, and to some africans they are the familiars of witches, demons and evil spirits. It is perhaps not surprising that these extraordinary insect hunters, which are many and varied, should have acquired such a bad name, for they look rather like miniature prehistoric monsters, some of them having little knobs or horns on the head. They also have the disconcerting ability to move each of their eyes independently and to change the colour of their body—characteristics that perhaps lend additional support to the local myths and legends. Yet this evil reputation has in a sense been their salvation for the superstitious local peoples leave them alone, neither trapping nor hunting them. So they are free to live in peace amongst the foliage, patiently awaiting their prey.

The grotesque appearance and unusual behaviour of the chameleon serve a double purpose, one offensive and the other defensive. Anyone who has tried to catch a fly or a butterfly in the hand will be able to appreciate the uncanny dexterity and accuracy with which the chameleon shoots out its long, sticky tongue to capture its prey, thanks mainly to remarkable vision which allows it to gauge precisely the distance this natural weapon has to travel; and the reptile's slow, languid movements as well as its colour-changing capacity are both valuable assets in self-defence, inasmuch as they avoid startling the victim and escape the attention of enemies.

Africa, including Madagascar, is a paradise for chameleons, for almost every species is found on the continent, with the exception of one from southern India and Ceylon. Some of them are exclusively tree-dwelling but others, furnished with a short, non-prehensile tail, spend most of their life on the ground. Active during the day, chameleons generally seek out thick areas of brush towards nightfall where they can hide. All their movements are closely conditioned by the temperature of their surroundings, for unless this is sufficiently high their body metabolism will be slowed down. They are in fact capable of withstanding very intense heat in dry regions, though if conditions permit they prefer districts with a high humidity content or where there is a

Facing page : The aardwolf, with its thick mane, looks in some respects like a striped hyena, in others like a domestic dog. But it is much smaller than the hyena and although it sometimes feeds on meat and carrion, it is basically an insectivore.

good water supply.

The most celebrated feature of this reptile is of course its ability to change colour. It should be remembered, however, that other lizards, including agamas, anoles and some geckos, share this ability. Nor is it something that can be switched on or off at will, as is generally assumed, for it depends on other factors besides the animal's immediate background surroundings. Investigation has shown that light, temperature and emotional stimuli are even more important.

The deadly insect hunter

The protractile tongue of the chameleon is its specialised weapon for hunting and capturing insects, which form the major part of its diet. The tongue is situated in the floor of the mouth and the tip is furnished with a sticky sucker. When the reptile is stimulated by the presence of prey, often an insect on the wing, the tongue shoots out at an incredible speed; when fully uncoiled its length can exceed that of the reptile's body and tail combined. Obviously success depends on the chameleon's aim being absolutely true and the distance to be covered is calculated with extreme accuracy. To do this the chameleon moves around very slowly indeed, swinging its body like a pendulum from side to side, casting wary glances in every direction without moving its head and thus pinpointing the victim with mathematical precision prior to seizing it with the deadly tongue.

Exceptions to the insect-eating rule are seen in several East African species such as *Chamaeleo melleri,* which eats birds, and the giant chameleon of Madagascar, *Chamaeleo oustateli,* which appears to be able to digest small mammals, such as young mice, as well.

The large, well-developed eyes are completely covered by scaly lids which leave a single opening in the centre, directly in line with the pupil. Their most remarkable feature, however, is the capacity to move independently of each other, turning through a field of 180°, providing both monocular and binocular vision. Thus one eye can look forwards at the same time as the other is looking backwards, up or down. In this fashion it can bring its prey within convenient range while making certain that no enemy is lurking in the vicinity.

Although the chameleon can go without food for fairly long periods it is normally a voracious eater and needs to drink at regular intervals.

Most species live in shrubs and trees and movement along stems and branches is made possible by pincer-like toes. The front feet are furnished with three toes pointing inwards and two pointing outwards; on the hind feet the arrangement is exactly reversed, with three outer and two inner toes. In the genus *Chamaelio* the tail too serves as a fifth foot for it is exceptionally strong and by curling round a branch can support the whole weight of the reptile's body. In other genera (*Brookesia, Leandria* and *Rampholeon*) the tail is short and incapable of grasping objects; in others it can be curled up on itself like the spring of a watch. But their movements are at all times measured and wary, almost as if they

Some species of chameleon have fleshy growths on their head which emphasise their grotesque and frightening appearance. By extending the length of the body these growths may also play a part in camouflaging the reptiles in the shrubs and trees where they usually hunt their prey.

were afraid to fall or slip, strange behaviour for such small creatures.

Almost all species display some kind of epidermal growth on the head, whether a wart, a spine, a crest or a pair of small horns. These may be used as weapons but are just as often a means of dissuasion. The male has strong territorial instincts and will permit no rival on his private hunting ground. It is therefore comparatively rare for two chameleons to meet and engage in active combat for the intruder will in most cases yield ground to the owner of the territory in face of the latter's intimidating manoeuvres. A strange female, however, will be readily accepted by the male, even outside the actual mating season.

The majority of chameleons are oviparous and this poses a considerable problem for the females which are forced to come down from the trees to lay their eggs. Here they are vulnerable to the attacks of many predators. The egg-laying season occurs towards the end of the summer and in the autumn, the females digging a hole about eight inches long and four inches wide, either in the bare ground or in a piece of dead wood. In this hole they deposit from twenty to forty eggs. Other tree-dwelling species do not run such risks for they are able to lay their eggs directly on the leaves by means of a sticky adhesive substance. Some South African species are even more fortunate in being ovoviparous (the eggs being hatched inside the female's body). All offspring emerge from the egg fully developed.

The extraordinary vision of the chameleon enables it to pinpoint insects with the utmost precision, prior to capturing them with its long, sticky tongue. The tongue, with a sucker at the tip, is in many species longer than the reptile's body and tail combined. The toes are arranged in such a way as to allow the chameleon to grip stems and branches and the tail often functions as a fifth foot.

ORDER: Tubulidentata

The aardvark or earth-pig is a placental mammal which, because of its unique characteristics, has been allotted a scientific category of its own. It is in fact the sole representative of the order Tubulidentata.

This strange animal has a remarkable capacity for burrowing and for capturing termites, which make up the basic portion of its diet. The shape and structure of its body are thus closely bound up with these specialised activities.

The bites of hundreds of termites can make little impression on the thick, tough skin and since there are comparatively few hairs on the body the aardvark is not in the least handicapped in its subterranean movements. The tail, broad at the base and tapering towards the tip, is also no encumbrance as the animal turns about in its confined space.

The forefoot lacks a first toe but the remaining four toes have large, strong nails which, according to Professor Grassé, could be compared to hooves if they were shorter. There are, however, five toes on the hind feet and the claws are not quite so long. The second and third toes are the most highly developed and are joined by a wide web.

The aardvark is digitigrade and when it senses danger supports its body on the kangaroo-like tail and hindquarters, then sets about digging a burrow with astonishing speed. This burrowing skill is in large measure due to the muscular strength of the forelimbs. The power of the animal's feet and the sharpness of its claws are invaluable too for breaking down the most solid of termite mounds. Having accomplished this, the aardvark then scoops up the insects with its long, sticky tongue.

The teeth are also closely related to the animal's specialised feeding habits and are one of the chief reasons for its being classified in a separate order. The first set of milk teeth are quickly replaced by a new batch. These permanent teeth are cylindrical in shape and more or less equal in size. They are completely devoid of enamel but covered by a layer of cement. Each tooth is made up of a number of six-sided ivory prisms, each traversed by a tubule or cavity (hence the name of the order) enclosing a diverticulum of the central pulp cavity. The teeth grow continuously but drop out fairly easily since they have no roots and are not implanted in well-defined sockets. There are no teeth at all in the fore part of the jaw and in fact not many are functional—usually five in each half of each jaw, though the number varies from four to seven depending on the individual. Incisors, canines and first premolars are not generally present in the permanent set, either because they have not been replaced or because they remain embedded in a vestigial form in the gum. This rudimentary dentition, plus the form of the snout and the tongue, caused scientists to classify the animal for some time among the Edentata (true ant-eaters).

The aardvark is mainly nocturnal, with poorish eyesight but with large, mobile, rabbit-like ears which afford keen hearing. The sense of smell is also well developed, the muzzle being long and the olfactory lobes of the brain voluminous. The cerebral hemispheres have few convolutions and do not cover the cerebellum. The sphenoid bone at the base of the skull is linked to the tympanic cavity of the ear.

Despite its strange appearance, the aardvark's anatomy is relatively simple. The digestive, respiratory and circulatory systems show few signs of specialisation. There is a double uterus and the placenta is zonary, like that of carnivores. The female has two pairs of teats, one in the groin and the other on the abdomen. The male's testes are in the groin but below the skin.

There is only one genus and species of aardvark, *Orycteropus afer*, with a range extending over nearly the whole African continent south of the Sahara, coinciding with that of the termite population.

Facing page : The aardvark, with its long snout, looks superficially like a domestic pig, but the tapering body and tail are convenient for entering and moving about in the burrow which the animal digs with its strong feet and claws. It is not a true insectivore, despite its termite-based diet, but the only representative of the order Tubulidentata, the latter name being derived from the unusual structure of the teeth, which are traversed by tubules.

CHAPTER 12

A springtime paradise for birds

Spring, though of short duration, transforms the African bush into a wonderland of colours, scents and sounds. Wood and forest soak up the tropical rain and parade their fresh foliage in a subtle, ever-shifting range of greenery; the evening breeze is delicately perfumed by the flowers of the acacias and baobabs, their nectar pillaged by swarms of wild bees; and the cool air resounds at dawn and dusk to the excited chatter of millions of migratory and native birds.

The birds with which we are most familiar in Europe are sombre and ordinary in comparison with their innumerable African relatives. The typical sparrows of the bush–the celebrated weaver-birds–are green and yellow, with black or reddish facial masks and splendidly vivid markings that are far removed from the sober, modest hues of their northern counterparts. The glistening plumage of the African starlings ranges through every imaginable shade of green to cobalt-blue, flecked with yellow, ochre and scarlet. The long, translucent beaks of the hornbills, as they perch on the tops of the acacias, flash in the first light of dawn. The bush too is the realm of the predatory shrikes or butcher-birds which hunt large insects and small vertebrates, earning their name by transfixing their victims through the body with sharp thorns, leaving the carcases to putrefy, and returning a few days later to devour them at leisure. This is also the habitat of the pygmy falcons, most diminutive of raptors, which possess the powerful and harmonious outlines of their more famous relatives but are themselves hardly larger than starlings.

A few days after the arrival of the seasonal rains the different species of weaver begin building their elaborate nests on the slenderest branches of the acacias, secure from the ravages of egg-eating snakes. These African sparrows, unlike their European

Facing page : The weaver-birds of the African bush are related to the European sparrows. Their nests, built of interlacing pieces of grass and vegetable fibre, hang from the branches of trees. They are cup-shaped, with long entry tunnels which protect the occupants from predators, particularly snakes.

counterparts which conceal their nests beneath tiles and between the stones of old buildings, have to provide their own means of natural protection, weaving a form of long tunnel at the base of the nest so as to bar entry to the many reptiles that glide through the branches. What is more, the birds construct false nests on the thickest forks of the trees which further deceive their enemies, so that the would-be pillager has to embark on a tiresome and frustrating search in order to locate the genuine nest.

Dry trees without leaves attract large flocks of rollers, some of them local species, others migrating from Europe. The little birds that arrive from the north to spend the winter in Africa share food with their sedentary relatives but the latter are easily distinguished by their far brighter coloration, the breast being brilliant violet, and the two lateral feathers decorating the tail, giving it a forked shape. These birds are extremely bold and self-reliant insectivores, feeding on crickets, grasshoppers and caterpillars.

This rich and varied bird population is supplemented during the rainy season by guinea fowl, francolins, partridges, stone curlews and many species of wader—converting the bush into a veritable bird paradise.

Wading birds of the bush

Most birds greet the dawn with a babel of chatter and song, but the stone curlews or thick-knees are creatures of the dusk and the night, whose noisy croaking is a characteristic sound of the early evening as the sun sets over the African plains.

The stone curlews represent the family Burhinidae of the order Charadriiformes. Their plumage is grey-brown, their large eyes are yellow and their long legs (the swollen joints of which give them their alternative common name) have only three toes, the hind one being missing. The comparatively drab plumage serves as an effective form of camouflage during the day when the birds are resting among shrubs or piles of pebbles. By night they venture out in search of insects, worms, molluscs, lizards and small rodents.

In the breeding season no nest is built and two or three eggs are laid directly onto the ground. The colour varies from white to fawn, with irregular markings that blend perfectly with the natural tones of the surroundings. Not only is it almost impossible to spot the eggs but it is just as hard to detect the brooding female as she guards them. The chicks are nidifugous and flatten themselves against the ground at the first sign of danger, necks outstretched and not a muscle moving.

The three very typical African species of stone curlew all belong to the genus *Burhinus*. The spotted stone curlew or thick-knee (*Burhinus capensis*), the water dikkop (*B. vermiculatus*) and the Senegal stone curlew (*B. senegalensis*) all have a fairly wide range. Sometimes, in northern Kenya and Uganda, one may also come across the European stone curlew (*B. oedicnemus*), which migrates to Africa for the winter.

The Charadriiformes include many other wading birds of varying sizes, most of which are found on river banks or in

Vulturine guinea fowl
(*Acryllium vulturinum*)

Tufted guinea fowl
(*Numida meleagris*)

Kenya crested guinea fowl
(*Guttera pucherani*)

Crested francolin
(*Francolinus sephaena*)

Superb starling
(*Spreo superbus*)

Social weaver
(*Philetairus socius*)

Buffalo weaver
(*Bubalornis albirostris*)

Yellow-necked spurfowl
(*Pternistis leucoscepus*)

Stone partridge
(*Ptilopachus petrosus*)

Red-billed quelea
(*Quelea quelea*)

Ground hornbill
(*Bucorvus leadbeateri*)

Silvery-cheeked hornbill
(*Bycanistes brevis*)

Yellow-billed hornbill
(*Tockus flavirostris*)

The crowned lapwing (*Stephanibyx coronatus*) is one of the most spectacular birds of the African savannah and bush. It will courageously defend its territory against wild animals and human intruders, uttering angry cries which are rather like those of certain falcons.

swampland, though some of them are inhabitants of much drier regions. The latter species have legs that are especially adapted for rapid running. Among African genera ideally suited to life on plain and savannah are various coursers, lapwings and plovers. Notable among these are Temminck's courser (*Cursorius temminckii*), the wattled plover (*Afribyx senegallus*), and the blackhead plover (*Sarciophorus tectus*), with a crest resembling that of the European lapwing.

There are several plovers of the genus *Stephanibyx* which do not display either a crest or wattles; but perhaps the most characteristic and remarkable bird to be found is the crowned lapwing (*Stephanibyx coronatus*), particularly widespread on the open plains of the Serengeti. Like many of its relatives, this bird is markedly hostile towards any strangers that happen to invade its territory. It is not uncommon to see a pair of these lapwings swooping above a group of baboons or even a roaming jackal or lioness, emitting piercing cries which, in their insistent rhythm, recall those of the peregrine falcon. With its small scarlet feet, its celebrated black crest and its luminous eyes, this bird—nesting on the ground—is one of the most colourful residents of bush and savannah.

The fleet-footed guinea fowl

The visitor to East Africa comes away with many unforgettable impressions and one of the most beautiful sights is surely that of a huge flock of guinea fowl. The journey from Mombasa to Nairobi takes one across an almost unending expanse of gently undulating plain and hardly a moment passes without a glimpse of a group, of these sturdy ground birds—wave upon wave of them—providing a most remarkable and exciting spectacle.

These birds feed on all kinds of vegetation, deriving the

maximum benefit from their chosen environment. They seldom stray far from the protective cover of trees and shrubs, though they are sometimes found on the fringes of the savannah. Since they are basically ground birds they are especially vulnerable to the attacks of predators, for all their fleetness of foot. But tree cover does at least afford a certain measure of security against the most implacable of their enemies, the martial eagle.

One morning, during the dry season of 1969, a group of naturalists stopped their Landrover to look at a family of lions on the banks of the Seronera river in the Serengeti. While the famished cubs were stretched out asleep and a number of lionesses were wandering about in the undergrowth, keeping a watch on a nearby herd of Thomson's gazelles, a flock of helmeted guinea fowl busied themselves scrabbling for seeds in the loose dust of the parched savannah. They did this in the same manner as domestic chickens, disturbing the earth with their feet, then stepping back a pace or two to peck at any seeds or grubs that might have come to light.

Suddenly there was a shrill cry and the birds lumbered off towards the river. Almost at the same moment a couple of very beautiful Bonelli's eagles swooped down on them. The peaceful scene was transformed into a battleground, the raptors scything

Following page : The various species of guinea fowl are ground birds, rather like small turkeys in appearance. The largest is the vulturine guinea fowl (*top*), with elegant blue plumage, striped and speckled in white. All are gregarious birds, gathering in large numbers round waterholes.

The helmeted guinea fowl (*Numida mitrata*) has a slender body and the 'helmet' is a horn-like growth on the head. Like other birds of the genus it feeds on the ground but spends the night roosting in trees.

the air with their huge wings, the guinea fowl churning up clouds of dust as they frantically made their escape bid. One of the lionesses, concealed in the brush, took advantage of the confusion to swipe with her paw at one bird which was half-running, half-flying, but failed to bring it down. Nor, for all the disturbance they were creating, did the eagles manage to plant their talons in the body of a single guinea fowl. The entire episode lasted only a few seconds, with land and air predators alike ending up empty-handed. The scientists were amazed to see how expertly the ungainly-looking guinea fowl evaded the clutches of their formidable enemies, partly due to their initial alertness and partly to their natural turn of speed.

Guinea fowl belong to the order Galliformes and the family Numididae and are thus related, as their appearance and behaviour suggest, to the partridges and pheasants of the family Phasianidae. But they differ from the latter in several ways. The male and female forms are difficult to tell apart, their shape is more thickset, the tail is short and carried low, and there are naked coloured zones on head and neck. They are quiet and wary birds which fly somewhat laboriously, so much so that, as in the example quoted above, they prefer when danger threatens to rely on feet rather than wings. If hard pursued they will take to the air but they will come down to perch on the first convenient bush as soon as conditions permit.

The guinea fowl belonging to the genera *Phasidus* and *Agelastes* have spurs on their tarsi, though these are smaller than those of pheasants. Other species, however, do not possess these spurs. The dominant colours are dark blue or grey but the plumage shows delicate white stripes or spots against the dark ground.

Savannah, bush and lightly covered forest, often at altitudes of up to 6,000 feet, are the favourite habitats of these birds, which may gather in flocks of as many as a thousand individuals. During the day they walk unhurriedly from place to place, often covering many miles. At nightfall they fly noisily up into trees to roost, with a babel of metallic, clacking cries reminiscent of those of New World turkeys. It is particularly fascinating to watch a long column of guinea fowl advancing with measured tread towards a river or waterhole, in well-organised Indian file formation. The gregarious habits of the different species are particularly marked during the dry season and the flocks considerably larger. Their food consists in the main of seeds, berries, tender shoots and small invertebrates.

Any small depression in the ground will serve as a nesting site and from six to fifteen eggs are laid, yellowish in colour with a hard, grainy surface. As a rule the incubation period lasts a little more than a month.

The tufted guinea fowl (*Numida meleagris*) is undoubtedly the most characteristic African species. It has a yellowish crest and naked red caruncles on the face. The latter vary considerably with the age, sex and regional distribution of the bird. The *Numida sabyi* species from North Africa was known to the Ancient Romans as Pharaoh's chicken. The helmeted guinea fowl (*Numida mitrata*) is an inhabitant of the eastern half of Africa from Somalia southwards to the Cape and has particularly spectacular colours,

☐ *Numida mitrata*

☐ *Numida meleagris*

▨ *Acryllium vulturinum*

Geographical distribution of guinea fowl.

AFRICAN GUINEA FOWL

Class: Aves
Order: Galliformes
Family: Numididae

Number of eggs: 6–5
Incubation: just over a month

HELMETED GUINEA FOWL
(*Numida mitrata*)

Total length: 20–22 inches (50–55 cm)
Wing-length: 10½–11¾ inches (26–29 cm)

Notable for yellow crest and copper-coloured caruncles. Body covered by bluish, white-tipped feathers.

TUFTED GUINEA FOWL
(*Numida meleagris*)

Total length: 22–25¼ inches (55–63 cm)
Wing-length: 9¼–11½ inches (23–28.5 cm)

Head and neck naked, apart from a thin line of feathers from top of head to back. Nasal openings and caruncles red. Crest, beak and feet brownish. Plumage grey-white, speckled with white spots.

VULTURINE GUINEA FOWL
(*Acryllium vulturinum*)

Total length: 24½–29½ inches (61–74 cm)
Wing-length: 11½–12¾ inches (28.5–31.5 cm)

The head resembles that of a vulture, with broad naked areas, brilliant blue, the base of the beak red. The breast is white, with grey markings on a black ground, with a lighter central line bordered in blue. The upper parts of the body are flecked with small white patches. The flanks are blue with white spots encircled in lilac.

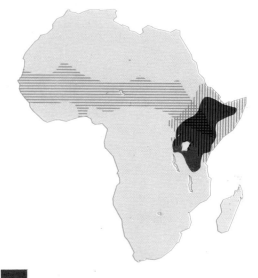

Geographical distribution of francolins and stone partridges.

the crest being yellowish, the beak red, the neck blue and the dark plumage speckled with tiny white spots.

Although its egg production is poor, the flesh of the guinea fowl is extremely appetising. For this reason, and also as a result of its docile temperament, the bird is reared in farms throughout Europe and America and is also displayed in zoos all over the world. It is an efficient guardian of farm stock, giving instant warning of any prowling predator, though not universally popular because of its noisy nocturnal habits.

The largest member of the family is the vulturine guinea fowl (*Acryllium vulturinum*), common in the tree-covered high plains and subdesert wastes of Somalia, Kenya and Uganda. It is sometimes referred to as the royal guinea fowl by reason of its magnificently variegated plumage. The lanceolate breast feathers are grey on a black ground with a white median line and bordered by a band of blue. All the upper parts of the bird's body have scattered white spots resembling pearls, encircled by black borders. The flanks are blue with large white patches, outlined in lilac.

The Kenya crested guinea fowl (*Guttera pucherani*) and others of the same genus have heads ornamented with an erect, thick crest, made up of long black feathers. The neck is naked. The plumage is black and dotted with uniformly-arranged patches of pale blue. The birds of this genus live in dense forest regions.

Francolins and stone partridges

The francolins are small members of the family Phasianidae, the African equivalents of the European partridges. They too are birds of steppe and savannah, most of them being grouped together in some 35 species of the genus *Francolinus,* and each showing distinguishing features in overall colour and particularly in the markings displayed on breast and belly. They are of fairly modest size, none of them exceeding 16 inches in length. Both males and females are furnished with leg-spurs, the males of certain species having two on each leg. The nest is a rough-and-ready affair, built on bare ground or in the grass. Seven or more eggs are laid, their colour ranging from light yellow to chestnut-brown.

Very similar to the francolins and sometimes known by the same name are the stone partridges, the best known and most characteristic African species being the stone partridge (*Ptilopachus petrosus*). As a general rule these birds have no spurs on their legs and lack the splendid markings on the breast.

One of the most distinctive features of the behaviour of the African francolins is their strident and penetrating cry. The clamorous call emitted by these birds as the sun rises is in volume and rhythm closer to that of quails than to partridges proper. The early morning alarm may not be all that welcome. In the Amboseli reserve of Kenya, for example, many a visitor has had his sleep rudely shattered at first light by the din of these birds, which may sometimes remain hidden in the grass but are occasionally to be spotted perching on a dead tree or on the top of a termite mound.

The egg-eating snake

The frantic cluckings and agitated movements of a female francolin suddenly draw the observer's attention to a clump of bushes where her nest is hidden. It has evidently been disturbed by a green, dark-veined snake, barely three feet in length, which is about to steal an egg. The snake curls itself around the egg, which is larger than its own head, gripping it firmly and running its forked tongue over the surface. Then, incredibly, its jaws open wide and it swallows the egg whole. The egg's diameter is fully double that of the snake's throat which is now grotesquely inflated. But now an even more astonishing thing happens, for the snake suddenly resumes its normal shape, the egg having apparently vanished. After a few spasmodic movements, the reptile regurgitates the shell and underlying membranes in a shapeless mass, then glides silently towards a second egg, intent upon repeating the entire process.

This agile nest-pillager is the egg-eating snake (*Dasypeltis scaber*), only member of the subfamily Dasypeltinae, part of the family Colubridae. It is an inhabitant of equatorial and southern Africa, with an almost cylindrical, slightly compressed body, a small head, elliptically-shaped, vertical pupils, and ridged scales.

Other snakes occasionally eat eggs by breaking the shells under

The francolins of Africa, inhabitants of plain and savannah, resemble the European partridges not only in appearance but also, to a certain extent, in their call, though that of the francolins is rather less strong and penetrating.

The egg-eating snake is one of the most persistent egg-stealers of all African animals. Special internal structures enable the reptile to swallow and dispose of eggs several times larger than its own head. Weaver-birds are frequent victims but so too are ring-doves and francolins.

muscular pressure and swallowing the contents, but none feeds in the specialised manner of the egg-eating snake. The latter's mouth and neck have a phenomenal distensible capacity so that when the snake is at rest the inside of the throat is arranged in folds. Furthermore the articular processes of the bones of the neck (hypapophyses) are long, sharp and covered with very hard bone, penetrating the dorsal wall of the esophagus and forming a kind of saw with eight or ten points. These, assisted by the powerful neck constrictions, rip the shell as the egg is swallowed, freeing the albumen and the yolk. Then a series of special muscles come into operation, expelling the parts that cannot be assimilated, while a valve opens to allow the edible portions to enter the stomach. The snake's small, rudimentary teeth also sink briefly into the shell and help to extract the liquids.

The only other snakes that possess similar articular processes are members of the genus *Elaphe* (chicken and rat snakes).

The egg-eating snake is also noted for the peculiar sound it makes by rubbing its scales together, similar to the action of certain vipers of deserts in Africa and western Asia.

The ingenious weaver-birds

The weaver-birds of the family Ploceidae are so named because of their instinctive and inherited ability to build their nests by weaving together scraps of grass, straw, stems and vegetable fibres. These small, gregarious birds are found on plains and savannahs and in forested regions over much of Africa, and though divided into several subfamilies, all have this remarkable nest-building habit. They lay their eggs, varying in number from 2–8, twice a year (or even more frequently), the incubation period lasting for two weeks.

The social weaver (*Philetairus socius*) belongs to the subfamily Passerinae and builds an extraordinarily massive nest, about 12–15 feet in diameter. Two or more pairs of social weavers may work together to construct it, devoting the greater part of their day to the task. The first essential is to find a solitary tree, usually an acacia, and then to start fashioning a protective roof. After that, by interlacing bits of straw and grass, the birds build the framework of the communal nest. Inside it they construct galleries and tunnels leading to an upper section, consisting of a series of compartments shaped like bells or retorts, where the eggs (2–4 for each female) will be laid and the chicks reared. The latter are eventually fed with insects and a large assortment of seeds and grains. Year after year the same couples return to the identical tree, building a new nest on the site of the previous one. This communal nest sometimes becomes so large and heavy that the branches snap beneath the weight. One such nest measured 30 feet by 20 feet at the base and was 5 feet high. It contained nearly a hundred nests and was probably over 20 years old.

The social weaver is not much more than $5\frac{1}{2}$ inches long and is closely related to the familiar house sparrows of hedge and garden. The male in particular resembles its northern counterpart with his dark head and chin, the feathers here forming a kind of bib. The pointed wings allow fairly rapid and sustained flight, the tail is small and truncated, and the entire body is covered with a rather sparse plumage. The beak is conical, short and quite strong, well suited for breaking the hard husks of seeds and for weaving the nest. To do this the bird grips one end of a grass stem with its feet and uses its beak to twine the other end.

The sparrow's African relatives

The tropical African representatives of the subfamily Ploceinae include the black-headed weaver (*Ploceus cucullatus*) known in West Africa as the village weaver. It is among the largest of the weavers although itself only about $6\frac{3}{4}$ inches long. In behaviour it too resembles European sparrows, living close to man. But because it is so numerous it causes much damage to crops.

During the breeding season the male has a black head and throat, with a V-shaped mark on the shoulders, the rest of the body and the breast being golden-yellow. At other times the plumage reverts to brown, with irregular patches of yellow or olive-green. Prior to breeding the birds hang their pear-shaped nests from the branches of trees not far from villages, the males being responsible for constructing them while the females simply put the last shaping touches to them. Each nest has a long central gallery leading to a lower section where the entrance is situated. The female lays 4–5 eggs and incubates them herself. The young do not leave the nest until they are about three weeks old.

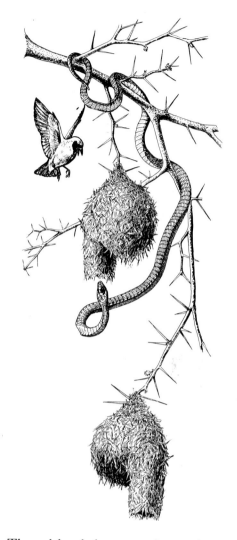

The red-headed weavers do not always use the nests they build. Some of them are left empty and these serve to dupe the egg-eating snakes and to keep them away from the real nest.

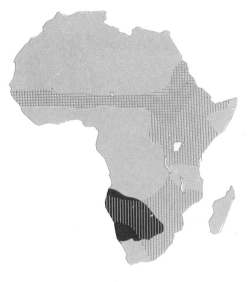

■ *Philetairus socius*

||||| *Quelea quelea*

≡ *Bubalornis albirostris*

Geographical distribution of social weavers (*Philetairus socius*), red-billed queleas (*Quelea quelea*) and buffalo weavers (*Bubalornis albirostris*).

AFRICAN WEAVER-BIRDS

Class: Aves
Order: Passeriformes
Family: Ploceidae

SOCIAL WEAVER
(Philetairus socius)

Total length: 5¼–5½ inches (13–14 cm)
Wing-length (closed): 2¾–3¼ inches (7–8 cm)

Fairly drab plumage, predominantly brown; there are darker marks on breast and flanks. The feathers of face and chin are also darker, forming a kind of bib.

RED-BILLED QUELEA
(Quelea quelea)

Total length: 5¼–5½ inches (13–14 cm)
Wing-length (closed): 2½–2¾ inches (6–7 cm)

Sexes clearly distinguished; the female is brownish, the male's facial mask and bib are black; face, head, breast and belly are pink. Both sexes have red beaks and feet.

BUFFALO WEAVER
(Bubalornis albirostris)

Total length: 10 inches (25 cm)
Wing-length (closed): 4¼–5¼ inches (11–13 cm)

Largest of all the weavers. Sexes clearly distinguished; the male is black with white-edged wing feathers; the female is pale grey. The female's beak is clear whitish-horn, but the male's has reddish tints.

The vitelline masked weaver (*Ploceus vitellinus*), also about the size of a house sparrow, is abundant in Central and East Africa. The sexes are sharply differentiated in appearance, the male's plumage being especially brilliant—chestnut red on the head, yellow on the neck and fawn on throat and breast. These weavers display considerable excitement during the breeding season and devote themselves unsparingly to the construction of nests on the outermost twigs of the acacias. They are round, with an entrance at the base and fashioned from grass, twigs and palm-fibres. The branches sometimes break under the great weight.

The members of the subfamily Euplectinae are known as bishop birds. The red bishop (*Euplectes oryx*) is of typically small build and both male and female are clearly differentiated at breeding time. They build oval nests with paper-thin, almost transparent walls. The females lay 3–6 eggs, incubating them alone. The fledglings, on becoming subadult, join together to form large flocks and embark on a nomadic existence, often causing considerable damage to fields of sorghum, the cereal which is their main source of food.

The red-billed quelea

The weavers of the genus *Quelea* are included in the Ploceidae and have a wide distribution throughout equatorial Africa. The red-billed queleas (*Quelea quelea*) are also about the size of house sparrows and in the dry season they congregate in immense numbers, causing extensive harm to cereals. Science has not yet found a way to control their ever-growing populations for they seem to be quite indestructible. Toxic chemicals, asphyxiating gases, fire and explosives have all been tried, without appreciable success.

A colony of queleas may consist of literally millions of birds, spread over an area of several hundred acres. The male is in charge of nest-construction, the female not lending a hand until it is nearly completed. Mating then takes place immediately, without any obvious form of courtship, and the first egg is laid 24 hours later. The female incubates the eggs at night and both parents during the day. This incubation period lasts two weeks. The nest-building activities begin at the start of the rainy season, and a few days before the first downpour the trees, still stripped of foliage, are already overburdened. All the eggs hatch at about the same time and are often so numerous that their shells cover the ground below the trees in a thick calcareous layer. This is the time when many predators are attracted to the nesting sites and they have some effect in limiting the prolific increase of the quelea population.

The ornithologists H. J. Disney and A. J. Marshall believe that the astonishing rate of growth of the species is due principally to the tendency of the birds to move freely from place to place in enormous flocks, seeking new nesting grounds each year. Almost any site will suit them, for their nests are relatively simple and quick to construct, but the timing will always depend on the arrival of the rains. Another contributory factor is that the young are capable of breeding before they are one year old.

The many species of weavers build nests that vary considerably in size, shape and internal structure. It is always the male, however, which plays the dominant role in nest-building, continually twittering and fluttering his tail to attract the female's attention. The nest, woven of grass, straw and vegetable fibres, is generally suspended from the slenderest branches of a tree, often an acacia, and 'false' nests are sometimes added that help protect eggs and brood from egg-eating snakes. Acacia branches are even stripped of thorns by some species, so impeding the reptiles' movements. The entrance to the nest is usually at the base, through a long 'tunnel'.

The buffalo weavers

The so-called buffalo weavers which belong to the subfamily Bubalorninae differ from other species chiefly in the shape of their beak. This is large and convex, extending in a straight line from the forehead. The mode of life and general behaviour of these weavers is similar to that of the oxpeckers of the genus *Buphagus*, for they too are often seen in the company of large mammals. Their favourite habitats are desert and subdesert regions, where they feed mainly on seeds taken from the excrement of domestic and wild animals.

The most characteristic member of the group is the white-billed buffalo weaver (*Bubalornis albirostris*), a gregarious bird which builds its nest on the thorns of acacias. Unlike that of other weavers, this nest has no interior transverse framework which could prevent the eggs from falling. The female lays 3–4 brown or grey eggs, which sometimes have additional black markings on a white ground. When the chicks hatch they make a kind of whistling noise so loud that, mingled with the cry of the adults, it can be heard hundreds of yards away.

The Layard's black-headed weaver is an East African species, often seen in the undergrowth, on river banks and on village outskirts. It nests in trees—usually in large colonies—and the female lays two or three white eggs.

The curious hornbills

The hornbills, belonging to the family Bucerotidae, order Coraciiformes, are large, sociable birds that often live close to human habitations. Their enormously large beaks, usually provided with saw-like edges and transverse furrows, are sometimes additionally furnished with horny growths or casques—more developed in males than females—which give the birds an even more grotesque appearance. But despite its size (and in a species such as the casqued hornbill the cylindrical casque almost completely covers the down-curved bill), beak and casque together are fairly lightweight for they are usually hollow and supported inside by spongy, fragile bony tissue.

All hornbills have black lashes on the eyelids, these being especially long in the ground hornbills. The latter also have very sturdy feet, the second, third and fourth toes being partially joined and the rear toe being mobile and well developed. Plumage is generally sober in colour—black and white, for example—and the feathers soft and loose, with several areas of coloured naked skin. The white-crested hornbill of Ghana is exceptional in possessing extremely vivid plumage. The colours of both male and female are similar in most species, the distinction being in the size and shape of the bill.

All these birds are outstandingly noisy in flight and a flock may make a sound not unlike that of a passing train. The reason seems to be that when they flap their wings the air whistles through the remiges, the bases of which are not surrounded by covert feathers. This enables the air to pass through more easily.

Hornbills live in well-wooded regions, from tropical virgin forest to the bush proper. Ground-dwelling species are sometimes encountered on the savannah, in groups of six or seven, walking about with calm, measured tread in search of food. They eat almost anything, including large quantities of fruit, seeds and insects. The white-crested hornbill tracks monkeys high in trees, catching on the wing any insects disturbed by the animals. Others feed almost exclusively on termites and few will turn down the chance of capturing a small mammal, fledgling or reptile. Groups may even band together to attack fairly large snakes. As an example of their catholic tastes, the stomach of one Abyssinian hornbill was found to contain a fragment of antelope hoof, feathers, a lizard, a frog, some dung-beetles, a large water scorpion, a caterpillar, a centipede and an assortment of insect eggs and bean husks!

The hornbill's tree-prison

The Roman writer Pliny, in his famous *Natural History*, was the first person to note and express amazement at the singular breeding habits of the hornbill. Modern ornithologists are none the less fascinated by the birds' behaviour at such times, and their detailed study has revealed interesting variations. In most cases the site of the hornbill's nest is a hole in a tree, sometimes as high as 100 feet up. The female enters this hole and then barricades herself inside, plugging the entrance with bits of dung

■ *Bucorvus leadbeateri*

▦ *Bycanistes brevis*

▤ *Tockus flavirostris*

Geographical distribution of ground hornbills (*Bucorvus leadbeateri*), silvery-cheeked hornbills (*Bycanistes brevis*) and yellow-billed hornbills (*Tockus flavirostris*).

AFRICAN HORNBILLS

Class: Aves
Order: Coraciiformes
Family: Bucerotidae
Number of eggs: up to 5
Incubation: about 50 days

GROUND HORNBILL
(*Bucorvus leadbeateri*)

Total length: 42 inches (105 cm)
Wing-length (closed): $20\frac{1}{2}$–$23\frac{1}{2}$ inches
  (51–59 cm)

Large black bird with short, thick feet. The white primary wing feathers are visible in flight. Face and throat red. Nests on the ground.

SILVERY-CHEEKED HORNBILL
(*Bycanistes brevis*)

Total length: 26–$29\frac{1}{4}$ inches (65–73 cm)
Wing-length (closed): $12\frac{3}{4}$–$15\frac{3}{4}$ inches
  (32–39 cm)

With the exception of the white covert feathers above the tail, body and wings are completely black. The male's casque is yellow, that of the female is smaller and dark, like the beak.

YELLOW-BILLED HORNBILL
(*Tockus flavirostris*)

Total length: $16\frac{3}{4}$–20 inches (42–50 cm)
Wing-length (closed): $7\frac{1}{4}$–$8\frac{3}{4}$ inches
  (18–22 cm)

A medium-sized bird, with a yellow-orange beak and no casque. Overall plumage colour brown or dark grey, almost black. White marks are sometimes visible on wing coverts; orbital stripe, sides of neck, breast and belly are also white.

Cross-section of a silvery-cheeked hornbill's nest. This is situated in a natural cavity in a dry tree, the small entrance hole being sealed with mud and dung so that only enough room is left for the male to introduce food. The female is virtually imprisoned in the nest while she incubates the eggs and later rears the young. The beak, topped by a characteristic casque, is powerful enough to help her defend the nest against mongooses, crows or any other animal attempting to interfere with the eggs or the fledglings.

Facing page : Hornbills are typical birds of the dry plains. Though all possess a huge downward-curving bill (with or without a casque), shapes and colours vary enormously. Shown here from left to right, top to bottom, are four species—Van der Decken's hornbill, yellow-billed hornbill, red-billed hornbill and ground hornbill.

or mud brought to her by the male, until there is only a narrow slit showing, through which food can be introduced. Some species lay one or two eggs, others—though more rarely—three, four or five. After laying her eggs the imprisoned female, carefully attended by her mate, begins to moult; sometimes all the wing and tail feathers are shed and completely replaced.

The extraordinary nesting procedure of the hornbills poses many problems. The female has to adapt herself to a prolonged period of incarceration while the male, who is responsible for transporting food to the nest, often appears to abstain from eating altogether. One silvery-cheeked hornbill (a species that has been particularly closely studied by the ornithologists R. E. and W. M. Moreau) was observed to visit his mate a couple of dozen times in the space of ten hours. The scientists noted that the incubation period was about seven weeks and that a further seven weeks elapsed before the fledglings reached full development. Thus the mother was immured in her nest for more than three months. In all this time the interior of the nest was kept perfectly clean, the female defecating precisely and at high velocity through the entrance slit and various commensal insects getting rid of any excrement left inside the nest, together with scraps of uneaten food. What could not be determined was at what age the fledglings learned to eliminate waste matter in a similar fashion nor how the insects resolved the problem up to that point. At the end of the incubation period the male, for no obvious reason, brought his mate bits of bark, berries, fruits and flowers.

There seems to be a definite connection between the female's moulting and her nesting habits. A female yellow-billed hornbill taken from her nest experimentally was found to have moulted and could not fly. Later observations showed that she leaves the nest after renewing her plumage, to help feed the nestlings. After the mother leaves the nest the four or five young birds promptly close up the entrance hole, apparently without the assistance of the father, using scraps of food and dung for the purpose. This, however, does not appear to be a general rule for in other species raising fewer fledglings, the mother hornbill will not abandon the nest until the young are ready to accompany her.

The ground hornbills of the genus *Bucorvus* have completely different nesting habits, the female never being imprisoned in the manner described. Nests are simply formed from a hole in a tree or an opening in the rocks and it appears to be the male rather than the female which incubates the eggs.

Mr and Mrs Moreau were the first naturalists to draw attention to another interesting feature of hornbill behaviour—the fact that in some species, including the silvery-cheeked hornbill, communal roosting sites are regularly used by several hundred birds at a time.

Hornbills vary considerably in size. The enormous ground hornbill (*Bucorvus leadbeateri*), an inhabitant of the open plains and bush of Kenya, Uganda, Tanzania and parts of Central Africa from the southern Congo down to South Africa, is as large as a turkey; the red-billed hornbill (*Tockus erythrorhynchus*) is, by contrast, the size of a partridge. There are in all five African genera, grouped into more than 25 species. Among other common

species are the trumpeter hornbill (*Bycanistes bucinator*) and the silvery-cheeked hornbill (*Bycanistes brevis*), both of these being forest birds found all over East Africa; the grey hornbill (*Tockus nasutus*) and the yellow-billed hornbill (*Tockus flavirostris*), inhabitants of the East African bush and some parts of Central Africa through Rhodesia to South Africa; the crowned hornbill (*Tockus alboterminatus*), the Abyssinian ground hornbill (*Bucorvus abyssinicus*) and the white-crested hornbill (*Tropicranus albocristatus*).

Related to the hornbills are kingfishers, bee-eaters, rollers and hoopoes – all members of the order Coraciiformes and found in tropical and temperate regions throughout the world.

Ring-doves

One can hardly imagine a film being made about the animals of the African bush without an accompanying sound track; and to capture on tape the dawn chorus of thousands of birds is surely to evoke the essence of the wildlife scene even more dramatically than through the visual images of the camera. Listening to this excited warbling and chattering, one cannot fail to be struck by a familiar sound which seems to dominate all the others – the soft, rhythmical cooing of the ring-doves.

These graceful, delicate members of the family Columbidae (doves and pigeons) find in the bush ideal nesting conditions. In the rainy season thousands of their roughly constructed nests can be found in the forks of acacia branches. Of the many species, few have the fragile charm of the namaqua dove (*Oena capensis*), about the size of a lark but with a longer tail (the central rectrices alone are nearly four inches in length). The sexes are well differentiated, the male with a black mask over forehead and face, with similar black marks on the beak, the throat and part of the breast. The female has no such markings on her uniformly brown plumage. Bluish tints are reflected from the outer side of the wings.

These doves are often seen at ground level but when not actually in view are extremely difficult to locate in the grass, for they are able ventriloquists. Their nest, like all members of the family, is a rudimentary affair, composed of twigs and placed low in a shrub or bush. The female lays two cream-coloured eggs and the chicks are hatched within two weeks.

The laughing dove (*Streptopelia senegalensis*) is a much more thickset, sturdy bird, the female being slightly smaller than the male. Not surprisingly, the latter has the more brilliant plumage. This is a sedentary species with a marked preference for built-up areas, often being seen in gardens. It is sometimes discovered nesting in eaves and rafters, the female laying two white eggs. Its cooing is like mirthless laughter.

Among other common and reasonably abundant species of African ring-dove are the red-eyed dove (*Streptopelia semitorquata*), which is roughly the size of a domestic pigeon; the pink-breasted dove (*Streptopelia lugens*); the emerald-spotted wood dove (*Turtur chalcospilos*); and the ring-necked dove (*Streptopelia capicola*).

Facing page : Ring-necked doves are plentiful in the African bush, sometimes elusive to the eye but identifiable by their soft, persistent cooing. They frequently flock in large numbers, together with weavers and other birds, round permanent water courses.

CHAPTER 13

Birds of prey in the bush and savannah

When the birds of prey of the Holarctic zone – namely those born in Europe and northern Asia – cross the Sahara and the Arabian peninsula to spend the winter in Africa, they find a large number of competitors already spread out on the plains and savannahs. But these fertile, sunny expanses are vast enough to support both the native populations and the migrants; and from November until February the East African landscape is notable for its unparalleled concentration of predatory birds.

The great raptors of the African continent are fortunate not only in enjoying ideal living conditions but also in being allowed to roam freely everywhere. Since man can neither eat nor commercially exploit them they are of no interest to hunters or poachers. They are intelligent and adaptable creatures, sufficiently docile to permit ornithologists to make patient and exhaustive studies of their behaviour. Even casual tourists have been rewarded with spectacular photographs of these birds.

Among the largest and most imposing of the indigenous species are the martial eagle (*Polemaetus bellicosus*), a typical raptor of plains and savannahs; the Verreaux's eagle (*Aquila verreauxii*), hunter of rocks and mountains; and the bateleur eagle (*Terathopius ecaudatus*), with its unusual tail-less silhouette. But in addition to these giants whose outspread wings may each measure more than 6 feet and whose body weight may be nearly 13 lb, there are many other species of varying sizes, down to the pygmy falcons or falconets which tip the scales at a little over 2 oz and which often shelter in the nests of the weavers.

Between these two extremes there are many wonderful birds of average size – eagles, buzzards, falcons, goshawks, kites and sparrowhawks – each of them using different methods for satisfying their special food requirements, according to their size,

Facing page : The bateleur eagle is one of the most impressive African birds of prey, characterised by remarkable acrobatic display flights in the breeding season. It feeds on small vertebrates and occasionally carrion.

The chanting goshawk is a medium-sized raptor feeding on reptiles, birds and small mammals. Unlike most other birds of prey, which utter sharp, piercing cries, this species is a melodious singer.

strength and natural endowments. And these birds are everywhere. A visitor may stop his car beneath an acacia in the middle of a stretch of empty savannah and be amazed to see a superb martial eagle perched motionless in the branches, patient and inscrutable as it waits to pounce on an unsuspecting mammal or large bird; and many a sign-post at the side of a dusty road will be occupied by an augur buzzard (*Buteo rufofuscus augur*), a brown bird with a white breast, on the lookout for rodents. The harriers or marsh hawks almost shave the grass as they swoop low in their characteristic hunting flight, as dramatic in its way as the sensational nose-diving of the native peregrine falcon (*Falco peregrinus minor*) or the winter-visiting Siberian falcon (*F. p. calidus*). But perhaps for those who are accustomed to thinking of birds of prey as gliding and circling high in the sky and scouring the ground below for victims, one of the most astonishing sights is the stately secretary bird with its tuft of plumes, strutting about on its long legs, indefatigably searching for the reptiles, frogs, rodents and insects on which it feeds.

The birds of prey are particularly dependent on the African continent for their winter quarters. Certain insect-eating species that nest north of the Tropic of Cancer seek refuge in these parts as soon as their regular habitats are swamped by the first rains and food becomes scarce. That is why colonies of lanners, which nest in India, and the red-footed falcons, from eastern China, journey south to Africa for the winter. Such migratory birds try as far as possible to avoid crossing over broad expanses of water; thus these Asiatic species do not normally travel by way of the Indian Ocean but enter Africa through the Suez Canal region, travelling across the Nile valley and ending their journey in East Africa.

Even more important are the migrations of falcons from northern Europe and Asia; they follow the flocks of wild ducks and geese and other water birds, preying on these birds when they eventually alight on the banks of the same lakes and rivers at journey's end. Thus on Lake Naivasha in Kenya and on the huge lake in the Ngorongoro Crater the visitor may often catch a glimpse of these raptors diving down to snatch and carry off the smaller aquatic species.

The winged hunters and their prey

There is hardly a single species of animal in East Africa, be it insect, mollusc, crustacean, fish, amphibian, reptile, bird or mammal, that is not a potential source of food for one or other of the winged raptors or scavengers.

Some of these birds have extremely specialised tastes. One such is the bat hawk or Andersson's pern (*Machaerhamphus alcinus*) which, as its name suggests, feeds on bats, swooping on these nocturnal creatures as they swarm out at dusk from the pitch darkness of the caves in which they live. The fish eagle and the secretary bird too have their specialised food preferences. But other raptors, such as the kites and the tawny eagle (*Aquila rapax*) enjoy a very much more varied diet, being capable of swallowing and digesting any living creature of small or medium

Verreaux's eagle owl
(Bubo lacteus)

Chanting goshawk
(Melierax musicus)
adult

Augur buzzard
(Buteo rufofuscus augur)

Red-tailed buzzard
(Buteo rufofuscus rufofuscus)

Verreaux's eagle
(Aquila verreauxii)
adult

Chanting goshawk
(Melierax musicus)
immature

Martial eagle
(Polemaetus bellicosus)

Verreaux's eagle
(Aquila verreauxii)
immature

Wahlberg's eagle
(Aquila wahlbergi)

Bateleur eagle
(Terathopius ecaudatus)

Tawny eagle
(Aquila rapax)

size and even, on occasion, feeding on carrion.

In certain situations, when there is a sudden and perhaps unexpected abundance of prey in a particular locality, different birds will converge upon the same spot in the expectation of sharing a meal. For example, Verreaux's eagles, tawny eagles, kites, chanting goshawks (*Melierax musicus*) and pygmy falcons may sometimes be found gathered together around a termite mound, intent upon capturing the tiny insects as they swarm out on their nuptial flight.

Any animal that weighs less than 20 lb or thereabouts is threatened, both day and night by these fierce birds of prey, as has been proved by minute scientific examination of the latter's feeding habits. Yet some raptors also have to beware of others of their kind, and cases of parasitism are not uncommon. The black kites, for example, are a plague to the fish eagles, tormenting them mercilessly until they drop the fish they have recently caught.

For obvious reasons, there are more birds of prey to be found on the open plains and lightly wooded regions than in the dense forests. In the wooded areas the largest and most powerful bird of prey is the crowned hawk eagle (*Stephanoaetus coronatus*), while on the savannahs a comparable ecological niche is occupied by the martial eagle and the Verreaux's eagle. All three species prey on mammals weighing between 2–10 lb. Deeper in the forest one finds the Ayre's hawk eagle (*Hieraaetus dubius*) and the great sparrowhawk (*Accipiter melanoleucus*), both of which feed on other birds; and on the savannahs the chanting goshawks and a number of falcons pursue the same type of prey.

The long-crested hawk eagle (*Lophoaetus occipitalis*) is also a bird of the forest, whereas the small Wahlberg's eagle (*Aquila wahlbergi*) is a creature of the savannah. Nevertheless, the nesting areas of these two species sometimes tend to overlap. The birds may even make use of the same shelters and there has been a case described of the first actually incubating the eggs of the second species.

But no matter whether they live in the woods or forests or on the plains and savannahs, the various African birds of prey take

Each bird of prey has a different diet and each has a particularly favoured spot for building its nest. In this diagram the outlines of some of the most characteristic raptors of the African plain and savannah are shown (in flight), together with the sites where they generally construct an eyrie. 1. Bateleur eagle (male and female). 2. Secretary bird. 3. Wahlberg's eagle. 4. Martial eagle. 5. Tawny eagle. 6. Verreaux's eagle. 7. Augur buzzard. 8. Peregrine falcon. 9. Chanting goshawk. 10. Pallid harrier. The peregrine is rather a specialised case since it lays its eggs on any kind of sheltered ledge, without preparing any nest material.

advantage of any form of terrain which can provide them with the twin necessities of life–food and shelter. In 1952, for example, eleven pairs of Wahlberg's eagles were found nesting in the 140 square miles of Kenya's Embu savannah region; in this same area there were three families of martial eagles, each virtually owning a territory of almost 50 square miles. In the Nairobi National Park it was estimated that a single pair of secretary birds lorded it over a piece of terrain about 10 square miles in extent; and two species of chanting goshawk roamed over portions of territory roughly twice as large. These figures give some idea of the vast dimensions of the individual pieces of territory controlled by some of these birds of prey.

One would imagine that the size of a chosen piece of territory would be determined to a large extent by the abundance or lack of available prey, as in the case of many predatory mammals. But some interesting and perhaps surprising facts in this connection have been revealed by a detailed survey of the food habits of the above-mentioned Wahlberg's eagles. It has been estimated that each of these birds requires about 3–4 oz of food every day. Thus, assuming that they feed exclusively on small mammals and that their own population remains steady, a single family would need to find about 1,460 such animals in a year. Each pair of eagles occupies roughly 10 square miles of savannah, and considering the density of the small mammal population within such an area, it is clear that only a very insignificant proportion can actually be caught and eaten by the raptors. Even taking into account the fluctuating nature of the mammal population in any given area, it can be reckoned that perhaps 50,000 might be found within the bounds of the eagles' territory, so that the possible loss of 1,500–as many as would be needed

The augur buzzard is a common bird of prey throughout East Africa, perching on top of a rock, a mound or a sign-post in wait for its prey. This usually consists of a small vertebrate; adult birds and strong, fleet-footed mammals are generally avoided for the augur buzzard is not a fast flier. It performs a useful service to farmers in preying on rats, mice and similar harmful rodents.

for a year's food supply—would have very little effect on the total numbers.

Similar calculations and conclusions can be made concerning the food habits of the martial eagle, which feeds mainly on bustards, guinea fowl and hyraxes and which appears to require about 9 oz of food daily. This would mean that each adult bird would need to find not more than some 290 victims in a year, ranging over about 50 square miles of terrain. Obviously this is an insignificant part of the total bird and mammal population in such an extensive area.

It is evident, therefore, that no single species of raptor—whether it be the Wahlberg's eagle, the long-crested hawk or the augur buzzard—is capable of exercising much influence on the population figures of its prey, although close collaboration between certain species in any selected area might have an effect, even if only a temporary one, on their numbers; and as we have seen, particularly in the case of the martial eagle, it is probably not the abundance or shortage of food that determines the density of the raptor population, but rather the dimensions of their hunting grounds, from which all other members of the same species—though not necessarily of rival species—will be expelled.

The Verreaux's eagle

In its massive build, outline and general behaviour, the Verreaux's eagle strongly resembles the better-known golden eagle. The main difference is of course the shining black adult plumage with its lighter patches on the back and on the secondary wing feathers, giving the bird the alternative common name of black eagle.

The beak of the Verreaux's eagle is strongly curved, the powerful talons join like a pair of pincers round their victim, the feet and cere are bright orange, the large, glittering eyes orange-yellow. As in all members of the family there are feathers right down to the roots of the toes. It is in fact an extremely striking bird and the contrast between the jet-black hues of the legs and wings and the fiery orange of the claws give it a singular beauty.

The Verreaux's eagle is a hunter of the hillsides, kopjes and mountain peaks, hovering in wait near the top of a rock or on a dead tree and plummeting down on its victim, often from a considerable height, in a spectacular nose-dive. Like the golden eagle it relies on a surprise attack of this nature to catch the hyraxes which are its favourite victims, hurling itself against the steep slopes where the fat little mammals congregate, seeming to cling precariously to the kopje walls and giving the terrified creatures no opportunity of scurrying off to safety among the holes and fissures.

It is true that the Verreaux's eagle also hunts guinea fowl, francolins, reptiles, hares, rats and other rodents. But just as the Alpine marmot is the special favourite of the golden eagle, so is the rock hyrax the chief victim of the African raptor. In fact the continental distribution of the Verreaux's eagle almost coincides with that of the hyrax population, the latter providing

over 80 per cent of the birds' food requirements in some regions and at certain times of year. Thus the eagle is found all over Africa south of the Sahara, as far north as Sudan and Somalia, ranging over high mountains, savannahs and subdesert zones, but never straying far from cliffs and rocks. In Ethiopia and on the high plains of East Africa the nests or eyries of this impressive bird of prey have been found at heights of over 13,000 feet.

The Verreaux's eagle normally breeds at the end of the dry season, the period being to some extent determined by the ravages of fire which lay waste to large stretches of its regular habitat every year. By raising a brood at this particular time both the parent birds and the fledglings are able to find plenty of food in the shape of innumerable small animals which fight for survival on the scorched grasslands, many of them having been driven by the flames from their customary refuges.

The nuptial displays of these eagles consist of a series of remarkable gliding flights during which the birds remain absolutely silent, in this respect behaving quite unlike other eagles. Only at the actual moment of coupling do the birds emit a soft whistling or throaty sound, something like the gobbling of turkeys.

In its shape, outline and behaviour, Verreaux's eagle is not unlike the golden eagle. Its plumage, however, is almost entirely black so that it is also known as the black eagle.

Facing page : Verreaux's eagles frequently roost and nest among the rocks of kopjes and steep cliffs and mountains. Here they are in a position to keep a vigilant lookout for small animals, especially hyraxes, their favourite prey.

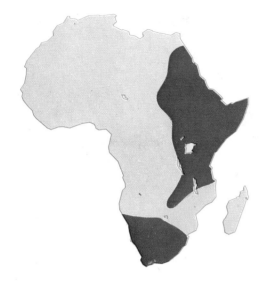

Geographical distribution of Verreaux's eagle.

VERREAUX'S EAGLE
(*Aquila verreauxii*)

Class: Aves
Order: Falconiformes
Family: Accipitridae

Total length: 30–36 inches (75–90 cm)
Wing-length (closed):
    male 22½–23¾ inches (56·5–59·5 cm)
    female 23½–25½ inches (59–64 cm)
Wingspan: 74–84 inches (185–210 cm)
Weight: male 7¾ lb (3·5 kg);
        female 7¾–12 lb (3·5–5·5 kg)
Diet: flesh (hyraxes, guinea fowl and other
    medium-sized animals)
Number of eggs: 1–2
Incubation: 43–46 days

Adults
Plumage black, except for white rump, white marks on primary wing feathers and V-shaped mark on back. The iris is dark. Cere and toes golden-yellow.

Immature birds
Reddish-brown plumage, boldly marked, lower sides of wings white. Dark iris. Cere and toes pale yellow.

Young
Covered with white down.

Four months before the eggs are laid, the two eagles begin to build an eyrie, either high in a tree or on a cliff ledge. The site chosen for the nest is always very small in relation to the size of the bird itself. As the incubation period continues both birds become noticeably more aggressive. Not only will they not tolerate the presence of any other large bird near the nest but they will not even allow an intruder, large or small, within their territorial bounds.

Naturalists studying the behaviour of one breeding pair on the Guan'g hill in northern Tanzania observed that the female was twice forced to abandon her nest in order to help the male to defend it. The first occasion was during the latter half of the incubation period when the eyrie was assailed by her own off-spring of the previous year; the second came after the eggs were hatched when two buzzards and a pair of white-necked crows launched a concerted attack. She did not bother to come to the assistance of her mate, however, when the latter was challenged by a single buzzard, a tawny eagle and two crows, a combination which the male was apparently able to cope with unaided. It was noticeable that as a rule the female's fighting instincts were much more sharply developed than those of her mate, who seemed to avoid clashes with intruders whenever possible.

Although both parent birds share the incubation duties, the female devotes more time to it and after a period of 43–46 days one baby is usually born. It frequently happens that the second egg does not hatch at all; sometimes it hatches later than the first one. In the latter instance the new arrival is at a grave dis-advantage, the firstborn chick continually tormenting the new-comer and preventing it from taking any food. Eventually the second chick has the strength neither to defend itself nor to feed and simply dies of starvation. Strangely, the parents appear not to intervene in these fratricidal conflicts. Only once during the Guan'g survey was the adult male seen to lower his head in the direction of the squabbling young who interrupted their fighting for a brief moment to bring their beaks into contact with that of their father.

During incubation and after the hatching of the eggs both parents were observed to make a series of journeys to and from the nest, bringing back branches in their beaks and between their claws. The male, however, appeared to be largely respon-sible for tending to the needs of the newborn chick. After capturing his prey he would perch a dozen or so yards away from the eyrie and begin to dismember his victim. After devouring the head and viscera he would deliver the remains to the female. She continued tearing it up, eating the tougher parts herself and passing on the more tender morsels to the greedy youngster.

The quantity and variety of prey brought back to the nest depends mainly on the age of the offspring. At the beginning food will consist chiefly of guinea fowl and francolins but in due course bird victims become fewer and there is a larger supply of hares and hyraxes, which are more difficult to tear apart and to digest. The parents are generally content to share the same type of food but they may vary their diet with a newborn antelope or, on rare occasions, mongooses and snakes.

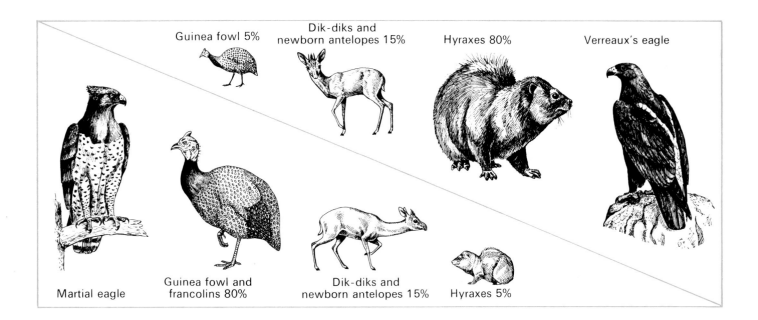

Guinea fowl 5%

Dik-diks and newborn antelopes 15%

Hyraxes 80%

Verreaux's eagle

Martial eagle

Guinea fowl and francolins 80%

Dik-diks and newborn antelopes 15%

Hyraxes 5%

Life in the eyrie

The young Verreaux's eagle, which at birth is covered with white down, soon starts moving clumsily about by supporting itself on its wings. At a month old the dark primary remiges begin to appear and the eaglet is able to stand upright. Gradually its appearance changes until it is enveloped in brown plumage. When about seven weeks old it flutters its wings experimentally; the plumage is now becoming darker and the bird is gathering strength and mobility. At eleven weeks it executes a strange kind of dance over the nest, keeping its head lowered; in another two weeks it is fully developed, ready to leave the nest and embark on its first flying lessons, sometimes clutching a hare or a hyrax between its talons. One day, while its mother is resting, the youngster may decide to launch out on its great adventure. It clambers on to her back and she, without a moment's hesitation, takes off. When she is a few yards from the ground and directly above the nest, the young eagle spreads its wings, makes a short solo flight and returns to the eyrie. Next day it may be sufficiently confident to attempt a longer flight without her assistance.

After it is able to fly about on its own the eaglet remains in the neighbourhood of the eyrie for at least another month, continuing to accept food from both parents. In the ensuing weeks, however, it will join the adults on their sorties but will not stay aloft for any considerable period. Later it accompanies them on hunting forays and becomes increasingly familiar with their hunting techniques.

Three or four months after leaving the nest for good, the eaglet is able to fend for itself in every way. The family, which until then has been a closely-knit unit, now breaks up, although parents and young continue to share the same territory. When the latter is about nine months old the adults may be ready to return to the old site to make another nest, and this will be the time for them to serve warning on their offspring that its presence is no longer welcome.

On the steppes and savannahs of Africa there is a concentration of birds of prey seldom equalled in other parts of the world. In many cases their various diets complement one another as can be seen by comparing those of two of the largest raptors, the Verreaux's eagle and the martial eagle.

This was the pattern of behaviour followed by the family nesting on the Guan'g hill. The observers noted that in addition to augur buzzards and white-necked crows, kites and white-backed vultures also made occasional attacks on the eyrie or carried out intimidatory manoeuvres, and that the eaglet too tried to beat the assailants off—aggressive bearing that doubtless stemmed from inexperience rather than a calm calculation of odds. But when other birds such as Egyptian vultures and pelicans flew over the eagles' territory, provided they kept well away from the nest, there was no hostile response from the occupants. As far as land carnivores are concerned, leopards appear the least acceptable to Verreaux's eagles and clashes between bird and mammal are frequent.

The martial eagle

The magnificent martial eagle is an even more powerful and persistent predator than either Verreaux's or the golden eagle. Its head is more rounded than those of other raptors, its beak is relatively short and strongly hooked, and only the goshawk can match the beauty of its golden eyes. Like the latter, the martial eagle has very long muscular legs and slender tarsi, covered with feathers down to the root of the toes. These are as long as those of most birds of prey and the powerful claws are characteristic of a raptor accustomed to hunting other birds in preference to mammals (for which shorter, thicker claws are more suitable).

The martial eagle mounts patient guard on the bare branches of the highest acacias, then with a noisy beating of wings launches itself as unerringly as an arrow at its victim—as like as not a plump guinea fowl. Alternatively, it will use its immense wingspan (greater than that of the golden eagle) to glide high over the steppe or savannah—like a hawk or a buzzard—and then drop almost vertically in free fall, braking at the last moment and skimming along close to the ground, skilfully avoiding the thorny undergrowth. Eventually it sinks its talons in the neck of a guinea fowl—surprised on the ground—a solitary dik-dik or a newly-born gazelle.

About two-thirds of the martial eagle's regular diet is made up of birds—mainly guinea fowl, then domestic fowl, francolins and bustards. Small mammals such as hyraxes, dik-diks, baby impalas, monkeys and lambs will also be attacked when the opportunities offer. The eagle has been seen—though admittedly on rare occasions—to prey on jackals, servals, storks, mongooses, large snakes and lizards.

In the breeding season the male does not indulge in any especially spectacular form of courtship display, but both birds emit a characteristic call which can be heard from some distance, whether they are gliding aloft or perched on a vantage point in the branches of a tree. The nest is always built in a tall tree (50–90 feet) and often in the highest branches. The eyrie itself may measure up to 15 feet in diameter, though generally smaller. Sometimes several will be found on the same site for the bird constructs a new one every year, perhaps using new and old

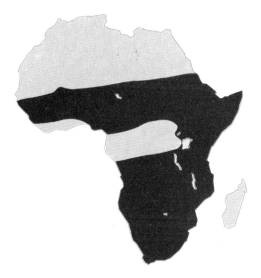

Geographical distribution of the martial eagle.

MARTIAL EAGLE
(*Polemaetus bellicosus*)

Class: Aves
Order: Falconiformes
Family: Accipitridae

Total length: 29–36 inches (72–90 cm)
Wing-length (folded):
    male 22–24 inches (56–61 cm)
    female 24–27 inches (61–67·5 cm)
Wingspan: 86–100 inches (215–250 cm)
Weight: male 7¾ lb (3·5 kg)
        female 10½–13½ lb (4·7–6·2 kg)
Diet: flesh (birds, small mammals)
Number of eggs: one
Incubation: 45 days

Adults
Lower parts of body white with darker spots; back, throat, neck and breast grey-brown. There is usually a tuft of feathers on the head. Iris yellow; cere and toes blue-grey.

Immature birds
Throat, breast and lower parts white, with no dark markings. Light marks on back and wings.

Young
Covered with dark grey down.

Facing page : The martial eagle frequently mounts guard on a high branch or the stump of a dead tree, waiting for its favourite prey—birds and small mammals. Although the bird in the lower picture, an immature martial eagle, has just killed a hare, the species preys more often on guinea fowl and francolins.

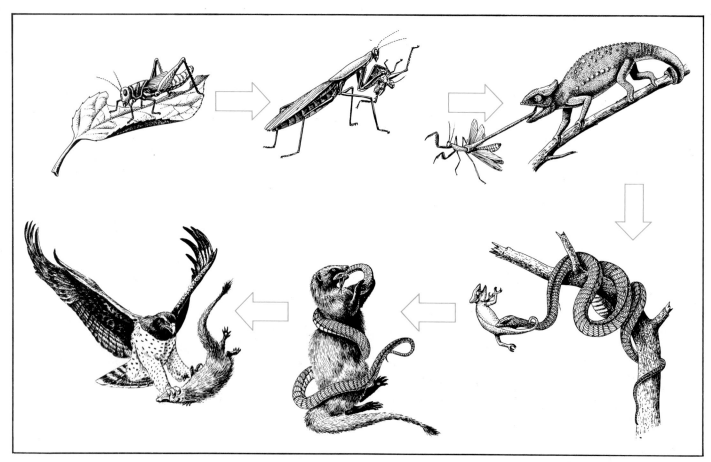

On the African steppes the various food chains are often highly complex. Thus part of the energy accumulated in vegetation such as leaves is passed on in turn to the locust, the praying mantis, the chameleon, the snake, the mongoose and finally the martial eagle. The body of the raptor may then be devoured by a hyena.

Facing page : The modest brown plumage of the young bateleur eagle (*above*) contrasts strongly with the spectacular attire of the adult. Despite their similar shapes they might well be taken for different species.

alternately. The nest-building takes about six weeks and eventually one egg is laid. Timing is variable, depending on the district. In Sudan, for example, the female lays the egg in November but in South Africa it may occur between March and July. The incubation period is about 45 days, the female assuming egg-guarding duties and the male feeding her. Breeding habits of the species are in fact somewhat haphazard. In one survey 31 pairs of birds were seen to build a nest, but only 18 eggs were found to have been laid and of these only 13 finally hatched out.

The chick is completely covered with down until well into its third month. When the time comes it is quicker in learning to fly than, for example, the crowned hawk eagle, but is not itself ready to breed until it is three years old.

The bateleur eagle

The most impressive African bird when actually in flight is without any doubt the bateleur eagle. Its wings are comparatively long and sharply outlined but the tail is very short so that when the bird is flying the red feet can clearly be seen protruding. It is interesting to watch this bird as it soars high above the plains in the midday heat. Its speed, complete confidence and amazing acrobatic ability as it executes complex aerial patterns are quite breathtaking—yet it hardly appears to move its wings at all. The only time it makes obvious use of its wings is when it takes off, about an hour after sunrise, from the ground or a tree-top; and even then it requires only a few

Geographical distribution of the bateleur eagle.

BATELEUR EAGLE
(*Terathopius ecaudatus*)

Class: Aves
Order: Falconiformes
Family: Accipitridae

Total length: 24 inches (60 cm)
Wing-length (folded):
   male 19–22 inches (48·5–55 cm)
   female 19½–21½ inches (50–55 cm)
Wingspan: 71 inches (180 cm)
Weight: 4½–6½ lb (2–3 kg)
Diet: flesh (carrion, small mammals, reptiles)
Number of eggs: one
Incubation: 42–43 days

Adults
Very short tail, chestnut like part of the back.
Lower surface of wings almost pure white. Females have a lighter patch under the wings. Iris black, cere and toes red.

Immature birds
Colour uniformly brownish-red; tail longer than that of adult; cere greenish, toes grey.

Young
Covered with dark down, cere creamy-white, toes whitish.

powerful thrusts for it to become airborne, using the rising thermal air currents to gain altitude, and adjusting its flight to the strength and direction of the breeze by altering the angle of incidence of its large wing feathers. The nuptial displays during the breeding season are particularly astonishing, the birds twisting and tumbling through the sky in a fantastic exhibition of aerial acrobatics, spending the greater part of the day aloft.

As the eagle gains height the silvery-grey tones of the lower part of its body merge with the opaque colour of the sky above and the eye has difficulty in distinguishing its outline in the shimmering heat rising from the plains below. Some experts believe that this camouflage effect plays an important part in the bird's surprise attacks on small mammals which make up part of its normal diet.

The bateleur eagle's average speed is 30–50 miles per hour so that it can easily cover 200 miles in a single day, scouring a vast area for signs of carrion–the basis of its food requirements. To this end it takes advantage of the movements of other scavengers, following in the wake of vultures and flapping its enormous wings to frighten them off when the site is located. But despite these threatening gestures there is seldom cause for serious conflict with other species.

In addition to carrion the bateleur eagle feeds on reptiles and small mammals such as mice, hedgehogs, squirrels and young hares. The raptor has also been seen to attack poisonous snakes, though this is probably an error on its part, a sleeping reptile being easily mistaken for a dead one.

The eyrie is constructed in an acacia, usually one ranging from 20–70 feet high. The nest is comparatively small, about two feet wide and a foot deep, but with new touches added every spring to a nest of the previous season, such constructions can become rather more voluminous. When the nest becomes too old or battered for re-use the eagles often resort to nests built by other birds of prey.

It often happens, either during the building of the nest or during the period of incubation, that another bateleur eagle takes up residence near the eyrie but this does not seem to cause any disturbance. An outsider has even been seen perching unconcernedly on a branch within a few feet of the brooding female, though no proof has yet been given of this third eagle playing any share in the actual incubation of the eggs or the feeding of the young. It is possible that this type of behaviour has some bearing on the eaglet's habit of remaining for some length of time, sometimes more than a year, close to the nest where it has been born and reared; this in spite of the fact that it is quick in learning to fly, and may leave the nest at the age of three months.

Should a human approach too close, the bateleur eagle often shows itself to be more aggressively inclined than other birds of prey. On the other hand, having made a great show of disapproval, the parents may spoil the effect by leaving the nest for several hours or even abandoning it completely, sometimes when the chick is not yet fully developed.

The female lays a single egg, almost uniformly white, and indications are that she alone incubates it. During the 42–43 day incubation period she is fed regularly by her mate, as is the case with most birds. The season for nest-building varies considerably from one region to another. The chick is born with an enormous head and is very awkward in comparison with eaglets of other species. The first feathers make an appearance in the fourth week and by five weeks they cover the whole upper part of the body, the tail feathers being the last to develop. At six weeks the bird can eat by itself and between three and four months it is ready to leave the eyrie, although it returns to it many times for lengthy periods. The male occupies himself with feeding the fledgling during the first few days and weeks–to a much greater degree than is the rule with other species.

In East Africa bateleur eagles do not seem to follow a regular breeding cycle. It is five or six years before the birds acquire their permanent plumage and these immature individuals make up about a quarter or a third of the population.

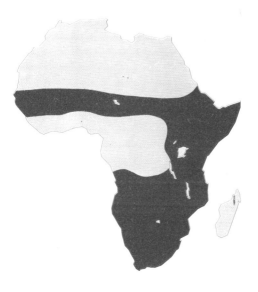

Geographical distribution of the secretary bird.

The secretary bird

The typical birds of prey all look more or less alike, though they vary considerably in size, from the diminutive pygmy falcon to the gigantic martial eagle. Their bodies are usually strong, their legs shortish and their wings broad and powerful. There is, however, one striking exception–the secretary bird (*Sagittarius serpentarius*). For this raptor is about the size of a small crane and its legs are just as long as those of the wader, to which it is in no way related. It walks instead of flying over

The secretary bird, a true bird of prey despite its unusual appearance and habits, keeps a close watch on the grass for the tell-tale movements of well-camouflaged reptiles.

SECRETARY BIRD
(*Sagittarius serpentarius*)

Class: Aves
Order: Falconiformes
Family: Sagittariidae

Total length: 40 inches (100 cm)
Wing-length (folded):
    male 25–26½ inches (63–67 cm)
    female 24–26 (61–66 cm)
Wingspan: up to 87 inches (220 cm)
Weight: 7¾ lb (3·5 kg)
Diet: flesh (lizards, snakes, insects, small
    mammals)
Number of eggs: 2–3
Incubation: 45 days

Adults
Distinguishing features are the long legs and the dark crest of head-feathers. Body plumage is mainly grey; remiges and some scapulars are black. Cere yellow, tarsi pink, naked red areas around eyes, which are chestnut-brown. The whitish beak is pointed, hooked almost from base to tip, and shorter than the head.

Immature birds
Differs from adult mainly in that the facial mask is tinted with yellow rather than red, and the central tail feathers are on average longer.

Young
Newborn chick is white or pale grey, but covered with darker grey down at two weeks. Feet and face yellow.

Facing page : On the rare occasions when it takes to the air, the long-tailed secretary bird resembles a child's kite. Nesting on the ground, the parent feeds its offspring with small reptiles, mammals and insects. Note the unusually long legs and the characteristic crest of plumes.

steppes and savannahs and even when attacked tries to run away rather than take to the air. Seen from a distance, in fact, there is nothing to suggest that the bird is a raptor at all; but closer inspection shows that the beak is strongly curved and that its small toes are furnished with pointed black claws. The head too is not unlike that of an eagle, though ornamented by a distinctive crest of feathers–each of them like the kind of quill pen once used for writing–which explains the derivation of its common name. At the time when Europeans were first becoming acquainted with this bird, in Africa clerks and secretaries wore wigs and used quill pens. They had the habit of keeping a number of spare pens handy by pushing the quills into the backs of their wigs. There is no room for doubt that this a real bird of prey, though a strange one.

The secretary bird is a hunter of snakes, lizards, grasshoppers and other insects, and small mammals, the structure of its body being admirably adapted for its specialised form of predation. It ranges all over Africa south of the Sahara, its habitats including steppe, savannah and bare ground frequented by its favourite kinds of prey. It struts through the sparse vegetation with long, elegant, confident strides, erecting and flattening the plumes of its head-crest, occasionally pausing to tap a tuft of grass with one foot in the hope of flushing out a reptile or insect. The long legs and sharp talons are quite capable of dealing with the largest or most venomous snakes, closing round the slippery body like a pair of pincers. If it manages to surprise a reptile without betraying its own presence, it will stalk it warily and then jump on it, several times if necessary, trying to break its body. Feet and claws will be used jointly to grasp the snake's neck and a blow from the beak will then crush its head. Then in a flash the reptile will vanish into the bird's crop.

If the first attack is unsuccessful or if the reptile is unusually large and has suffered only a slight wound, it may defend itself. This provokes the secretary bird to great excitement and agitation. It hops rhythmically up and down, rapidly opening and closing the ornamental head feathers, and spreading its wings wide. The intention is clearly to confuse the reptile, which is at a loss to know what part of the bird's body to strike at. Eventually, sheer fatigue lays it open to a final, fatal blow of the beak.

Despite the bold manner in which it tackles large poisonous snakes the secretary bird is not naturally immune to their venom. Only speed and mobility save it from succumbing to the serpent's fangs. It normally relies on fleetness of foot to keep out of harm's way, though if danger is imminent it may decide to use its wings. But over the ground, with wings only lightly deployed, the bird is capable of running faster than any man, as well as most animals.

The secretary bird does sometimes take to the air during the breeding season for nuptial display. Seen in flight–with its short, broad wings and extremely long central tail feathers, the bird looks in outline rather like an enormous toy kite.

The eyrie is built during the spring at the summit of a tree, usually a thorny species, at a height ranging from 10 to 30 feet.

270

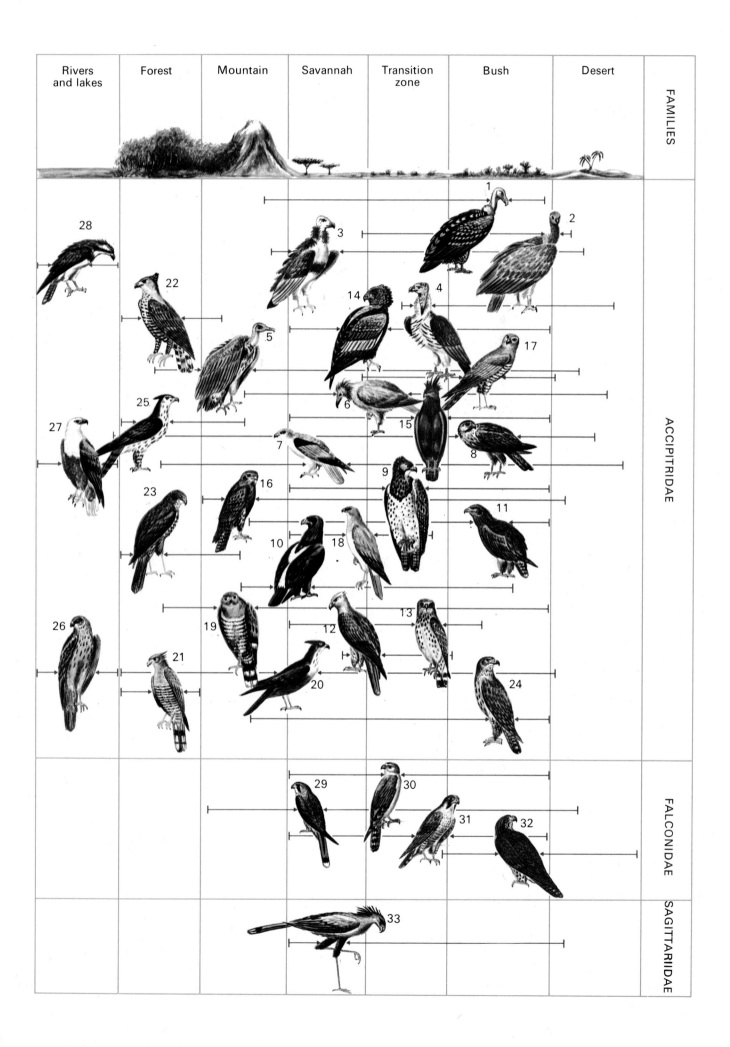

| Rivers and lakes | Forest | Mountain | Savannah | Transition zone | Bush | Desert | FAMILIES |

The nest is composed of branches lined with grass, sometimes reinforced by mud or clay. Although it may measure up to 6 feet in diameter it is often hard to locate amongst the foliage.

Secretary birds pair for life. The female, which is slightly larger than the male, lays 2–3 eggs which are on average 3 inches long and 2 inches broad. She alone incubates the eggs for 45 days. The fledglings are not provided with special food, being reared on the customary kind of prey taken by the adults. The parents initially tear the food up into very small pieces but later pass it on whole. The chicks stay in the nest for about 3 months or sometimes longer. When they leave it they already look like the adults.

Rodents and their foes

Africa is of course celebrated for its large animals. The handsome hoofed mammals are extremely photogenic and provide an unforgettable spectacle as they depart on their annual mass migrations from the high plains. The carnivores that prey on these grass- and leaf-eaters are the epitome of sleek strength and power. It is not surprising that these beautiful creatures should occupy the forefront of the stage, making it all the easier to ignore the world of the smaller mammals, the birds and the reptiles – all of them an integral part of the panorama of African wildlife, and all displaying their own specialised methods of survival in this grimly competitive arena.

The herbivores and carnivores form a perfectly balanced animal community, pitting speed, strength and cunning against one another so that hunters and hunted are evenly poised, both playing their predestined role. But the carnivores also prey on smaller mammals, including rodents, and here there is an even more subtle interaction between the hunters and their victims; the adaptations of the latter to obtain the maximum amount of energy from the vegetation on which they, in their turn, feed, are almost unbelievable.

Since they are normally incapable of escaping their enemies by outrunning them, the various rodents of Africa have to rely on natural camouflage or concealment. Those that spend the greater part of their lives above ground or perhaps in shallow holes to shelter from the light (and which venture a little way from such refuges into the surrounding grasslands in order to find food) are largely dependent on cryptic coloration. Their coat colour largely matches that of their environment. Other rodents, despite their modest size, are amazingly fast and agile, so that they have time, provided the distance is not too great, to scuttle back into specially constructed burrows when they are attacked by predators. The most spectacular animal of the latter group is certainly the Cape jumping hare (*Pedetes capensis*), which moves in a series of long leaps, each of them more than 30 feet long, without the front feet even touching the ground!

A jumping hare, or springhare, has been reported to travel 20 miles (32 km) in one night for water during a drought.

Among the rodents that live on or near the surface are ground squirrels, mice, long-tailed rats, white-tailed rats and other

Facing page : The African birds of prey are found in all the typical habitats, but as this chart shows, the majority are inhabitants of steppe, bush and savannah. 1. Rüppell's griffon. 2. White-backed vulture. 3. White-headed vulture. 4. Lappet-faced vulture. 5. Hooded vulture. 6. Egyptian vulture. 7. Black-shouldered kite. 8. African hawk eagle. 9. Martial eagle. 10. Verreaux's eagle. 11. Tawny eagle. 12. Wahlberg's eagle. 13. Harrier eagle. 14. Bateleur eagle. 15. Long-crested hawk eagle. 16. Augur buzzard. 17. Chanting goshawk. 18. Pallid harrier. 19. Harrier hawk. 20. Bat hawk. 21. Cuckoo falcon. 22. Crowned hawk eagle. 23. Great sparrowhawk. 24. Bonnelli's eagle. 25. Ayre's hawk eagle. 26. Marsh buzzard. 27. African fish eagle. 28. Osprey. 29. European kestrel. 30. Pygmy falcon. 31. Peregrine falcon. 32. Lanner falcon. 33. Secretary bird.

AFRICAN MOLE-RATS

Class: Mammalia
Order: Rodentia
Family: Bathyergidae

BLESMOL
(*Cryptomys hottentotus*)

Length of head and body: 4–7½ inches (10–19 cm)
Length of tail: about 1 inch (1–3 cm)

Spindle-shaped body covered with short, soft, mole-like hair. Tiny eyes; rough, naked skin around nostrils. Solitary habits, active by day and by night, feeding on roots and bulbs. Female gives birth to 1–3 young at a time.

NAKED MOLE-RAT
(*Heterocephalus glaber*)

Length of head and body: 3½ inches (8–9 cm)
Length of tail: 1½ inches (3·5–4 cm)

The very rough skin has only a few scattered hairs, allowing the rodent to tolerate high temperatures. It usually lives near ground level, seldom venturing far from its lair by day. Feeds on roots, herbaceous plants and insects. A creature of the desert and subdesert steppe, its presence is given away by the small mounds of earth thrown up as it digs its burrows.

SILVERY MOLE-RAT
(*Heliophobius argentiocinereus*)

Length of head and body: 4–8 inches (10–20 cm)
Length of tail: 1–1½ inches (1·5–2 cm)

External appearance similar to the blesmol; has 28 teeth – unusual among rodents. Feeds on *Hyparrhenia* grass which grows throughout its East African habitat. Solitary habits. The female has two litters of 2–4 young each year, which she looks after for 2–3 months.

species, which feed variously on grass, leaves, grains, bulbs, roots, bark, wood and insects.

It stands to reason that because the range and freedom of movement of such animals are severely restricted, they cannot possibly undertake the long migrations that enable the large herbivores, when it becomes necessary, to abandon arid regions for more humid districts. But some species are able to go into estivation (the exact opposite of hibernation), which means that they spend the long summer months plunged into a condition of torpor or semi-lethargy. At such times their metabolism is very low and they hardly require anything to eat. What vegetable matter they do need will have been hoarded up when plentiful during the preceding rainy season.

There is, however, one group of African rodents that either as a result of the competition encountered from their prolific parents or in order to escape their carnivorous foes—perhaps a combination of both—have taken an evolutionary step quite contrary to that of their fast-running or expertly-jumping relatives. These are the so-called mole-rats, creatures that spend the greater part of their days, often their entire lives, underground, digging long tunnels where they can shelter from predators and feed on the roots, rhizomes and bulbs of the subsoil. The bodies of these strange little creatures are perfectly adapted to this

African rodents are preyed upon relentlessly by a large number of carnivorous mammals and birds but because they are such prolific breeders remain very numerous themselves. They are hunted during the day by raptors such as the kestrel and at night by such birds of prey as Verreaux's eagle owl. Although many burrow inside long galleries, these provide scant protection against the ferret-like zorilles, snakes, jackals and bat-eared foxes.

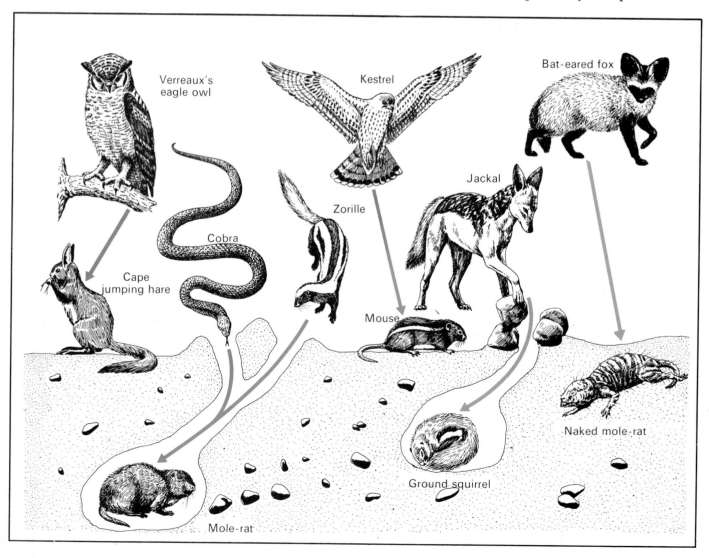

subterranean existence, though seen by daylight they would appear to be quite incapable of defending themselves or surviving. They do not burrow with their front feet (like moles) but make use of their highly-developed incisors which, with their bevelled edges, are transformed into sharp shears. The jaw muscles operating these teeth are so powerful that the tiny creatures can go to work like miniature excavating machines, while their back legs are used to throw out the loose mounds of earth.

An ingenious internal mechanism prevents the mole-rat's mouth filling with dust and soil during its burrowing activities. There is a fold inside the cheeks which separates the mouth into two sections. Thus when the animal draws in its lips they fall into position behind the incisors. Looking at the head of the mole-rat one would imagine that the teeth sprang directly from the skin and that they were not even connected with the jaws. But when the rodent feeds, the lips fall apart and the vegetable matter cut by the incisors passes into the rear part of the mouth cavity. This is possible because of the diastema, the gap between the incisors and the cheek-teeth, a feature of all rodents.

Nevertheless, despite their specialised form of self-defence, mole-rats—like rodents the world over—often fall prey to their numerous enemies. As in the never-ending struggle between herbivores and carnivores, here too, on a less dramatic plane,

Naked mole-rat
(*Heterocephalus glaber*)

The sharp, pointed quills of the porcupine can inflict painful wounds on would-be predators.

PORCUPINE
(*Hystrix cristata*)

Class: Mammalia
Order: Rodentia
Family: Hystricidae

Total length: 26–32 inches (65–80 cm)
Weight: 40–60 lb (18–27 kg)
Diet: vegetarian (fruit, roots)
Gestation: about 63 days
Number of young: 2–3
Longevity: 8–12 years, maximum 20 years

Adults
Head and neck have long chestnut-brown or white hairs. Top of body and tail are covered with long, pointed quills; those of the top part of the back are black, those of tail white; others are striped black-and-white.

Young
Born without quills, but these begin to show at three days old, becoming hard about a week later.

BAT-EARED FOX
(*Otocyon megalotis*)

Class: Mammalia
Order: Carnivora
Family: Canidae

Length of head and body: 14 inches (35 cm)
Length of tail: 12 inches (30 cm)
Height to shoulder: 12 inches (30 cm)
Weight: up to 11 lb (5 kg)
Diet: mainly insects, also rodents, lizards, fledglings, eggs
Gestation: 60–70 days
Number of young: 3–5

Adults
Looks rather like a small jackal, but legs are shorter and ears much larger, both in height and width. In the East African subspecies the head and ears are black, as are the feet and the tip of the tail. The overall colour is silvery-grey, reddish or yellow.

Young
Very lively and playful, roundish in shape. Often preyed on by larger raptors.

Facing page : Although the bat-eared fox often makes use of the abandoned lair of a porcupine, it will rarely make the mistake of attacking this largest of all African rodents.

the hunters have evolved the means of counteracting and negating the manoeuvres of their victims. So although the rodents are effectively camouflaged or hidden, the predators outwit them by means of their exceptional powers of hearing–their chances increased immeasurably by their own nocturnal habits. Some of these hunters are so specialised that, like Verreaux's eagle owl, they rely exclusively on hearing to pinpoint their prey. Hearing, in fact, plays a prominent role in the hunting techniques of all owls. True, they are ideally equipped to move about in the dark, thanks to the sensitivity of their retinas to dim light and their capacity for silent flight; laboratory experiments under infra-red light have shown that an owl will launch itself unerringly on a mouse as long as the latter makes a noise, but that when the rodent remains absolutely still and quiet the bird has no means of locating its prey. In the same way, when an owl's ears are stopped up with wax it cannot find its victim in the darkness. This has been most fully investigated in the barn owl, which can catch mice in absolute darkness, provided they move.

Another animal which relies on keen hearing to stalk small mammals in the dark is the bat-eared fox (*Otocyon megalotis*), its distinctive feature in fact being its enormous ears.

Foxes and jackals have additional highly effective methods of catching rodents, for they persistently dig away at their tunnels, forcing the occupants into the open. Many of the Canidae use this technique, coupled with a keen sense of smell, to prey on a wide range of burrowing animals. What is more, rodents are also frequently attacked by snakes–such as the Egyptian cobra, the spitting cobra and the common puff adder– all of which have no difficulty in gliding silently through the narrow, twisting underground galleries.

Genets, civets and mongooses–small carnivores with fairly primitive hunting techniques–use hearing and sight but above all smell to capture rodents.

Without delving too deeply into the complicated interaction between rodents and their predators, it is important to mention that the former manage to keep their population at a very high level by reason of their very high rate of reproduction. This alone would not be sufficient to assure their survival were it not for the fact that the smaller the size of the rodent, the less it is hunted. A hunting dog or leopard will obviously concentrate on a type of prey which is likely to provide a large number of calories in return for the least expenditure of energy.

It is perhaps for this reason that the largest rodent in Africa, the porcupine (*Hystrix cristata*), which weighs up to 55 lb and can therefore be classified as a 'worthwhile' prey, not only spends its day inside secure burrows but is also protected by its long, sharp quills. Even a lion or a leopard may sustain a painful wound if venturing too close.

The many African birds of prey also include rodents in their diet. The augur buzzard is one of the more specialised rodent-catchers, lying in wait for them for hours from the top of a rock or a tree. But none of them, from the martial eagle to the chanting goshawk, will overlook a tasty rodent should the chance be offered.

CHAPTER 14

Somalia: the sub-desert steppe of Africa

Tana, to the west by the Ethiopian massif and the heights called the 'horn' of Africa, is bounded on the south by the river Tana, to the west by the Ethiopian massif and the heights forming a dividing line between the basin of the Nile and Lake Rudolf, and to the east by the Red Sea and the Indian Ocean. The major part of this immense region is covered with thorny scrub. In some places the landscape is similar to the most inhospitable sections of the Sahara—endless expanses of dunes; elsewhere the arid terrain is broken here and there (depending on the season) by dusty soil or patches of grass.

Rainfall, never very abundant, is also extremely irregular. In certain areas it rains twice a year, in April or May and in November or December; in other districts there is one wet season lasting from April until August. But in none of these regions is there sufficient rainfall to allow the grass to grow in continuous fashion. Thus the vegetation cover consists only of scattered tufts of grass which becomes yellow when the winter ends and when the only other signs of life are the thin, stunted trees just managing to hold on.

Despite the very harsh climatic conditions in these parts there is a flourishing animal population. The herbivores have to wander continually in search of those places where occasional showers encourage the growth of a little grass, whereas the leaf eaters are a little more fortunately situated. Among the former group is the Somali wild ass (*Asinus asinus somaliensis*), its small population nowadays confined to the frontier of Somalia and Ethiopia. The survival of this species will ultimately depend upon the successful transportation of selected individuals to the new Awash National Park in Ethiopia. If this fails, the Somali wild ass will undoubtedly suffer the same fate as the Nubian

Facing page : Wild asses still roam freely over the subdesert steppes of Somalia, but it is not always possible to tell whether they are of pure stock or whether they are domestic animals that have reverted to the wild state. One species is already almost extinct, another will only be saved if it finds full protection in reserves.

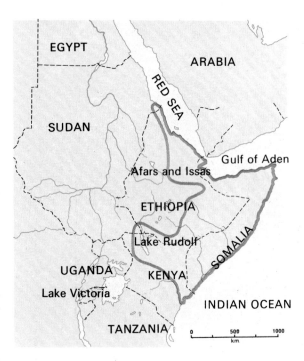

Map of the 'horn' of Africa.

AFRICAN WILD ASS
(*Asinus asinus*)

Class: Mammalia
Order: Perissodactyla
Family: Equidae

Height to shoulder: 40–53 inches
   (100–135 cm)
Weight: 460–615 lb (210–280 kg)
Diet: grass
Gestation: 330–375 days
Number of young: one

Adults
Its head, with long ears, is disproportionately large in relation to the rest of the body. There is a short mane on the upper part of the neck and a tuft of dark hairs at the tip of the tail. The animal is grey or pinkish-grey, depending on subspecies, with belly, muzzle and inner surface of limbs white. There is a narrow black band on the back and another transverse stripe across the shoulders. Lower part of legs often with black-and-white rings.

Young
Very shaggy and stands high on slender legs.

Subspecies
The Nubian wild ass (*Asinus asinus africanus*) is a little larger than the Somali wild ass (*A. a. somaliensis*), with a less uniform pelage. The former sub species is now almost extinct.

---

wild ass (*Asinus asinus africanus*), which may already be extinct; for the animals still found in the Sahara are believed to be domestic asses that have returned to the wild state and are thus not of pure stock.

Another species is the dibatag (*Ammodorcas clarkei*), an antelope which looks rather like the gerenuk but which does not carry its neck in a horizontal position when it runs. It was long feared that this species too was close to extinction, but it is now known that there are fairly large numbers left in parts of Ethiopia and Somalia. The dibatag lives for preference on plains strewn with shrubs and covered with tall grass; since it stands barely 3 feet high at the shoulder it is not easily seen in its typical habitat. It feeds on grass, leaves and acacia flowers, and also browses on the thorns of the *Commiphora*, shunned by other ruminants. Like the gerenuk, it sometimes rears up on its hind legs against a tree trunk or branch while eating. The male is distinguished by its horns.

Dibatags generally live in pairs or in small groups of three to five individuals. The early morning hours until noon are spent looking for food. When it gets hotter the animals rest in the shade of the acacias or in a natural depression. If danger threatens they pause for a few moments to see what kind of animal is disturbing their repose, then make off, lifting their tails and stretching their necks backwards so that both seem almost to be touching.

Mating takes place at any season but occurs most frequently between March and May. The newborn antelope is unable to follow its mother around immediately after birth and remains hidden in the undergrowth where the mother suckles it till it is able to fend for itself.

Another typical creature of the subdesert steppe is the oryx, a magnificent antelope with huge, straight horns. Well adapted to endure both heat and drought, the oryx has been able to survive in these inhospitable regions as a result of an ingenious system of internal temperature regulation.

When the outside air temperature is high and the oryx has plenty of water to drink, it eliminates part of the absorbed liquid in the form of sweat which, in evaporating, helps to keep the body temperature steady. This method of regulation, common to many living creatures, is supported by another mechanism which comes into play when the animal is short of drinking water. The problem at such a time is not to lose a drop of precious liquid when breathing. In this situation the oryx, as a result of its body temperature being higher than that of the surrounding atmosphere, neither absorbs nor loses heat. Dr G. Taylor has been able to show that this is an incredibly advanced form of adaptation, for in order to avoid the delicate brain structure becoming dangerously overheated, the carotid artery branches out into a fine network of arterioles which pass close to the veins; the latter, carrying cooler blood from the muzzle area, absorb some of the heat before entering the brain.

Pelzeln's gazelle (*Gazella pelzelni*) is another species perfectly adapted to an abnormally dry environment, as is Soemmering's gazelle (*G. soemmeringi*) which replaces Grant's gazelle in

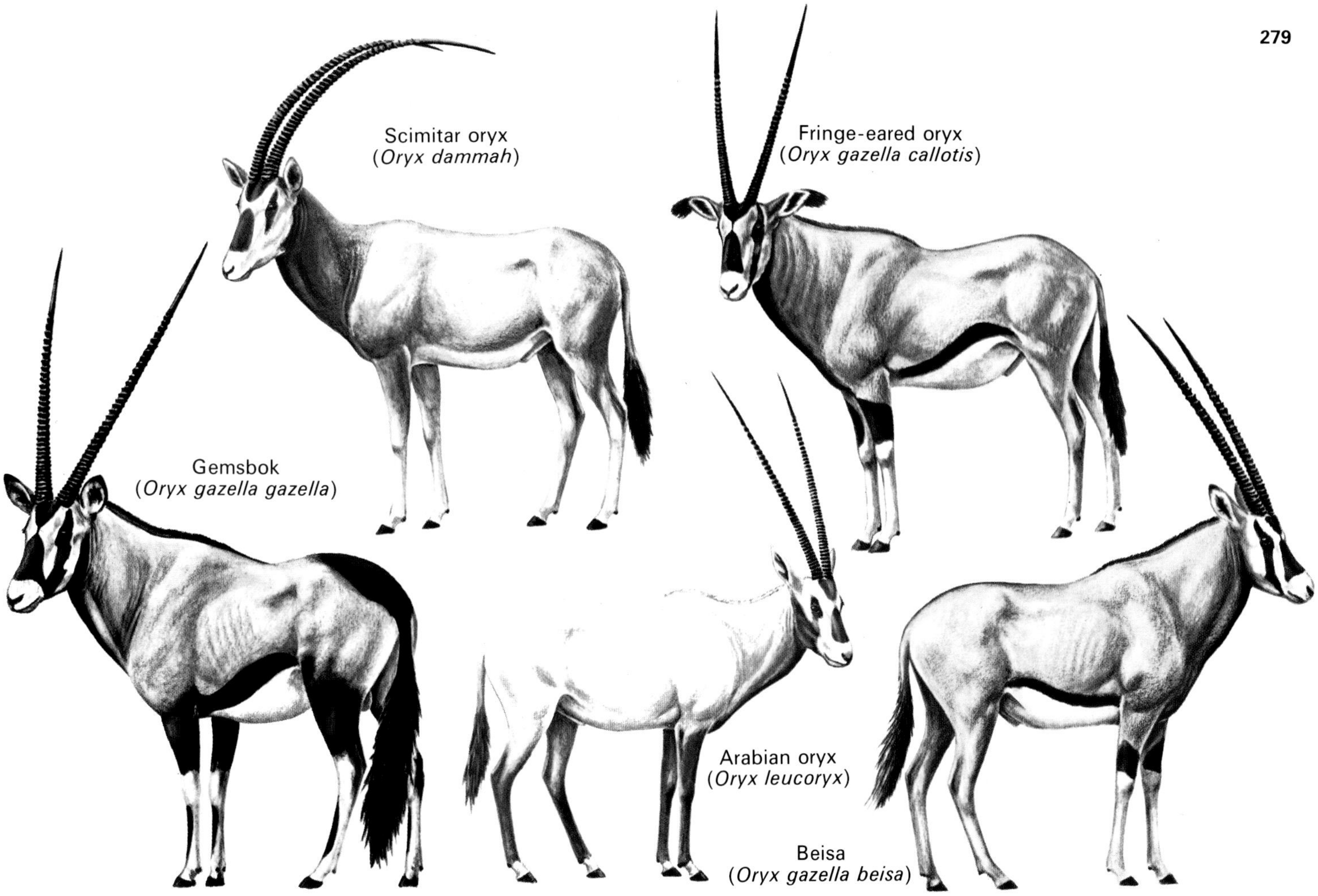

Scimitar oryx
(*Oryx dammah*)

Fringe-eared oryx
(*Oryx gazella callotis*)

Gemsbok
(*Oryx gazella gazella*)

Arabian oryx
(*Oryx leucoryx*)

Beisa
(*Oryx gazella beisa*)

certain areas which the latter will not tolerate. Grévy's zebra and Hunter's antelope (*Beatragus hunteri*) are two other herbivores that flourish in these regions, together with the dik-dik and the giraffe.

Predators of the subdesert steppe include lions, hyenas and jackals, which usually hide in the bushes bordering the rare streams and waterholes where the large ungulates drink. Cheetahs also pursue the gazelles across the empty plains.

In some parts of the Rift Valley, during the dry season, the temperature may rise as high as 75°C (167°F), and the most astonishing thing is that there should be such an abundance of wildlife in such an apparently hostile environment. The birds, of course, since they are more mobile, find conditions ideal for breeding and many species are particularly numerous in these parts. When the rains arrive, the immense deserted plains, with their stunted acacias, rocky outcrops and massive termite mounds, come alive once more—even if only for a brief period. The weavers build their basket-nests in the shrubs and trees, and their fledglings grow fat on the swarming insects. Inevitably, the long dry season soon returns and the landscape is once again a wilderness, but the little birds will just as predictably be back the following year; and there are guinea fowl, francolins, bustards, sand grouse, bitterns and raptors such as pygmy falcons, Verreaux's eagles and lappet-faced vultures to complete the count of local birds.

Another characteristic animal of these East African wastelands is the beira antelope (*Dorcatragus megalotis*), a shy and wary creature which stands about 2 feet at the shoulder and moves about in small herds. Until quite recently this animal was

There are three species of oryx, of which one is further divided into several subspecies. The Arabian oryx (*Oryx leucoryx*) is about 3 feet high, found today only in south-east Arabia, although once widely distributed over the whole peninsula. The scimitar oryx (*O. dammah*), also called the white oryx, lives in the subdesert steppes south of the Sahara. The species *O. gazella*, larger than the other two, includes the gemsbok (*O. g. gazella*), the beisa or East African oryx (*O. g. beisa*) and the fringe-eared oryx (*O. g. callotis*), with a more southerly habitat than the beisa in the subdesert steppes of Kenya.

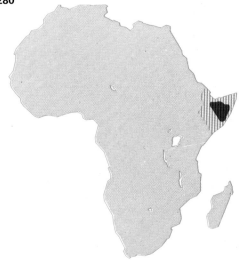

■ *Ammodorcas clarkei*

||||||| *Dorcatragus megalotis*

Geographical distribution of the dibatag (*Ammodorcas clarkei*) and the beira antelope (*Dorcatragus megalotis*).

DIBATAG
(*Ammodorcas clarkei*)

Class: Mammalia
Order: Artiodactyla
Family: Bovidae

Length of head and body: 60–68 inches
  (150–170 cm)
Length of tail: 12–14½ inches (30–36 cm)
Height to shoulder: 30–35 inches (77–87 cm)
Weight: 55–77 lb (25–35 kg)
Diet: vegetation (grass, roots, shoots)

Long, slender body with a very long neck. The straight ears are black-tipped and the horns (in males only) are ringed, curving forwards. The overall colour is reddish-grey and the tip of the tail is black. There is a dark mark, surrounded by white, on the face.

BEIRA ANTELOPE
(*Dorcatragus megalotis*)

Class: Mammalia
Order: Artiodactyla
Family: Bovidae

Length of head and body: 32–36 inches
  (80–90 cm)
Length of tail: 4–5 inches (10–12 cm)
Height to shoulder: 20–24 inches (50–60 cm)
Diet: vegetation (grass, leaves, straw)

Neck and back covered by grey, white-tipped hairs. Lower parts of body yellowish, fork of legs and groin pure white. Upper part of legs and rump light red. Eyes bordered with white. Ears large, horns (in males only) lightly curving, not exceeding 5 inches in length.

---

rarely seen by travellers and hardly known even to naturalists. During the period of the big game massacres towards the end of the 19th century, people spoke vaguely of certain gazelles inhabiting the dry hill regions of Somalia; but it was not until Captain Swayne of the British Army caught a few of these delicate animals that London's Zoological Society first exhibited them to visitors in 1898 under their now-accepted generic name.

The beira antelope has a restricted range of distribution – the mountains and high plains of Somalia and Ethiopia – where it lives among the rocks and on steep, precipitous slopes. It is remarkably agile, leaping about as confidently and acrobatically as the klipspringer. Like the latter it keeps its balance on the treacherous inclines and narrowest cliff ledges by means of its short, cylindrical hooves and the cushion-like soles of its dainty feet.

The small herds usually consist of not more than twelve animals, most of which are females, with perhaps one or two males. Each little band makes its home on a separate hill and it is to this portion of territory that the antelopes return regularly, even after being chased away by hunters.

Not much is known about the breeding habits of beiras. It is believed that the young are born at the beginning of the rainy season, as is the case with most other antelope species in these arid parts.

The animal feeds chiefly on the hard and fibrous grasses of the subdesert steppe as well as on the leaves of dwarf acacias. It is thought to be able to go without water for lengthy periods, deriving sufficient liquid content from grass, leaves and morning dew.

The locust—plague of the Bible

Some animals, in the course of their evolution, have acquired characteristics that enable them to endure all manner of natural handicaps imposed upon them by their environment. Such species are usually fairly large, have a relatively low rate of reproduction and take some time to attain sexual maturity. Individuals grow very gradually and the population increases slowly. Other species, by contrast, see their numbers decimated dramatically whenever natural conditions become unbearable. But to make up for these losses such species have a high breeding potential and a short life-cycle, so that the population grows in an uncontrollable manner as soon as external pressures are relaxed. These population explosions result in veritable plagues.

It is in the subdesert steppe regions of Somalia and the coastal plains of the Red Sea that we find the locust—the Biblical symbol of divine wrath and punishment. For thousands of years the locust has plagued man and his crops. Nowadays, thanks to scientific research and international co-operation, the worst effects of these insects have in many countries been mitigated. But the age-old dream of totally exterminating the species remains unrealised. Consequently, for some three million inhabitants of Africa and Asia the voracious locust remains a permanent menace.

The aerial invaders

In 1951–2 there was a massive plague of desert locusts, which began in Somalia and spread through the Middle East to reach India and Pakistan. Several swarms veered westward into Ethiopia and Sudan but the bulk of the vast aerial army crossed the Red Sea into Arabia. Anti-locust teams were recruited from the United Kingdom and Egypt, joined by contingents of the Arab Legion. By February 1952 the locusts had reached Iraq and American aircraft were called in to help contain the invasion which then branched out in two directions, towards Jordan (where Turkish, Syrian and Lebanese troops were rushed in, supported by specialists from the United Nations) and Iran— where military action was directed by scientists from India, Pakistan, the Soviet Union and the United States. It was a remarkable example of international co-operation.

Despite all these warlike preparations and activities the locust hordes pressed on to the east and arrived in India and Pakistan during the monsoon season, finding conditions there highly favourable for breeding. The swarms regrouped and ruined crops over an enormous area. After the rains, several months later, the locusts turned back and flew westwards again. By

The fringe-eared oryx, with its long, straight horns, is a resident of the subdesert steppes of Kenya.

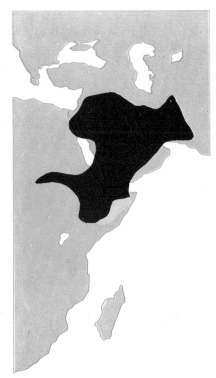

Locust swarms originate in clearly defined areas of the subdesert steppe and spread their destruction to lands far from their point of departure. Thus the plague which originated in the area of the map marked green towards the end of 1951 extended in the following months to all the regions marked red. The insects, completely uncontrollable, destroyed all the vegetation in their paths of invasion.

October they were once more over Arabia and by the end of the year were back at their original departure point. Then they suddenly vanished without trace, as mysteriously as they had appeared a year earlier.

It is hardly surprising that the unannounced arrival of this army of insects, leaving a grievous trail of destruction and famine in its wake, and its equally sudden disappearance, should have reinforced local superstition that here was a clearly demonstrated symbol of divine anger and punishment. These desert locusts, after all, were the very creatures reputedly sent by God in Biblical times to plague Pharaoh and the Egyptian nation; and although modern science is now able to explain more or less why these locust plagues occur, there is no denying that they constitute one of the most astonishing sights imaginable, and it is easy to understand the terror which they have inspired throughout the ages.

Seeds of destruction

The locust plague may be triggered off by nothing more dramatic than a sharp shower of rain bringing to an end a period of drought in the subdesert steppe. The locusts living in this arid region are already sexually mature, as indicated by their bright yellow colour, and the sudden change in temperature and atmospheric conditions now stimulates breeding activity. After mating, the female plunges the tip of her abdomen two or three times into the damp earth. With every lunge she deposits 80–100 eggs, each the size of a grain of rice and each enveloped in a secreted substance which, when it dries, forms a hard protective coating. The eggs are incubated by the heat of the sun and hatch two weeks later. In northern Morocco the incubation period may last a week longer. All the insects in the same nest are born together, within several minutes. At this stage the tiny, long-legged green insects look perfectly harmless—and so they are. During the first few days they cannot even jump. But appearance, in their case, is deceptive. If one were to examine the head of the tiny insect, magnifying it many times under a microscope, the size and power of the jaws would immediately be revealed, for in proportion to the creature's body they are larger

Locust invasions do not occur regularly but may break out quite unexpectedly, which means that there must be continuous surveillance over a wide area. There were no further serious outbreaks after 1951–2 until 1967 and 1968, both of which erupted simultaneously in different parts of Africa and Asia. The outbreak areas and direction of the migrations are shown on the map.

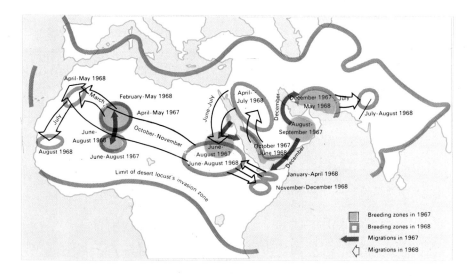

and stronger than those of the most massive carnivores!

A few hours after birth the body colour of the locust alters from green to black and during the ensuing month or month and a half it moults several times until the wings appear and the insect takes on its adult guise. Soon it will begin to attempt short flights, falling back into the centre of the throng. But it is not long before it is sufficiently developed to take wing and to move about freely during the daytime, though immobilised at night by the chill subdesert temperature.

Were it possible to discover and destroy the locust larvae when they are still incapable of flight, the plague to come might be averted. After that it is too late. These growing insects spell danger in the very near future, not only for people and crops in the immediate neighbourhood but probably for countries hundreds of miles distant. One morning, as soon as the sun's rays have warmed their numbed bodies, millions of these insects will swarm into the skies with a great buzzing sound, steadily gaining height and gathering reinforcements as they go. To get some idea of the extent of damage they are likely to do to crops it must be borne in mind that each locust eats a daily quantity of food equal to its own body weight, and that a single swarm may consist of up to 10 milliard (10 thousand million) insects, weighing about 50,000 tons! Little wonder that strong branches snap under their combined weight and that vegetation vanishes as if consumed by a devastating prairie fire.

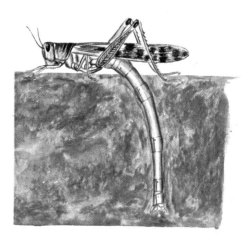

The female locust uses an abdominal appendage to dig a hole in the damp earth where she lays her eggs. These are enclosed in a protective envelope called an ootheca.

Dr Uvarov's experiments

It became evident early in the present century that the locust problem could only be tackled by intensive scientific research and combative measures on an international scale. The fact that locust plagues can now be controlled, even if not entirely eliminated, is due in large measure to the work done by Dr B. P. Uvarov, a British entomologist of Russian birth, who in 1932 was appointed first director of the Anti-Locust Research Centre, with its headquarters in London. It underlines the international nature of scientific research, that this far-reaching result should have had its origins in a country entirely free of locusts.

Dr Uvarov had begun his work on the subject around the year 1920, using two types of locust, one of which was green, the other black-and-orange. Although the majority of the insects obviously belonged to one or the other category, the situation was complicated by the presence of a number of individuals with intermediate characteristics, which were consequently hard to classify. Despite their physical similarities, the two main types showed distinct behaviour patterns. The green locusts had solitary habits, seemed relatively inactive and appeared to be potentially no more harmful than any other kind of insect. The black ones, on the other hand, were gregarious, very active and demonstrably possessed of a voracious appetite. Clearly the latter were capable of causing widespread destruction.

One morning Dr Uvarov returned to his laboratory after a few days' absence to find several black locusts in the same cages as green ones. Presuming negligence on the part of his assistant, he

After a succession of moults this migratory locust has developed wings and taken on its final adult form.

The desert locusts in their solitary and
gregarious phases look and behave
differently. The gregarious insect (*below*)
is far more active and destructive.

Facing page : Despite preventive
measures, locust invasions still constitute a
threat for millions of inhabitants of Africa
and Asia. In their gregarious or migratory
phase the insects travel hundreds of miles,
consuming a daily quantity of food
equivalent to their own body weight and
destroying crops as completely as if they
had been devastated by a prairie fire.

rebuked the latter, who hotly denied having been guilty of a
mistake and claimed that the intruders must somehow have
appeared of their own accord. Highly intrigued, Uvarov then
conducted a series of experiments which led him to an unexpected
conclusion. The quiet, solitary, inoffensive green locusts, if kept
together, would, after a given time, be transformed into vigorous,
gregarious, greedy black locusts. There was thus no question of
there being two separate species, but only one, taking on
successive and different appearances – existing in fact in two
forms, subsequently known as solitary and gregarious phases.
Uvarov later showed that the progeny of the black locusts would
even revert to the solitary phase when isolated. The other
locusts simply represented a transitional form, the progression
from one phase to another being a gradual one, not less than
three generations being necessary for the green locusts to acquire
all the characteristics of the black ones, and vice-versa.

This discovery was of tremendous importance in trying to
understand how locust swarms originated and subsequently
disappeared – phenomena which until then had remained a
mystery. Scientists who had long dreamed of getting rid of the
plagues simply by exterminating the swarms the moment they
appeared now realised that such a radical solution was quite
impracticable.

What happens is that for several successive years the locust
population of a so-called outbreak area may be no more numerous
or harmful than any other related type of grasshopper. The
insects breed in these relatively congenial surroundings while
still in the solitary phase, but their population is not so vast as to
be uncontrollable. Then the climatic conditions may change
very slightly – a heavy shower, for example, may terminate a long
period of drought (creating ideal situations for egg-laying) or an
exceptionally bad year may reduce the number of available
nesting sites and compel the locusts to crowd together. Under
such conditions the mystifying processes leading to the gregarious
phase are unleashed, and should the crowding last for a further
two generations, the steppe will soon be swarming with an
enormous locust population.

Several months after hatching each individual grows wings
and the swarm takes to the air, collecting others as it heads for
distant lands. As long as the locusts find favourable conditions
in the course of their journey they will continue to breed and
swell their ranks. This gregarious or migratory phase may last
for twenty generations or thereabouts before the reverse trend
sets in and there is a gradual return to the solitary phase. This
may happen as a result of the migratory swarms being decimated
by parasites or by adverse climatic conditions. Then the locusts
vanish once more into the desert.

The enormous problems confronting the anti-locust brigades
can now be seen in proper perspective. The invasions do not
necessarily occur at regular intervals. As soon as their numbers
are drastically reduced the locusts revert to the solitary phase
and pose no special danger; but changing conditions eventually
result in a population explosion and before long the destructive
insects are again on the rampage.

If, within a given breeding area, an especially large number of eggs are laid, the hatched larvae may develop into the destructive gregarious phase, though for the moment wingless and unable to fly. If breeding conditions are unfavourable they will remain in the harmless solitary phase.

The hard exoskeleton protecting the young locust's body prevents continuous growth. From time to time the insect sheds this layer which is then replaced by a larger one.

War against the locust

Dr Uvarov's experiments were carried out on the widely-ranging migratory locust (*Locusta migratoria*) but his findings were clearly applicable to other species throughout the world, including the desert locust (*Schistocerca gregaria*), responsible for the above-mentioned Middle East plague of 1951–2. Some species are, however, more destructive than others. The Anti-Locust Research Centre has, for example, established that the outbreak areas of the African migratory locust are comparatively few and localised. These areas can therefore be subjected to continuous scrutiny and as soon as signs of the gregarious phase appear the locusts can be destroyed *in situ,* before they are capable of taking flight. Indeed, by definition a locust is merely an innocuous grasshopper until it swarms, the term 'locust' being restricted to the swarming stages of these insects.

The fight against the desert locust is not so simple for the habitats of the species are not nearly so well defined. This locust ranges over a broad band of territory stretching from North Africa to the Middle East, India and Pakistan (swarms sometimes appear in southern Spain but conditions there are not conducive to their entering the gregarious phase). Thus the area of the species' distribution is so immense that it is quite impossible to survey it thoroughly or continuously. Efforts are therefore concentrated on establishing teams in areas likely to be affected, giving them forewarning whenever possible and enabling them to take preventive measures prior to the arrival of the invaders, whose numbers and direction can often be accurately predicted.

When the locusts fly close to the ground they make journeys of only limited range and duration, without any clear directional purpose. But the migrations that take the insects on flights of hundreds of miles occur at heights of 10,000–20,000 feet, and with favourable winds the swarms can travel at an average speed of 10 miles per hour. It is noticeable that they head towards areas of low atmospheric pressure. This is a cardinal condition of survival for it is in these low-pressure regions that rain is most frequent, bringing the ideally humid conditions for egg-laying and development. Rain also encourages vegetational growth, providing an abundance of food for the newly-hatched larvae.

There is a wide belt of low pressure which, depending on seasonal conditions, tends to move slowly across northern Morocco to the southern boundaries of the Sahara and back again, and the locusts keep pace with it. This simple pattern is unfortunately modified by currents of low pressure which prevail in the northern hemisphere during the winter over the Mediterranean and the Persian Gulf, as well as by irregular and unpredictable movements of air fronts.

Detailed knowledge of what actually encourages the gregarious phase constitutes one of the most powerful weapons in the war against locusts. Plotting the movements of low-pressure fronts can help naturalists to predict the probable course of the migrating swarms and to put in hand the requisite neutralising measures. Once a swarm is located, a variety of combat methods can be attempted. Scattering bran, soaked in insecticide, in the path of the locusts may be effective but if the creatures are already swarming in a densely-packed cloud it may be necessary to spray insecticide from the air. In one such operation in Somalia a single aeroplane was able to exterminate 400 tons of locusts in 40 minutes. Attempts have also been made to spray crops with specific chemicals but this may have serious contaminating effects which can spread to other animals feeding on the vegetation at a later date and thus upset the balance of the local ecosystem. The most encouraging prospects would seem to be linked with space exploration. Scientists at the Anti-Locust Research Centre are hopeful that artificial satellites, equipped with infra-red ray detection devices – capable of pinpointing variations in vegetational development anywhere on the earth's surface – will be able to show where desert grass is growing as a result of recent rains. These are the sites where locusts are most likely to breed and it would then be feasible for teams of scientists to be flown to the potential danger areas to take the necessary precautions.

Natural selection, which has for millions of years determined the structure and behaviour of living creatures in all the world's most inhospitable regions, has reached a pitch of incredible refinement in the case of locusts. The insects are able to escape adverse conditions simply by emigrating in large numbers to distant lands, thanks to a radical change in their appearance and behaviour triggered off by external agencies. The peaceable solitary locusts are capable of withstanding all the rigours of the subdesert steppe for years; then one day the process will begin whereby they are transformed into gregarious creatures, soon reaching plague proportions and wreaking havoc for hundreds of miles around. It is not surprising that in pre-science days such plagues were assumed to be influenced by the supernatural.

Locusts belong to the family Acrididae, which includes all the insects loosely termed grasshoppers. As a general rule they have long, powerful hind legs, suitable for jumping. Other distinctive features of the anatomy are the well-developed organs of hearing, with a stiff, projecting tympanic membrane situated on either side of the first abdominal segment, and the impressive feeding mechanism with its huge jaws that can grind down vegetable matter at an immense rate. The female also has two pairs of short, strong abdominal appendages used for burrowing into soil or rotted wood for egg-laying purposes. The characteristic noise made by some species results from the rubbing of the rough inside edge of the femur against a protruding nerve on the front wing, which by vibrating amplifies the sound.

Predators sometimes help to keep the locust numbers down. Parasitic larvae of other insects may devour the eggs, and other species, including ants, watch for the appearance of the developing locust larvae to kill them with their powerful jaws. And when the locusts enter the gregarious phase, foxes, jackals and hyenas, gazelles, birds and even local peoples find them edible, especially the females with their swollen, egg-filled abdomens – rich in protein. But predators alone are incapable of making serious inroads on the total numbers, so that direct action by man is really the only possible answer.

The complex mouth-parts of the locust, with their extremely powerful jaws, enable the insect to nibble vegetable matter with great speed and efficiency.

CHAPTER 15

The dry lands of south-west Africa

In the flat or gently undulating plains of East Africa and South Africa it is noticeable that the physical appearance of the terrain changes according to the incidence of rainfall, especially as this becomes progressively rare and irregular. In the Sudanese savannah, dense regions of tall grass alternate with areas where large trees and shrubs provide ample foliage. The open savannah, with its short grass and isolated, scattered acacias, offers pasture during the rainy season for immense herds of ungulates. The bush, sparsely covered with grass and strewn with thorny scrub, supports comparatively few grass-eating animals but abounds with leaf-eaters, large and small. Even the subdesert steppe, where there is barely enough rain to allow human habitation, has a flourishing animal population, some species being nomadic, others physiologically adapted to endure drought and dispense with water. From the fertile savannahs bordering Lake Albert in Uganda, with a larger concentration of animals per square mile than in any other part of the continent, to the wastelands of East Africa, with a more dispersed but still abundant animal population, only the variation in wildlife density clearly identifies those regions impoverished by lack of water. Yet even in near-desert conditions, the animals somehow manage to survive, and the ways in which they do so form a fascinating story.

The parts of the African continent south of the Sahara where the most unfavourable conditions for flora and fauna occur are in the south-west. The Namib, the Kalahari and the Karroo are excessively dry regions which are usually classified among the world's deserts; but even in this harsh terrain there are signs of vegetation—if only the occasional tufts of grass and stunted trees—sufficient nevertheless to sustain a variety of animals similar to those found in the neighbouring steppes, including antelopes,

Facing page : The oryx is one of the most handsome of African animals. The subspecies living in the Kalahari—the gemsbok—is the largest and strongest of them all.

Three characteristic stages of a ritual fight between two rival male oryx.

gazelles, an assortment of large and small carnivores and a generous miscellany of birds. If many local forms of wildlife have vanished over the years it is not hunger and thirst that have driven them away but the guns of hunters and the competition posed by domestic herds, in addition to widespread alteration of the habitat for agriculture.

When the sun rises behind the dunes of the Kalahari, the weavers leave their enormous communal nests and fill the air with sparrow-like twittering. A sandy-coloured caracal may be glimpsed at rest behind a bush. The temperature will not have fallen below freezing-point during the night and the morning air has a spring-like freshness. At such a time it is hard to imagine that one is in a spot which is generally described as a desert. Even the famous reddish-brown sand-dunes look more like hills for their slopes and summits are often dotted with shrubs and broken by patches of green grass. Still more untypical of true desert are the solitary trees, some of them quite tall; in their shade sprout more clumps of tough, nutritious grass. In the brief periods of rain the valleys between the dunes and the stretches of plain beyond are green with burgeoning vegetation; and to shatter all one's preconceived notions about desert regions, a splendid herd of oryx may unexpectedly appear outlined against the cobalt-blue horizon.

A photo-safari is just as likely to surprise a herd of springbok bounding away to safety with the white hairs on their hind-quarters bristling in alarm. Gnus and elands are not uncommon and there may be a glimpse of a lion (its mane much darker and shaggier than that of its relative of the subdesert steppe), a leopard or a cheetah. There is enough enticing prey for packs of hunting dogs, jackals and brown hyenas to roam freely in these parts; and the sight of giraffes browsing on acacia leaves or the appearance of smaller mammals such as ratels and mongooses will confirm the visitor in the belief that the much-maligned Kalahari is in many ways a haven for wildlife.

Most of these animals are in fact protected within the bounds of the Gemsbok National Park, a sanctuary set up in the Kalahari itself not only to assure the survival of the remaining wildlife species but also to provide a refuge for the Bushmen, that hardy nomadic tribe which has been living in this wilderness for thousands of years.

The oryx

Each zoological community on the African continent boasts at least one animal which is outstandingly beautiful in appearance and deportment. The king of the Kalahari, without any doubt, is the oryx. The name given by the Boers to this magnificent animal was gemsbok and it is fitting that this should also be the name of the Kalahari's fine game reserve.

The gemsbok (*Oryx gazella gazella*) is the most handsome of all the oryx subspecies—animals that roam the steppes and sub-desert regions from Arabia down to the Kalahari and the Moçâmedes Desert of Angola. It is splendidly built, with graceful, flowing lines. The body is thickset and massive (the animal weighs up to 450 lb), the chest deep and the withers high. The rump is something like that of a horse, as is its tail which falls to just above the hocks and ends in a tuft of thick black hairs. The legs are fairly long but extremely muscular, the hooves being larger than those of most antelopes, almost as if tailor-made for an animal which has to keep its footing in soft sand. The coat colour is pearl-grey, with fawnish tints and a black horizontal stripe outlining the flanks. There is another short black line along the spine. Dark markings on the face give it a mask-like appearance, recalling the pictures of primitive tribal warriors with painted faces.

The most distinctive feature of the gemsbok is its pair of long, narrow, prominently ringed and sharply pointed horns. These not only influence its looks but have certainly played a vital part in its pattern of behaviour. They are not shaped in any unusual or wayward manner, as are the open, curving and more or less lyre-shaped horns of the impala, the bubal hartebeest or the topi; nor do they resemble the impressively spiralled horns of the kudu. The gemsbok's horns are like strong lances, powerful enough to pierce the body of a lion or seriously wound a rival in

The Kalahari is not as arid and empty a desert region as the Sahara. Although the major part of it is covered by sand-dunes, there are scattered patches of grass and even occasional shrubs and trees. These provide food, especially in the rainy season, for a wide range of animals.

Mating ritual of the oryx.

ritual combat. An injured gemsbok, cornered by a hunter and desperate, will also make effective use of its horns. In the Namib naturalists trying to catch the animals with a view to saving them from dying of hunger, have been subjected to fierce attacks. Though themselves secure inside their Landrover, the sides of the truck were scarred and dented by the horn-thrusts of the aggressive antelopes.

Another unusual feature of the gemsbok is that the young are born with horns, though obviously only just sprouting and very minute. The horns of the adult male may exceed 46 inches and those of the female are even longer—up to 48 inches. They are twin lances set on a head carried on a thick powerful neck, a formidable weapon for goring and tossing even large predators.

The tireless runner

The gemsbok is an extraordinarily energetic creature, apparently tireless. This is a tremendous advantage in the circumstances, for in a sparsely vegetated region inhabited mainly by light-weight gazelles and small rodents, predators look on the gemsbok as a valuable source of nourishment. Were it not for its stamina and sturdy defensive weapons, the species would not have survived long in this hostile environment.

The herds of the Kalahari generally consist of not more than twelve individuals and the animals roam boldly and rapidly over an extensive area. They are particularly active during the night and early morning, chiefly because the rough grasses, shoots, bulbs and fruit which make up the major part of their diet possess a high water content (up to 42 per cent) at night, whereas in the full heat of day the liquid proportion is reduced to barely one per cent. As we have seen, animals that live in deserts and other dry regions have to take advantage of every possible source of liquid refreshment—including desert succulents and morning dew.

The small herds make no attempt to move about during the hottest period of the day but spend their time ruminating in the shade of shrubs and acacias, the grey coats with their black stripes being hard to pick out in the sun-dappled undergrowth.

When the gemsbok is faced with imminent danger it gallops off, not as rapidly as a gazelle, but sufficiently fast to carry it well out of harm's way. The thoracic cage is especially well developed and the muscular structure so powerful that when it comes to sheer stamina there are few African animals to challenge them. In the Namib, when efforts were being made to save the animals from dying of starvation, helicopters tracking the gemsboks had to keep pace with them for 10–15 miles at a stretch—and that in the scorching mid-day heat over treacherous sandy terrain.

Letting off steam

The oryx, like any other animal furnished with potentially dangerous offensive and defensive weapons, adheres instinctively to certain rules of conduct which avert serious confrontations between members of the same species. Obviously these very heavy animals with their spear-like horns are capable of doing considerable damage to one another in the course of intraspecific fights. During the mating season the territorial instinct is especially marked so that it is important for the antelopes to adopt ritual attitudes designed to dissuade rivals without actually harming them. These ritual attitudes allow the contestants to weigh up each other's strength without actually coming to grips. They also show the determination of the other's threat.

The sexually aroused male will take up a position close to a small tree or hillock and there await the arrival of a potentially receptive mate. Should two contenders dispute the possession of a female, they face each other in simulated combat which is evidently more of a game than a serious quarrel. In any event it is rare for either antagonist to be hurt in such a confrontation. Should one animal be wounded, the reason will probably be that it has not yet mastered the rules of these ritual struggles.

In their preliminary menacing postures both animals stretch their necks and lower their heads slightly as they advance towards each other. This is followed by three distinct ritual phases. The first consists simply of pushing heads together with a view to forcing a retreat. In the next stage of combat the horns are interlocked and there is a complicated, noisy, but essentially harmless bout of fencing. In the last phase of the encounter both antelopes lower their heads and try to twist the other's neck, the object being to catch the rival off-balance and topple him. At no time does either animal draw back, lower its horns and run full-tilt at the opponent. The only occasion when an oryx charges impetuously with horns at the ready is in the event of it having to defend itself against a predatory lion or leopard.

Should a gnu, an eland, a gazelle or another ruminant venture too close to the territorial bounds of an oryx during the mating season, the latter will have no hesitation in chasing the intruder away with similar threatening gestures.

A rough courtship

For anyone who has not previously seen the procedure, the preliminaries of the oryx courtship are strongly reminiscent of the earlier behaviour of rival males as they arrogantly measure each other up to defend their property. The male now approaches his partner with a marked lack of gallantry—in fact, quite brutally. She is a match for him and responds to his advances in an equally brusque fashion. Both male and female are inclined to be aggressive at such times. He has already demonstrated it in his hostile attitude towards potential rivals and intruders; and she will later prove it if called upon to defend her young against predators. In theory both could damage the other severely with their sharp horns in the course of their rough love-play but in fact no harm results. These antelopes have evolved a pattern of behaviour which inhibits their naturally aggressive instincts so that, as in the case of the rival males, the sexual encounters are also highly ritualised.

After the initial show of apparent mutual hostility, the animals lock horns and begin to push heads against each other, moving

The positions adopted by the male gnu (1) and the male greater kudu (2) for copulation are characteristic of all antelopes, apart from the oryx, which holds his head high. The reason is that both the male and female oryx have long, sharp horns.

The oryx can run fast for long distances, travelling with long strides.

294

||||||| *Oryx leucoryx*

\\\\\ *Oryx gazella gazella*

▢ *Oryx gazella callotis*

■ *Oryx gazella beisa*

//// *Oryx dammah*

Geographical distribution of the Arabian oryx (*Oryx leucoryx*), the gemsbok (*O. gazella gazella*), the fringe-eared oryx (*O. gazella callotis*), the beisa (*O. gazella beisa*) and the scimitar oryx (*O. dammah*).

GEMSBOK
(*Oryx gazella gazella*)

Class: Mammalia
Order: Artiodactyla
Family: Bovidae

Height to shoulder: up to 48 inches (120 cm)
Weight: 400–500 lb (180–225 kg)
Diet: grass, shoots, roots, bulks
Gestation: 260–300 days
Number of young: one

Adults
A large black stripe, extending down to the upper part of the legs, separates the white belly from the rest of the body, which is grey with delicate fawn overtones. The front and sides of the face have a black pattern on a white ground. The tail and some marks on the rump and upper legs are black. The horns are straight, divergent and prominently ringed—up to 48 inches long for the females, 46 inches for the males.

Young
Brownish-red coat with a black line under the eyes and a black tail. The horns are already visible.

---

around in wide circles but not straying outside the area designated as nuptial territory. This contest of wills lasts until the female acknowledges defeat and runs off, though again not very far. Her submission coincides in fact with the period of highest sexual receptivity, namely ovulation.

When the female eventually comes to a halt the male leans his head on her back and lightly places one of his front feet between her hind legs, in the manner of other Bovidae. During this ritual the male holds himself stiffly and she lowers her head. The procedure may be repeated several times before the animals actually couple. Finally he mounts her hindquarters, gripping her haunches firmly with the front legs, his head held high while she inclines her head in a submissive gesture. The sexual act takes only a few seconds.

The gestation period lasts 260–300 days and the young are usually born in the rainy season, between September and January. Together with their mothers they soon rejoin the herd and are well protected and fiercely defended against hyenas and other predators.

Experiments in the Munich Zoo confirm the observations made in the wild concerning the natural aggressiveness of the oryx. Even in captivity the antelope from the Kalahari will not accept the presence of other animals of large or medium size, but goes for the intruder immediately, with horns pointing straight towards it.

When a herd of oryx settles down to rest, a circle is formed, each animal turning its rump towards the centre, with head facing outwards so that it can keep a close watch on what is going on in every direction.

The nomads of the Kalahari

In the sandy depression of the Kalahari and on the high plains of South Africa lives the springbok (*Antidorcas marsupialis*), an antelope which the naturalist Buffon once described as the 'gazelle with a pouch on its back'. This animal, now South Africa's national symbol, looks rather like the Thomson's gazelle of East Africa but is larger, runs faster and has horns of a different shape. The characteristic behaviour of the species can best be seen when a small herd, perhaps grazing close to the swamps of Okavango or in the grassy areas of the Karroo, is startled by a sudden noise or movement. Halfway down each animal's back and extending as far as the tail is a fold of skin which in normal circumstances can hardly be seen. Under the stimulus of possible danger this pouch opens to reveal a thick crest of long, white hairs. Legs rigid, head lowered, back arched and hair bristling, one springbok suddenly jumps 6 feet into the air. Alerted by this signal, all the others react in similar fashion, erecting the white hair of their hindquarters and executing acrobatic leaps in their turn. Within seconds the tranquilly grazing herd is transformed into a panic-stricken throng whose agitated movements provide clear warning to other animals in the vicinity that some kind of danger is near.

The springboks have been the victims of the white man's brutal massacres and his gradual expropriation of land which once served them as pasture in the course of their migrations. The 19th-century mass-migrations of the springboks must indeed have been astonishing spectacles, the immense herds blackening the plains as far as the eye could see, destroying all the vegetation in their path. The Boers in fact considered the springboks' migrations to be as damaging as locust invasions.

Quite apart from their seasonal travels from the highlands where they had spent the summer back to their winter quarters in the heart of the Kalahari, the springboks used to embark on other journeys, apparently at random and with no discernible objective. Herds of up to 2,000 animals would collect together to form an enormous army comprising hundreds of thousands of heads. Sometimes they would be joined by zebras, gnus, elands and other antelopes but even when unaccompanied by other species the herds would stretch to the distant horizon.

In the course of these mysterious migrations the springboks seemed to change character completely. They showed themselves to be extremely nervous, taking fright for no evident reason, darting off aimlessly in different directions and even shedding

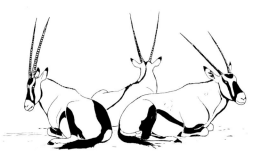

Like other social antelopes the oryx, when at rest, will form a circle, turning their rumps inwards and their heads outwards, so as to be alert for signs of danger.

With its brown and white coat, and black markings on face and flanks, the springbok looks like a larger version of Thomson's gazelle.

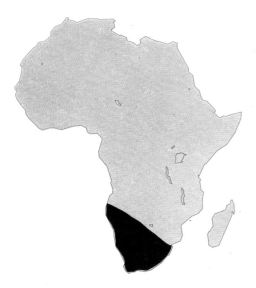

Geographical distribution of the springbok.

SPRINGBOK
(*Antidorcas marsupialis*)

Class: Mammalia
Order: Artiodactyla
Family: Bovidae

Length of head and body: 48–60 inches (120–150 cm)
Length of tail: 8–13 inches (20–32 cm)
Height to shoulder: 27¼–36 inches (68–90 cm)
Weight: 40–100 lb (18–45 kg)
Diet: grass, leaves, shoots
Gestation: 170 days
Number of young: one

Adults
Much like the Thomson's gazelle in appearance but slightly larger. Both sexes possess lyre-shaped horns, up to 16 inches long, those of the male being longer and stronger than the female's. The overall colour is light fawn and there is a black stripe along the flanks. The lower parts of the body and the hindquarters are white. The face is white with two black lines from the ears to the muzzle. A pouch of skin, running from the centre of the back to the root of the tail, opens when the animal is alerted to reveal long white hairs. The tail terminates in a tuft of black hairs. The slender feet are supported by small hooves.

Young
Sandy coloured, the baby is fully dependent on its mother for six months.

Facing page: In the 19th century springboks, far more numerous than they are today, used to embark on mass-migrations in their millions, destroying vegetation as they went. Although many of these journeys were seasonal, in quest of food, others seemed to have little obvious purpose, ending in the deaths of vast numbers of the antelopes in rivers or in the ocean.

their normally shy manner to make their way into towns and villages. Dr J. L. Cloudesley-Thompson, professor of zoology at Khartoum University, described how in 1849 a group of springboks broke into the streets and gardens of the township of Beaufort West. When the antelopes departed three days later they left an unbelievable trail of destruction behind them.

After 1887 there were four vast springbok migrations in the Prieska district, three northwards and one heading to the south and west. An eye-witness, Mr T. B. Dabie, left a vivid account of one of these episodes:

'When the herds were on the move all you could see was one vast mass of springboks wherever you looked. The whole country-side was seething with them. With the single exception of locusts they could not be compared to any other group of mammals or insects. They stretched in a straight line, as far as the eye could see, along the road from Prieska to Draghoender, 45 miles away. The animals moved steadily forwards, never stopping, not even to get out of the way of carts.

'During one of these migrations the owners of a farm at Witvlei stationed themselves around a well which they had not yet had time to cover. The father, son and son-in-law had armed themselves with rifles while their women did their best to drive the oncoming antelopes away with sticks and stones. The well was the family's only source of fresh water for the carcases of thousands of springboks that had been trampled by their companions blocked the nearby canal. Eventually the farmers were forced to retreat and the antelopes surged round the well. In a matter of minutes it was brim-full with their dead bodies. Fortunately the survivors left before nightfall, except for a few late-comers, and the family were able to clean out the well and get it working again. A few days later the whole herd had vanished, its destination unknown. . . .'

In the 1888 'invasion' Mr Dabie described how Dr Gibbons, a naturalist, tried to count a springbok herd:

'We left at dawn and soon found ourselves completely encircled in a virtual ocean of antelopes. The doctor admitted that it would be quite impossible to count them so he decided to make a rough calculation. Pointing to a fairly large enclosure, he asked a colleague how many sheep he thought could fit into it. "About 1,500" was the reply. "Well," said the doctor, "if 1,500 animals can be accommodated here, an acre will take 8,000. Now I can see about 10,000 acres covered with antelopes, which means there must be getting on to 100 million of the creatures. And what about the millions that we can't see?" At that point the doctor, not surprisingly, gave up. After breakfast we left Nelspoort and for more than four and a half hours rode on horseback through the sea of springboks, which hardly broke ranks to allow us to pass.'

It frequently happened that a herd would become entangled with groups of domestic animals. Calves and lambs would be mindlessly trampled underfoot and on one occasion two young shepherd-boys suffered the same fate. Even a lion was once crushed to death in the course of the springboks' relentless advance. Sometimes the animals would turn westwards, striking

298

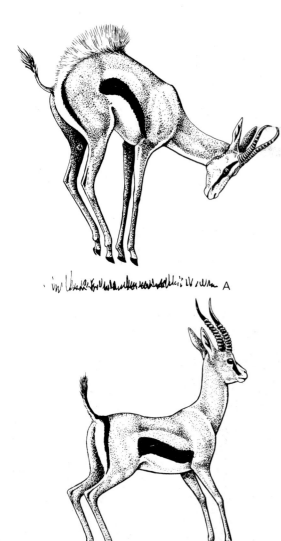

Both the springbok (A) and the Thomson's gazelle (B) leap high in the air when alarmed. The former erect the white hairs of their hind-quarters and the latter vibrate the black stripes on their flanks. Both actions serve as warning signals for others of their species.

blindly on until they reached the sea, where millions were drowned. One eye-witness near the mouth of the Orange River described how the water was choked with countless bodies which piled up along the banks to form a dike 25 miles long.

The last massive migration of springboks in South-west Africa occurred in 1896 but by this time there were already many fewer animals than on previous occasions.

Scientists still lack the information which would explain the real causes of these migrations and their significance both for the local animal population and the species as a whole. They may have constituted a kind of 'safety-valve' designed to reduce the size of the springbok population in a given area when their numbers were so great as to threaten their survival, as is the case with the 'explosions' of lemmings.

The caracal

A couple of hours before the sun rises over the Kalahari the air resounds to a strange, dry, whirring noise. This is caused by the repeated, rhythmical wing-beats of flocks of sand-grouse on the way from their nesting sites to a distant waterhole. The birds are about the size of pigeons and their flight, in close formation, is a twice-daily routine—there and back. When they arrive at their destination all seems tranquil. But the birds are being watched by a pair of enormous green eyes. They belong to a sleek feline with triangular, pointed ears that end in long brushes of stiff hair. The creature guarding this waterhole so attentively has a soft, silky, plain reddish-brown coat. Pressed to the ground, motionless, feet folded beneath the body, it takes the trained eye of a Bushman to make out the animal's shape as it crouches in the thin grass.

This splendid member of the cat family is the caracal or desert lynx (*Lynx caracal*). But although it is a true lynx some naturalists prefer to bracket it with the serval. Certainly it is a much more streamlined animal than the northern lynx, its coat softer and thicker, its ears larger, and its tail—extending to the hocks—more fully developed. What is more, unlike the European and Canadian lynxes, the caracal has no ruff. Be that as it may, the feline is a genuine lynx of the desert, found throughout the dry regions of Africa—albeit in small numbers—and from Arabia and South-west Asia as far as the western provinces of India.

When the sand-grouse have drunk their fill and flutter their wings in preparation for the long flight home, the patient caracal launches its attack, springing arrow-like from its hiding place and leaping up to 10 feet in the air to bring down one of the plump birds as it takes off. It is indeed an expert in capturing birds on the wing, and given the choice between a mammal and a bird will almost always go for the latter. Size is no deterrent for naturalists have come across the remains of eagles that have clearly been killed by caracals. With its slender, powerful limbs and muscular, streamlined body it can bowl over its prey with an impetus unmatched by any other member of the cat family. Its speed and jumping prowess made it a favourite at one time with Asian royalty and nobility, who trained it for hunting. It was said that a caracal could surprise and kill ten pigeons in a single pounce.

Few birds, whatever their size, can escape the clutches of the desert lynx, but the favourites appear to be sand-grouse, guinea fowl and francolins. A strutting bustard is also fair game and there have been reports of the carnivore attacking an ostrich as she incubated her eggs. The caracal evidently goes for the bird's neck and throttles her in a few seconds. Small mammals and rodents such as jerboas are acceptable alternatives to birds, as are young antelopes. One case has been recorded of a caracal killing a baby kudu.

Bird hunter of the desert

Like most members of the Felidae, the caracal can operate both by day and night. In its desert habitat hunting expeditions seem to be dictated as much by temperature as by light. In the hottest period of the day it will lie outstretched in the shade provided by a rock or a leafy tree; alternatively it may select a comfortable spot on a hillside where there is a cooling breeze. Eyes half-

Geographical distribution of the caracal.

The caracal is a rapid runner and expert jumper, catching birds on the wing.

With its long, tufted ears, large eyes and powerful, streamlined body, the caracal or desert lynx is one of the handsomest of all felines.

CARACAL OR DESERT LYNX
(Lynx caracal)

Class: Mammalia
Order: Carnivora
Family: Felidae

Length of head and body: 24 inches (60 cm)
Length of tail: 10 inches (25 cm)
Height to shoulder: 16–18 inches (40–45 cm)
Weight: up to 42 lb (19 kg)
Diet: flesh (especially birds)
Gestation: 9 weeks
Number of young: 2–4

Adults
The coat colour varies slightly according to the surroundings, but is generally a uniform sandy-brown, except for the lower parts of the body which are lighter and sometimes spotted. The large, triangular ears are tipped by tufts of long black hair. The eyes are also large and the tail is longer than that of other lynxes.

Young
Very similar to the adult, but lighter in colour.

---

closed, the animal continually twitches its long ears to ward off the flies pestering it. Then, as the shadows lengthen and the day draws to a close, the caracal nonchalantly gets to its feet and strolls off, ready for the hunt. Everything favours the nocturnal foray—the animal's inconspicuous sandy colour, its silent tread, its keen eyesight and the sensitive, tactile hairs on its face. In addition there are those enormous ears, comparable to those of the serval, thanks to which it can detect the faintest sounds in the surrounding darkness; even the imperceptible noise of a rodent nibbling or scuttling through the dry grass will lead the predator unerringly to the spot.

Felix Rodriguez de la Fuente has provided the following description of the desert lynx, having studied it in the wild and kept it in captivity:

'The grace, versatility and power of the animal's movements are incomparable, as is the manner in which it has adapted itself to its chosen method of hunting. Not only can it jump with all the sureness and agility of a cat but it can run, at least over a short distance, almost as fast as a cheetah, thanks to its strong, slender legs which are longer than those of any member of the cat family, apart from the cheetah itself. Looking at this splendid creature, conditioned as it has been by its harsh desert environment, one can well understand why Persian and Indian noblemen esteemed it so highly as a trained hunter and why the ancient Egyptians chose to immortalise it by embalming it or portraying it in their sculpture. For the Bushmen of the Kalahari the female caracal is said to be the "bride of the dawn", the name applied in local legend to the morning star. And surely these nomadic tribesmen, whose knowledge and experience of African wildlife is unequalled, could have chosen no more felicitous description.'

The caracal normally lives by itself, only joining others of its kind during the mating season and in the ensuing family-rearing period. It is a territorial creature, marking its domains by urinating at the foot of trees, on tufts of grass or on any other conveniently located landmark. If cornered it will spit and miaow like a domestic cat, but in normal situations its cry is similar to a leopard's, though deeper.

Between September and December, after a gestation period of 9 weeks the female caracal heads for an abandoned aardvark burrow, a hollow in an acacia or a natural opening in the hillside, there to give birth to 2–4 (sometimes 5) cubs. These remain in the lair for several weeks, suckled and ferociously defended by their mother. It is not known whether the male plays any part in hunting on their behalf (as does the leopard) or whether he considers his duties over as soon as he has mated (like the cheetah). Certainly it is the mother which gives instructions in hunting techniques to her young during the first few weeks of their life.

Like all lynxes, caracals are not easily or frequently seen, for in most regions they live a secretive existence. Only the tracks of their padded feet betray their presence around water holes. In Asia—doubtless because so many were once caught and trained for hunting—they are even rarer than in Africa. Nevertheless, they can still be found throughout their former range.